PENGUIN BOOKS

Dorothy Einon was educated at Durham University, where she gained a B.Sc. Honours in Psychology, after which she was selected for research at New Hall, Cambridge, where she gained a Ph.D. From 1975 to 1979 she held the Pinset–Darwin Research Fellowship in Mental Pathology at Cambridge and from 1979 to 1981 an MRC Research Award at Durham University. Since 1981 she has been a Lecturer in Psychology at University College London. Dorothy Einon's academic career, centring on the behavioural sciences, has encompassed much work play and child development. She is a frequent contributor to radio television as an advisor to parents on bringing up children, and written many articles for both the academic and popular press on behaviour. Her other publications include *Parenthood: The Whole Story*, *Playing with Your Baby*, *Playing with Your Toddler, Creative Play* and *Time to Play*, co-written with Jane Asher

CHILD BEHAVIOUR

Dorothy Einon

PENGUIN BOOKS

PENGUIN BOOKS

Published by the Penguin Group
Penguin Books Ltd, 27 Wrights Lane, London W8 5TZ, England
Penguin Putnam Inc., 375 Hudson Street, New York, New York 10014, USA
Penguin Books Australia Ltd, Ringwood, Victoria, Australia
Penguin Books Canada Ltd, 10 Alcorn Avenue, Toronto, Ontario, Canada M4V 3B2
Penguin Books (NZ) Ltd, 182–190 Wairau Road, Auckland 10, New Zealand

Penguin Books Ltd, Registered Offices: Harmondsworth, Middlesex, England

First published by Viking 1997
Published in Penguin Books 1998
1 3 5 7 9 10 8 6 4 2

Copyright © Dorothy Einon, 1997
All rights reserved

The moral right of the author has been asserted

Conceived, edited, designed and produced by Duncan Petersen Publishing Ltd
31 Ceylon Road, London W14 OPY

Typeset by Duncan Petersen Publishing Ltd
Film output by SX DTP, Rayleigh, Essex
Printed in Slovenia by Delo-Tiskarna

Important

At intervals throughout this book, you'll find the heading Milestones, followed by a summary of the characteristics of a baby or child at a particular stage in his or her development.

In reading these, remember that children vary, and that generalizations such as these, although useful as a broad measure, need to be treated with caution.

If the picture given mentions only a few of your baby's or child's characteristics, don't worry: your child's development is probably 'normal'.

If your baby or child bears no resemblance at all to the picture given, and shows none of the specific characteristics, then you probably don't need to worry either. But in this case it may be sensible to mention it on your next visit to the doctor.

He or she?

In order to strike a fair balance between the sexes, and in common with other childcare books, I've used 'he' and 'she' in alternate sections as the personal pronoun to describe your baby or child.

CONTENTS

The first few months
A family's first months –
the baby's point of view

Everyone has a history, even a newborn baby. Whatever else your baby may be, she's not a blank slate, and won't behave like one. In the first weeks outside the womb, the baby is curled up tightly in the foetal position, eyes closed. The womb is a newborn baby's only history and at first she is none too pleased to have left it behind. It was secure, safe, unchanging. Try to remember this as the first weeks give way to the first months and years. Babies like change only when most of their world remains constant.

Think of your baby as needing to reach out to explore from a secure base, adding items one at a time to an increasing store of experience. Don't bombard her. A bombarded baby will protest, become 'difficult'. What else can she do?

If you can provide that womb-like security and the means and desire to reach out to bring in new experiences – and do it well – you will be as close to the perfect parent as any child could want. If you force a child into an unceasing round of stimulation, she may never get that inner security and calm which enables her to be self sufficient. What is true now is true always. The basis of a child's security will change throughout life, but, baby or child, teenager or adult, she will succeed in life if she always steps out from a secure base. The need for a constant round of stimulation, or a world without calm spots is not conducive to contentment. Ultimately, it can be a difficult road to ride.

Which is not to say that all children are the same, or have exactly the same needs. They are not and do not. They vary just as all people vary. They all need calm and excitement, flopping and finding out. The mixture can be different for different children, or for one child at different times. Sensitive parenting requires you to read your child's needs and respond to them. It does not require you to give in to every whim, or always to put your child first. Everyone must live within a wider social group. A baby you 'pussyfoot' around becomes a difficult and demanding child. So does one who has to fit in with your needs. Somewhere between the extremes there is a yellow brick road. Finding it is not difficult if you remember one simple rule: everyone in your family has rights. Each of us should sometimes come first. Each of us should sometimes come last.

A new baby has a very small brain because women are not designed to give birth to big heads. That brain (and head) will grow during the first years, rapidly in these first six months and then more slowly over the years to adulthood. Reflecting this growth, children develop and change by the week, then by the month and finally (as they approach puberty), hardly at all. At first they can only learn the simplest things and understand things in the simplest ways. They see only in a very short-sighted and rather rudimentary fashion; they can hear high-pitched sounds better than low-pitched. They are especially attuned to the female human voice, but they cannot tell where it is coming from unless you stand right in front of them. They know you by smell within hours, by voice within a day or two and by sight within a week. But they do not remember you when you are out of sight. If you go away for a couple of days, they will forget you entirely. They rock themselves very gently in time with the rhythm of your voice. (You rock back.) Getting into tune. It is an anthem we should remember. If we pull a face at them they may well make the same face. Even at this age they can copy some of the things we do.

Babies can remember very little, and that not for long. As they grow and develop they can learn and understand more complex things, and remember over longer periods. But even at ten years of age their thought processes are not quite like an adult's. Their interpretation of events is simpler, more naïve, less hedged around with ifs and buts. But although they are not like adults until they are fully grown, they quickly become rather like us. A child of two is in fact much more like an adult in the way she perceives, thinks and remembers than she is like a newborn baby.

You cannot warn a baby in advance that something is about to happen, so a sudden change can be totally disruptive (even if it is a pleasant change such as going on holiday or having Grandma to stay). On the other hand, babies cannot remember for very long either – so even a major trauma (like losing a parent or being left all day with a babysitter they had not met before) only causes transient upset. As their memories improve, a sound or a smell associated with an earlier trauma can make them uneasy and fearful, but they do not necessarily remember why, and they will not be disturbed for long. When a baby is distracted she forgets what went before, even an injury if it no longer gives pain. A small baby's day is like a mystery tour – dragged from thought to thought by the things that grab her attention.

Babies learn from us what we teach them: no more and no less. They cannot work out what we intended them to learn because they cannot understand complexities. If you always come to them when they cry they believe crying makes your face appear. If spitting out carrots brings on the chocolate pudding they think that spitting made it happen. They only have two ways of communicating: they can draw us to them by their happy and endearing ways or they can demand attention by their niggles, restlessness and screams and cries. All babies do both! Some babies are encouraged to do more of one than the other. Sometimes fate steps in. A baby who has cause to niggle (such as persistent earache), and a parent who knows the cause and can act with sympathy and understanding will set up a pattern which is difficult to break. The baby gets into the habit of crying. You get into the habit of sympathizing when she does. It is not wrong to be sympathetic. What else could you do? There is only a need to be vigilant. To be firm when tears are used without just cause.

Babies are born unique. Something of the individual that they will become is there in those first days. If you are lucky your baby will be sunny and adaptable. Maybe she will be more cautious and shy, though happy once she feels secure. On the other hand she could be a good deal more difficult, quick to protest, easily disturbed by any change and slow to settle to anything new. Most babies are a mixture of these things. They have their easy points, and their difficult ones. They might, for instance, be sunny and happy, yet fussy about their food. Even the sunniest baby has an off day.

There are obvious reasons why some children are difficult: birth trauma, colic, illness, or frequent pain can make the world seem a pretty inhospitable place for those who cannot understand what is happening to them. In time, a cause can become a lifestyle. A baby who finds cries of pain bring you running may learn to cry even when there is no pain. However, most babies are the way they are for no very obvious reasons. Sometimes the difficult child finds herself in the sort of easygoing and optimistic family which can cope with her demands and perceives her good points as far outweighing the bad. Sometimes such a child finds her own difficult behaviour reflected in other family members.

The prognosis is different for each child. She is born. For a very short time she is the way she was at birth. Soon the interactions between the child, her family and her experiences come to play a bigger role in the way she is; difficult children can be made more difficult by constant ill health or clashes with their parents. A sunny child can become more difficult given similar experiences.

Opposite: Babies do not need an unceasing round of stimulation. They need to return to the security of womb-like rhythmic sounds, enclosure, monotony and calm. Between the excitements they must flop, curl up, feel secure.

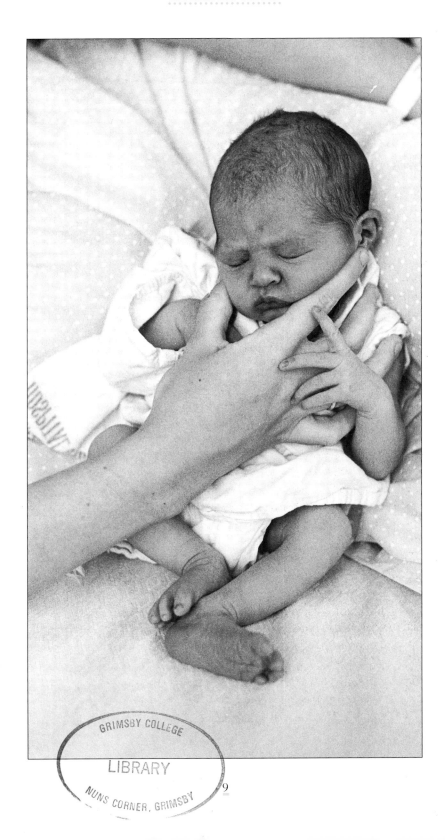

Different types of babies

One of the most interesting scientific studies of infants' temperament con-
centrated on a large group of babies growing up in New York over a
period of ten years. Parents described their children at different times
and in different contexts. The children could be roughly classified into
four different groups.

◆ Easy children who were quick to settle, easy to feed, ready to
accept change. An easy baby is likely to sleep through the night
sooner than the baby next door. An easy baby will switch to a
bottle and solid food without fuss, have regular bowel movements,
like food and readily accept a new taste. An easy baby welcomes
new toys, new people and new places. Easy children are easy to
have around: and easy to settle with a babysitter. They make first-
time parenting more manageable. Many babies stay like this. Some
are trained to be like this.

◆ Children who were slow to warm up, shy and reluctant, or even
withdrawn when approaching something new. They will spit out
food, they are more difficult to settle at night – especially in a new
place – and are easily disrupted by change. In time, as things
become more familiar, they are more accepting and more open.
With people they can be easy and outgoing. Most of the problems
for a slow-to-warm-up child are transient rather than lasting. One
does not have to tiptoe around their moods – it is enough just to
understand the initial shyness and fear. These children can be given
the confidence to be easy. They can also have what little
confidence they possess taken away by insensitive parenting.

◆ Difficult children who protest at every change and are irregular
in many of their habits. They will not settle easily to sleep, to a
new babysitter, new food, to any sort of toileting routine or indeed
anything very much. These are the children who are still not
sleeping through the night aged one, are difficult to wean, settle
into school, leave at a party, dress, or take shopping. They cry
more. They have more tantrums. They spit out their food, may
only eat chips and chocolate pudding. They find it harder to get on
with other children.

Most children do not have to be this difficult. With firm, loving
and consistent treatment they can become easier.

◆ 'Mixed children': children with some of the characteristics of one or more of these types. Easy except when it comes to bedtime. Difficult except when it comes to food.

Excitable baby/placid baby

Some people are tigers and others are sheep. For a tiger, life is not worth living unless it contains risks and excitement; sheep find it difficult to cope unless everything moves along smoothly and quietly.

Some people need much more adventure than others. They ski down steep slopes, adore roller coasters, and go free-fall parachuting. Faced with a few weeks without such excitement, they are likely to drive their cars a little too fast or to pick a quarrel just in order to raise the tempo.

Others rarely stray from their hearth. A night out once in a while is excitement enough. One of the differences between those who love adventure and those who love peace is thought to be the underlying level of activity in the cortical centres of the brain. Those who already have high levels of activity in these centres do not need much excitement in their lives. They are more cautious and introverted. Those with low levels of activity in these cen-

THE WRONG WAY TO TREAT A BABY

✖ *Don't assume that all babies are the same, and that if you keep pushing you can in time overcome reluctance, shyness or difficult behaviour. On the contrary. Forcing them to do what makes them fearful is likely to make them more withdrawn and more difficult. Sometimes you need to look at the causes of bad behaviour: for example, a baby who is often difficult may often be in pain.*

✖ *Don't always put the baby first. Every family member has a right to be first in line sometimes: and that includes parents. If your baby will only sleep with a dummy, so be it. If she will not eat vegetable purée, give her fruit purée (on nutritional grounds there is little difference).*

✖ *Don't fit your lives entirely around your baby, however difficult she is – in doing so you simply teach her that difficult behaviour pays.*

✖ *If you find it difficult to love or to care for your baby, or to take an interest in her needs, ask for help now and keep asking. These are symptoms of post-natal depression, a condition which affects one woman in ten. It can happen at any time in the first year after a baby is born and frequently goes unrecognized, even by a woman's family or doctor.*

THE RIGHT WAY TO TREAT A BABY

✔ *Children need a combination of understanding, security and firmness: sympathetic treatment and discipline. They need to know there are no upper limits to your love and support, but that there is a very definite bottom line to your tolerance. A tiny baby will not really recognize any of this since she can only remember from moment to moment. But from about five to six months babies begin to remember from day to day and they can learn that some behaviour (such as refusing to go to bed in the evening) is unacceptable.*

✔ *You cannot appeal to a baby's finer feelings because they do not exist. You cannot appeal to their understanding of right and wrong, or of safety and danger. All a child under two can do is to learn to obey the rules.*

✔ *As children grow up, unquestioning obedience needs to be modified with concern for others. But all this comes later.*

tres need to spice things up. They have a greater need for excitement of all sorts and are in general more extroverted. Whether or not this is true, many parents will agree that a particular child always seemed to be extroverted, or that another was always shy and cautious. There are those who look before the leap, and those who leap before they look.

And you?

Only the baby comes naked to the World. The rest of us carry our baggage of expectations, history and roles. We choose to have babies, but few of us have them for purely altruistic reasons. We expect to get something out of it – even if we are not quite sure what we expect. In that jumble of unexplained motives there are sometimes the seeds of individual discontent and/or disagreement between parents. There are also the seeds of failure. A baby you thought would bring you together could in reality drive you apart. One seen as just the icing on the cake of life can become the cake. One who was to bring joy brings only sadness and depression.

Before you have a child it is difficult to imagine the power she will have over you, or the all consuming attention she will demand. It is impossible to foresee the sheer panic you feel as she runs a high temperature or falls down stairs. Your children are the most loveable, demanding, exasperating, heart-warming and potentially heart-breaking people you will ever encounter. And they (or the emotions and ties associated with them) will never go away. It is

ENCOURAGING AN OVER-CAUTIOUS CHILD

✔ *Never force children to do something that makes them afraid. It will only increase their caution.*

✔ *Always stay with your cautious baby in new situations. You are her security.*

✔ *Remember that there is no race. If your baby rocks back and forth for six weeks before crawling, it does not matter.*

✔ *Praise each little step along the way.*

✔ *Introduce your baby very gently to new toys, foods and activities. If she only eats two different sorts of food, what does it matter? As long as she has milk she will be OK. Nor does it matter if she hates her jack-in-the-box.*

DISCOURAGING A FEARLESS CHILD

✖ *Babies have no sense of danger. You cannot tell a baby to be careful. You have to be a baby's eyes and ears.*

✖ *Childproof your house as soon as your baby becomes mobile.*

✖ *Introduce periods of quiet play. Turn the volume down on some games. Jog a little more gently. Speak more softly.*

✖ *Sometimes we encourage our children to be daredevils and to enjoy high levels of stimulation by the way we play with them.*

✔ *Gradually introduce a little 'rough' play. Jog your baby just a little bit faster, swing her just a little higher. Take it slowly. Never go further than she wants you to go. Making her more nervous defeats your purpose.*

✔ *Remember that sometimes your nervousness is transmitted to your child.*

the strength of these emotions which surprises us. Had we known all this in advance, we would have been less naïve about assuming we could slot them into our well organized lives.

It is hard to explain to those without children quite how it feels to know that someone has the power to break your heart. To know that if anything happens to this child it will indelibly mark your life for ever. Complete vulnerability is frightening. There is no way to escape. As you check for the 37th time that she is still breathing, understand that in reality you are simply trying to come to terms with the enormity of your commitment. Second babies are never as difficult because by the time they are born you have come to terms with the potential heartbreak of being a parent.

The relationship each of us has with our own parents is complex. Embedded in it we find love, anger, resentment, gratitude, pride, oppression, embarrassment, shame, fear, loss, rejection and much else besides. For each of us, the cocktail is different (and the relationship with each parent may also be different). Whether we turn out as parents in their image, or try to correct what we see as their mistakes, we are destined to relive some aspects of the way our parents were to us, just as they were in turn coloured by the ways of their parents. If there is good, 'enabling' parenting on both sides of the family, the outcome is likely to be less traumatic than otherwise.

In times of stress we are likely to retrace our steps, to return to the first ways we knew. We play through our own personal parenting scripts and find ourselves out of tune with our partner. Histories are not always compatible. Parenting used to be mainly women's work. Fathers were disciplinarians and teachers. Now fathers are more active co-parents and many parents use babysitters, childminders and nursery-school teachers as part-time helpers. There are more parenting styles, more opportunities for disagreement and inconsistency and less time to sort them out. It is small wonder that there are often problems.

Can parental disagreement hurt a baby?

Disagreement cannot affect a baby directly, but a parent's unhappiness about such disagreement might. However, even this is not clear. One parent may be engrossed in their own unhappiness and switch off, another might withdraw their love from a partner and heap it on the baby. A tiny baby cannot sense an atmosphere. There is nothing subtle about her feelings. As long as she has someone to care for her, she is happy. She is not upset when her mother storms out, slamming the front door (although her elder sister may well be).

However, stresses and strains can aggravate any tendency to depression in parents; this is potentially serious and could ultimately affect the baby. But quarrels and disagreements in the first few months of parenthood are unlikely to have any direct consequences.

Laying the foundations

Although it is good to get it right first time, we all make mistakes. The more we live by our mistakes, the harder it becomes to change bad habits. Fortunately, babies have very short memories, and this is especially true of small babies. There is nothing we teach them in these first weeks (intentionally or unintentionally) that cannot very easily be undone. The problem lies more with us.

If you got it wrong...

◆ Relax, and remind yourself that a new baby cannot remember. She can only recognize that something has happened before. Nothing you do wrong now is being stored away for future reference. There is plenty of time to change tack and try another route.

◆ Bear in mind that a new baby can only recognize something familiar for 24 hours. Take it away for an interval, then re-introduce it,

THE WRONG WAY TO BE A CO-PARENT

✖ *Openly disagree. Small children see things in black and white, not shades of grey. They need consistency if they are to learn. As they grow up, children exposed to inconsistency may learn to play off one care giver against another. You are going to have to learn to agree to disagree.*

✖ *Don't impose your views on your partner. Discuss and compromise, at all costs. If you expect your partner to share the childcare, then you must both operate the same rules. Children need consistency. If parents have basic disagreements, they cannot provide it. Discipline and independence are both necessary traits, and getting the right balance between them is difficult. Basic disagreements about whether discipline or independence should be emphasised is unlikely to help a child reach the right balance.*

✖ *Don't slip into contrasting roles; don't let one parent be the 'good guy' and the other the 'bad guy'.*

✖ *Don't kid yourself into thinking that the way children turn out is all encoded in their genes, and that nothing you can do will have any real impact on the outcome.*

THE RIGHT WAY TO BE A CO-PARENT

✔ *Talk about your own upbringing with your partner. Be honest in describing what was good and what was bad about it. Look around families and friends, comparing their styles of raising children with the results. Do you see the sort of children you want? Who do you know who has got it right?*

✔ *Decide where you can be flexible and where you cannot. Children need to be kept safe, but where the question of safety does not arise they need a combination of love and security, independence and discipline. The cocktail needs all these ingredients, but the measure of each does not always have to be exactly the same. You can be strict about rudeness, lax about bedtime (or viceversa). No single formula can be exactly right: the mix can be richer in independence or richer in discipline. The only rule you must follow is that you are consistent day to day.*

✔ *You need to agree on the everyday rules, even if you cannot agree on overall policy. For instance, if the father is generally much more liberal than the mother, and doesn't believe in strict timekeeping, you should try to sort out instances where the mother's rules are sacrosanct – such as going to bed at 7.30 and no argument. In return, the mother should allow flexibility in some other area of her partner's choice. Likewise, talk together in principle when you would consider smacking a child: if you have basically different attitudes, settle some cases where there will be smacking and others where there won't.*

✔ *Remember that you don't need to apply the same formulae to each child, and that you may need to control one child more strictly than another.*

and she will treat it as something she has never experienced before. By three months she can extend this recognition period to four or five days. By six months, she can remember new tricks for at least 15 to 16 days. At this age she can apply a trick learned in one place to a different place. The older she gets, the more she can generalize. This means that you have to get your act together by, say, the time she is six months old. You have a short period of grace in which to adapt to the new presence, and to work out with your partner how you can be consistent. The older the baby, the more pressing this need becomes.

◆ Remind yourself that parents are babies who grew up. The rules they learn can be remembered for ever and are easily applied in all sorts of contexts. Early mistakes are remembered by parents. They get into bad habits which are sometimes difficult to break.

Confronting fear

Most parents have fears for their children, often exaggerated by stories in newspapers or on TV, and perhaps the lack of the reassuring presence of Mum around the corner and a couple of sisters in the next street. Here are some of the most common fears, and ways to deal with them:

◆ **Sudden infant death syndrome (SIDS)**. This is not nearly as common as the news media would sometimes have you believe. Although it is a cause of death in otherwise healthy babies, it happens very rarely. Research suggests that babies who sleep on their tummies are much more likely to suffer SID. So the most important and practical way to allay fears of SID is to put your baby down to sleep on her side or her back. Since it is also possible that SID occurs more often when a child has a cold and some other infection, never put a poorly child to sleep on her tummy.

There is some evidence that SID is lower amongst populations who spend much time carrying children, as African, Chinese and Japanese women do. Carrying a baby so that she sleeps upright against your body may make it easier for her to breathe (as lying on her back does). It is known that when we hold babies next to us they fall into our breathing pattern, much as people walking together fall into step. It is thus also possible that the rhythm of your breathing when you hold a child against your body helps her to continue breathing in times of stress.

Bottle feeding has also been associated with slightly higher levels of SID, but whether this is to do with breast milk, or with the higher levels of damp housing and parental smoking amongst bottle feeders, is unclear.

◆ **A baby being kidnapped or snatched**. Whenever someone takes a baby, there is a huge amount of publicity. This can make even the most level-headed believe that the kidnapping of babies is common. It is not. It is much more common in TV serials and psychological thrillers than in real life. While it is wise to be cautious, there is little real cause for concern.

However, your baby should never be given to someone you do not know. This is particularly important when the mother is still in hospital after the birth. Do not let a strange nurse or doctor take the child away for 'tests'. Go with them or check with the ward sister that they are telling the truth. If you cannot do this, insist that the tests will have to wait. Second, never leave a child outside a shop. Use a baby carrier when shopping if the pram or pushchair is too awkward. Third, don't leave a small baby with an unknown babysitter. If you have to use a stranger, ask for references and check them.

◆ **Accident.** Dreadful accidents do happen, but fortunately they are rare and you can minimize the dangers by ensuring that children are safely strapped into car seats and pushchairs. Use safety catches on folding prams and pushchairs and ensure that brakes are applied before you let go of the handle. Never put a bouncing cradle chair on a raised surface and walk out of the room, and never leave a baby in a bath. Don't leave a baby alone with a pet, however much you trust your dog, cat or ferret. Cats can sit on babies' faces. Dogs and ferrets have been known to kill. Never leave a mobile child where she has access to fire, poisonous plants, sharp edges or stairs. Check that there is nothing within her reach that will cause her to choke. Toys for babies are clearly marked. Warnings on packaging mean exactly what they say.

◆ **Hidden problems.** One in ten children are born with a minor problem, and most (like extra toes and clicking hips) are easily put right. More serious problems are almost always recognized within a few days of birth. Doctors see hundreds of babies: they get to know the tell-tale signs. Some problems – deafness is one – may not be picked up until later, when the baby is tested at about five months, although many parents will have noticed the child's lack of response by then, especially if she is profoundly deaf. If you have not been told that your child may have a problem before you leave hospital, there is unlikely to be anything wrong.

◆ **Mistreatment.** Of all the fears we confront, this is probably the one which worries us least; but it is the most likely to occur. Perhaps because we feel more in control of our own environment – and ourselves – than of the world outside, we think the child is safe. Yet most children who are abused – whether physically or sexually – are abused by a parent, step-parent, carer or close relative. Stepfathers rank high on both lists. And it happens in all social classes. Most abusers are men, though some are women. Sexual abuse of small babies is exceedingly rare; physical abuse, unfortunately, is not.

Few of us want (or need) to confront the possibility that a loved one or trusted carer could harm our child. Unless there is a reason for suspicion, it would be very disruptive. But if a child has an accident which you did not observe, and which has no obvious explanation, it is time to ask questions. (The hospital will often do so, even if you do not.) Whenever a child is returned to your care with bruises, burns or broken bones, you should consider whether the explanation fits the facts. (For instance, a child who pulls over a cup of hot tea is unlikely to have burns mainly on her back and bottom). A second accident should always ring alarm bells. Older children are sometimes accident-prone, but small babies are not. In such instances, it is wise to remember that even an accident-prone child is unlikely to have more accidents when with another carer than she does when with you. Accidental bruising is more common on those parts of the body which are easily seen; intentional bruising on those parts which are hidden. Children do not get two black eyes from a fall, or walk repeatedly into burning cigarettes. Handicapped children are more likely to be abused than normal children. Seek help.

◆ **Harming your child**. Until you have children, it is hard to believe that anyone could harm them. Now you do, you discover that there are moments of anger and desperation which, taken to the extreme, might just mean that you were capable of lashing out harder than you should.

If you feel that you could harm your child, and that there is a realistic possibility that you will do so, you must ask for help. If you feel that you have difficulty controlling your anger towards your baby, tell your partner and a friend or relative whom you can phone when you need help. When you feel your control slipping, put the baby in her cot and walk away. Speak to your doctor or health visitor, who may be able to put you in touch with a self-help group or arrange for counselling. In an emergency, telephone the Samaritans, and/or put the baby in her cot and go around to a neighbour and ask for help. People will be far more sympathetic and understanding than you think. Although people find it hard to forgive those who harm their children, few will turn away someone who is trying to keep such impulses under control.

Sharing childcare

Martha and Tom have always shared most chores. Martha cooks one week, Tom the next. They share the shopping and housework. Now, in principle, they share the baby. They are working parents, but Martha has taken a few months maternity leave. The scenario is quite a common one. So is the outcome. Martha, like most women, goes into hospital to have the baby. Tom stays for the birth and then goes home. Martha spends the first day with her baby. Tom visits. Neither parent knows much about babies, but Martha is learning fast. Tom learns nothing. Compared to Tom, Martha is an expert by the time she is home. As she watches Tom holding the baby, she cannot help but interfere. When he tries to bath her, she stands over him. She even tells him what programme is needed to wash the baby's clothes. (This to a man who has been doing his own washing for 15 years.) When he cannot get the baby to stop crying, she takes the baby and offers the breast. How can he compete with that?

While Martha is in hospital, Tom busied himself about the house getting it ready for their return. Come Monday he goes back to work. When he comes home from work, he is tired (the baby woke him in the night). He flops in front of the TV. Martha offers a drink. She makes dinner. (Well, she is at home). Tuesday it is the same. "We need milk," he says as he leaves for work. Pretty soon Martha is the complete housewife - cooking, shopping, cleaning and looking after baby. (There is not much point in him going to the baby during the night: he does not have a breast to offer.)

Months pass, and it is time for the housewife and mother to return to work. Life has been turned upside down by the arrival of the baby. Once we had a working couple. Now a housewife and mother lives with a male provider. When she returns to work, there should be two working parents; but a pattern has been set. It only needs a little guilt on her part ("I really should not be leaving the baby") to compound it - to ensure that she not only works, but sees to the baby, makes the dinner, does the shopping, gets home to take over the childcare and takes days off when the baby is ill. She has become an old-style housewife and mother – and a working woman. He retains his role as old-style male provider.

If you think that it could not happen to you, think again. Surveys show again and again that this is the most common arrangement amongst working parents. Couples who share before the birth of a baby, frequently stop sharing after it arrives. New men become old-style men. New women take back all the old roles while hanging on to the new. No wonder the divorce rate rises: something has to give.

Ghosts from the past

We all have in our heads a map of the world as we know it: a picture of how it was, is and should be. We use it to guide our behaviour. When a baby enters our lives, we need to redraw our maps; to write the words 'mother' and 'father' into our picture of ourselves and of our partner. We may not like what we now see. Perhaps we picture a father as stern and controlling, and a mother as soft and yielding, sexually off limits, not glamorous or demanding.

In the weeks after the birth of a baby, it is useful to confront our ghosts – to look at views we may have taken for granted, and to ask questions. Relationships have a habit of recurring. In the love we have for a partner, there may be a little parental love, a little of what we learned at our mother's knee. She 'parents' him. He 'parents' her. In our expectation of love there may be something of the child remaining. We may not quite stamp our foot and demand, but we still expect certain ministrations: fetching slippers, dinner on the table, tea in bed. A baby gives us someone else who needs ministration. Suddenly, you find that you miss being the child; that you never grew up completely; and that it is difficult, all of a sudden, to become a complete adult at a time of stress and change.

If mistakes were made in your upbringing, you may want to avoid making them again with your children. But how? Memory is selective. Some people remember all the good bits; others remember all the bad. A childhood that one person wishes to avoid may not be that different from one that someone else remembers as idyllic. The differences arise not from how our parents performed their roles but from the influence of siblings, cousins and friends, and from circumstances beyond parental control. Memory is not static - it slips and slides, until there is only a loose connection with the facts. When we recall, we usually draw up our last thoughts on the subject rather than the facts. We put back into our memory banks new experiences which combine all that went before with our current interpretations.

THE WRONG WAY TO NEGOTIATE FAIR SHARES

✖ *Feel resentful about her relationship with the baby, but don't mention it.*

✖ *Feel resentful about his freedom, but say nothing.*

✖ *Feel guilty because mothers should look after their children and compensate for that guilt.*

✖ *Drift: let things slide into a new pattern. The longer it is before you address a problem, the harder it is to make changes.*

✖ *Assume that everything will come right once the mother returns to work.*

✖ *Expect your partner to keep a tally of debts to you. If you have taken over home and baby by force, you cannot expect him to notice when you want to go back to the old ways.*

✖ *Become obsessive about breast feeding. It is not as important as shared parenthood and a long and happy relationship. Indeed, it is not very important at all.*

Reality becomes a movable feast. For those who see life through rose-coloured spectacles, it takes on a rosy glow. To others it looks gloomier than it needs to be. That is not to say that 'bad parenting' is a myth. Unfortunately not. One only has to stand in the supermarket queue to see how unfair some parents are, and how easily the children become the brunt of parental bad temper. As you stand there unencumbered by badly behaved children, it is easy to see why other parents have manipulative and disruptive children. Harder, of course, when you are the tired, stressed parent.

In order to lay the ghosts...

To give yourself a chance of avoiding the mistakes made in the generation before:

◆ Remember that, in preparing for a baby, you do not often consciously think of the change in your self-image. Instead, it may well nag away at you at some other level. Don't let it nag; think about it openly.

◆ After the birth of a baby, find time to reaffirm your relationship with your partner, even though you are both tired. The basis of the relationship is changing, and you both need time to yourselves in order to accommodate such changes.

HOW TO SHARE PARENTHOOD

✔ *Recognize that having a baby is stressful, and that in times of stress we all revert to less than adult behaviour, and to the sex roles instilled in us as children. Don't blame each other if this happens. None of us is immune to society's pressures.*

✔ *Discuss new roles. Set up new work divisions. Discuss what is fair now – and what will be fair if she returns to work. If Saturday is his day off, Sunday should be hers. Do this before the baby is born. Do it when the baby is a month old. Do it again before she goes back to work – and after you have settled back into the joint parenting/working roles. Be flexible. There will be times when each one of you will need to do more than your fair share, times when one of you needs to do less. Stresses and strains are not constant: nor are external pressures and demands.*

✔ *Don't expect others to read your mind. Tell your partner what you want.*

✔ *Don't hold on to responsibility while shedding tasks. A father is not Mummy's little helper: he is a co-parent, with equal responsibilities.*

✔ *Treat fathers as if they are adults. If he goes out for the day and forgets the spare nappies, that is his problem. Babies do not come to any harm by being wet or dirty for an hour or so.*

✔ *Dummies and bottles are wonderful inventions. Use them when you need them. Don't feel guilty. The breast-feeding lobby is sometimes stronger on dogma than compassion. If the odd bottle feed seriously undermined your child's health, perinatal mortality would not have dropped in the last fifty years. Life expectancy would not be rising, either.*

BONDING DOES NOT DEPEND ON:

◆ Hormones or giving birth. Fathers, grandparents and adoptive parents bond.

◆ Timing. Bonding does not depend on loving babies from the moment of birth. Parents who adopt also bond.

◆ Breast feeding has nothing whatsoever to do with loving.

◆ Being with the baby constantly. It is easier to bond with a baby you can hold and cuddle, but parents bond to babies who are in special care. Fathers bond to babies even though they often have to leave soon after the birth.

BONDING IS HARDER WHEN:

◆ You are on edge. The more you worry about not falling in love, the harder it is to fall.

◆ A mother is suffering from post-natal depression. This is probably the most common reason for bonding problems. Seek help.

◆ The baby is separated from the parents for long periods.

◆ The baby is handicapped.

Get a babysitter and go out. Be a couple as well as a parent. The older you are, the more important this is.

◆ Acknowledge that memories of childhood are fallible. If you have siblings, re-create with them an accurate picture of what your upbringing was like. In times of stress, you are likely to re-create these patterns, automatically, with your children. You have a better chance of avoiding the errors if you are clearly, rather than hazily, aware of what they were.

◆ Once you are clearly aware of themes in your childhood, beware of over-compensating. If you felt you were not loved enough, it's all too easy to love too much. Too much love and care can feel like smothering; too much independence can seem like desertion.

◆ Remember that you will never be a perfect parent, and that if you were you'd be the dullest parent of all. How could your children compete?

Bonding problems

You can see someone across a crowded room and fall in love. It is rare, but it happens. You can grow to like someone, then learn to love them. You can even dis-

THE FIRST FEW MONTHS

like them on first meeting, yet love them on the second. As with men and women, so it is with babies.

Some perfectly ordinary people do love their babies at first sight. Most equally normal people do not. In fact, the most common reaction, after the excitement of the birth, is to feel nothing at all. For most, the bond grows gradually over the first weeks and months. It may happen with the first smile. It may happen even later. In a lifetime of loving, one week here or there is quite irrelevant. The baby will never remember that you did not love her at first sight: as long as you love her later.

How to deal with bonding problems

◆ If you are depressed, go to a doctor quickly. There is nothing shameful about this. You owe it to yourself and to the baby to get back on an even keel.

◆ Remember that love does not happen when you are tense.

◆ Try to find time for your new self and to keep in touch with the old one. Often we are afraid of becoming lost if we fall in love. If you feel strong and secure, you can take the leap.

COPING WITH ENGORGEMENT

◆ Have faith. It happens to everyone, it does not last long.

◆ If your baby will not or cannot feed, express a little milk and give it via a bottle – but see below.

◆ Use a nipple shield with a teat for feeding if this helps.

◆ Run a bath. Sit in it and cover your breasts with warm towels. Let them drip.

◆ Don't express all the milk: it will only create more – although you may need to express a little to enable the baby to latch on.

◆ Cold flannels (or frozen peas) may soothe. But do not keep them on too long. Some people suggest alternate warm and cold poultices.

◆ As to feeding, there is only one thing to do: hang in there. You will adjust.

◆ Cry if it makes you feel better.

◆ Find a moment (and someone) to cuddle.

◆ You are not a failure because you did not have a natural birth, cannot breast feed, or do not seem able to cope. You are probably depressed.

◆ Accept the baby you have: forget the one you hoped to have. It is always more difficult to begin to love a handicapped child. You need to express the anger you feel. Don't bottle it up. Anger is, after all, appropriate. Your dreams have not been realized; nor have your child's. Until anger is expressed, it can sit beneath the surface blocking other emotions.

◆ Make life easy for yourself. Forget the housework. Eat frozen food. Have the baby in bed. Give her a bottle. If there are things you resent doing, they will stand in love's way.

◆ Remember that she cannot tell love from duty - not at this age, anyway.

Third/fourth-day restlessness

The after-effects of the birth last a few days for all concerned. Both babies and parents are more sleepy than normal. The excitement of the birth still buoys you up. Parenthood is not easy, but a sleepy baby makes it possible. It all seems surprisingly manageable. Then, on the third or fourth day, you wake to breasts which feel like concrete, with a demanding baby and the blues. Take heart. Nobody has ever coped well with this combination. The baby's demands arise, perversely enough, because newborn babies don't need food. They live off fat stored before birth, which is why they always start life by losing weight. After using these pre-birth fat stores for a couple of days, they begin to feel hunger for the very first time, and they yell. Hunger always produces restlessness. It is what eventually gets us up and sends us out looking for food. Just now, it is what draws you to the baby's side.

Some facts about depression

◆ Post-natal depression affects one in ten women. It is more common in first-time mothers and those who breast feed. Women who suffer from post-natal depression may not have been depressed before. They may never be depressed again. This frequently goes unrecognized by family or by doctors. There is about a one in seven chance that the depression will occur with subsequent

If you are breast-feeding, your child's hunger usually coincides with breast engorgement. He wants food, and you have food by the spadeful. The problem is, he is now hungry and impatient, wanting more than the comfort of sucking. Your milk is less obtainable. It is hard for a naïve baby and an inexperienced mother to feed successfully.

children, although then it may not be so severe.

◆ From the age of 15 onwards, women tend to get depressed more than men. They are treated for the condition more often, given more drugs and admitted to mental hospitals more frequently. Marriage protects men from the risk of entering mental hospital. Single, widowed and divorced men are more unhappy than married men.

◆ Marriage does not protect women. Single, widowed and divorced women are less unhappy than married women.

◆ Being employed protects both sexes from depression.

Can depression spoil your relationship with the baby?

Yes. Depression is one of the major causes of dysfunctional relationships between parents and children, and thus one of the major influences on child behaviour. A depressed mother withdraws from her child. The child chasing love and attention makes heavier than usual demands on the mother, who withdraws further. So the spiral goes. At some point, the child decides to step aside to minimize her hurt. She shuts off. She may thus mirror her mother's depression in a lack of interest in the world about her. Later, she may develop an abnormal 'attachment' to her mother, avoiding involvement, though needing it; showing a devil-may-care attitude when she leaves her and unconcern when she returns. Because the initial attachment between the child and her mother serves as a model for future relationships, this can have far-reaching consequences.

It need not. Fortunately, you have a little time on your side. During the first few months, your behaviour towards the baby, however depressed you are, will not undermine attachment. A tiny baby loves you when you are there. She does not miss you when you are gone.

◆ Nothing happens within the first two years which cannot easily be undone. A child can learn to love if you can too.

◆ Nothing happens in the first five years which cannot, with effort, be undone. The longer it is left, the more effort it will be to correct the failing, the less the chance of success. But nothing is ever absolute.

◆ A child's world does not contain just one adult. He does not form just one attachment. A child has two parents. It is the responsibility of both to love her. It is perhaps unfashionable to speak of the responsibilities of the extended family, but they too should love. A child who knows that she is loved by many people has the strength to tide herself over her mother's periods of depression.

◆ It is unfair and incorrect to suggest that a depressed mother always causes lasting emotional problems in her child. They may, in spite of her depression, have a loving relationship; but if, in addition, her relationships with others are fragile, then it is easier for her to be knocked off course by depression.

28

COPING WITH TRUE POST-NATAL DEPRESSION

It is normal and natural to feel a little blue a few days after giving birth. It is nothing that needs attention beyond a shoulder to cry on and a sympathetic cuddle. True post-natal depression is altogether more serious. It may become so severe that a woman is a danger to herself and her child, and may need to be admitted to hospital. An illness this severe can have lasting affects on her child, especially if it is untreated. A woman who feels very depressed often finds it impossible to begin to love her child. Such failures add to her depression and her sense of worthlessness. She feels angry with the child, and with herself, because things have not turned out in the way they were supposed to.

Post-natal depression always needs outside help. There are many forms: drugs, therapy, self-help groups, extra help with child care, and, just as important, understanding from family and friends. More than anything else, women need to confide in and express their feelings to others.

Some months after childbirth, another sort of depression, often mixed with phobias, anxiety and obsessiveness, can develop. In mild form, it can pass for fatigue, worry or obsessive concern for the child. Unrecognized and untreated, it can last for months. Because it is thought that post-natal depression happens immediately after birth, we think of it as caused by hormones. There is no evidence that it is. Because we tend to think it is caused by giving birth, we often fail to recognize post-natal depression when it has a delayed onset. We are less forgiving and less understanding. Our response is often to suggest that the mother 'pull her self together'. Marital discord, and poor mother–child relationships, are common in such cases. Untreated, this late-onset depression can have lasting effects on all family relationships.

Finding a way through depression

◆ Depression does not go away. The longer you wait, the more damage is done to the relationship with your child. Get help now.

◆ Your child does not need an attachment with you particularly; but she needs one with someone. If you cannot give much to her just now, try to find someone who can.

◆ If you can afford a childminder, it will help your child and give you some child free time. It may be easier to love for a few hours than to try all day to give something it is hard to give. A relative may be able to help, or in certain cases it may be possible to get help from childcare services.

◆ Do not be afraid that your child will love someone else more than you. Love is not like that. There are no ration books. The more people there are to love her, the more she can love in return.

◆ Do not withdraw completely.

Jealousy between parents

The first weeks are filled with love, fear, contentment, anxiety, calm and frustration; with tiredness and stress, too. One could blame the see-sawing feelings on her hormones if he did not feel them too. Birth has a way of unleashing insecurity. Where love meets insecurity, we are never immune from jealousy.

It's tough being a man

Within each relationship lie two more: his and hers. While women suffer more from childbirth than men do, men's relationships often suffer more from the arrival of children. Men require things from the relationship – like the monopoly of her attention and her ministrations – that women need less. Before she had children, she liked to give those things. Now she resents the demands. He can feel pushed to one side by her relationship with the new baby. Men rarely feel entirely neutral about their partners' new, close relationship with the baby, or about the fact that it is 'unearned'. While he fights for recognition in the workplace and worries about the responsibility of supporting his family, he cannot fail to notice that she just has to be a mother. She has to be exceptionally bad at it before she loses the job. You do not have to earn a baby's love the way you have to earn the respect of an employer.

THE RIGHT WAY TO DEAL WITH JEALOUSY

✔ *Discuss. Feelings which are open are always less destructive than feelings which are hidden.*

✔ *State the facts without judgement. Don't say you understand how someone feels; say you're trying to understand. You can only try; you cannot be in their shoes.*

✔ *Accept that adjustments are necessary. Look for solutions. Accept that life may have to change more than you thought it would, and talk though your options.*

✔ *Change your mind if necessary. You may not have wanted to go back to work. Now you are not so sure: or vice versa. Nothing is written in stone.*

THE WRONG WAY TO DEAL WITH JEALOUSY

✖ *Ignore. Jealousy does not go away because you pretend that it is not there.*

✖ *Blame your partner. Jealousy never made anyone feel proud of themselves. Don't add to his/her feeling of low self-esteem. If you do, things will get worse between you.*

✖ *Belittle. If you belittle someone's emotions, they will get angry, and rightly so. We cannot help our feelings – we can only learn to control them.*

✖ *Tell yourself that you have everything you ever wanted. It is a lie. We never have everything.*

✖ *Be angry. If you show your anger towards your partner, it will be returned with righteous anger.*

✖ *Make a competition out of your problems. The other side of the hill is not greener.*

✖ *Withdraw from problems. Turning your back helps no one.*

It's tough being a woman

The contrast between a woman's day of baby care and his day of work can lead to misunderstandings. Even if she is not jealous of him going back to work, she may be jealous of his independence. He can read his paper on the train without looking up every minute to check on the baby. He can call in for a drink on his way home and sit there without anyone making demands on him. The fact that a new mother can rarely get on with her life without interference comes as a shock. So, in many cases, does financial dependence. While she was earning she did not feel guilty about spending. Now she may do – and it matters more than you think.

We feel guilty. A dependent woman's little treats are more likely to be guiltily and quickly consumed. That men do not feel these restrictions (or are perceived as not feeling them) can feed into our jealousies. Once upon a time we were defined by the church we attended and who our relatives were. Today we are defined by what we wear, the way we decorate our home, the car we drive, and what we buy at the supermarket. Restricting spending restricts self-expression - a real problem for many new mothers.

Can you 'spoil' a baby?

You cannot give a baby too much love or too much indulgence. Since a tiny baby cannot remember anything for more than a few moments, today's indulgences are hardly going to cause tomorrow's problems. All a baby can learn is that A is followed by B: that if she cries, she is swooped up in a cuddle; that if she smiles, you talk. But until she is about four months old, even this simple sort of learning needs much practice and is only remembered when she is in the place she learned it. After a day or two, it is quickly forgotten. So if she learns that crying in her cot at night causes cuddles, she will not remember this trick when lying on the sofa. Nor will she remember it for more than a day or two unless you go to her again. All this suggests that you cannot spoil a baby until she is at least five months old.

Whether you can spoil her after this depends on what is meant by spoiling. You can teach her not to sleep at night; to spit out dinner to get pudding; to cry to be picked up. But is that spoiling? Not all babies who do not sleep, are fussy or bad-tempered have been taught by parents to be this way. There are other reasons for these behaviours.

THE RIGHT WAY TO 'SPOIL' A BABY

✔ *Let her know you have heard her cries. Use a soft word, a rock of the cot, her name spoken in a friendly sympathetic way. If you are attending to another child, making her bottle, or engaged in something you cannot leave, let her cry for a little while. But don't make a principle of it. If she always has to cry hard to be picked up, she will learn to cry hard.*

✔ *There are always two ways of asking. You can do it pleasantly, or you can make demands. Because we all lead busy lives, it is often easier to wait for the demands of our children, to get on with our own affairs while they are being good. In the long run, this makes them into very demanding people. We need to switch those biases, to teach them how to use charm to get their way.*

✔ *Don't ignore crying – any more than you should ignore smiles and gurgles when you are busy. When she cries, you should always acknowledge her: say her name, rock the pram. If she is in pain or afraid, pick her up and comfort her. If she is hungry, make the space to feed her. Deal with older children, finish the chore in hand and/or prepare her feed. If she is bored, put her where she can see you. If she is restless, turn on the vacuum cleaner. If the first line of defence does not work, pick her up and comfort her. When all is said and done, this is a baby's due.*

THE WRONG WAY TO 'SPOIL' A BABY

✖ *Pick him up every time he cries, but leave him when he is good.*

✖ *Give your all, but leave no time and space for him to give his.*

✖ *Always put him first.*

✖ *Never put him first until he demands it.*

Always let her know that you love her smiling face and happy gurgles, even if it's just a word and a smile of encouragement. If she is awake when you need to be busy, keep her with you.

Sleepy baby, wakeful baby

A small baby sleeps a great deal: but not always as much, or for as long, as you think. She sleeps more by night than by day, but can take up to six weeks to fall into this pattern. Most babies are not sleeping through the night at six weeks, 12 weeks or even six months. By ten months, one in four babies are still not sleeping through. By two years, there are still a few stragglers.

The typical pattern for a newborn baby is to wake, look about for a while, spend 30 to 60 minutes on feeding, burping and being changed, and then fall back to sleep. She will sleep for another couple of hours, and the pattern will start again. Gradually the waking times between feeds will increase.

HOW TO KEEP A BABY AWAKE AT NIGHT

✖ *Change her nappy. Babies soon grow to love the social interaction of a nappy change. It perks them up. Babies do not mind wet nappies. They are a bit like a wet suit: pleasantly warm against the skin. Crying because they are wet is a complete myth. Babies cry for the attention we give when cleaning their bottoms. They are quite happy to have the old nappy back. If you are worried about nappy rash, use a towelling nappy at night. Add a little vinegar to the rinse water (this makes it harder for the bacteria to breed) and tie the plastic pants loosely so that a little air can get to her bottom.*

✖ *Put her in a separate room. By the time you have reached her to feed her, she will be wide awake.*

✖ *Warm her bottle. Although babies do not like bottles straight from the fridge, they do not need them to be warmed to body heat.*

✖ *Sit up, get out of bed or try to keep awake while you feed her.*

✖ *Worry about falling asleep with a baby in your arms.*

✖ *Burp her. It really is not necessary. Feeding sends small babies to sleep. Being held upright and having their backs patted wakes them up.*

HOW TO KEEP YOUR BABY SLEEPY AT NIGHT

✔ *Keep her in your room. Most babies, taking the world as a whole, sleep in their mothers' arms. So could yours. As long as you are sober, she will come to no harm.*

✔ *Breast-feed. You will always have food on tap.*

✔ *Bottle-feed at night. See box.*

BOTTLE FEEDING AT NIGHT

Sterilize a flask and a bottle.

 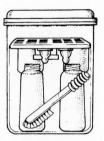

Measure the formula into the bottle.
Cap it. Boil water and let it
cool to just above
blood heat.

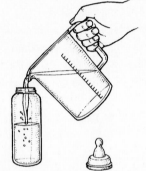

Put it in the flask. Add to the bottle
when needed in the night. If she is
likely to wake twice, prepare two bottles.

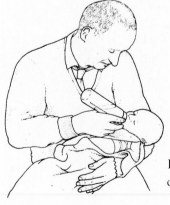

Do not keep bottles warm;
it is dangerous. Do not worry
if the water has cooled too much.
Cool milk is as nourishing as warm.

Do not burp her – it's unnecessary.

If you both fall asleep while you feed,
don't worry (assuming you are sober).

Crying for hours: six to 12 weeks

All babies cry sometimes. Most babies cry more between six and 12 weeks than they cried before. You will find that there are times during the next few years when your child is happy and easy, and times when she is upset and difficult. This is one such time. Nobody is quite sure why, but most difficult periods coincide with accelerated growth and change, most easy periods with slower growth and consolidation.

One reason why babies cry at this time may be that they are hurting. Growing is a painful business. If you have ever ached after exercise, you will know how it feels to grow muscles. Exercise breaks down muscle. The pain we feel is caused by the rebuilding. Another sort of growing pain occurs when she cuts a tooth. Even before it breaks through the surface of the gum, a tooth hurts. Now imagine how it feels to have growing bone and muscle in every corner of your body. It must surely hurt. The sheer rate of growth in these early months is amazing - in fact, the baby is growing faster now than she ever will again. She does not grow a little bit every day: she grows and pauses, then grows again. She can grow by as much as half an inch in one day. Between six and 12 weeks, most babies are growing very fast, changing in several ways. They have uncurled; they are looking at and listening to what goes on around them. They are beginning to realize that their arms and legs belong to them and that they are separate from you. Change usually causes stress. By six weeks, she can tell night from day and spends longer periods awake. She can control her breathing, which may be another clue to her frequent crying. At birth, a baby breathes in slow and out fast, a pattern which is not much good for crying or speaking. Between six and 12 weeks, she learns to breath in fast and out slow, which is just what she needs for a good cry.

How to deal with crying babies

◆ Rock them. Babies are soothed by gentle rocking. Rocking in the motion of a swing (rather than side to side as in a rocking cot) mimics the movement of a baby on the body as his mother walks. Rocking in your arms or pushing a pram back and forth gives this motion. Some babies find it more soothing.

◆ Cuddle. If there is a natural place for a baby to be, it is in your arms. Cots and prams are a modern invention.

◆ Swaddle. Small babies like to be wrapped up tight.

◆ Sing. There would not be lullabies in most languages if they did not work,

◆ Give them monotonous sound. Vacuum cleaners and car engines work well.

Colic

Colic, a form of indigestion, causes repetitive crying at a certain time each day, most often the early evening. It lasts for about an hour. During this time there is nothing much you can do. The problem usually starts at about six weeks and lasts until about 12 weeks. Occasionally it lasts longer.

No one is sure why some babies have colic. It may be that carrying a baby as much as possible will lessen the chance of colic, but this is is not certain. Babies who have colic are not more likely to cry later, have eating, sleeping or feeding problems or to be difficult toddlers. It is a short-lived and isolated problem.

DEALING WITH COLIC

If you are breast-feeding, your diet can exacerbate her problems. Dairy products are the major culprit (milk, cream, yoghurt, butter, cheese, ice cream), but cabbage, sprouts, beans, nuts and chocolate can upset her too. Check them out. Keep a diary of what you eat and try and relate your intake to her colic. Cut out certain foods and see if things improve. If nothing has changed within five days of eliminating an item from her diet, it is unlikely to be the cause. Remember that you will need to cut out all dairy foods.

Gripe water helps some babies.

Try soothing sounds, rocking and swaddling.

Take it in turns to look after her. If it is not your turn, get out of earshot.

Crying after 12 weeks

Some babies cry a good deal throughout the first year. A baby who always cries on and off during the day is not suffering from colic. Colic is much more specific. Babies usually have a reason to cry. If your baby cries a great deal:

◆ Keep a diary of when she cries, what you/she eats and where you are when it happens. Is there any obvious pattern?

◆ Look for a reason. Is she off colour? Does she have a cold? Has she just been fed? Is she upset when she goes to bed?

◆ Persistent crying is often associated with earache. Get the doctor or clinic to check that there are no medical reasons for her tears.

◆ Sometimes children associate certain places with crying. It becomes a habit. If this is the case, make changes.

◆ Does she gain more by her tears than by her quiet behaviour? If so, stop rewarding her for crying. Start rewarding pleasant behaviour.

◆ If you are breast-feeding, check that nothing that you are eating is upsetting her.

◆ If you have introduced solid foods, check whether something she has eaten may have caused the problem.

◆ Try carrying her in a sling or back pack. This sometimes helps. If this is not possible, leave one of your jumpers with her. Your smell may make her feel more secure.

◆ If there is no apparent reason for her tears, try giving plenty of attention when she is happy and less when she is sad

Smiling

A baby who is born a couple of weeks early will smile late. One who was overdue will smile early.

Smiles appear in a sequence. Her first smiles always happen in sleep. Sometimes they are just little 'half face' smiles. Some call them windy smiles, but they are not due to wind; they happen as babies move from deeper to lighter sleep. Later, sleepy smiles occur when your sleeping child hears your voice or another high-pitched sound.

By the time she is five to six weeks old, she will give her first real smiles, brought on by high-pitched sounds and movement. The best stimulus is a female head, talking and nodding, but rattles and bells are quite effective, too. Later, she will prefer a talking face, but she will still like the head to move. By four months she appreciates stationary faces. By six, she prefers the people she knows. By the time she is eight months old, she may only smile at her friends.

◆ All babies smile. It is their way of talking to you. Do not worry if she is later starting to smile than the baby next door. This has no implications for her behaviour, now or later.

◆ Babies smile more often if you smile at them.

◆ Babies like to take turns in smiling. They smile at you and you smile back, several times, one after the other.

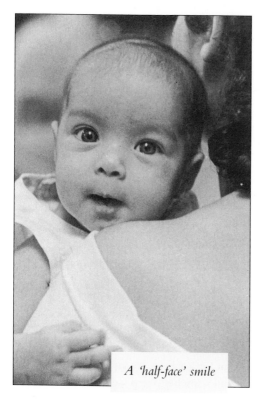

A 'half-face' smile

Taking turns

Being a good parent means being sensitive to a child's needs. One of those needs is to have her turn, whether it is her turn at being first (or last), or saying her piece. Even a tiny baby demands her turn. If you keep on talking without letting her have her say, she will make her exit. This carries on being true during the first weeks and months. She is programmed to know what she needs from you, but has only one way to communicate it. When you get it right, she will shower you with attention. When you get it wrong, she will switch off. Unless you give her a chance, she cannot tell you how to change.

◆ Always pause after you speak to your baby, so that she can answer you. It may only be a flick of the eyelids, but it matters.

◆ Always be guided by her needs. Stimulation is when you give her what she wants: not what you want or feel like giving. Over stimulation is likely to lead to withdrawal.

◆ Stop when she says stop.

◆ Treat them as individuals. Parents still tend to assume that, when a girl cries, she needs comfort, and when a boy cries, he needs stimulation.

The sexes

The tendency to treat boys and girls differently is deeply rooted in our culture. It is easy to change pink bows into denim overalls, much harder to address some of the underlying messages, because we are often not aware of them.

How we often treat baby girls and boys

◆ Often, the first word the new mother of a baby girl says to her partner is, "Sorry." Often, the first words the mother of a boy says to her partner are, "Oh, it's a boy."

◆ When you 'rough play' with a girl, you are gentle. When you 'rough play' with a boy, you are rough.

◆ When a boy cries, you go to him faster than to a girl.

◆ When a girl crawls, you get her back if she strays too far. You let a baby boy crawl right across the room.

◆ When a boy talks or shows us what he can do, you act as if what he says/does is more interesting than if he was a girl.

◆ You talk more to a girl.

◆ You allow a girl to dress like a boy, play like boys, act like a boy. You buy her boys' toys. You are less likely to let a boy dress like a girl, play like a girl or act like a girl. You do not buy him girls' toys.

◆ If you think you are even-handed, ask yourself how you would react if your six-year-old son and daughter asked if they could have their ears pierced. How you would react if your four-year-old son wanted to go to the park in high-heeled shoes and a sequinned boob tube?

I want to go back to work

By the time their children have started school, most mothers have returned to work. It used to be a choice; now, it is becoming a necessity. It is increasingly difficult to live on one income. Many mothers have returned to work (at least part time), by the time children are ready for nursery school.

Increasing numbers are returning within a few months of the birth. Many careers depend upon the swift return. Many women would make this choice even if they did not have to.

There is nothing special about a mother – nothing she gives a child that cannot be replaced by a well-chosen carer. In the past, children were rarely raised by their mothers (or parents) alone. Amongst the wealthier classes, women had nannies or nursemaids. They even passed the feeding on to wet nurses. Amongst the poorer classes, children were often passed around the family. If you look at the census returns of countries in Western Europe from the middle of the 19th century, you will find many records of small children living with relatives – especially grandparents. Indeed, in certain areas, it is rare to find grandparents without a grandchild or two living with them.

There is no limit to how much a child can be loved; nor to how much a child can love. When somebody thinks you are wonderful, you glow. Research suggests that multiple attachments are just as positive for children as single ones. If four people love you to bits, it is likely that you will feel really rather special.

But: not everyone who plays the role of carer plays it well, and not everyone who cares stays. It can be very disturbing for a child to be cared for by unsympathetic or downright bad carers. It can very disruptive for a child to love and lose too many times. After a while, the child may become reluctant to become involved with yet another fleeting carer.

It has become fashionable to imagine that everything your children are and become is fixed in their genes – as if somehow it does not matter what happened to them in the years that followed conception. Convenient as this feeling is for those who have lost yet another mediocre carer, it is untrue – as anyone who has grown up feeling unloved and unwanted will surely agree. It matters whom we ask to replace us as parents.

How to choose and keep a carer: home care

If you can afford to do so, having someone come into your home to care for a child (whether daily or live-in) has obvious advantages. But it has some quite serious disadvantages too.

THE ADVANTAGES OF HOME CARERS

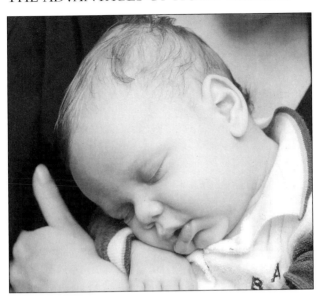

✔ *You do not have to take the child anywhere in the morning or pick up at night.*

✔ *Care can be provided when the child is sick.*

✔ *It is usually easier to make adjustments to cover emergencies.*

✔ *The cost does not double if you have a second child.*

✔ *Your child has one-to-one care.*

✔ *Your child is in the security of her own home, with her own toys, her own bed for naps. She can make trips out to shops, parks and other places. Her life is thus relatively normal. There is less contrast between her weekday care and the care you offer at weekends.*

If the carer is a trained nanny, she (or nowadays, occasionally he) will have been independently checked at some stage.

THE MAJOR DISADVANTAGES OF HOME CARERS

✖ *Good nannies do not come cheap (though sharing one can bring down the cost).*

✖ *Having a live-in carer can be inhibiting and disruptive*

✖ *If the carer is a mother's help, she may have had no training and no experience of looking after children or much love for them. But then, parents are not trained, either. Mothers' helps can be excellent – but do check references very carefully.*

✖ *Au pairs often have no experience of childcare. They are supposed to work part time in exchange for their keep and pocket money. If you expect long hours of cheap childcare from an au pair, do not be surprised if that is what you get. An exploited teenager is hardly likely to put your child's needs before her own. Sometimes even a well-treated one does not. There are good au pairs, but since you often have little choice, who you get is a matter of luck.*

✖ *Nannies often do not stay in one job for long. Au pairs rarely stay more than six to 12 months. Changeovers can be very disruptive.*

✖ *Although qualified nannies are observed during training, other home carers are not. You are the only people who can check on the quality of care. Where care is shared between parents, there are a number of people who can make daily checks.*

By contrast, nurseries and registered child minders have to meet official standards; and you do not have to cover when a nanny or other home carer falls ill.

✖ *One-to-one caring, without the intrusions of housework or even shopping, can make a child over-demanding. It is not good always to be first in line.*

The only way to be certain when leaving a child with a stranger

◆ Take up all references and check them very carefully. Who is giving the reference - a friend or previous employer? Talk to the last employer and, if possible, someone at the college where she trained. If someone is coming to you from an agency, ask for the carer's last employer, and check with them directly. Do not trust agency checking. In my experience, agencies ask previous employers only to fill in a brief report form. Anyone can claim to be a previous employer.

◆ Be wary of anyone who has flitted from job to job.

◆ Choose someone you like and who likes you. Arrangements work best when you have shared values: particularly values associated with childcare. A warm, outgoing personality is always a plus. Avoid anyone who seems depressed.

◆ If neatness matters to you (or the carer), it is best if you share this feeling. Neither of you will feel comfortable in the long run if there are large differences.

◆ Some time during the new carer's first week, pay a surprise visit so that you can check that the carer is looking after the baby as you would wish. A carer who resents this is not worth employing. Anyone capable of loving your child will understand that you cannot leave a baby with a stranger simply on trust. If you are still unsure, pay another surprise visit. If you are still unhappy, find someone else.

◆ Even after the initial check it is wise occasionally to turn up at home unexpectedly ('forget' something or 'finish early'). Things (and people) can change.

◆ Do not exploit carers. Give them a contract which states the hours you expect them to work for you, their duties, and pay. Extra hours and extra duties should be paid for with extra money or time off.

◆ Unless you have employed a nanny for sole care (and are paying her for the long hours this entails), do not expect her to care for the child when you are not working.

◆ You are much more likely to keep someone you treat well. Do not expect someone who is caring for your child to do all of your heavy housework and shopping. Tidying the house and doing the baby's washing can be included in her duties: but this must be agreed between you.

◆ Do not try to hire someone for as little money as you can get away with. You are likely to lose them to the first person who makes a better offer.

◆ Au pairs are fine for school-age children, but they should not be left in sole care of a small baby all day. This is exploitation.

ADVANTAGES OF DAY CARE

✔ *The environment is constant, so children will be less upset by the loss of a particular carer.*

✔ *The facility is checked, both by the authority who licenses it and by the other parents who use it. Individual carers will be monitored by their workmates.*

✔ *Your child will be raised with other children. He will have plenty of playmates and he is likely to turn out with good social skills. This can make him much more adaptable and help him to settle well into school.*

✔ *The facility is always there: even if one carer is sick.*

How to choose and keep a carer: day care

Good day care is expensive. A well-equipped nursery with quality carers costs money to run. There is no way you will get this cheaply unless it is subsidized by an employer or social service agency. Check out more than one nursery before making a choice. You get a better idea of what is good and what is bad if you can make comparisons. Always:

◆ **Visit the nursery**. Does it feel right? Do you like the staff? Are they interacting with the children or with each other? How many staff are on duty? Although one carer can look after a group of four or five three- and four-year-olds, she cannot look after such a big group of tiny babies. If one baby can walk and three can crawl, the one who is left in her cot is likely to get little attention.

◆ **Do the children look happy?** What happens when they are upset? Are the carers sympathetic? Would you be happy if your child turned out like these children?

◆ **Can you see a baby being cuddled?** When you talk to the carer, does she still watch and interact with the children? Who comes first?

◆ **Are there baby chairs, mobiles, and toys** in the baby section?

◆ **What happens when babies cry?** A good nursery puts children first. It provides a warm, caring and stimulating environment.

DISADVANTAGES OF DAY CARE

✖ *It can be every expensive, especially if you have more than one child.*

✖ *You have to take the child to the day care.*

✖ *The child cannot go when ill. He is likely to pick up more colds and illnesses than at home.*

✖ *Difficult children can sometimes miss out on attention because the easier children – the 'charmers' – get more than their fair share.*

✖ *Hours are less flexible than with a home carer.*

✖ *Children used to having playmates can find it harder to amuse themselves at home.*

How to choose and keep a carer: childminders

Childminders are women who care for children in their own homes. Often they have children of their own. In Britain and other countries, registered childminders have to meet certain standards. Unregistered ones elsewhere do not. The number of children a registered childminder is allowed to care for is strictly regulated, as are the care and facilities she provides. Unregistered and unsupervised carers can be good, but they need very careful monitoring. One person cannot look after half a dozen children under five.

THE ADVANTAGES OF A CHILDMINDER

✔ *They are relatively cheap.*

✔ *They are monitored by those who register them and/or other parents.*

✔ *It is relatively easy to make adjustments to cover emergencies.*

✔ *They are usually very experienced in looking after children.*

✔ *Your child is part of a family atmosphere and usually has playmates.*

DISADVANTAGES OF A CHILDMINDER

✖ *Your child will be sharing a carer with a number of other children (which could mean she gets much less attention).*

✖ *The carer may live some way from your home: you will need to travel with your child.*

✖ *If the carer (or your child) is sick, you are without back-up arrangements.*

✖ *Your child is likely to pick up more illnesses than at home.*

Choosing a childminder

◆ Visit her at home. Check that she is providing a stimulating and warm environment and that the children in her care seem happy and reasonably well behaved. (But make allowances; no one can be expected to have a group of little saints.) Check that the place looks clean; that there are toys and playthings.

◆ Watch her with the children. If she sits down for a natter and ignores the children, she is not for you. Ask her what she does with the children in a typical day.

◆ Avoid anyone who seems depressed or you feel is cold or will not stimulate your child.

◆ Ask for references from other parents who have used her services.

Jealous of the carer of your child?

You want her to be loved. You want her to be happy. But you still want to be number one. It is foolish, but who is not foolish about such things? The love your child has for you is exclusive to you, just as your love for her is exclusive to her. She will not love you less because she loves the baby sitter. She will almost certainly love you less if she hates her. An unsympathetic and unlovable carer seriously damages the child's ability to love. If she greets her with smiles and showers her with kisses, be glad that you have chosen your substitute wisely.

Yes, she will probably get more of those slobbery kisses than you do; hear her first word; see her first step and be with her when she is at her best and most endearing (five days out of seven). You will get her when she is tired, when you are stressed and when there are other demands on your time. For you, childcare is shared with filling the washing machine, getting her to the childminder, making supper or doing the weekly shop. The childminder has all the leisure to sit and play. Everything has its price. Whoever said you could have it all?

In the long term, the price is small. You may indeed miss those first steps, that first word (even if they were discrete and missable events, which they are not); but they have very little to do with the joys or responsibilities of parenthood.

It is possible to miss out on your children's childhood. Long hours at work and frequent travel can keep parents from their children rather more than is good for either of them. A child who learns to love (whoever teaches her) can surmount such barriers when a parent knows how to demonstrate, their love and can easily become involved. It is harder when they are less demonstrative, and awkward in their child's presence.

The working mother

There are good parents and there are bad ones. Some are men and some are women. Some work outside the home, some in it. A few are full-time carers with no other responsibilities. This does not make them good mothers. There are good substitute carers, good facilities, good nurseries and schools; and bad ones as well. Some have safety nets of supporters to pick up the pieces, while other parents and children do not have support to fall back on. Trying to look for cause and effect in such variety is doomed.

Some working mothers are not successful parents. But whether or not there are more of them than there are among mothers who do not work outside the home is impossible to judge. How would we measure a mother's success? By her children's monetary success? Happiness? School attainment? Ability to sustain a happy marriage? No doubt we would find

As you regretfully say 'good-bye', take comfort from the fact that although she may want her carer more than you today, she will love you more tomorrow. Carers and teachers come and go. You are constant.

little correlation amongst such measures.

Mothers have always worked. Caring for half a dozen children, washing, sewing, mending, cleaning, shopping and cooking is hard work - probably harder and more demanding of time than working as a part-time teacher. Add to this the need to tend the garden, keep the chickens, work in the fields, take in washing or sewing to make extra money, and it is not clear that yesterday's women had more time for dedicated babycare than today's working mother. Today, babies almost certainly get more individual attention than before. It may not come from the mother – but it did not in the past, either. Historically, children were raised by a variety of carers: mother, father, siblings, aunts, uncles and grandparents. In many parts of the world (including Britain) babies were often cared for by older sisters (or young aunts) who carried them around much of the day, and/or by grandparents who might take over the entire responsibility after weaning. Modern arrangements whereby parents rely on a paid carer are no further removed from the 'normal' rearing environment of most of the world's children than is the woman who raises children in the isolation of her own home.

She won't take a bottle
Women who breast-feed sometimes have difficulty switching babies from the breast to the bottle before returning to work.

Milestones: the settled baby, four to six months

What should a well-adjusted baby be like as he ends his first six months? It is useful to have a yardstick against which to measure, but if he's somewhat different, don't worry. A wide range of variations from the picture which follows is perfectly 'normal'.

Babies change very quickly. The helpless newborn living from moment to moment quickly becomes a child who sits crawls, reaches out to explore, and sustains attention for a moment or two. By four months, your child is able to turn to you as you come into the room. She smiles and coos in answer to your voice. When you show her something, she looks intently, then puts out a hand to touch. Her fingers close around anything placed in her hand, and it goes to her mouth for exploration.

By six months, she will be reaching out to pick up a toy; banging it on her high chair; even beginning to let things drop from the chair. She will be able to sustain attention for longer, so that her behaviour appears less disjointed, less dragged along by external happenings. She will remember from day to day, week to week, and you will see evidence of this in her behaviour. She is expecting a bath when she hears the water. She reaches out to pull her bottle to her mouth. She gurgles and babbles back to you when you speak.

By four months, a baby has usually settled into a routine. She takes feeds at more regular times, fills her nappy at the same time. By six months, she will be ready for solid food, to begin using a cup. Some babies sleep through the night at four months. By six months almost half of all babies do so. All sleep more by night than by day. Between sleeps, she lies (or sits) awake and happy, looking around, watching, playing, listening, 'talking'. Her body has uncurled. She lies flat, kicking and waving her arms when her nappy is removed or when she is bathed. Seeing your face, she looks intently, smiling, gurgling and responding to your interest in her by he interest in you.

By four or five months, parents have also settled into a routine. They are more used to the broken nights, to having the baby around, to being parents. While the child sleeps, they can switch off for a few hours in the firm expectation that their child will survive without their watchful eye. Thus freed from constant thoughts of parenthood, they can think and talk of other things, go out for a drink, read, watch TV. Life is settling into a new routine.

BREAST OR BOTTLE

✖ *Don't try to breast-feed exclusively. Books dedicated to breast feeding often suggest you can carry on feeding while working. There is no need, reason, sense or point in trying to combine work with exclusive breast feeding unless you are working under the same roof as your baby. Anyone who suggests you can easily express enough milk to provide a hungry baby with a day's worth of feeds and then change into a smart suit and clean blouse and do a day's work has clearly never tried it. Expecting a baby to go hungry so that you can offer her a breast when you get home, or a carer to accept a baby screaming for food because you are delayed by traffic is unreasonable, selfish and dotty. There is absolutely no evidence that hygienic bottle feeding, with milk which is correctly diluted, does babies any harm whatsoever. Those who believe otherwise have misinterpreted the statistics. Bottle-fed babies are more likely to be admitted to hospital with gastro-enteritis and chest complaints than are those who are breast-fed. But so are the children of teenage mothers, lower-class mothers, mothers who smoke and those who live in damp housing. Mothers who breast-feed tend to be older, middle-class, non-smokers living in centrally heated homes. When one compares like with like (ie working-class smokers who breast or bottle-feed) one sees no difference between the two groups.*

✖ *Do not wait until a few days before you have to go back to work before introducing her to a bottle. If you know you are returning to work before she is six months old, introduce a bottle in the first weeks and continue offering an occasional feed by this route. The problem for a child asked to make a late switch is that she has developed a breast-sucking technique rather than a teat-squeezing one. A baby who sucks a dummy is used to having a rubber teat in her mouth.*

You can combine breast and bottle feeding if you wish. Breast-feed the baby in the morning and when you get home in the evening. You can also give a ten o'clock night feed, though this may need a top-up with a bottle. If your baby is still taking a night-time feed, you may find it easier to give a bottle at ten and breast-feed during the night. A baby who wakes for food more than once in the night may not be getting enough milk from the breast.

If she will not take a bottle, don't panic. She will make the switch. A baby likes starvation even less than she likes a rubber teat when she is used to skin. If she gets hungry enough, she will take a bottle.

Starting to play

A tiny baby looks. She responds to you by sometimes copying your facial expression. She may even shake a rattle if you wedge it in her hand. She does not play in the sense that older babies play. One does not see that constant, voluntary, self-initiated interaction with the world that gives playing children such obvious pleasure. At first, interaction is an altogether more serious activity.

Encouraging play

◆ Play with your child. Small children cannot always motivate themselves. Talk to her, smile, interact frequently when she is awake. Show her toys, pictures, books. Jiggle her on your lap. Play tickle, peek-a-boo. Hand her toys.

MAKING PLAY SAFE

◆ Children's toys have to be safe. Household objects do not. Once a child can reach and grab, never leave her alone with anything which is not designed for baby-play.

◆ Watch your baby often and keep one step ahead. You need to remove things before she starts to grab them, to have a fireguard before she starts to creep forward.

Once she is strong enough, prop her up. A seated baby can see more than one who lies on her back, and it makes it easier for her to find her playthings. Or put her down on her tummy. It is not safe to sleep this way, but quite all right for play.

Learning

Even a tiny baby can learn that A follows B; but she will not remember it for long. One of the main differences between a two-week-old and a five-month-old is that the older child can remember what she learned last week. This means that she can build on what she already knows. She does not have to keep starting from scratch as a tiny baby does. The other big difference is that the older child has a much longer memory span. A newborn baby's thoughts are but a moment long. She thinks and it is gone. Then she thinks another thought. Because that second thought also quickly disappears, she cannot put two thoughts together. The things she learns have to be repeated often, to occur in the same context, and to happen very close together in time. As she begins to think about what is happening now and also remember what happened before, she begins to see

patterns of action. Putting on her coat means you are going out. Going to the park means she will have a go on the swing.

But memory brings fears

◆ Once she can put two things together, she can learn things you do not wish her to learn – such as the fact that crying gets your attention.

◆ Babies are slow to learn, and see only those things that are obvious. They understand your actions, not your words.

◆ Babies learn best when they are happy and relaxed.

◆ Babies need to consolidate the things they learn. This means quiet times in which to cogitate, rather than a constant round of stimulation. Be guided by your baby: when she is happy, she is learning.

Introducing solids

Babies do not need solid food. In the past, most would have lived exclusively on breast milk well into their second year, sometimes longer. The introduction of early weaning (and six months is early) was made possible by the introduction of potatoes into our diets. Potatoes are much easier for babies to digest than wheat.

A baby is ready for solids when:

◆ She likes having things in her mouth.

◆ She is at least five to six months old.

◆ You feel ready to start weaning.

◆ She can sit up when propped.

◆ A baby needs about 3 oz/85 ml milk for every pound of her weight per day. A 10-lb/4.5-kg baby needs about 4.5 full bottles of

Opposite: *Make sure that a waking child has things she can watch, listen to and later touch and hold. Put things where she can reach them.*

WHAT TO FEED A BABY

Baby rice or mashed potato mixed with milk is a useful first food. Because gluten is difficult for babies to digest, wheat should not be introduced into a baby's diet until she is at least six months old.

Babies need milk. In the early months, add solid food to milk rather than replacing milk feeds with solid food.

Start by giving only one or two spoonfuls of something rather milky and bland. She will spit most of it out. Packet foods are probably the most convenient to use at this stage. Food should be given as a runny purée.

If she takes your first offering, settle her on that taste for a day or two, then try something else. Again, make it milky at first. Once she is happy with this, you can introduce something new. (It is often easiest to do this by mixing a little with something familiar.) Good starter foods are avocados, cream cheese or cheese sauce, cereals, strewed puréed fruits and vegetables, eggs, meat stock gravy, soups thickened with potato or cereal, fish mashed with potato or rice, lentil purée, egg custard, chicken livers – indeed, anything that can be made into a smooth paste. Take it slowly, introducing one new taste at a time. If she does not like it, give her something familiar. (This is where packet foods are especially useful.)

Once she is taking more food it is worth considering both home- made and commercial foods. I think that there are better ways to spend one's time than always cooking specially for your baby. If you are eating something suitable, by all means share with her. When you are not, cook something simple or open a can. You may feel differently. One of the advantages of giving a baby 'adult' food is that she will learn the family tastes and may be more likely to sit down to family meals later, but don't count on it. An over-zealous attitude to good home cooking gives a child a clear insight into ways and means of protest and/or manipulating you to his advantage.

Babies don't have to eat bland food. If you like strong-tasting, spicy food, introduce it early on. Children often do not like hot chillies in sauces, but will tolerate mild chilli sauces, and are quite happy with other spices, garlic, olive oil, herbs and strong flavours such as liver or blue cheese. They do not need to take food in a 'pure,' simple form. Puréed peas are fine if you are just cooking for her, but she may prefer a little of your spaghetti and sauce, coq au vin or paella; she might even like some pizza as long as you can make it into a purée first.

milk. A 25-lb baby needs ten or 11 full bottles.

◆ Young babies take in this milk over a series of feeds. Even though a 7-lb baby only needs three full bottles of milk, she is likely to spread this over six to seven separate feeds. Breast-fed babies tend to take a little less at each feed than a bottle-fed baby of the same age and weight (and may have an extra feed or the odd top-up between feeds to compensate). As babies get older, they start to take in more milk at each feed: and may only have four to five by the time they are five to six months.

A baby's stomach can take only about 7 oz/170 ml of food at a time. Once she has reached this limit, any extra food has to be taken in as additional feeds or in the form of solids. It is a matter of convenience which you choose. In the past, women would have given the extra feeds, particularly if they were carrying babies or working in the fields. A one-year-old would need about ten or 11 bottle feeds a day and might require slightly more breast feeds. Once the daily requirements for breast (or bottle) feeds start to rise, most women find it easier to introduce solids.

Although there is no date by which a baby has to have solids, it is possible to start to early. A tiny baby's digestive system is not ready to deal with solid food, nor does she find it easy to swallow. Most doctors suggest that babies younger than five months should not be weaned on to solids.

Nothing is gained by forcing the issue. If she is unhappy, wait a couple of weeks and try again.

Six months to 24 months
Milestones: six months

The most obvious differences between a new-born baby and one entering the second six months of life is his individuality. By nine months this little character has more in common with older children than with himself as a new born baby. Rapid brain development is one reason for these changes. His brain is now almost twice the size it was at birth and his head has grown to accommodate it. What does having more brain mean for the child? First, and most obviously, he is beginning to get more and more of his body under control. Now he does not just move his arms and hands in excited waving motions, but he puts them where he wants them to be. His body is beginning to serve his needs rather than to act automatically in response to stimulation. It all began in the first weeks with control over his face (which enabled him to copy your facial expressions and to beam his delighted smiles). Then it moved down to his neck and shoulders, so he could hold up his head and turn to look at you. Control then passed down the body and out along the arms.

Now, at six months, he controls his hands but not his fingers, this will not begin until a little later - see the picture caption on page 60. His back may be firm enough for him to sit up, but not yet to hold him while he stands. As control moves out to his fingers, it also moves down his back and extends to his lower limbs. As he takes over control of more and more of his muscles, he will be able to sit unaided, crawl, creep, stand and eventually walk. It will not be long before you have to watch out for any loose object within his reach.

Brain growth also underlies the development of memory, language, and understanding. This does not mean that experience is unimportant. The relationship between brain growth and experience is circular. Experience kick-starts development and keeps it moving apace. Without it children may simply stop growing or developing. Development enables the child to gain more experience, and so the circle starts again.

There is, for example, an acceleration in all children's development just after they become mobile. Mobility gives them more to explore. It also means parents have to watch them a good deal more than in the preceding weeks. All this means that, initially, early crawlers and walkers are more advanced - not just mobile, but brighter, better communicators, more skilled than their sedentary peers. But after a while, things even out. A late walker enjoys exactly the same parental involvement in the end, the same new world to explore. When he becomes mobile his development rushes forward and he catches up.

Another fascinating example of how stimulation can alter development was discovered when researchers investigated the effects of famine on children's development. They found that babies who were fed supplements by spoon were much more advanced even if the food on the spoon had very little nourishment in it. When you breast-feed or bottle-feed a baby you do not need to interact. After you latch him on, you do not even need to look. Try giving food by spoon without coaxing, smiling and talking to him.

The child's new ability to hold more than one piece of information in his mind at any one time now means that he can start making simple comparisons between what is happening now and what happened a moment ago. The first time you will notice this is probably when he holds something in his hand, drops it on to the floor and looks over the side of the cot at it. At this stage he will not watch something you drop. He is only interested if he does it: all he can do at the moment is compare the object which was in his hand with the one now on the floor. Most babies start to do this between about seven and ten months. Soon afterwards you will see him hiding things behind doors, or putting things into boxes and peeping in to find them again.

By eight or nine months you will start to realize that he is beginning to communicate and to make requests. He has, of course, been manipulating you for months, but in a passive way. Now he starts to do it with intent. Nothing elaborate at first. He may just stretch up his arms and make a noise, so you pick him up. By about ten months he might hold a toy, look at you, then drop the toy for you to pick up. When you do, he drops it again. He is beginning to realize that he can control you. Over the next two years he will practise this controlling game many times, and in many contexts.

Asking (or telling) others to do something for us is one function of language. Doing what we are told is another. Once a baby starts to communicate his intentions and to respond to yours, he has the potential to be naughty, stubborn and disobedient. He will scream and shout to get you to do things; say 'No'; spit out food in order to annoy. From small beginnings such as these, behaviour grows.

Opposite: Sometime between six and ten months, he will begin to use each finger separately and his thumb in opposition – the facility which makes human hands so skilled.

Teaching a baby to sleep

To understand how your baby sleeps, you need to know how adults sleep.

No one just falls asleep and stays in exactly the same state until they awake. Nor do they sleep through the night without waking. Sleep goes in cycles: it gets deeper and deeper and then comes up rapidly to lighter levels. As we sleep we sometimes toss and turn or move about. From the deeper stages of sleep we often slip into dreams. Dreaming sleep is a distinct state – the brain is as active as if we were wide awake. But our bodies – apart from the eyes, which twitch and turn – are perfectly still. You could not move them, even if you wanted to. After dreaming, you return to non-dreaming sleep. The cycle lasts one to two hours, then you start again. There is less deep sleep as the night passes.

Scientists who watch people sleeping have noticed that when we come up from deeper sleep to a lighter one, or finish a dream, we sometimes 'overshoot': wake up momentarily, turn over and go back to sleep. It happens to most of us a couple of times every night. If you do this from a dreaming sleep, you will briefly remember your dream, but forget it once you go back to sleep. What enables us to go back to sleep after these brief awakenings is familiarity – familiarity with surroundings, with the whole process, which is why we sometimes wake in the night when sleeping in a strange room or have had a strange dream.

Babies sleep just like adults, except that they dream rather more. In their brief awakenings, little things can conspire to keep them longer awake: mild growing pains, strange places, colds. They do not turn over and go straight back to sleep. A child who expects his parents to be there singing lullabies or stroking his hair (as they do every night at bedtime) will cry out. If you go to him, you will set, and reinforce, a pattern. You become a necessary condition for the relaxation he needs in order to sleep: a part of every sleeping routine. On the other hand, a child who has learned how to fall asleep by himself will not call out unless he is in pain or afraid.

The art of getting a baby to sleep through the night is teaching him to fall asleep by himself. You can do this by letting him sleep (and go off to sleep) near you or in a room by himself. If you want him to fall asleep without you in the night, he must do so in the evening. The easiest way to get a baby into a sleeping routine is to start as you mean to go on – never begin the routine of strokes, songs and sitting beside the cot until he is asleep. Failing this, you will need to retrain him.

If your baby sleeps with you at night, you may find it easier to put

THE WRONG WAY TO PUT A SIX-MONTH-OLD BABY TO BED

✖ *Put him in his own bedroom. Stay with him until he is sleeping, always come back to his bedside if he catches you creeping out of the room.*

✖ *Stroke him and sing to him until he is sleeping. Start again if he demands you do so.*

✖ *Go to him in the night whenever he wakes and repeat the bedtime routine.*

✖ *Put him down to sleep in one place — and then carry him to his night-time bed (unless he sleeps in your room). He will not relax without your sounds and smells.*

✖ *Give him a bottle. It can ruin his teeth. Baby bottle tooth decay is the biggest cause of bad teeth in small children. Milk is just as bad as juice.*

✖ *Letting him suck your (empty) breast in order to go to sleep is asking for trouble. Breasts are fine for feeding babies, but when they become comforters, you create a demand that only you can fill. This may be fine by you — but it does rather exclude his father from doing anything except the traditional fatherly things such as playing and disciplining.*

✖ *Inconsistency never works. One rule one day, another the next leads to confusion and unease. Babies need simple rules.*

him down to sleep in pram or on the sofa where he can hear you. Your smells and sounds are part of his sleeptime security. But this is not always necessary. Wherever he is to go to sleep, put him down, say goodbye, and let him go off to sleep. Once asleep, leave him until you are ready to take him up to bed with you. He can either sleep in your bed or beside it. What remains constant between going to sleep in the evening and falling back asleep in the night in the night is that you remain close by.

The other strategy is to put him down for a sleep where he is to spend the night, say goodbye, give him a kiss and walk away. This can be in a room by himself, in your bed or in a cot in your bedroom. The key point of both strategies is that you leave the child to fall asleep by himself. A child who has always been put to bed in this way will be able to get back to sleep when he wakes in the night. even if you are not there. Daytime sleeps should be taken where the child is to sleep at

THE RIGHT WAY TO PUT A SIX-MONTH-OLD BABY TO BED

✔ *A familiar routine helps. Give him a bath, kiss everyone goodnight, cuddle and feed him in the bedroom. Tuck him up with a teddy. Switch on his musical box. The unchanging nature of a ritual really does reassure. Marking the event makes it clear that bedtime is nigh. In time, it will also make him feel sleepy.*

✔ *When a child is teething, ill or very unhappy, you will find it easier to let him fall asleep next to you on the sofa and to carry him up to bed later. If this disrupts an established routine, you will need to reinstate it once he is well again.*

✔ *The first stages of any sleeping routine should be putting him down to sleep in the same place every time. Kiss him goodnight, turn down the lights and leave (even if you only go and sit on the other side of the room). A baby who will not easily fall asleep on the sofa or in his pram should be taken to his cot.*

✔ *If he protests, check that there is nothing wrong and then leave.*

✔ *If he protests some more, tell him it is time for bed. Stay with him until he calms down a little, then leave.*

✔ *If he still does not settle, harden your heart and leave the room. Get yourself a drink and some ear plugs and let him cry it out. He will eventually fall asleep. Next night do the same, and the next. By the fourth night, most babies are putting themselves to sleep.*

✔ *If you find you cannot be so hard-hearted (and sometimes you cannot) try a more gradual approach. Stay with him for a shorter time each night. Talk to him rather than stroke him. Put on a story tape or some music to replace your voice. Eventually you can establish the tape as part of the 'good night' routine. Keep it short or he will expect it in the night as well. If this does not work, you will have to be tough – or accept his nightly demands.*

✔ *If even the gradual approach is too difficult, let him fall asleep on the sofa, then tuck him into bed beside you. It will make it harder to leave him for an evening or to talk to visitors, for he will certainly stay awake if there is any excitement or change. But he will almost certainly sleep through the night, and so will you. It is possible to break the habit of sleeping in your bed (if it was not, most of the people in the world would still be sleeping with their parents). The getting tough programme can be instituted at any age. Do get a big bed.*

night, or fall asleep in the evening.

Problems arise when you sit with him until he goes to sleep in the evening; or let him sleep on the sofa where you stroke and soothe him during the day – then expect him to go back to sleep alone in his cot at night. If you sit with him soothing and singing until he is asleep, he will need this soothing to put himself to sleep.

Waking in the night

A baby who can put himself to sleep without your help will be capable of going back to sleep when he wakes in the night. A baby who needs someone with him in order to fall asleep will call for you.

How do you stop him calling for you?

◆ Be there already. If he sleeps in your bed, there is no problem.

◆ A baby who always sleeps in a completely dark room is comforted by the darkness and, on waking, quickly goes back to sleep. Most babies in continental Europe sleep in completely dark rooms. Started soon enough, it is not frightening.

◆ If you do not want him to sleep in your bed, or to have to lull him back to sleep each time he awakes, a wakeful baby is better off in his own room. If he niggles in the night, leave him. If he cries, check that nothing is wrong, say 'Goodnight' and go back to bed. If he cries again, leave him. (Cover your head with a pillow until he has fallen asleep again.)

A child who cries every night may be hungry. One who suddenly starts to cry after weeks of sleeping through may be in pain. One who is obviously unwell needs comfort. Take him into your bed (or the spare bed) if you need to sleep.

◆ It is always easier for a baby to sleep in your room in the first months. You can reach out and pop his dummy back into his mouth, and feed him without completely waking up. Once he no longer needs a night feed, you may find he sleeps better in his cot if he is in a room of his own. A baby who screams to be picked up will scream longer when he can smell and hear you beside him. He knows you are there.

◆ Because babies start to miss their parents at about seven or eight months, this is not a good age to make the move to a separate room or out of your bed. Wait until he has passed the clinging stage.

◆ When a baby becomes capable of missing his parents, he often cries from loneliness. A comfort object helps him to feel less lonely. He can hug it and go back to sleep. Encourage him to sleep with a teddy, or put the edge of the quilt in his hand. Some children become attached to dummies, but these are harder for a baby to find in the night.

◆ Babies who sleep in their parents' beds soon return to sleep if they awake to find themselves in their parents' arms.

Refusing to go to bed – or back to bed

At about seven or eight months, a baby begins to understand that you continue to exist even when he cannot see you. Until now, he never missed you. Once your baby misses you, he will cry when you leave him, cling when you want to go and protest after you leave. A child who has been happily going to bed for months may start to protest when you say goodnight. The problem is exacerbated by teething, which often occurs at this time.

◆ As babies grow up, they need less sleep. If he is not sleepy in the evening, you may need to cut down on his daytime sleeps. Also, some babies need much less sleep than others. But there are no rules. If he is waking at six and still lively at eight, he probably does not need to sleep for a couple of hours in the day. It is obviously easier to get a child to go to bed if he is tired.

◆ A teething, frightened child needs indulgence. When he is very unhappy you may not be able to put him to bed as usual. Give him something to relieve his pain. Soothe him by rocking his pram or taking him for a drive around the block. If he cries in the night, go to him. Take it in turns with your partner to sleep with him. At these times it is often easier to let him sleep in your arms.

◆ Once he is well – and at all other times – be firm and consistent. Go through the sleep routine. Put him in his cot and leave.

◆ Familiar routines help him relax. A bath, a feed, dim lights and monotonous sounds will make him sleepy. (Covering his cries by vacuuming the stairs is a useful tactic).

◆ It is easier to be firm if you and your partner can agree and can support each other through the nights of protest.

◆ Some children sleep better once they are out of their cots and into their own beds. You will need to guard stairs. Be prepared for him to walk to your bed in the morning.

Getting him out of your bed

As I've noted elsewhere in this book, it is often convenient to have a small baby in bed with you – especially if you are breast-feeding. Babies sleep soundly in bed with their parents and mothers barely need to wake in order to breast-feed. Once he is latched on to the nipple, everyone can go back to sleep. It is a helpful system for mothers who have to go out to work in the early months of parenthood. Even if he sleeps in a cot, he will almost inevitably spend some time in bed with you – unless you are very vigilant. But why should you be? Having small children in your bed in the morning is one of the delights of parenthood - as long as they do not arrive before dawn. The problem arises when they come in at 3 am and toss and turn until seven

◆ A small child who has come into your bed during a time of illness or stress can be returned to the old routine simply by putting him into his cot and insisting he stays there. Expect tears and protest. Whoever is the most persistent will win: make sure it is you. If he sleeps through the night, returning to the old routine should not be too difficult.

If he does not, you are in for a couple of rough nights. You may need to move out to the sofa or spare bed unless his cot is in a separate room. It will help if you make sure he is really tired before going to bed. Avoid afternoon naps for a day or two. A hot water bottle may help.

◆ A baby who has always slept in your bed can be weaned from it in the same way as a child can be weaned from his cot to a bed. Make it important and special. Choose the bed and covers; make plenty of fuss about being 'a big boy'; tuck teddies into beds; have a table beside the bed for music or story tapes. Always put him to sleep in the new bed (even in the day) and leave him to go to sleep by himself (see above). It will help if you have already trained him to do this when sleeping in your bed. A hot water bottle may comfort a child who is used to a warm body next to him.

◆ A child who can climb out of bed (or his cot) and walk to you is more problematic. He will come to you when he wakes. The best way to ensure he does not wake until morning is to make sure he is tired. Keep him up a little later. As babies grow, they need less and less sleep. Some tiny children make do on eight to ten hours per day. Mine certainly did. If you want him to sleep at night, cut down on the daytime sleeps and keep him up later. Dividing up sleep into two or three blocks means we do not need quite as much. In countries where people sleep for an hour or so in the afternoon, they may sleep for only four to five hours at night. If he does wake and walks to your bed, take him back.

◆ An older baby can be delayed on his morning trip to your bed if you leave a little surprise for him in his room each morning. Nothing elaborate: just a toy he has not played with for a while. A drink of juice. A bowl of sand on a table.

How to stop constant crying

Some children are always unhappy. There are reasons, and there are excuses for this. You can (and should) do something about it. A child who is always crying is more difficult to love or to like. The most obvious cause of constant crying is pain. Ear infections, eczema, persistent colds and infections are the most common causes. See your doctor. He may be able to prescribe something to help.

Another common cause is family upset and stress. Even small children pick up signals and can reflect our unhappiness with their own. Young children cry because this is often the easiest and most reliable way to get your attention, and this is especially the case when we are distracted by our own unhappiness. Even if they only break through to your bad temper, they are reassured. A depressed mother may find it difficult to offer the stimulation and affection that keeps a baby smiling, interested and happy. Her child may hover between withdrawal and making demands.

Of course, some babies are easier and sunnier than others. One who starts out difficult can be moulded into sunnier ways by rewarding his good behaviour and ignoring his bad. A difficult child can be confirmed in his ways if you give in to him when he is naughty and ignore him when he is good.

THE RIGHT WAY TO DEAL WITH CONSTANT CRYING

✔ *Look for, and deal with, any apparent causes.*

✔ *When your child is being good, show him how much you appreciate it. Give attention, cuddles, play with him. Teach him that he will get his way more quickly and more often if he asks nicely. Always count to 100 before responding to his whinges.*

✔ *When your child is happy, join him. Laugh with him. Give plenty of attention.*

✔ *Try to minimize the attention you give when he cries without reason. Respond slowly (or not at all) to bad-tempered demands. Leave the room.*

✔ *Head off bad temper and tears. If he is unhappy, cuddle and comfort before he has to cry to demand it.*

✔ *Ignore manipulative crying. Walk away. Come back when he stops. If this is impossible, scoop him up and cuddle him very firmly. Hold him very tight until he calms down.*

✔ *If you are depressed or finding it difficult to cope, ask for professional help.*

✔ *If you find it hard to keep your temper, tell someone. Walk away. Ask for help before you harm him, not after.*

HOW NOT TO DEAL WITH CONSTANT CRYING

✖ *Always go to him and offer sympathy when he cries. Say he cannot come into your bed/have a biscuit/sweets/ice cream and then change your mind and allow these things if he keeps on crying.*

✖ *Help him more readily if he cries than you do if he does not cry. Pass things to him when he cries for them. Take away his dinner if he cries because he does not like it.*

✖ *Call him difficult and expect a different standard of behaviour from him.*

✖ *Tip-toe around him. Never confront him, contradict him or in any way teach him that being sunny or easy is a more reliable way to get what he wants.*

Shyness: can you change the way he is?

Some babies are slow to warm to people or to new places. While those children who seek excitement are probably always going to be more extrovert and outgoing, shy children do not have to be withdrawn. Babies who grow up rarely interacting with other people are almost inevitably shy with strangers and in new places. All babies have a phase of shyness and fearfulness from, say, nine to 12 months. Those who often go out and meet new people and do new things grow in self-assurance. Those who stay at home may continue to feel uneasy. Most children are shy when they have to break into a group which has already formed. The less experience they have, the harder they will find it.

Is he really shy?

◆ Small children always need to check with you that people, places and action are safe. This is not shyness.

◆ Babies may be interested in other children, but do not initiate play or talk with them until they are about two years old. It is entirely normal for your one-year-old not to want to play with other children.

◆ Babies can be drawn into 'conversation' with other people, and can initiate interactions with adults and older children they know well. A couple of toddlers will not talk or laugh together or share toys, because they do not know how.

◆ At about nine months, all babies withdraw from strangers, and will cry if you try to force them to interact with strangers or people they have not seen recently. Children have to learn to feel secure with new people. If they rarely meet anyone new, it will take them longer. It is practice which makes this easier.

◆ Most children are uneasy, and cling when in new places. This is something else which begins at about nine months and can continue into the school years or beyond. Again, practice is important. A child who rarely leaves home is bound to feel insecure when he does so.

◆ Most babies have to learn how to feel secure when not in physical contact with you. When visiting a new place, they may insist on playing at your feet or holding on to your skirt. Even after they have been in a new place for some time, babies do not move very far away from their parents. They will constantly check that you are watching them. It is normal for children to do this when you are near.

◆ Whenever a baby tries something new or meets someone new, or if you move away from his vicinity, he will look to you for reassurance. Only when he can count on your support will he venture further. If you ignore him when he looks for this support, he may remain shy and clinging.

◆ If you have a baby girl, you are more likely to retrieve her if she starts to crawl away from you than if it is a boy. You are more likely to stop her talking to strangers or playing boisterous games. Not only are parents often more tolerant of their daughters' shyness; they may actively encourage it.

HOW NOT TO HELP A SHY CHILD

✖ *Try to force him to play with others. Tell him not to be so silly.*

✖ *Assume a baby will settle with a stranger, or with a relative he has not seen recently.*

✖ *Lack sympathy – or patience. If a child feels insecure, he needs more support, not less.*

✖ *Ignore a child when he is in new places or with other people.*

✖ *Carry on with your social life and leave him to carry on with his.*

✖ *Get irritated and withdraw support when he clings. Shout at him or smack him. Tell him – in words or action – to go away.*

✖ *Tell him not to be a baby when he needs to hug his teddy.*

✖ *Label him as the 'shy one' by what you say, how you act or what you expect of him.*

HELPING THE SHY CHILD

✔ *A child who is securely attached to more than one person will find it easier to interact with others. A child who spends all his time with his mother will find it hard not to be shy.*

✔ *A child who is used to new people and places will be less worried by them. Practice is important here. Find a mother and baby group, visit the park. If you do not interact with others, how is he to learn?*

✔ *He gets his security from you. If you can give this at a distance, he is more likely to venture forth. If he goes one step further than his present confidence allows, he will need a confidence booster. This may be no more than a smile across the room. Given at the right time, it can allow him to explore further. Sometimes he gets frightened and needs to come back for a quick cuddle. If, when he seeks reassurance, you communicate unease rather than confidence, or if you are too busy to notice, his fears will grow. Next time he is more likely to stay close to you.*

✔ *A toddler does not interact with strange children until after his second birthday. But he will sit next to them. A baby who is sitting with others can watch how conversations begin. He may be drawn in by older children. When he is ready to start a conversation himself, he is in the right place. A child who has never mixed with other children has much more to learn. He will inevitably be a little shy at first.*

✔ *A child who knows you have confidence in him will feel that confidence. Always let him know you appreciate his efforts.*

✔ *Children who like excitement are less likely to be shy. Boisterous play may help a child to overcome some shyness. But turn the volume up slowly.*

✔ *There is some evidence that a comfort object (teddy, rag, blanket) helps children to deal with new places and people. (This is true even for ten-year-olds.)*

Missing you: clinging and fear of strangers

From about seven months, when he is able to think about you when he is alone, he can miss you. Once he can miss you, he begins to dread your going, and will look for signs that you are about to go. When he sees them, he will protest. If he can crawl, he may follow you around from room to room and will cling on tight as you kiss him goodbye, and howl as you go through the door. A child whose parents leave and come back often (as working parents do) soon learns that the parting is not for ever. There may still be protest, but it becomes milder.

HOW NOT TO DEAL WITH A CLINGING BABY

✹ *Start back to work just as he begins to realize he can miss you. That is between about seven and nine months. If this is impossible, do make a practice of spending a little time away from him before you start work, so that he can adjust. It is painful for you to have to leave a screaming child.*

✹ *Leave without saying goodbye, especially at seven months and older.*

✹ *Leave him with a total stranger.*

✹ *Ignore him. Respond only when he demands.*

✹ *Be cold and unsympathetic if he makes a fuss.*

HOW NOT TO DEAL WITH HIS FEAR OF STRANGERS

✹ *Say "Don't be silly, this is Grandma."*

✹ *Pass him to a strange person and expect him to get used to them. Remember, a stranger to him could well be a familiar person to you.*

✹ *Shout; get upset.*

✹ *Leave him when in a strange place, with someone he does not know, or in a room full of strangers.*

HOW TO DEAL WITH A CLINGING, FEARFUL BABY

✔ *If you are returning to work after your child is six months old, always make sure he knows the person he is to be left with, and the place he is left in. If necessary, spend time with him on his first day.*

✔ *Do not make the first day of work the first time you have left him. Go out in the evening some days before, leaving him with a baby sitter. Leave him with a friend (whom he knows) for a few hours while you go shopping. He needs to feel confident that you will return. A whole work-ing day is a long time for him to feel that he has lost you for ever.*

✔ *If he is frightened of strangers (even Grandma), be sympathetic. Wait until he is used to them before handing him over. Your concern is with your child. Grandma may be upset, but she is old enough to look after herself.*

✔ *Expect him to be clingy in a new place. When the place is more famil-iar, he will be more adventurous.*

Late walking

Some children walk at nine months. Most walk at 13 to 14 months. A few do not walk until they are almost two. For a few of these late walk-ers, there may be an underlying reason for their slower physical devel-opment – such as cerebral palsy or Down's syndrome. Most parents will be aware of such problems. If a child is not walking by two, his physical development needs to be checked. He may, for example, have problems with balance, or his sight may be poor.

Because the brain matures in a set pattern, and at a fairly constant rate, a child who is late holding his head up is likely to be delayed in reaching all later milestones, including sitting, standing and walking. This delay may be quite unrelated to other skills such as learning to talk. (There is almost no correlation between speed of physical maturity and later intelligence.) It may, however, affect certain other physical skills, including hand and finger control. A late walker is also likely to be a late picking up his peas, piling up bricks or tying his laces.

Although there is no correlation between mobility and later intelli-gence, mobile babies are initially brighter than immobile ones. This is probably because parents spend much time watching, talking and gen-erally interacting with babies when they first start getting about. They have to. Mobile children have many more things to explore, manipulate and see. They are motivated to plan. Because they can go across the room to pick up a toy, it is worth planning how to get there and back and what to do next. Rooted to the spot, the immobile child has less need to consider a sequence of behaviours. However, the boost to his intelligence does not last long, and immobile children soon catch up.

Premature babies are almost invariably late reaching developmental milestones. Development is associated with gestational age (time from conception). At seven months you can expect a child born two months premature to be like a four- or five-month-old. It can take them a full two years to catch up. Remember, being born early is in itself stressful, and that stress can add its own delay. Since prematurity is more frequently associated with birth damage, one should never be complacent about developmental delay in such children. They should receive regular checks in the first year.

SOME FACTS ABOUT PHYSICAL DEVELOPMENT

◆ Some racial groups mature faster than others. The average Afro-Caribbean child is walking before the average European.

◆ Girls mature a little faster than boys, probably because they are a little lighter.

◆ The speed of physical development seems to be largely pre-programmed. Identical twins walk within days of each other. Non-identical twins are no more alike than any other two children from the same family.

◆ Plenty of practicewalking around the furniture or in a baby-walker can speed things up a little: but the effects are quite small.

◆ A child who receives very little general stimulation can be considerably delayed, as can a child who is neglected.

◆ Children who bottom-shuffle are often slow to start walking. This is probably because there is little motivation: they can get about and carry objects just as they are. A crawling child can do this only if he carries things in his mouth like a dog.

What to do about late development

◆ If he is a just a little below average, stop worrying: this is not a race or an intelligence test. Early walking runs in families.

◆ If your child is late reaching his early physical milestones (such as supporting his head) ask your clinic or your doctor for a developmental check. You will be referred to a specialist if they think there is a problem. Remember that published tables show averages: half of all babies born will be at or below these averages.

◆ A child who is reluctant to become mobile may have other problems. If he was sitting at the normal time, but is still not walking or crawling by 18 months, consult your doctor or clinic and ask for a developmental check.

◆ A child who is slow becoming mobile may be very frustrated. Consider buying a baby walker. Do not leave him in this for long hours every day. It can cause damage to the ankles. It also stops your child investigating or handling objects. He practises using his feet at the expense of his hands.

How to wean a child who is using the breast as a comforter

◆ It is best not to offer the breast when he is upset. Most of us do not realize that we have been doing this until it is too late. If he finds comfort in sucking, is it possible to substitute a dummy or a bottle? Your partner may need to give it to him. He is unlikely to take a substitute when he knows the real thing is available.

◆ Find a convenient time when you are both free from stress.

◆ Offer another comforter – a teddy, a blanket or a bit of rag he can hold. Give it to him when he is going to sleep or sitting quietly. Give him a teddy when he is feeling upset. Combine it with a drink in his cup if that helps.

◆ If he hurts himself, scoop him up for a cuddle together with the comforter.

◆ You will need to reduce access to the breast except at feed times. Wear a dress if he tries to help himself.

◆ Restrict comfort sucking to certain places – the house at first, then perhaps your bedroom. Restrict the times. Stop comfort feeding during the night (if this is easiest), then during the day, finally cutting it out before bedtime. For many babies, this last is the most difficult hurdle.

◆ You may have to approach these steps in a different order with different children.

◆ If he protests about either type of restriction, and refuses to adapt, you may feel it is easier to get it over in one go. In this case, do make doubly sure that there are no other stresses for either of you.

◆ If he is very attached to the breast, it will not be easy. You may have to stand firm and let him cry.

Weaning a child from a comfort bottle

◆ Since there is often little urgency to wean the child from a comfort bottle, it often happens much later.

◆ Find a suitable time when no stresses or changes are on hand.

◆ Either restrict access slowly – as to the breast – or, if he is older, set an agreed target, perhaps after half term if he has just started at nursery. Most children of this age will voluntarily restrict their access to their bottle: they do not want their friends to see.

◆ Exchange the bottle for some special treat. Always praise him for trying. Few of us find it easy to give up our comfort habits.

◆ My mother organized a funeral for our bottles. We buried them in the garden: but then, most of us did have them until we started school.

Weaning a child from the breast or bottle feeding on to a cup

◆ Cut out breast and bottle feeds one at a time, substituting a cup of milk.

WEANING PROBLEMS

Babies can be weaned from the breast or bottle on to a cup from
about seven months. But since they are still taking a large
proportion of their nutrition in the form of milk at this age, they
need to be quite proficient with the cup.

Just because a baby can be weaned does not mean he has to be.
Nor does it mean that it is necessarily a good idea. Babies like
sucking. They are comforted by it, and if you are quite happy to
continue giving the breast or a bottle, this is perfectly OK. Nor do
you have to wean him from the breast to a cup. You may find it
easier to wean him to a bottle. If this is what makes your baby
happy, it is the right thing to do.

There are no hard and fast rules: it really is a matter of taste and
convenience. In the past, children were often exclusively breast-fed
until they were three or four years old, and may have continued to
have the occasional feed until they were as old as seven. You do
not wean children on to solids in order to improve nutrition. You
do so because it is more convenient. You no longer have to rely on
breast feeding for contraception. By the time a baby is nine or ten
months old, he would need feeding at about two- or three-hour
intervals to obtain sufficient milk. Most women probably do not
want that sort of tie. If you want to continue with exclusive breast
feeding, however (or partial breast feeding for that matter), there is
absolutely no reason why you should not do so. Nor is there any
reason why you should completely wean from a bottle to a cup.

Bottles and breasts comfort them. If feeding was the only
function of the breast, it would be easy to switch a child over to a
cup. It is the comforting aspect from which is often difficult to
wean him. At about seven months, most babies become rather
clinging and fearful, and often become attached to those things
that reduce their fears and make them feel more secure. Breasts and
bottles are often on their list. Whenever he is unhappy and/or
afraid, a few sucks will set him to rights.

◆ The night feed is usually the first to go. By six months, most children have also dropped the late evening feed. If you are switching a younger child from breast to bottle, he may still need a bottle at these times.

◆ By the time he is having solids three times a day, he is probably only having four or five feeds: early morning, breakfast, lunch, tea and just before bedtime.

◆ Substitute a cup of milk for the breast or bottle at breakfast, lunch and tea. If he has milk with his cereal, he could have juice with this meal. After he is settled to this regime, replace the early morning bottle. If you have tea in bed, let him join you.

◆ The late bedtime feed is always the most difficult. Children are tired and easily upset at this time and many find that this last feed is part of the going to sleep routine. I found the easiest way was for one of us to sit with the child while he had a bedtime drink.

◆ There is no harm in taking a bottle or sucking cup to bed, as long as it does not contain a sweet drink.

◆ If you cannot get a baby to sleep unless he sucks a night-time bottle, what does it matter? As long as you take the bottle from him as soon as he is asleep and/or give him a bottle of water.

THE WRONG REASONS FOR WEANING A CHILD

✖ Because you are told it is about time.

✖ Because he has reached a certain age.

✖ Because you are about to start work or go on holiday.

THE WRONG TIME TO WEAN A CHILD

✖ If there are major changes in his life: going to nursery, parental separation, parental illness, mother returning to work.

✖ If the child is teething or ill.

✖ When you are about to go on holiday or move house.

✖ Any time his confidence is low. Any time you are under stress.

Is he late talking?

Children begin to understand their first words at about seven to nine months. If you look carefully you may begin to see his first 'sign word' at this time. He may stretch out his hands to say "Give me"; screw up his face when you try to give him food he does not like; or lift up his arms to be picked up. By about ten months, some children are adding sounds or words to these signs. They may also point and say something like "Psst" when they see a cat. Most children probably have one such word by the time they are about 13 or 14 months, although it may not be very clear, Within weeks of this first word, they have probably added another three or four. Once under way, the words come thick and fast. By the time they are 18 months, most children have about one hundred. By the time they are two, this will have increased to about 250 and they will have begun to put words together to form simple sentences. At two he may make over a thousand different statements every month.

A small percentage of children (mostly boys) have language difficulties. Some of these may be deaf. An even smaller percentage (1:2,500) may have early infantile autism. Some may have a general learning disability. Such children will have difficulties understanding language as well as speaking. Amongst children who are late speaking (but can nonetheless understand language) there are those who later stutter; some who speak rather unclearly – and may need some speech therapy; and some who will later have dyslexia or poor spelling. All these problems are more common in boys. Many have a family history. By no means all children who are not speaking at two have such problems.

Is he deaf?

Because deaf children can be helped to understand and use language by providing them with hearing aids and teaching them sign language, early diagnosis is essential. Sometimes early problems arise because of ear infection and/or large amounts of wax in the ear. Other conditions can be corrected by simple operations.

◆ Make sure that your baby has all the scheduled checks on his development. These include hearing tests.

◆ If you suspect a hearing problem, you can carry out some simple tests yourself. Does he turn towards a loud sound? Is he upset by sudden loud noises? If you call him from one side of the room, will he turn to look at you, or does he need to catch sight of you before he turns to you full face? Does he turn if you whisper?

◆ If you suspect deafness, don't try to ignore it – you may well be right. Remember that most children don't suffer total hearing loss. If he passes your informal tests. there may still be some kind of hearing loss: see a doctor.

◆ Hearing loss is sometimes missed in a child with multiple problems.

How to help a deaf child

◆ Speak to the child face on, and exaggerate lip movements. Children become surprisingly adept at lip reading.

◆ Speak loudly and clearly. He may have some residual hearing.

◆ If you know he has a problem within a specific hearing range, try to use whatever range he can process.

◆ Remove background noise. Radios and TVs or noisy washing machines make it very difficult for those with hearing loss to make out what is being said.

◆ Use signs. Point, mime action.

◆ Do not give up. Deaf children need more communication, not less.

◆ Books can help him understand signs and lip movements: just as they can help a hearing child to learn words. But do look at him as well as the book.

◆ Deaf children can learn to communicate using sign language sooner than hearing children can communicate with speech. If your child is profoundly deaf, learn and use sign language with him.

◆ Understand his frustration, but do not make too many allowances. A deaf child needs to be tough and strong if he is to succeed in a hearing world. Sometimes it may seem cruel when you force him to speak, but he will thank you in the long run.
Let him know how important he is. Build up his self-esteem.

Above all, let him know how much he is loved. Because other children find it difficult to communicate with him, he may have fewer friends than they do.

Autism

Autism is first noticed in early childhood. It is characterized by an inability to relate to others and to respond to attempts to communicate by remaining mute. Self-injury or preoccupation with objects may also be symptoms. These children tend to be aloof and unresponsive to those who care for them; they lack social skills and appear to be very alone.

◆ Autistic children are physically normal. There is often, but not always, associated learning disability. It is usually very difficult to diagnose any problem in the first year: most children are diagnosed between two and three.

◆ Children with autism have severe language delays. Some autistic children have no language. Some simply echo what they hear. Others have a limited proficiency. This improves as they get older.

◆ Autistic children are likely to keep repeating the same movement, such as rocking back and forth.

Milestones: 12 to 14 months

The period between 11 and 14 months is often a very happy time for parents. The baby is growing up and life is often very much easier for him. He is beginning to communicate his needs and to share his experience. He shows his delight when you walk into the room. He is also becoming more independent and can amuse himself with his toys for much longer periods. He will love his bath, trips to the park, and outings such as visits to the fire station. He will also love being with other children, although he will not yet know how to interact with them. When he does, he will laugh and scream with delight.

On the down side, he needs constant watching. He is beginning to have his own ideas about what he likes and dislikes ('No' is in most children's early vocabulary).

Because he is more active and independent than before, it is easy to over-estimate what he can do. A child of this age has little idea of self. He will know he is a boy, but not that he will grow up to be a man. He will not even recognize himself in a mirror or in a photograph. He still thinks that you share all his thoughts and feelings. If pulling your earrings does not hurt him, how can it hurt you? He can be obstinate, but not yet really naughty. He can do things to attract your attention (and if naughtiness works best he will learn to do naughty things), but he does not set out to deliberately upset people.

His attachments are important to him: the rocks on which he builds his gradual emergence from his family. A child who is securely attached to a number of carers and siblings is secure and happy, playful and ready to learn.

Self from six to 18 months

In their first half year. babies fall in love with their carers. The people they love are altogether wonderful. They look eagerly for their faces and when they find them they communicate that love. They smile, gurgle and laugh. As the second half-year progresses, this need to communicate increases, and the means of communication become more complex. The baby begins to show various emotions and express them in response to the effect of people on their existence. They cry when left. They answer happily when called. They look to a loved one for reassurance, or to check before exploring. He may woo you, and by nine months is beginning to develop an organized way of responding. If he wants a biscuit, he may take your hand and lead you to the cupboard. He may tug on his father's sweater to be picked up.

These actions are usually interpreted as showing that the child is beginning to develop an idea of himself as a person: someone with his own specific needs and emotions who can communicate with others. He shows joy and elation and knows he wants to be loved and cuddled. He experiences anger and fear, anxiety and petulance when his wants are not fulfilled. By 18 months, he may even feel shame and defiance.

Helping the development of self

◆ Let your child know you understand his requests.

◆ Name what he is asking for, so he not only understands that he has communicated with you, but also learns the words to do this.

◆ Respond to your child's emotions.

◆ When he 'checks' with you whether something is OK, let him have an answer: a word of encouragement, or the reverse.

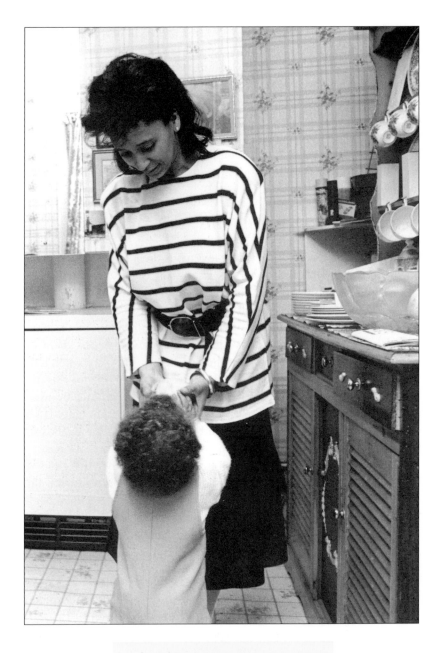

He is better able to understand what others want from him because he is better able to understand what he wants for himself.

◆ Defiance is frustrating: but it is a necessary stage in the development of his sense of self. Try to remember this: when he is being playful and teasing, respond playfully.

And when you come home from work...

Most working mothers will have arrived home and peered through the window at a happy, angelic child. They will also have opened the door to find that angel transformed into a whirlwind. Trying you is a way of ensuring that you love them. When you leave a child five days a week, he may need to test you harder and more often than otherwise. Children do play their parents off against their other carers. But children play all their loved ones off against one another. It is nothing special.

The bond between a mother and her child has long been considered an important pillar on which later social and emotional development is built. But while that bond is clearly important, there is no evidence that a child needs just one attachment figure, needs this attachment in the first year, or that being cared for by a number of different people is necessarily bad. Early studies which suggested that separation from the mother had long-term bad effects on a child's emotional life were flawed. They confused separation with a generally poor environment in which the child was being raised. When children who lived in otherwise loving and supportive homes were studied, maternal deprivation in the first two years had no long-term influences on development.

Nonetheless, it must be said that formation of an attachment between a working mother and her child can be delayed because of her absence, especially if she works more than 35 hours per week, just as the attachment between a working father and his child is often slower to develop when he works longer hours than this. No one has shown that this is necessarily damaging for the child, as long as he is secure in his environment and with his carers. There is, for example, no evidence that children reared in Israeli kibbutzim, where they live in nursery peer groups and see their own parents for only a few hours per day, have any more social, emotional or developmental problems than children reared by their mothers. Children can change attachment figures (or take aboard new ones) without devastating effect. Late adoption often works well. Whether a child can cope with a long string of indifferent carers while his parents work long hours is another matter. On a more positive note, children raised in day care are more social, adaptive, playful and explorative than children cared for at home in these first two years. They're also more confident and less fearful. On the negative side, they are also more aggressive.

Research suggests that day care does not disrupt attachments if:

◆ Children are securely attached to their carers. This is by far the most important factor.

◆ Children come from a stable family.

◆ The care they receive is good.

◆ Babies and mothers are temperamentally alike. If time together is short, it is easier to mesh with someone you recognize.

◆ Mothers are sympathetic to their children's needs.

◆ Marriages or relationships are happy.

◆ Mothers – especially of boys – do not work more than 35 hours per week.

◆ There is a low level of stress within the family.

◆ Parents are warm and accepting.

◆ Children are not put into day care between six and 12 months, or between 18 and 24 months.

◆ Mothers enjoy working.

WHAT NOT TO WORRY ABOUT IF YOU ARE A WORKING MOTHER

✖ *That you are not always there. He needs good care 24 hours per day. You do not have to be the only one providing it.*

✖ *That a happy and healthy child seems more attached to his full-time carer. Be happy he can love. Do not weigh by how much.*

✖ *That your child seems to play up when you come home. He is just testing.*

✖ *That he is playing you off against his carer. All children do this.*

✖ *That maternal deprivation causes long-term problems. There is no evidence for this as long as children form secure attachments with you and their carers.*

WHAT TO WORRY ABOUT IF YOU ARE A WORKING MOTHER

✔ *The quality of your carer(s). That the child is developing a warm emotional bond with them.*

✔ *That carers will not stay and that there is no security or certainty in his life. Children are affected by the departure of loved ones. For younger children and babies, the effects are fairly transient. Too many changes could effect the development of early attachments, especially if you are working long hours.*

✔ *That there is time for you and your partner to develop a close relationship with your child. Quality time is no substitute for real time.*

✔ *That your child is growing up in a supportive and stimulating environment.*

✔ *That your child is not being placed in a punitive environment.*

✔ *Don't expect 'genes' to out. What you put in after conception matters.*

The developing bond

There is now quite substantial evidence to show that the type of initial attachment a child makes with his care giver remains true to type over time. Those who make poor parents in the first year often do not improve. Poor attachment (and poor 'parenting') can influence many other aspects of a child's life. The earliest attachments are thought to be especially important for future development because they serve as secure a base for the child as he tries to make sense of his world and the people in it. The parent is the anchor and safe haven he holds on to, somewhere to turn when he is afraid. He does not have to divert energy into worrying. Anyone who has ever felt unloved by their partner will know how distracting this can be. Attachments also form a pattern for later social relationships. But note the plural. If he turns out to be rather anti-social, it is not just down to his mother. There are other people in his life and his attachment with them can shield and support – or undermine – his confidence. Attachments do not have to be made in the first year. There is plenty of evidence that children can form very good and stable relationships with step-parents.

Although most research in this area is concerned with the effects of poor attachment on later behaviour, it should be remembered that it is virtually impossible to separate poor attachment from poor 'parenting'. A mother who is unsympathetic to a toddler is unlikely to turn into a model parent the moment the child turns four. Over the years, habits are formed on both sides which become more and more difficult to change. Studies which suggest that attachment quality remains stable for most children reinforce this. They do not, however, show that the delay in attachment between a working mother and her child necessarily means that there will always be difficulties. It may take longer to mesh together, but that meshing can still be good. We know this to be the case because children do form good – but late – attachments with working fathers.

There are three separate factors which are assumed to underlie attachment. The first factor is separation anxiety, which, as the name suggests, is the child's fear of losing a loved one. This is strongest when the child is between seven and 30 months. The second is concerned with negotiating a balance between attachment and exploration. You might think of this as the interplay between the desire to be with the mother and the need to go out into the wider world in order to explore. When a child toddles away from you and looks back to check you are watching, you can see this interplay at work. Security is the final component. A secure child feels confident enough to leave his loved one and for her to leave him. It is a measure of his certainty that he (and she) will be together again.

Types of attachment

◆ A securely attached child feels comfortable when he is with his parent. Their behaviours mesh together. They are two people who are obviously in love. He is quite unhappy if she leaves him in a strange place or with strange people. But he quickly and happily greets his mother when she returns to him. He does not show any anger or bear grudges. He does not need to cling to her. He may stay near to her for a while, but after he has settled, he will be ready to venture out to explore. Secure children have mothers and carers who are accessible, consistent and sensitive. They respond to their babies' cries, smiles or other signals. Their children are confident that they are loved and that the parent has their interests at heart.

◆ An insecure/avoiding child does not mesh with his parent. When they are together he may appear uncomfortable, even uninterested. If she leaves him he may not cry, but will actively avoid her when she returns, looking away, carrying on with what she is doing when she calls him, squirming if he is picked up.

Mothers of insecure, avoiding children tend to be rather self-centred parents. They respond to their children only if they themselves are in the mood for it. Their children have to fit in with them. They are less sensitive to their children's needs and often dislike physical contact. It is as if neither is as involved with the other as they should be.

◆ Ambivalent children tend to cling to their parents, but that clinging seems to bring little comfort. Sometimes mothers cuddle them in return, sometimes they lose their temper. When the mother leaves, the child may become completely distraught. When she returns, she brings little comfort. The child may cling to her one minute, crying piteously, but avoid her the next, struggling to be put down if she picks him up. It is as if he needs to punish her, as if neither the child nor the mother know what they want. The mothers of ambivalent children tend to be inconsistent. Cuddling one minute, ignoring the child the next.

◆ Disorganized/disoriented children display a variety of disorganized behaviour patterns. Their behaviour is full of contradictions. One minute they avoid, the next they show an intense desire to approach. They seem dazed, unsure and lacking in any coherent way of interacting with the parent. Parents of such children are often abusive.

Factors that can influence early attachment

◆ Gentle, sensitive, available mothers generally have securely attached children.

◆ Mothers do not find it more difficult to become attached to difficult babies.

◆ Parents who are willing to show their emotions have more securely attached children.

◆ If a mother is depressed and stressed, she could well also be inconsistent with her baby. Distracted by her own problems, she may not always respond to her child.

◆ Working more than 35 hours per week. There is some evidence that leaving children for longer than this delays the formation of attachments, especially in boys.

◆ Culture. Different cultures have different ideals. Mothers in Germany encourage independence in their children and are often more emotionally distant than British or Japanese mothers. Mothers in Japan rarely leave their children for a moment, sleeping with them and never using baby sitters. Their children are clearly much more dependent. That each culture produces well adjusted individuals (as well as badly adjusted ones) suggest there is not one 'true' way.

Factors which promote early security

◆ What children need is consistency: consistency in the expression of love, and in the expectations of independence. The means of expression and the level of independence which is encouraged is relatively unimportant. Children need to know where they stand, what they can do, and that they can always depend upon you. How you show this is less important, but your accessibility is important. They need your confidence, to know you encourage their independence. Whether this allows them to crawl halfway across the room or the whole way is less important than knowing the limits are clearly defined.

◆ Children need carers to respond to their requests – even if it is to say no.

◆ A child and his carer need time to form attachments.

Early education?

Although there is probably a large genetic influence on intelligence, the course of development is by no means set by the genes a child inherits from his parents. Early studies of children adopted from very disadvantaged backgrounds show that they can be stretched by good, supportive and stimulating adoptive parents. While peers who remained in bad orphanages often grew up with severe learning difficulties, the fortunate children who were adopted into caring homes grew up to be normal, intelligent children. Parents, care givers and educators can and do influence the way children develop. So do life events. Even the place of birth may be important: urban children tend to be rather brighter than rural children. When parents divorce, a child may stand still for a while, even falling behind his peers. Most bounce back. The older the child is, the longer the effect of any disruption may last. But most overcome these problems; the older the child, the longer recovery may take.

Children who develop into highly intelligent adults are described, when children, as independent, problem solving, self initiating and able to get on with things without constant prompting. These are all things that parents can begin to encourage from an early age. They can also spend time talking and reading to children, although the amount of vocalization a parent engages in with her small child seems to correlate with intelligence only in girls. Perhaps the best evidence that early input matters is that the quality of active and interactive play predicts later intelligence.

Studies in America suggest that a supportive, warm home is associated with high achievement, and a critical, punitive home with low achievement. Although we cannot formally educate children at this age, we can encourage their inquisitiveness, praise their efforts and enable them to play. Sometimes we should allow them to find out; at other times we can show or tell them how something is done. Exactly how we blend the elements depends upon the child. Successful boys tend to have warm mothers who are involved and interested in what they do. Successful girls have mothers who push them. But this may be more a reflection of society than the needs of the children. You probably have to be more pushy to succeed as a woman. Probably the most important

HOW NOT TO EDUCATE YOUR BABY

✖ *Lose interest in what he is trying to do. Tell him he cannot do it before he even starts.*

✖ *Be critical of the way he tries and the way he plays. Ignore his play.*

✖ *Take over. Of course he cannot do it as well as you can. But if you set the standard so high, why should he try?*

✖ *Show by your actions that you have no confidence in him.*

✖ *Punish him for getting things wrong, making a mess, or not succeeding.*

✖ *Never notice when he gets it right.*

✖ *Never (or rarely) play with him.*

✖ *Think of him as not very bright. Tell others he is the 'sweet one' and that his brother is the 'clever one'.*

✖ *There is often a very fine balance between stretching a child and pushing him too hard. No one can be educated every minute of the day. Education works best if there is time to rest and consolidate in between work sessions.*

HOW TO EDUCATE YOUR BABY

✔ *Treat him with warmth.*
✔ *Praise him whenever there is an excuse to do so. Show interest in what he does,*
✔ *Play with him. Talk to him. Interact as often as possible.*
✔ *Never say he is only playing. Play is learning.*
✔ *Have high expectations of his abilities and show that you have confidence in him. Encourage him to try to solve problems: but help when he needs helping.*
✔ *Encourage his independence.*
✔ *Encourage him to play by himself, to initiate activities, to get on with things without constant prompting. But don't expect too much. Children need gradual, gentle stretching, not forcing.*

element is to believe that your children can succeed, and transmit this belief to them. If he knows he can do it, and believes you know this too, he is halfway to succeeding. Parents who are always critical of their child's efforts (whether when teaching them or when watching them play) have less successful children. Studies suggest that mothers are more important than fathers in all these matters.

Does it matter what he eats?

There is a current obsession with healthy eating that makes it difficult to view the eating habits of many small children with anything short of alarm. Most of us probably believe that, left to themselves, children and young people would eat nothing but unhealthy fast food. Surprisingly, however, experiments suggest that. left alone, children actually select quite balanced diets for themselves.

The reason? Doing anything else makes them ill. A child who is missing some vital ingredient in his diet is sick and listless. If your child is full of life and energy, and growing well, he is getting all the nutrients he needs, even if they do come from hamburgers and baked beans.

Because most of us come to parenthood with very little experience of raising children, we are prey to all sorts of concerns. Many of our fears about what our children eat are fuelled by insecurity about being good parents. It the past, being a parent was an inevitable consequence of a relationship and marriage. Now that we choose it, there is more of an onus to do it well.

Food has become an icon for care – a hot topic, like everything else we spend our money on. Many of the fashionable concerns are non-sense. If the choice is between persuading him to sit down with a book and a hot dog or spending the time preparing him brown rice with crisp fresh vegetables, there really is no contest. The story is much the best brain food. Children can survive, grow and blossom on a pretty basic diet. Children all over the world have been doing so for thousands of years.

Facts about children's diet

◆ Children do not need a varied diet. If what they eat provides them with all the nutrients they need, it does not matter if it is the same every day.

◆ Children do not need a huge amount of protein. If it forms about 2 per cent of their diet, that's enough. This is not very much. Most European children get far more protein than they need. Hamburgers, fish fingers, sausages, peas, baked beans on toast, yoghurts and ice cream provide more than enough.

◆ Children do not need a vast array of vegetables. Many of the vitamins and trace elements vegetables provide can be found elsewhere. They are, for example, added to cereals, found in tomato ketchup and fruit juices, present in yoghurt and ice cream. If in doubt, you can always give him vitamin and mineral drops.

◆ If nature intended children under two to live on anything, that something is milk. If in doubt, supplement his diet with milk, or milk products such as full cream yoghurt or cheese.

Does he eat too many sweet things?

◆ Sugars provide energy for all the cells in the body and the brain. You can break food down to provide the necessary sugars, or take them in directly. Most small children burn off all the sugars they consume. Very few toddlers are skinny. They are not meant to be. Sometimes they need to grow half an inch in the night. They need stores on hand (or should we say tummy). If your child is no plumper than average, is active and energetic, always has his teeth cleaned after meals, eats food other than puddings, and does not have more than one or two sweets and biscuits a day, there is probably no need to be worried by his sugar intake, unless you or your husband are very overweight.

◆ Once children taste sweets, they often refuse to touch savouries. Sometimes I feel this is because the savoury foods we offer them are so bland, especially when compared with the sweet things on offer. A child who refuses his dinner may prefer hamburgers, ketchup and crisps because they have strong flavours. A little spice, garlic, herbs, tomato or pesto may help. Add a little at a time and go easy on the chilli.

◆ Sweet things can damage the teeth. Always encourage your child to clean his teeth after eating them.

◆ Do not bribe him with pudding if he finishes his main course. This makes pudding the prize and dinner the punishment.

◆ Stop worrying. Children love to wind us up. It demonstrates how much we care. If you are obsessive about food, he will learn that this is the button to press.

◆ Honey is no less fattening and no less harmful to teeth than other sweet things.

Does he eat too much fat?

◆ Children need more fats than adults because fats are essential for building cells. The walls of each cell in the body contain fats. As children grow, they build more and more cells (as well as replacing the ones they already have). So they need a rather higher percentage of fat in their diet than adults. This is why children should have full cream milk.

Although you should never restrict a baby's fat intake except on medical advice, it does no harm to keep a sensible eye on how much fried food the child eats: not because it will do him any harm now – but because it can turn into a bad habit for later.

Toddlers should have fat stores. If his doctor and clinic are not concerned about his weight, he is almost certainly not overweight.

Food allergies

◆ The concept of food allergy is often used as an excuse for behavioural problems which are caused by poor parenting. Food allergies do exist and have increased in recent years, but most allergic reactions have a physical form, not a behavioural one. They make a child sick, lethargic, come out in spots and skin rashes, or red and puffy. When large-scale trials have looked at the effects of common allergens on behaviour (these include the food colouring tartrazine) they have been unable to show that eating them causes hyperactivity or poor attention. If a child is badly behaved, his parents are more likely to be at fault than his diet.

◆ Children do develop allergies to foods. But those allergies are less common than people imagine. If you think a food is causing an allergic reaction, ask your doctor to have him tested.

◆ You can make some initial tests of your own by systematically excluding certain items from his diet. Leave them out for a week to ten days, then reintroduce them. If there is no change in his behaviour/fitness/happiness when you do this, an allergy to the excluded food is unlikely to be the cause.

◆ Extensive testing has failed to show that food colourings have anything to do with hyperactivity. This does not mean it is a good idea to eat a great deal. Since we do not know the long-term effects of additives in our diet, it is wise to avoid them when we can.

◆ The most common allergens are milk or milk products; wheat or gluten; nuts; and strawberries.

Stopping fads and getting children to eat

◆ The best way to reward faddy eaters is to be concerned.

◆ The best way to encourage your child to refuse his dinner is to make his 'problem' the centre of attention.

◆ The best way to discourage faddiness is to let him eat what he wants for a month or two. If he is active, energetic and growing, he does not have a problem. My daughter lived off beans, sausages, bananas and cereal for about three years. She has rarely been ill and frequently represented her school and local borough in cross-country races. She is slim and clever, too.

◆ Do not force-feed. Children do not starve themselves to death. They don't even make themselves ill by eating 'too little'.

Two to three-and-a-half
Milestones: the second birthday

What is a well-balanced two-year-old like? Obviously, she is mobile. She is also social and vocal. Even if she says very little, she understands a great deal. She is increasingly organized and helpful; also more loving and aware of herself. This can be a source of great delight: the behaviour of the typical two-year-old generates a fund of funny and endearing stories. Many of them will remain family memories. You will probably embarrass her in later years by dragging them up in front of friends.

On the downside, she needs constant attention because her curiosity and skill often outstrip her sense. She thinks she can carry her bike down stairs or take herself off to the park. And she will try. Most children have minor accidents attempting such feats. Fortunately they are still very flexible: bones are harder to break when a two-year-old falls.

At another level, the child is still very dependent, and will cry if you leave her without explaining why, and cling if you take her somewhere strange. This is normal and natural. It is the child who does not cry in such circumstances who may cause some worries.

These are the times when "No!" and "Me do it" are her favourite words; these are the years of growing independence. In short, she is delightful and infuriating in turn: like everyone. That is the essential point: at two she is much more a 'little person' than a baby.

Underlying the changes

Underpinning these changes are the gradual maturity, growth and development of the child's physical, social and mental abilities. By now she is able to use her hands in moderately skillful ways. She can grasp, explore, poke, prod, twist and turn, pick up and put down. She can place one block on another, scribble with a crayon and undo the straps of her car seat. She can walk, stop, pause and pick things up as she goes. She can walk up and down stairs one step at a time, push a cart, manoeuvre her sit-and-ride and pull a rabbit on wheels behind her.

She will feed herself (messily), use a cup, take off her socks, open doors and make a beeline for the open gate. Because she cannot visualize the consequences of her actions, she does not see what dangers lie ahead. She has to be watched at all times, which has the beneficial consequence that a carer is always interacting with her: commenting on what she does and expanding and interpreting what she says. On the whole, she gets more of this kind of attention than she did as a sedentary baby.

In return, she loves, completely and utterly and without any element of judgement. Even if her parents do their job badly, she will (initially) remain devoted to them. By two, a child will have formed most of her major and some of her minor bonds of love. In the centre are her parents, siblings and care givers, on the periphery, neighbours, family friends and other relatives. About half of all children will have some sort of comfort object, too. She watches what her loved ones are doing, looks where they look and cries if she loses sight of them. In a strange place, she will use them as a safe haven. When afraid, she will cling on tight.

There is a growing body of evidence to show that the nature of those early bonds has lasting effects upon the child's behaviour. A child whose early attachments are secure is able to build other friendships and love affairs in their image. A child whose attachments are poorly formed may go on to make further poor love ties. As the child grows, the security of these early bonds permeates other areas of her life: how she responds to strange people and places, how she relates to siblings and other children, how she explores her environment and how much other children like her.

Forming attachments

Attachment is facilitated by gentle, sensitive, available carers who look out for the child's needs and express their feelings and emotions, especially if that expression is physical.

It is difficult for a small child to form an attachment to a carer who is withdrawn and unavailable.

It is difficult for a child to form an attachment to a carer who dislikes physical contact, and/or withholds emotions and feelings.

It is difficult for a child to form an attachment to a carer who is very stressed, depressed and/or angry, because such carers tend not to be available to the child. They are too deeply engrossed in their own problems.

It is difficult for a child to form an attachment to a carer who is negative, withdrawn and/or unable to adapt to a young child.

Importance of memory

At the root of many of the changes in the way the child behaves as she approaches her second birthday is a gradual improvement in memory.

A baby's memory is quite a fleeting thing. She looks and she sees, but when she turns away, it is gone. Out of sight is literally out of mind. In the early months she lives only for and in the moment. When she looks at something (like you) she can recognize that she has seen you before, but the memory she has does not extend beyond that: she does not know when or why she last saw you. In that brief moment she may notice a change of hairstyle, but will not remember that you have been away at the hairdresser for the last three hours. In the child's first years there is a gradual increase in the length of her 'now' (the moment she lives in), and the extent and detail of her 'then' (those moments she remembers).

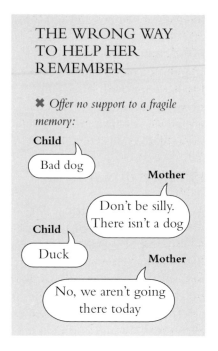

THE WRONG WAY TO HELP HER REMEMBER

✖ *Offer no support to a fragile memory:*

Child
> Bad dog

Mother
> Don't be silly. There isn't a dog

Child
> Duck

Mother
> No, we aren't going there today

When you take a two-year-old to the park, she does not just recognize that it is a familiar place; she also remembers some of the things which have happened there in the past. She can put together the 'then' memories with her 'now' experience. If, for example, a big dog once came up to her buggy and frightened her, she may remember that 'then' as she goes into the park, and say, "Bad dog," or begin to look a little anxious. She may also start to scream if she sees a dog.

By two, her 'now' is long enough to enable her to make simple plans, and to make her intentions and needs understood. Because she can hold on to more than one idea at a time, her behaviour is more fluid than before. It flows more and jumps about less.

Her joys and fears are more

THE RIGHT WAY TO SUPPORT A FRAGILE MEMORY

✔ *Instead of dismissing, acknowledge:*

Child
> Bad dog

Mother
> Bad dog's gone – there's no bad dog now

Child
> Duck

Mother
> Clever girl. The ducks are over there

immediate, obvious and individual. Because she can sustain and build on her moods, she is capable of great elation and glee but also of angry moods and petulance. Moods can swing from joy to tears quite quickly, and when a mood is over (however bad) she quickly behaves as if nothing has happened. You gently help her find her way through these swings by supporting the development of her memory. Obviously, it's not a process which can, or should, be hurried; but there are constructive, and unconstructive, approaches to memory development.

A sense of self at two

The sense of self is that feeling of being conscious and living within your body, knowing that you are seeing things through your eyes and hearing through your ears: the sense that you exist as a separate person. Babies do not have much sense of themselves as individuals. They cannot, for example, recognise themselves in the mirror. If you put a smudge of lipstick on a one-year-old's nose and show her her own reflection in the mirror, she will reach out and touch the red spot in the mirror. Ask "Who's got the funny nose?" and she points to the mirror. Do the same when she is two and she will start to wipe the smudge off

HOW TO ENCOURAGE SELF-AWARENESS

✔ *Refer to the child by name. Keep pet names unique and address her uniquely.*

✔ *Refer to her relationships with you and others. "My little girl." "Your big brother." "Your friend."*

✔ *Refer to her things. The child understands herself initially in the context of her possessions.*

✔ *Refer to the things she can do. The child understands herself by her competence.*

✔ *Mirror play helps her understand 'That's me'.*

✔ *Encourage independence. A child understands herself in the context of separateness.*

her own nose. Ask her who the baby is or who has a red nose and she says "Me." Creep up silently behind her and she will turn around to look at you, rather than simply watch the mirror and laugh as she would have done in the past. A two-year-old is aware of herself in a way that a one-year-old is not.

Being bad

Her growing sense of herself as an individual means that she is able to think about what she wants, and to contrast this with her family's rules and expectations of how she should behave. This enables her to become defiant, and to start to feel both shame and pride in what things she does.

By two-and-a-half, she may be afraid of things she imagines, and may offer simple explanations of why other

Some people have found that holding children very tight for 15 to 30 minutes each day eases their problems.

people feel certain emotions: "Mummy cross. I spill juice." She knows which actions should go with which feelings, so she might say: "I not cry now. I happy." She also knows that actions affect others and may say something like, "I cry. Mummy get it me." She can be deliberately naughty and hurtful, and is quite capable of making her baby brother cry. Yet, although she knows that hitting him makes him cry, she will not yet understand that she has hurt him. She is not yet aware that what others see, think and feel are different from her own thoughts and feelings. She hits, he cries. She did not hurt, so why should he? Her understanding of her naughtiness is more a case of 'because mummy said so' than realizing the harm she might do.

Hold firmly

The technique is simply to gather the child in your arms and hold very

THE WRONG WAY TO HANDLE A DIFFICULT TWO-YEAR-OLD

✖ *Set up a situation where she has to be bad to be seen or heard. Be available for him. Show her how much you like her to be good.*

✖ *Dismiss her feelings or efforts. Don't say: "You are being silly"; or "Don't be such a baby"; or "You are not trying hard enough."*

✖ *Be inconsistent. Don't say "No you can't have it," and then give way to keep her quiet.*

firmly. She may well resist: but don't let go. After a few minutes, she should calm down. Go on holding tightly. It should feel a bit like squeezing the badness out of her. Don't wait for her to be naughty. Some find that a daily holding session reduces the number of daily clashes. Others find that a holding session works well when a child is spoiling for a fight or is already behaving badly. It sounds bizarre, but it does work for many children.

Accept your limitations

Sometimes it is easiest to sidestep a battle. While it would be foolish to teach the child that she can gain by her bad behaviour, it is sometimes necessary to head off clashes, even when this means finding a compromise which is not entirely acceptable to you. If you need to keep the peace for your own sanity, it is better to give in a little in the beginning rather than a great deal at the end.

Apologize

If you lose your temper, tell her you are sorry. If she loses her temper, let her cuddle you until she is better.

Difficult two-year-olds

The personality of a baby is stamped quite lightly on her family. Life is turned upside down by her arrival, but most of that turmoil would be caused by any baby you took into your home. As the months pass, her individuality and personality become more firmly stamped on everything she does – as is your way of responding to her.

A cranky baby – one who is short-tempered and miserable and cries much of the time – can (in theory, at least) be put in her cot while you get out the ear plugs and try to read the paper. A cranky toddler is

THE RIGHT WAY TO TREAT A DIFFICULT TWO-YEAR-OLD

✔ *Always find time to show love. Let her have as many opportunities of showing her pleasant emotions as her nasty ones. When she is pleasant, make sure you tell her. "You are a very good girl to help." "What special hugs you give." "What a kind and helpful girl you are."*

Studies suggest that parents do not, on the whole, find it harder to love a difficult child than a moderate one. Children who are loved and attached to their parents are more likely to overcome their difficulties. Remember that a child who is frequently disciplined needs to know (just as often) that she is also loved.

✔ *Never compare her with better-behaved children. If she thinks she is a hopeless case, she will not try. Instead, say, "I think you know you could do it without crying." Refer to her normal, acceptable behaviour, without stating that some other child behaves that way.*

Help her to find solutions

"That shoe is hard for a little girl to put on. You did very well."

"Next time I think we need to put the shoes at the bottom of the stairs so you can step into them. Shall we see if that is easier?"

Show her how to arrange the shoes with the left on the left and to step from the step down into them. Then ask her to do it by herself.

✔ *Accept her frustrations: show her that you understand by taking her side. "It is hard." "No wonder it makes you bad-tempered."*

✔ *Appreciate that she tries. "You have been really good today." "I know you have been trying very hard to be good."*

✔ *Appreciate her efforts even when they end in temper. "You had been trying so hard all morning." "You had nearly got all your clothes on. It's those silly socks that cause the problems."*

never invisible. You cannot often walk away, so there are ample opportunities for her to manipulate you, and ample opportunities for you to respond to her bad behaviour with your own.

Although very cranky newborns tend to be rather cranky toddlers, the predictions are far from perfect. To some extent it depends upon the causes of her crankiness, and the way you have responded (and do) to it. A colicky child usually grows out of her nightly rages as suddenly as she started them. She is no more likely to be a difficult toddler than any other baby. A child who has been intermittently ill in the first year may become a short-tempered toddler, especially if the medical problems persist. Can you blame her? Persistent earache, one of the major problems, is not something that makes any of us particularly sunny. There is even some evidence that bad-tempered adults are more likely to have been sickly babies. Children who cry much in the first year (for whatever reason) also tend to be difficult toddlers.

There is something about extreme children (whatever the cause of their extreme behaviour) which makes us fit in with them. We tip-toe around the toddler who might otherwise scream for an hour and a half because, after a long and stressful day, you need the peace. Her initial crankiness is then compounded by the fact that she learns to use the threat of her temper to manipulate you. Although you know this, and are aware that, in the long term, it is probably unwise, it may still be necessary, and sensible, sometimes to put your needs first. It is not clear, in any case, that toughing it out is always the best policy with such children.

Difficult children fare best with sensitive, loving parents. The trouble with always toughing it out is that your anger and frustration may not dissipate as quickly as hers. It takes a saint immediately to calm down and cuddle a two-year-old who has screamed for one hour at the end of long and stressful day. If you are feeling fragile, try to head off clashes or to find other ways for her to show her anger and frustration. If this clearly is not working, remember that it is better to give a little at the start than a great deal in the end.

As she grows up, the child's difficult behaviour may centre upon problematic relationships with friends. If they feel unloved outside the home, they may need to manipulate the home situation to prove that you still love them.

Difficult children make you want to hit out or shout back. It is very easy to develop a confrontational style when faced with such confrontational children. Such patterns, once set, tend to continue to colour interactions with the child. In time, you might even find that you are using the child as a target for your daily frustrations; that it does you good to shout at her. Every parent has felt like this at times, but it is a feeling you need to keep firmly under control.

A few of these cranky toddlers later have behavioural problems. The vast majority do not, although they probably remain vulnerable characters. There is evidence to suggest that they are especially disturbed by family upsets or divorce. They are also (not surprisingly) more likely to remain the butt of their parents' anger, and are disciplined more harshly than the even-tempered child.

How middle-of-the-road children turn out is less predictable. 'In-between' children probably learn more than one behavioural trick for their repertoire: sometimes they charm, sometimes they demand in order to get the attention they need.

You reinforce her bad behaviour by giving way after she has been rude or had a temper tantrum. You give the message that, if she is bad enough, she will win.

Being good

Toddlers learn many things by imitating their parents, and

IMPULSIVE CHILDREN

Some children will always look before they leap; others invariably leap before they look. When faced with something new, one child will look carefully before she reaches out to touch. Another rushes in. Style – the way the child interacts with the world – tends to go on as it starts. Impulsive toddlers were probably impulsive babies, and may in turn grow up to be impulsive adults.

However, this can be overstated. Being reflective, the opposite of impulsive, is, as you might imagine, more likely to endear your child to her teachers. Reflective children initially do slightly better at school, but it is not as big an advantage as it might seem at first sight. Impulsive children are used to getting it wrong. They are more willing to 'have a go' and less likely to have their confidence undermined by what people think - considerable advantages.

because parents are generally helpful towards their children, toddlers are, on the whole, helpful and co-operative in return. Anything you do, they will try to do better. They are pleased with themselves when they have watered the plants or rolled some pastry. "I good girl," she says, and beams at the rather wet bathroom floor she has just mopped for you. Who would doubt it? Children like and enjoy being helpful.

As babies become toddlers, and toddlers turn into pre-school children, they become more and more co-operative, helpful and harmonious. Savour it. These helpful, thoughtful children are likely to become more competitive and selfish as they get older. This sort of 'goodness' tends to peak at about four. After that it is mainly downhill.

Studies have shown that the culture outside and inside the home influences the level of competition and co-operation children show. In the past, children were required to help about the house, to care for younger siblings. Many games were as much about co-operation and playing together as about winning. While this was the general ethos, co-operation probably persisted, especially among girls.

Society now values competition more highly than co-operation. Intense competitiveness is common. By the time children are in junior school, this competitiveness is likely to have driven out some (if not most) of the child's helpful tendencies. Seven-year-olds are less co-operative than they were before they started school, and often find it quite hard to work together.

Encouraging co-operation

◆ Children are more likely to help when they know how to help: so show them.

◆ Children are more likely to help when you show your appreciation of that help: so thank them, and don't be too critical.

◆ Children are more likely to help when they see their parents (and older siblings) helping each other: so set a family example. Quarrelsome and competitive parents have quarrelsome and competitive children.

◆ Create a 'we' environment. Co-operate at home. Children should help their parents and each other. Helping should not be a special favour. It is a case of: "Could you help your sister with that?" not: "Be a good girl and help your brother."

◆ Families should do things together, including talking, supporting, eating and socializing.

◆ Sometimes one member's interests should be considered first. Trying to be completely fair encourages competition. Remember, children know to the nearest crumb who has the biggest piece of cake, and to the nearest second how much longer they spent on the washing up.

◆ Do not try to share equally. If you are always even-handed, children spend their time looking for which one got the bonus. Everything they do becomes part of life's great competition. By not trying to be even-handed, you take out the competitive element.

Tantrums

About half of all two-year-olds have tantrums on a more or less daily basis. A few start having tantrums earlier than this, a few later. Some have regular tantrums for years; most grow out of them within two years. Some children never have tantrums at all.

Tantrums start with shouting or crying. There is usually a note of protest, ("No! I won't!"), a demonstration of anger (slamming the door, screaming, hitting, kicking, stamping the floor). At this point the child's temper is rising fast. As the tantrum gets under way, children wave arms, kick legs, stamp feet, arch their backs (especially if you are trying to strap them in a car seat or chair) or fall to the floor. They go red in the face and cry and scream. They may even deliberately kick you or the furniture and throw things. Not all children show all these behaviours.

Very young children seem to blow their tops especially quickly. The tantrum comes from nowhere and disappears quickly and completely. Once over, it is as if nothing at all has happened. In an older child, the tantrum is more likely to build, and to calm down more slowly. She is more likely to be sorry and upset.

Other classic features of tantrums include pushing away the mother; hitting or screaming at the mother; casting aside dummies and comforters if proffered. The child may even hurt herself, biting an arm until it bleeds, or banging her head until it is bruised. Such things are alarming, but bode no ill. Not all tantrums are so severe.

Tantrums have definite phases. Before they start, many parents report that the child was spoiling for a fight; that she was contrary, and easily frustrated. Tantrums are more common when a child is ill or tired, but also when the parent is ill or tired: which suggests they are about relationships – which indeed they are. Children have tantrums only when they are with people who care for and about them.

Sometimes, children seem to provoke a tantrum deliberately. They ask for something they know they cannot have (and have never been allowed to touch), or they ask for something in a voice we cannot hear or understand. If you try patiently to explain to them why they cannot touch the desired object or ask them to tell you clearly what it is they want, you do not avoid the tantrum. On the contrary, you more or less ensure its rapid onset.

Once under way, the tantrum is initially intense. This phase may be followed, particularly in older children, by a quieter phase where the child is sad and sorry. Sobbing replaces screaming, and she may come and sit or stand beside you, not quite making up. This sadness then

THE RIGHT WAY TO ENCOURAGE CO-OPERATION

Your two-year-old, Danny, wants to wash the table. His sister Sarah wants to carry on playing with her Lego.

Encourage co-operation and discourage competition:

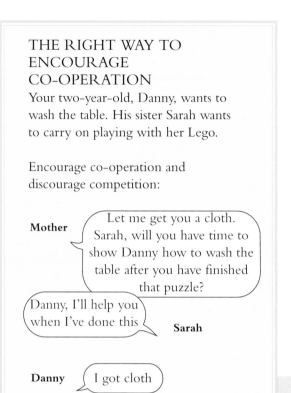

Mother: Let me get you a cloth. Sarah, will you have time to show Danny how to wash the table after you have finished that puzzle?

Sarah: Danny, I'll help you when I've done this

Danny: I got cloth

THE WRONG WAY TO ENCOURAGE CO-OPERATION

Stops co-operation and encourages competition.

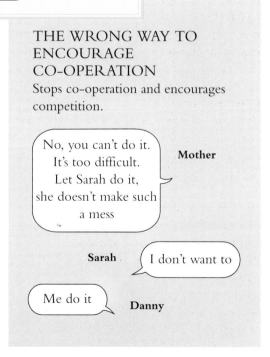

Mother: No, you can't do it. It's too difficult. Let Sarah do it, she doesn't make such a mess

Sarah: I don't want to

Danny: Me do it

gives way to a period of forgiveness when the child may need to be cuddled. In spite of the cuddling, some children show anger or remain in a bad mood for a while. Again, the older the child, the more likely it is that anger and bad moods will persist.

Tantrums — the causes

Tantrums always occur within a social context. It is a very rare child indeed who has tantrums when her mother or another major care giver is not present. About half of all the children who have tantrums when alone with their mothers also have them when alone with their fathers. Very few have them with nursery school teachers or playgroup leaders.

Help her to learn to express her feelings
Show her how to express her feelings in productive ways.

Keeping calm is very hard. Shall we put on the shouting music and shout?

or

It's hard not to lose your temper. Show me how bad you were feeling. Hit this cushion. That's bad. But how bad are you feeling now? Not so bad?

Let her know the limits.
Set limits clearly and try to be as consistent as possible.

I said you could not have a biscuit before dinner and I mean it

Stop. People are not for hurting

I am going to go upstairs. Come and see me when you have calmed down

I do not want to see such bad behaviour. Go to your room. Come back when you have calmed down

110

Even children who spend much of the day with a childminder may have serious tantrums only when at home with parents.

Most tantrums occur in the home, especially when the mother is engaged in an activity which excludes the child. Children have more tantrums when their parents are upset, feeling

The average child who is having tantrums has about one per day, and the average tantrum lasts about five minutes. But a few children have more than five tantrums per day, and a few tantrums last more than one hour.

TANTRUMS – THE RIGHT WAY

✔ *Head off*. *It is sometimes possible to distract or head off an impending tantrum by distracting the child. Read a story, engage in a boisterous activity or play a silly game. If she is spoiling for a fight, find something unusual to do.*

✔ *Ignore.* *Once the tantrum is under way, it is best to ignore it if you can. Just walk out of the room. Tantrums do not occur in a vacuum, they occur within the context of a relationship. If you are not there to witness it, she will stop.*

✔ *Be consistent.* *If a child knows what your bottom line is, she is less likely to fight against it. She will have no expectation of success when she asks for something she cannot have, and will be less frustrated by your 'No'.*

✔ *Hug.* *Hugging very tightly by gathering her up and trapping her in your arms can work well. It is particularly good when having to deal with a tantrum in the supermarket. The fact that you cannot walk away often drags out public tantrums for longer than usual.*

Tight holding induces tantrums, and it may be that you 'squeeze' the tantrum out. Who knows? The point is that it works. Some suggest that you should look the child in the eye as you hug, others that you should look away. It is worth trying both.

✔ *Cuddle.* *Children who are cuddled when they become sad and sorry have fewer tantrums than those who are left to fend for themselves.*

✔ *Talk.* *Talking about the causes of the tantrum, and how to avoid them in the future, seems to reduce the frequency, especially in older children.*

TANTRUMS – THE WRONG WAY

✖ *Slap*. *Slapping seems to increase the frequency and duration of tantrums. It also seems to be associated with especially violent tantrums.*

✖ *Give in*. *Children learn how to manipulate you by their temper. If they get what they want by having a tantrum, they will have more tantrums because it is worth it.*

112

down or ill. They also have tantrums when parents are talking to friends, concentrating on the shopping, or tired, fed up or in a hurry.

Of course, children also have tantrums at other times: when they are ill and upset; when they are tired or frustrated or fastened into a chair; and sometimes for no obvious reason at all. Tantrums are nonetheless about relationships: about love, attachment, security and anger. Just as we lose our tempers (and our cool) with those we love most in the world, so they lose theirs with us. Just as we shout and cry more easily when in the safety of our homes and cars or with our loved ones, so do children. Tiredness, illness, worry and insecurity – which make adults blow their tops – make them do so, too.

At bottom, tantrums between the years of two and three are no more or less than the result of child's inability to control deeply felt emotions. They are not, at this stage, a sign of instability.

Children who eat very little

It is sensible for children not to eat everything that is put in front of them. 'Parenting' would be very difficult indeed if they did. Imagine having to police the house and garden if children ate (not just sucked and chewed, but swallowed) everything which looked edible.

Children, like all animals, young and old, have a mechanism which makes them cautious about new foods. It is part of our inheritance, built into our genes. As we pass into adulthood, we learn that it is fairly safe to eat new things in certain contexts (in restaurants, for instance, or at other people's houses). But our willingness is almost certainly coloured by a wider knowledge and experience of foods.

Children have to learn about foods, and they do so in a variety of ways. There is a little evidence that particular tastes for certain foods might be passed on in the mother's milk, better evidence that we pass to our children a certain cultural pattern of food which gets designated as familiar and safe. Traditionally, a British or North American child would learn that carrots, potatoes and gravy were safe to eat, as was custard. Foods can then be slipped into the diet under the guise (or covering) of potatoes and gravy, or pudding and custard.

It follows that the easiest way to teach a child not to be fussy about food is to start with a familiar and accepted food, then add a very small quantity of something new. The child might try a few peas with pota-toes and gravy, and, once this was accepted, more peas. Each time, a new food is introduced in small quantities, so it hardly flavours the meal at all. The new element is gradually increased, and the basic elements reduced until the child accepts peas as familiar food.

ONLY EATS BAKED BEANS AND CHOCOLATE PUDDING – THE RIGHT WAY

✔ *Start with baked beans plus a quarter of a small cocktail sausage, chopped fine and added to the beans so it cannot be seen. Once this is readily accepted, increase the amount of sausage very gradually. Don't push: it may take two months to build up to a whole cocktail sausage.*

✔ *Cheese and potatoes can be introduced in the same way and the chocolate pudding can be used to mask egg custard, banana and cereal. If the child stops accepting it, go back a few steps. Sometimes the battle is not about food, but about independence, relationships, attachments: the battlegrounds, in fact, of most toddler disputes.*

✔ *Stop worrying and ask yourself the following questions:*
   Is the child growing normally? Is the child fit and healthy?
   Does the child have plenty of energy?

✔ *If the answer to all these questions is yes, she is getting an adequate amount of food. It is easy to become obsessed with the need for children to eat healthy food. Most children throughout history, and all over the world, are raised on a very basic, and a fairly monotonous, diet. Perhaps they prefer it that way. It does them no harm. The traditional Irish diet of milk, butter, potato and a small amount of vegetable is an excellent diet for young children.*

✔ *Children are more likely to eat if the family sits down at table together. Find things she will eat and give them to her. Defuse the battles before trying to extend her diet.*

✔ *Baked beans are a useful source of protein and roughage.*

✔ *All meat has trace elements and proteins; this includes hot dogs and hamburgers.*

✔ *Chips, crisps or even biscuits and cakes have plenty of carbohydrates and fats, which are essential for children. In fact, they contain rather more fats than sedentary adults or overweight children need. But fussy children are rarely sedentary; they are growing, and in any case they do not overeat. Similarly, although overweight children need to control sugar intake, sugar is hardly a problem for an active, picky child who eats rather little.*

   Banning all such foods, when they constitute the main portion of the child's preferred diet, is asking for trouble.

ONLY EATS BAKED BEANS AND CHOCOLATE PUDDING – THE WRONG WAY

✖ *Don't* introduce too many new foods to the child who is a fussy eater in the hope that she will like at least one of them. The problem for many of these children is that they only like very, very, familiar foods.

✖ *Malnourished* children are always lethargic, have stunted growth and are more susceptible to illness. If you are worried that she is not getting enough protein, or that she is not receiving all the trace elements she needs, relax. Disease has obvious symptoms. You would know if there was something wrong; so would your child. There is evidence (somewhat old now) that, left to their own devices, children select a diet which contains everything they need. Remember this. It is a well established principle that all animals (including man) have a mechanism which ensures that, if a diet makes them ill (as one seriously deficient in some element would) they reject it and try something new. If in doubt, get her checked at the clinic. If she is fit and well, she is getting the nutrition she needs.

✖ *Persist* in trying to get the child to eat the sort of food she does not like to eat and you will you make meal times a focus for all those battles that are nothing to do with food, and which inevitably occur between parent and child.

Food as a trigger for tantrums

Children pick up on our major concerns. If you are obsessed with giving her healthy, nourishing food, it can become useful to her if she's spoiling for a fight. She may well be flexing her muscles just now, trying to put some distance between your controls and her independence. For some children the battleground is refusing the pottie; for others it may be food.

THE RIGHT WAY TO COPE WITH AN IMPENDING FOOD TANTRUM

✔ *Offer her a familiar food. Let her feed herself using her fingers if she prefers.*

✔ *If she wants to leave the table, let her.*

✔ *If she does not eat, ignore the fact.*

✔ *Don't let others comment: the aim is not to let her fussy behaviour control you, or anyone else.*

✔ *If she is hungry, offer her a few foods that you know she will eat.*

✔ *Ignore whether or not she eats it.*

✔ *Don't let her split her parents on this issue. You and your partner should agree to try one approach for three weeks, waiting to see what happens.*

✔ *Pause and consider how you, and your partner, talk about food. If you are always saying, "I don't like this," or, "I like that," then it's unreasonable to expect a two-year-old not to have views either.*

✔ *It is often instructive to make a tape recording of how you speak to your child about food. If you were her, how would you react if spoken to in this way?*

Remember that junk food is nutritious. Sugar-coated cereals have added vitamins and are eaten with milk. They are no more fattening (and often more nutritious) than porridge with brown sugar. Some special high-protein cereals have more calories and respectable roughage.

Three-and-a-half to five

Milestones: your child at three-and-a-half

Why three-and-a-half and not just three? The answer is that at three-and-a-half your child has definitely stopped being a toddler and makes a sudden leap into childhood. Between two and three-and-a-half children change gradually. Between three and four they make a sudden leap.

By now your child no longer has that flat-footed toddler gait, feet planted firmly, legs rather far apart. Instead he walks with a spring in his step. His hands, though still rather clumsy, no longer give the impression that he uses his whole arm to move his hands.

By the time he is five he will run, jump, skip and hop; walk up and down stairs with alternate feet; wash, dress and feed himself; hold and use a crayon and fit puzzle pieces together. All these skills are not in place at three-and-a-half, but will be by the time he starts school. Shoe laces, small buttons and tight zips will probably still elude him at five.

His language skills improve gradually. By now he will be able to express recurrence: "More cars"; non-existence: "All gone juice"; attribution: "Pretty flower"; possession: "My coat"; nomination: "That cat"; agent-action: "Jamie hit"; and agent-action-object: "Lily catch ball."

He is adding "ing" to verbs to show that he is talking about the present: "I walking"; he can use words to show where people or things are: "Lucy in pram"; he can use plurals: "Two cows"; possessives: "Mummy's hat"; the past tense: "It broke"; and he can add the right endings to verbs: not "Lucy run" but "Lucy runs". He knows about 1,000 words and will add more than 200 in the next six months.

He becomes altogether more social, playing with other children rather than just playing alongside them. When he arrives at play school, he is delighted to see his friends and will run off happily to play. When he joins the activity table he does not just sit down, but greets the other children, talking, and laughing with them as he plays. He cannot understand jokes but will dissolve into fits of giggles at a rude word, and show mock horror when he hears that some other child has been naughty.

With very little encouragement he will race around, chasing and pushing with screams of delight. If confined to the classroom on a rainy day, he will explode like popcorn when the rain stops. He knows how to be naughty and can be very sanctimonious about the behaviour of other children. But his ideas of naughtiness are based on false premises. Intent does not feature in his rule book. The accidental breaking of two cups is a bigger crime than deliberately breaking one. Which is why breaking things accidentally can leave him so distraught.

The sense each of us has of being conscious, residing in our own body, seeing through our own eyes, hearing through our ears, develops gradually over the childhood years. The first clear sign we have that children are beginning to think of themselves as individuals is when they first recognize themselves in a mirror. This happens in most children between 20 and 24 months. The child's view of himself as a separate individual builds steadily from this point. In the pre-school years a child also defines himself in terms of attributes or possessions. He is, for example, the boy 'with the blue coat' and the 'boy who loves trains'. By seven, children are much more aware of their private selves, and of their own unique emotions and thoughts. If asked to describe themselves at this age, they will use relatively abstract terms, and make comparisons between themselves and others: "I'm best at reading in my class" and "I'm one of the smallest in my class".

Before three, children do not distinguish their own view from others', nor can they see themselves from another's point of view. At about three-and-a-half, children begin to realize that each person is a separate island of thoughts and feelings. This opens up all sorts of possibilities, good and bad. For a start, he now realizes that punching his baby sister does not just make her cry; it hurts her. He realizes that he can deceive you, and you him: although at this stage he will not be very good at it. He also begins to feel sympathy and empathy. He cannot respond to subtle changes, but if you are truly down he may spontaneously come and give you a cuddle. He still finds it hard to read the signs which say "I'm losing interest"; or "I'm losing my patience."

By three-and-a-half, most children are beginning to get their emotions under more control. For many, tantrums are on the wane, and by four most will have stopped, although those who had many tantrums may persist for another year. Because children are now able to stop and think before they act (although maybe not yet think twice), they are less likely to be lured into misbehaviour.

They are better able to plan activities. This ability to plan ahead means that tasks such as model building are less frustrating than before. So is dressing. However, plans are rarely thought out well enough to ensure that they all work out. There will still be a fair number of socks moodily cast aside. Three-year-olds are boisterous and happy, sad and brave, trusting, loving and giving. They have the bloom of innocence and that wide-eyed wonder that brings tears to your eyes. They are altogether easier to be with than they were a year ago (and will be next year). Most of the time they are pure delight. Part of that ease comes from their growing independence. They no longer need us within sight every moment of the day.

Self-esteem

Independence, happiness and security depend on love and self-esteem. A child with self-esteem does not need constantly to attract your attention by his bad behaviour. Learning how to give and share love with your growing children and how to instil and nurture their self-esteem is worth a thousand rule books. The way we act as parents changes as they grow. The benign dictatorship you ran in the early years has to become more democratic. Instead of simply teaching them what they must do, you need to teach them why they should behave in certain ways, and that they have to consider other people, not just themselves. The process is a gradual one, and at three it has barely begun. The tools you use to control their behaviour remain pretty much as they were: time out and cooling-off periods are the main methods. You might now begin to try to encourage responsibility by offering reasonable choices rather than simply making demands. For instance, asking, "Do you want a bath tonight or a shower?" makes it inevitable that the child will wash before bed, but also gives him a little say in how it is to be done. But choices are not always possible and your child will still need rules.

Reasoning

When they reach the age of about seven you can begin to reason with your children, but reasoning with pre-schoolers is pointless. Although by four they can understand that other people have different points of view, they cannot hold two points of view in balance. They cannot, in short, understand democracy.

If your child does not know (or forgets) that you are watching, he may forget to be good. At three-and-a-half he can't control himself from within. However, in the later pre-school years this begins to change and the child starts to internalize control. This will be a sure sign of true maturity: rather than allowing his behaviour to be manipulated by others, he relies on self-generated controls.

Self-esteem lies at the root of self-control because it affects how readily a child can internalize control. A child with high self-esteem has the confidence to act; a child with low self-esteem is still ruled by his

HOW TO COMMUNICATE LOVE

✔ *Just be with them. It is easy to get tied up in a constant whirl of doing things with children - easy to forget that sometimes just being with them is enough. Sharing is about unwinding together as well as winding up: "Come and sit down with me: it's been a busy day."*

✔ *Use your body to communicate. Posture and facial expressions are as eloquent as words. Look him in the eye when you speak; touch, smile, look interested; keep your body language opening and welcoming.*

✔ *Positive words, positive attitudes. Everyone needs to hear good things about themselves. If he knows that he brings you fun, he feels good.*

✔ *Take children seriously. If it is important to him, it should be important to you. The latest episode of his favourite programme does not have to concern you as it does him, but his report on that episode is too important to miss.*

✔ *Show that you're in step. You can communicate love across a crowded room just by the glance that says you know he's there, you understand what he's up to, and that you're happy he's enjoying himself.*

✔ *'Quality time' is one of the most abused terms of recent years: it doesn't have to be action-packed entertainment, nor earnestly pursuing some interest. It is a measure of what you mean to each other. Don't let it be a licence for being a minimal parent. Children are not fools: they can read the messages and this one is all too clear: "Sorry. There are more important things for us to do."*

HOW NOT TO COMMUNICATE LOVE

✖ *Don't be too permissive. Children need safe, reasonable limits. Saying "Do what you like" also says "I don't care what you do."*

✖ *Don't be over-protective. It means "I don't trust trust you to be capable."*

✖ *Not with toys and sweets. Indulgence has nothing to do with love.*

✖ *Not by self-sacrifice, which is not love but self-indulgence.*

✖ *Not by quantity time. Spending hours and hours together does not necessarily communicate love if you fail to become involved.*

✖ *Avoid conditional love. Never say 'I only love you when...' or even 'I love you because...'*

need for other people's attention, praise or disapproval. If a parent undermines self-esteem by relying only on superior power, or demeans a child, the child comes to view himself as helpless and unworthy. Although a child with this view of self can resist external control, he remains uncertain what to put in its place.

From attachment to self-esteem

In the earliest years the child's security comes almost exclusively from the bond he has with his family. The security of that bond pervades all aspects of his life. He loves, and because he loves he thinks others love him too. A well loved child is thus secure. A less well loved child, or one loved inconsistently or conditionally, is insecure.

As children grow, that initial bond is elaborated into a model - a 'script' for life. As his memory improves, what has gone before is carried forward to define how things are, how they should be, how he should act. Ultimately they define who he is. His script has some important sub-plots: what people outside the family think and do, how well he achieves the goals of society, what his peers feel about him. So does his name, how he looks, where he comes from, the culture he grows up in, and how well he achieves goals which are valued within his culture and social group.

When we gather together memories of things we have achieved or not achieved - people's praise and anger; the roles others have set for us ("Why can't you be as tidy as your sister?") - we end up with a view of ourselves in the context of others we which call our self-esteem. It is no more and no less than self-love.

A child who loves himself deeply and securely does not need to reassure himself by constantly pleasing others nor constantly behave badly to attract attention. A child who has self-love can reflect back the love of others with secure generosity, not simply absorb it. He has enough self-love to initiate loving. A child with self-esteem is in control.

The gift of self-esteem

It is hard to survive and prosper without others' esteem, and the safest source of this is self-esteem. So the best gift you can give a child is to teach him how to love himself unconditionally. Unconditional self-love means loving yourself because you are you. Self-esteem is a child's knowledge that he has a right to happiness and respect. It is not from self-importance or egotism, which more often arises from a lack of self-esteem. People who feel good about themselves do not need to put others down in order to feel better.

If esteem does not come from within, it has to be created from with-

WAYS TO GROW HIGH SELF-ESTEEM

✔ *Treat him uniquely. "I love you because you are Jamie." Honour idiosyncrasies, provided they don't harm others.*

✔ *Take him seriously, and his needs. "I know that thinking about monsters can be frightening." "Don't worry. If you talk about them it won't be so frightening."*

✔ *Believe in him. "I know you can do this." Give him a sense of personal power and choice, even when there is little actual choice. "Do you want to wear your red socks or your blue ones?" rather than "Put your socks on now."*

out, an altogether more chancy process. Without an inner core of self-love, people constantly search for other means of puffing themselves up; they go through life desperate for acceptance: people can rarely be be bothered to bolster someone else's ego.

You cannot give a child self-esteem directly. It has to be learned, nurtured; and, sadly, you can kill it. Learning to respect himself is easiest for a child if you respect him; learning to accept himself is easiest if you accept him. A child has to learn to esteem himself, but finds it easier if you esteem him.

Children soon learn that the world is full of downers and that there are a hundred chances for humiliation every day. No one can avoid them all. As well as building up self- esteem, you need to give your children strategies for maintaining self-esteem when it is under pressure. They have to be able to switch off when called names, and to play down failures so that they can start again.

Protecting self-esteem

Outlaw put-downs: "We don't call people names: that is a family rule."

Teach him to confront. A useful technique for small children is to say "Ouch" when words hurt or to hiss like a snake and point two fingers. Do it semi-humorously.

Teach him to pause, then ask "Is something wrong?" after someone says a hurtful thing. The pause is surprisingly uncomfortable for the other person, and the question - to which there is rarely an answer - can neatly dismantle their game. Or, if someone is being mindlessly nasty, "That says more about you than about me."

How to protect self-esteem outside the family: Tell him to withdraw. If people are being cruel, walk away and think about something else. Say to himself: "This is their problem, not mine."

THE WAY TO GIVE A CHILD LOW SELF-ESTEEM

✖ *Rejection. Lack of attention, being ignored, not being taken seriously, not being listened to:* "*Go away; stop bothering me*". "*Not now*". "*In a minute.*"

Loving a child uniquely

This is another key to self-esteem in children. If you go out for a meal, is the food more important than where you eat it? And is Italian food always better than Chinese?

Of course, you would not want to answer these questions with absolutes. The answers depend upon mood, on quite how good the food is, on who we are with, the needs of the moment. An open-air café overlooking the bay in some Greek island might be forgiven its awful food because the view was so beautiful, the experience unique.

Each of your children is unique, and you if you judge them absolutely you undermine their self-esteem. Love is not something you can divide up into parcels. You probably do love each of your children uniquely - but do you get the message across?

It's easy to send confusing signals. They watch you giving presents, carefully chosen for the same value, and assume that love can indeed be costed; they watch you sending them to bed in reverse birth order and assume that staying up an extra few minutes conveys power over your affections.

Children should not be treated equally

■ Give each child what he or she needs, not equal portions.
Buy a book for Jamie this week, some pencils for Claire next week. Offer each child a small piece of cake. Tell them that if they want a little more when they have finished, they only have to ask.

■ Give each child unique love, not equal love.

Never say,   (I love you just as much as him)

Say instead: (I love you because you are you)

■ Give each child the time they need, not equal time.
Some days Jamie needs more help, sometimes Lucy. Don't ration.
Or exclude:

(When I have finished listening to Lucy
reading, I will come and see your picture,
Jamie)

■ Avoid comparisons.

Not   (Why can't you behave like your sister does?)

Just state the facts: (It upsets me to see you behaving badly)

■ Let them feel what they feel.   ○○ (You must feel upset
about that)

not ○○ (You are making a lot of fuss about nothing)

■ Allow them to be themselves.
Monsters under the bed are not "silly".
Being afraid of lifts is not "babyish".

Children should be praised

■ When it does not quite work out:
**"It's frustrating. I bet you wish someone would make
children's socks without heels.
Now you're getting the hang of it. That's better."
"I'm proud of you. You really stuck at it."
"Don't worry; I know it's difficult. It takes time."
"I like the way you have painted the sky."**

■ When things do work out:
**"I love the way you have drawn that cat."
"That is really complicated. It must have taken ages."
"You should feel really pleased with yourself."**

Discipline techniques that work for the three-to-fives

Set limits which reflect growing competence

Your child will determine how they expand. Remember he cannot learn to be responsible if he is always controlled and dominated. Give him the structure but within that structure give options.

Set some house rules

For example:

"We do not call each other names or fight."
"We discuss problems and try to find solutions."
"We do not hurt people, pets or property."
" Even small people can be helpful."

Time out, withdrawing attention, keeping a poker face and cooling off are still the major tools. As children approach school age they can make their own decisions about when they have cooled off and are ready to come back.

Use cooling off time positively. "I think you need time to cool off; come back when you feel calmer" helps teach self-control. Let him know you need to cool off, too. Say, "I feel angry and need time to cool off" as you walk out of the room.

Continue to teach children how to behave. Reasons now become more important. Set limits ahead of time. "Lucy, we are going into town to buy Jamie a birthday present. It is his birthday and his treat." Then name a small figure Lucy can also spend. "If you make a fuss and start asking for more, we will come home without a present for you."

Try to use positive messages. "Jamie, come here and let me turn your volume down." "Ask with your polite voice," rather than "Don't."

Choice empowers children and lets them take control. Keep broadening their choices. "We need to clear the table for supper by the time the big hand is on the 6. You can clear up now, or finish what you are doing first."

Family meetings. These can be informal discussions over a meal, or more formal, when there is something to important to discuss. Each child should feel that his or her contribution is important. An agenda might consist of: 1 thank-yous and well-dones; 2 plans for the week; 3 sharing out weekly chores; 4 discussion of one family problem (for example, clearing up toys) and trying to find a solution; and 5 planning a family activity such as a picnic.

Keep out of their squabbles. The more people join in, the higher the

THINGS CHILDREN SHOULD NEVER BE TOLD

You stupid boy

✖ *We all do silly things. If he does something silly, describe what he did and how you feel. "You threw paper on the fire. That could cause a big fire in the house. That frightens me. Promise me you will not do such dangerous things again."*

Look what I gave up for you

✖ *You chose to have a baby. If you did not realize the consequences of that decision, it is hardly his fault.*

I wish you had never been born

✖ *The ultimate rejection. If you feel like saying it, walk away before you do.*

You could be so pretty if...

✖ *If you tell her she is plain, how can she feel pretty?*

You could be so clever if...

✖ *If you tell your child she is stupid how can she feel clever? There is research that suggests children reach the standard of their labels rather than their true potential.*

Why can't you be like...?

✖ *In other words, "I don't love you as much as I love the perfect boy down the road" - or worse still, "as much as I love your sister."*

Why do you always have to spoil things?

✖ *Don't label. Attack the behaviour, not the child.*

There is nothing to be frightened of.

✖ *On the contrary, if the child is frightened, there is.*

I'll tell your father

✖ *By the time you do, the misdeed will be long past. This just makes Daddy an ogre.*

I'll leave you unless you behave

✖ *If he believes you, this is cruel. If he does not, it is pointless.*

CHILDREN SHOULD BE TOLD:

I'm so glad I had you. You have always been a joy to me

✔ *Children should always know how important they are.*

✔ *If you make it worth arguing the case, they will.*

No means no

✔ *The message is clearer if you let children know when you have made a mistake.*

Everyone makes mistakes. It is OK

That was a stupid thing I just did

Telling tales is OK

✔ *If we tell children not to tell tales they may fail to tell us about tales that matter.*

✔ *Emotions are not bad.*

You can cry. You can feel sad. You can be afraid

✔ *You did that by yourself! Wow!*

You can say 'No'

✔ *Children do not have to do what others ask.*

✔ *Overplaying the dangers of life deprives them of the initiative and the freedom of childhood. The outside world is not full of bad men waiting to rape or kill them.*

It is all right to be a child

The world can be a good and safe place

It's all right to relax and do nothing at all

✔ *Children do not always need to be learning and doing.*

temperature gets, so turn a blind eye and a deaf ear unless it gets out of hand.

Avoid self-fulfilling prophecies. Telling children they are stupid is likely to make them stupid. There is convincing research suggesting that people live up or down to others' expectations. They may even die if they are told this will happen.

Problem solving

For the under-fives it must be kept simple. Suppose his sister is pulling faces at him. Start by accepting his anger and showing empathy. "My sister used to do that, so I know how you feel." Then describe the situation and/or the child's wishes. "Lucy is pulling faces at you when you are trying to draw and you wish she would stop." Just doing this can help him stand back a little from events, and creates a pause in which to consider solutions. "What do you think you should do?" "You could pull a horrid face. You could hiss like a snake. What do you think would be best? We don't want to make it worse."

Keeping your sanity

No one warns parents how stressful parenthood can be. There are times when even the best children drive you crazy. All children have difficult phases. Most have good phases. The two interleave. If things have been bad for a month or two, you can say with some certainty that they will get better. If they've been good, they will probably get worse. The phases are driven by the way in which children grow and develop: which is to say not in an even pattern, but by leaps and bounds.

When on a leap, a child is miserable. While you adjust to being the parent of the 'new' child, so are you. Then you settle into another new routine - until the next jump. There is a big jump about two, another about three-and-a-half and a third at about six to seven years.

If you are frantic with the child: take a few minutes every day to relax: a walk around the streets; lying on the grass; a gentle swim or simply taking a lazy bath. Learn how to relax muscles to reduce tension. A massage can do wonders.

Take a few minutes to yourself. Teach your children that there are times when you are off-limits. "Mummy is meditating" used to work for me. Settle the children with a video or TV. Go into an adjoining room (leave the door open) and lie quietly on the floor for five minutes. Relax all your muscles in turn, starting at the head. If this is some-

THE RIGHT WAY TO BRIBE

✔ *You can't always expect them to perform selfless acts.* Few adults do things for nothing all of the time. Bribery turns children into winners. Sometimes you can bribe them with a smile, sometimes with a gold star. Immediate rewards work best. The younger the child, the more instant the reward should be. When a reward has to be delayed, a token acts as visible and tangible stand-in. Since all young children like collecting, they have value in their own right. Counters in a pot, thank-you notes in a bag, or stars on a chart are all excellent.

✔ *Star charts.* Draw a chart setting out seven days. Divide into morning and afternoon if appropriate. Label the chart. You might call it 'Not shouting in the car,' for example. After each car trip unspoilt by shouting he gets a star, which he sticks on to the chart. At the end of the week the stars can buy a small treat. Big treats defeat the purpose, in fact often the stars are enough by themselves.

The technique works by drawing the child's attention to a particular behaviour. Keep it simple; one chart at a time.

✔ *Time*. Children cannot be good for ever. Sitting still for 15 minutes takes a deal of effort and needs rewarding. Set times with the kitchen timer or show the child on a large clock.

✔ *Appropriate rewards:* cuddles, silly things, outings, extras such as staying up, favourite meals.

HOW NOT TO BRIBE A CHILD

✘ *Give only for what the child does - never for what he is.* Children need to be loved and appreciated for who they are.

✘ *Give love only when the child performs.* Love should not be conditional.

✘ *Reward everything he does.* How will the child cope away from you if he always expects to be rewarded?

✘ *Give too much. Too much is meaningless.*

✘ *Food rewards. Best steer clear;* they can be the root of eating problems. An adult may over-eat when needing to reward himself; and under-eat when feeling bad about himself. This is not a habit you want to establish now.

thing you do every day, your children will regard it as normal. If they need to speak to you, they should stand next to you and wait quietly until you are finished.

Or, try visualization - see this page.

Get out of the house. Take a class, exercise, learn something you always wanted to do. Tap dancing? Playing the flute?

Visualization

Try to get warm and relaxed. Lie down, close your eyes, relax every muscle. Think about what happiness looks like. Is it waves lapping on golden sand? Snow falling, knee high? Mist in a green meadow? Think of the colours of happiness. Visualize those scenes and those colours. Let the sun shine even brighter, bathing your scene in a golden glow. Relax and let the feeling ride over you. Practise this every day until you are able to 'switch on' happiness. Now when you feel stress building, switch over to visualization.

Fantasise. What you cannot have in reality, have in fantasy. Pretend you are somewhere else taking a favourite walk - alone, calm and relaxed.

Join a parent group. Troubles are not so troubling when everyone else has them too. One of the commonest causes of stress is feeling you cannot cope. Just being in touch with other parents keeps this in perspective.

Start a telephone circle. This is a group of friends who agree they can ring each other up when feeling isolated.

Listening, asking and refusing skills

If you never listen to your child he will grow up thinking what he has to say is unimportant. Even with good communication skills, we are sometimes misunderstood. How much worse it must be when we do not have those skills.

A child who does not know how to ask is likely to grow up making demands. While families accept demanding, difficult children (because they think they have little choice) such children are unpopular with others. When peers choose friends, difficult, demanding children are often left on the outside with only like-minded individuals as companions.

Even basically pleasant, undemanding children can be ostracised by their peers because they do not know how to make themselves 'worth knowing'. Modern life does not encourage communication in families. Few of us sit down regularly to family meals. Whole evenings are spent in front of the TV, where we slump at the end of a stressful day.

Parents can be poor models in this respect. Some people feel that their family is an adequate social circle in itself; that acquaintances are enough. They say "Hello", but don't talk. Without social skills to copy from parents, a child can find himself on the outskirts of a social group. The habit can stick.

To communicate well

A child needs listening skills. They are easy for a child to imitate, so it's worth cultivating them. Children also need to learn the movements and postures associated with conversation. When two people are interacting, they tend to mimic each other's body language. They nod before the sentence is finished, look away while they talk. If you make the wrong moves, the other person may feel that you are not listening.

Although listening is important, it is never, on its own, enough. You can demand, you can manipulate or you can simply ask; but you can't listen your way into what you need. Males tend to be taught to demand, females to wheedle and to manipulate. There is not much to choose between these styles. Demanding and manipulating may get us what we need, but the expense is high. In addition to the bad feelings they create in others, they often make us feel bad in ourselves. If it takes two hours of moodiness, is it worth it?

It is easier for both parent and child if you teach him to say "Will you give me your attention?" rather than allowing him to go through the rigmarole of bad behaviour, falling out and making up before his needs can be addressed. Children do not learn to ask if they see you,

133

the parent, making demands and manipulating others at every turn. They are not born with the ability to manipulate: you teach it. And although they are born with the ability to make demands, they can easily be taught a less confrontational style. That is, after all, what civilizing them is supposed to be about.

Teaching children to ask directly for what they want empowers them and liberate you. You have to say "No" to wheedles and demands if children are to learn limits.

Be interested and look interested when he talks to you. Look into his eyes; get down to his height if necessary. Face him directly, lean forward and open your body to him. Do not cross your arms or hunch forward in an aggressive manner.

◆ **Don't judge** Let him have his say. Put yourselves in his shoes and try to see it from his point of view. Listen to him first; composing your answer after he has finished, not while he speaks.

◆ **Read between the words.** Small children do not deceive us - they don't know how - but older children can.

◆ **Let him finish.** Don't finish his sentences or interrupt before he has had his say. If you interrupt, do so only to encourage and to lead the story on. Your attention is a gift to your child. A child with many gifts has among them the gift of speaking.

◆ **Reflect on his feelings** ("You must have been upset") and on his point of view ("I can see why you think that isn't fair"). Do this even if you later go on to disagree. Express yourself in neutral tones. "That would make you angry."

◆ **Play conversational tennis**. Bat the conversation back and forth. It is his service game, but that does not mean you should expect to be entertained by a string of aces.

◆ **Establish a practice ground for communication.** The dinner table is traditional. A family conference may be just as good (see page 127). Make sure that the younger members have their turn. Sitting and listening to conversations he does not understand won't encourage a three-year-old to talk.

Beginning to let go

Your aim is to produce independent individuals who can function without you, think their own thoughts, make their own mistakes, and succeed on their own terms, which means that sooner or later you have to stand aside and let them do things for themselves. In these pre-school years, don't always dress him, tell him what to eat, suggest how he feels, or deny his experience. Avoid "You can't be hungry" or "Are you sure you don't want to pee?"

◆ **Start to encourage choices.** "What do you want for breakfast? An egg or cereal?"

◆ **Keep the flame of hope burning.** Never say "It's much too difficult;" say "Let me know if you need some help."

◆ **Show respect.** When he tries hard to be independent and comes a cropper, don't say "I told you so."

◆ **Stop the inquisition.** Don't ask too many questions. Leave him the privacy of his thoughts.

◆ **Let him try.** Don't rush in with the answers.

◆ **Let him spend his pocket money.** Put the money in a purse and let him take it out to pay.

◆ **Let him walk to the corner to post a letter.** Nothing bad can happen if you watch from a distance.

He won't do as I ask

Adults are always making demands on children. If you counted up the words you speak to your two- or three-year-old, a high proportion would be concerned with getting him to do things he hasn't chosen to do.

When not making demands we are often running down their choices. "You don't like that." "You're just tired." "You don't really feel like that about your brother."

Put yourself in his shoes. What do you do when an inner voice tells you to stop reading the paper and wash the kitchen floor? Or when the same voice tells you not to eat chocolate cake? Perhaps you do as you

HOW TO GET HIM TO DO AS YOU SAY

✔ **Don't nag.** *If it does not matter leave it.*
✔ **Don't dictate.** *Give him some say in what he does and thinks.*

✔ **Describe what you see.**
Or describe the problem.

> *There is Lego all over the kitchen floor*

✔ **Give information.**

> *It is dangerous. Someone could slip*

✔ **Say what you expect.**

> *I expect you to pick it up*

✔ **If he tries delaying tactics:** *Consider if this is reasonable. If it is not, say so.*

> *I need to cook. Everything must be picked up now*

If a delay is reasonable, repeat your request,

adding the new time scale. If he does not act, give him choices.

> *OK, you want to watch the end of your program. I want you to pick up the Lego as soon as the programme has finished*

> *Jamie, you can pick up the Lego or I will sweep it up and put it away for one week. It is your choice*

✔ **Remind with one word.** *When his programme is over, say*

> *Lego*

✔ **If he still does not act.**

✔ **If he still does not act.** *Sweep up the Lego and put it away.*

> *I see you have chosen to have the Lego put away.*

✔ **If he protests.** *Say*

> *Jamie, this was your choice. You can play with it next week*

HOW NOT TO GET A CHILD TO DO THINGS

✖ *Judge the child, not his behaviour. If the child thinks he, rather than the behaviour, is naughty he is more likely to be naughty again.*

✖ **Nag.** *If you keep telling him he is naughty, why should he try?*

✖ **Threaten.** *Threats are meaningless unless you always act; and pointless if you do.*

✖ *Always automatically punish. Discipline works best when there is mutual respect and trust. Punishment forces and coerces: it undermines respect.*

✖ **Blame.** *Blame undermines self-esteem. Without self-esteem, good behaviour is very difficult. See also pages 121-125.*

are told, but you are unlikely to do so with good grace. How would you react if our partner took over the role of that inner voice?

Children do not always do what we ask. It would, in truth, be pretty worrying if they did. Total obedience to all authority is not a characteristic most parents wish to instil in their children. We do, however, need to socialize them. There is, as in all things, a happy middle course.

What not to do when they wind you up

◆ **Don't blow up.** *He only does it to annoy.* Of course he does, because when you are annoyed you give him your whole-hearted attention. Good behaviour gets the odd smile and word of approval, which is shared with whatever activity we are engaged in at the time. You peel half a dozen carrots and smile once. On the other hand, his bad behaviour gets your undivided attention. Down go the knife and carrots, and we walk across the room to him. The more easily you blow, the more sure his technique.

◆ **Don't intervene** *Children wind each other up because they enjoy fighting.* Ignore them unless they are about to hurt each other.

◆ **Never act as a referee.** It becomes a full-time job.

◆ **Don't insist on getting to the bottom of each misdemeanour.** This gives bad behaviour too good a press.

Avoid situations which spark conflict

Don't allow children to play you off against your partner.

◆ **Favourites.** The problem is not having a favourite child but showing that you have one. It is perfectly normal to feel differently about each of your children, to treat them differently, to value them differently. What can be devastating to a child is to come in last on every count.

◆ **Be aware.** Sometimes you can show favouritism unconsciously in body language, the speed of our response, the tone of your voice or in your readiness to hear or to respond when a child glances across the room for reassurance. You need to watch yourself in your mind's eye and change if need be.

◆ **Don't compare one child unfavourably with another.** Never say "Why can't you be like your brother?"

◆ **Don't compare one child favourably with another.** Never say "Why can't your brother be like you?"

◆ **Don't label –** by expectation, by action or by words.

◆ **Don't try to be give equally.** You do not need to divide attention down the middle. It is impossible, and attempting to do so simply attracts the child's attention to everything that was not fair.

Respond to each individual child as an individual, showing interest when he or she needs it. However, while you do not need to divide your attention hour by hour or even week by week, children need to know that they are sometimes first in the queue and that there will be a time every day when they can swim in the light of your whole-hearted attention while others wait.

◆ **Give according to need** - be it time, biscuits or attention.

◆ **Show love uniquely.** Love them for themselves. Seek out what is special in each child, not just the favoured child.

Divorce

In some countries, typically Britain and the U.S.A., almost 50 per cent of marriages end in divorce. Many of these marriages have children. The child has no say in the break-up, no control over who they live with, or how often (or whether) they see the non-custodial parent.

They have no say in whether their parents form new relationships, or who they chose as partners: yet all these things have a profound effect on their life.

They have a right to explanations, and to feel angry about what is happening. Many young children believe that some of the fault must lie with them. They think it might have been avoided if they had been good. Such feelings are often reinforced by the distraction and bad temper of stressed parents in the weeks and months leading to the separation. If parents are cross, it is usually the child's fault. Why not now? You have to reassure them that nothing they did or could have done would have made any difference.

After the break-up, parents often withdraw into a protective shell. They do not mean to withdraw warmth and openness from children, but often do, and may remain too tangled up in their own unhappiness to know what they are doing. Sometimes the parent who is leaving the family home finds seeing the children too painful to contemplate, so makes a clean break. Children need both parents.

Some children expect their parents to separate; for others it comes as a complete surprise. They should always be told once the decision is made. Do not let them overhear plans, or learn from a secondary source. Give them time to adjust to the news, and encourage them to ask questions. Answer these as honestly as you can without placing blame on either parent. Both parents should talk to the children. There is no need for a formal statement solemnly given by both parents. If this is not your family style, such a departure from the norm would be frightening. Even if family meetings and discussions are your way of doing things, presenting the news in this fashion is probably too much for most small children to bear.

Allow children to show their feelings. They have a right to be angry and should be allowed to express that anger. Don't dismiss their fears with platitudes such as "I know you will like your new Daddy." He is not their Daddy and they almost certainly will not like him, now, or in the near future. They may come to tolerate or even like him in the distant future. Do not tell them it will "be all right." It will not be. Nor that they will be "happier". You may be. They will not. They may be all right and happy a year or two from now, but it will take time. Older

OTHER REACTIONS TO DIVORCE:

◆ Being fussy about food; refusing to eat.
◆ Doing badly at school or running away (typical of older children).
◆ Getting ill or even attempting suicide in an attempt to get parents back together again.
◆ Playing parents off against each other; being naughty and disruptive.
◆ Asking the same questions over and over again.

children may always dream of what might have been.

Expect rudeness, sullenness, blame, name calling, squabbles, even depression. Expect bad behaviour, poor relationships with peers, meanness and reversion to baby-hood ways. Wet knickers and beds and a need to hold your hand in order to go to sleep are common-place. Anger must come out. Let it. Help him to express his anger in constructive ways - kicking a cush-ion, throwing bean bags at a wall, shouting very loud.

Try to stay calm for them, and keep routines as normal as possible. Do not hide your feelings, only the excesses of feeling. If you complete-ly protect children from your unhappiness and anger, you send the message that their own reaction is excessive. You also suggest that you do not share their unhappiness - which is dishonest.

Avoid quarrelling in front of children, or laying blame on your ex-partner, either directly or by sly digs children can overhear. You must not just be fair when talking about your partner in front of the chil-dren: you must be more than fair. However badly a partner has behaved, he/she is still the child's parent. That relationship is important and will need plenty of nurturing. However hard this is for the custodi-al parent, it is important they do this. Children survive divorce. They survive it well if both parents respect the relationship between the child and the other parent. A very high percentage of non-custodial parents lose touch with their children. These children are more likely to be dis-turbed and disrupted by divorce. Making difficulties at this stage increases the likelihood of this.

There are many stresses associated with divorce. Children's bedtimes and meal times are often disrupted by your unhappiness and distraction. After divorce, parents are usually poorer, and many single mothers live in poverty. Children may have to move house, move school, change neighbourhood. Mothers who have not worked outside the home since the children were born may need to go out to work. Children may need to go to a child minder or to a relative. This can seem like rejec-

HANDLING DIVORCE – THE HARD WAY

✖ **Let the courts decide.** *Lawyers don't stop couples arguing. Once they take over, the problems tend to multiply rather than subside. It costs a fortune too. The money is almost always better spent on holidays.*

✖ **Fight access all the way.** *Children have a right to see both parents. Parents have a right to see their children except if they lose that right by harming them.*

✖ **Opt for a clean break with the children.** *Clean breaks may be easier for parents. They are never easier for children.*

✖ **Go by the letter of the law.** *If the court says alternate weekends, obey the letter of the law, but do better than that in spirit. Don't limit access just to weekends: children should feel they have access to both parents at any time. They should be able to see the non-custodial parent more often than the legal access allows if they wish too. If they want to ring up and say "Good morning, Daddy," that is their right.*

✖ **Expect children to slot into new relationships.** *There is nothing more likely to make children see the new partner as the wicked step-parent than having him/her hanging around during visits. Children need time alone with both parents.*

✖ **Make the non-custodial home child-unfriendly.** *Use children as spies. Don't ask questions.*

✖ **Expect to draw a line.** *Sharing children means that you cannot make a clean break from old partners. The sooner you accept this the happier everyone will be.*

HANDLING DIVORCE – THE MORE ENLIGHTENED WAY

✔ **Settle out of court.** *The sooner the fighting is over, the sooner children's lives can be rebuilt.*

✔ **Be generous about them seeing both of you.** *Do everything in your power to tend the relationship between your children and your ex-partner. It is hard, but loving always is hard. The children deserve this act of love. It was not their fault.*

✔ **Let a child see the non-custodial parent more often than once a week, particularly in the early months.** *If this is impossible, they should talk on the phone. Ringing up to say good night (or good morning) only takes a moment.*

tion and abandonment to a child who has lost one parent and now fears losing the other.

Discuss the future. Tell him what will be remaining the same and those things that will change. Where are thy going to live? Who will be living in the house? What is happening to the pets? What will happen to the furniture? Where is the non-custodial parent to live? Will there be room for the children to stay there? How much time will the child be spending with each parent? Don't funk the questions. Studies of children whose parents are divorcing suggest that children initially react to divorce with anger, fear and shock. Many become withdrawn and depressed. Most children eventually adapt, but where there is aggravation and continuing conflict between parents, adjustment can take much longer, and sometimes they never adjust. Difficult children have more problems adjusting. Boys usually show more behavioural problems after divorce. Girls have more problem adjusting to remarriage. The younger the child, the shorter the memory of what has gone before and the sooner they get over the break-up. Most pre-school children show signs of upset and withdrawal for about a year - school-age children for a year or two, and teenagers for a number of years. Even after ten years, many teenagers remain angry. Young boys are more affected than young girls, older girls more affected than older boys.

Remarriage

About 80 per cent of men and 75 per cent of women eventually re-marry and about 25 per cent of children will spend time with a step-parent before they are 18. Rather more than half of those parents who remarry will divorce again. The more often they remarry, the more likely they are to divorce again.

Remarriage is never straightforward. Younger children may come to accept it: older children often do not. This is especially true of older girls, who have particular problems accepting a mother's or a father's new partner. Younger boys have more problems with a mother's new partner. They may not even like them; or they may feel disloyal to their own parent if they do.

Don't foist your new relationship on to your children too soon after the divorce. Allow a pause for the children to get used to the idea. This will make the transition very much smoother. Don't underestimate how disruptive an unhappy and resentful child can be to a new relationship, especially where the new partner has little or no experience of dealing with children. Give things time.

Don't be gleeful if your ex-partner and his/her new partner are having a difficult time with the children. The children's hearts are the ones that break. Never applaud their behaviour from the sidelines. It is in the child's best interest to reduce stress. Sniping and gloating are natural, but keep it for your friends and family, out of earshot of your children.

Stepchildren

Stepchildren do not choose their step parents. Indeed they would probably prefer to be without them. There is no reason for them to like the new partner, nor to like their new step brothers and sisters. It would be pleasant to live as one big happy family, but unrealistic to suppose that you will.

◆ **Expect jealousy between stepchildren,** especially when your children visit stepchildren who are now living with the non-custodial parent. Remember that they too are having to adjust, and have probably gone through a period of stress. Two sets of stressed children pushed together by circumstance are not a recipe for harmony.

◆ **Give it time.** Children settle, and many come to co-exist fairly harmoniously.

◆ **Give in fantasy what is absent in reality.** Let children express their jealousy and their wishes. "You wish Luke was not living with Daddy. I can understand that; but it's happened and we have to try to get used to it." "I know you wish Jane didn't have to come and stay with us. But I believe you'll find it better in time."

Half-siblings

Children can often be very good with half-brothers and sisters they have known from babies, but may never learn to like stepchildren foisted on them by a parent's new relationship.

Physical abuse by step-parents

Divorce means that neither parent can oversee their child all the time. Parents are angry and stressed after divorce and may take this out on their children. Wicked step-parents are not just the stuff of fairy tales. Studies show that stepfathers are very much more likely to harm children than are natural fathers. When abuse occurs in families, parents often have some of the following traits:

◆ *A history of battering,* often as children. They are quick to anger, have poor control of impulses of any sort. A pattern of emotional or verbal battering may also be evident.

◆ *A distorted view of children and their capabilities,* and unrealistic expectations of children. They do not take the child's age or stress into consideration.

◆ *A tendency to expect too much from children.* They want the child to fill some basic need, and are disappointed when they do not.

◆ *A lack of warmth; poor communication skills.* They do not know how to listen to children, or how to give love.

◆ *A tendency to see children in negative ways;* they don't notice good characteristics or good behaviour.

◆ *They use, and abuse, power; they dominate.* But they are often weak and powerless in reality. They tend to over-use punishment.

◆ *They are often isolated and obsessive, and have few close friends.*

Children do fall and hurt themselves, walk into shelves, bruise themselves and burn themselves. Not all such injuries are unintentional. It is wise to recognize the signs:

◆ **Frequent bruising or injury** is always suspect.

◆ **Bruising or lacerations** which are hidden by clothes are also suspect. After a fall, a child usually has some visible sign of injury as well as those beneath clothes. Bruising and/or laceration is especially suspect when extensive. It might happen once by chance, but not two or three times.

If children are very clumsy, they hurt themselves both at home and at school. They don't get two black eyes.

If you feel that you might abuse your child, get help at once. There are parent self-help groups in most areas. Your doctor or library may be able to help. In the meantime, leave the room. Put distance between you and the child. Try to calm down. Take some deep breaths. Then call a friend or relative for help.

Death of a pet

Often the loss of a family pet is the child's first encounter with grief. Indeed, one strong argument for keeping short-lived pets such as hamsters or gerbils is that this teaches children to love and care, grieve and accept that death comes to everyone: that it is sad, but not necessarily frightening. Obviously, the death of a few pets will not in anyway prepare a child for the loss of a parent. Nothing can. But grieving over a hamster can help a child understand an adult's grief at losing someone close. It can also teach that bad things pass, that happiness can return.

A child's grief at the loss of a pet is real. Help by explaining that all creatures are born, live and die. If the death is the result of illness or old age, it will help if you prepare the child for the possibility that the pet will soon die. Explain that we cannot change things, however much we would like too. Help him to remember the good times.

Asking a child to assist you in burying the body can help him to accept the finality. Flowers and a gravestone show respect for the child's sorrow. Explain that, although the pet dies, what it meant and the happiness it brought, goes on. Do not rush into getting a new pet. Some children would rather wait; let the child dictate.

Death of a friend or relative

Death of someone close to us, however much we expect it to happen, is almost impossible to comprehend. We react to the news first by denial, then with anger and protest, and finally with depression and grief. Children under five have difficulty understanding the finality of death and will assume that the person will come back: as people in their life normally do. Although they use the word "death" or "dead", they tend to think of death much more in "cartoon" terms than reality. People die for a while, but then things get back to normal. This is not the result of watching cartoons but the way small children think.

Don't use euphemisms such as 'resting in peace' or 'passed on'. Children do not understand what they mean, and this might encourage their belief that the sleeping person will awake again, or make them afraid that, when they sleep, they may die. It is best to use the word 'dead'. Explain to the child in simple terms that the person is not coming back. Even if you are not religious, you may find it easier if you use words such as 'heaven' to indicate that the loved one is in a place from which they cannot come back. The idea that someone ceases to be is difficult for the under-fives to comprehend, especially when that person has been of central importance.

Don't bottle up your feelings. Children cope better if they share tears and sorrow. Do not be upset if you find him killing off his teddies or having funerals in the garden. This is his way of coming to terms with death. It is not disrespectful.

Don't shield children from grief. Talk often about the person who has died. Remember the good times. Emphasize that life goes on; that more happy times will come, and must be created, if only for the sake of the dead person, who after all would want it that way. What people were to us, they remain; nothing can take the past from you, but it should not cloud the future.

Let those who have died be both saint and sinner - don't construct perfection out of imperfection. A dead but 'perfect' sibling is an impossible childhood model. Keep photographs on view of the person who has died. Children cannot always visualize. They need to remember how they looked.

Be honest. Answer questions but do not try to be omnipotent. You can explain what caused the death but none of us can say why it happened. Sometimes the answer to 'Why' is that life could not continue as it was. "Grandma was hurting too much, she could not bear the pain and we could not bear to watch her suffering."

Grief - a practical approach

◆ **Prepare the child for the possibility of death** when someone is very ill. Do not keep children away from a loved one who is dying. Let them say goodbye. They do not need to keep watch if someone is dying at home, but should not be banned from the room because death is imminent. Nor should they be kept from the room after the death. They do not have to kiss the body goodbye if this frightens them. But it is good to say the words.

◆ **When a parent dies,** the child's first worry is often that the remaining parent will also die. He may become quite hysterical if you go out, come home late or are sick. Do not expect this to pass quickly. Try to keep the child's routine as regular and familiar as possible: meals on time, goodnight stories and regular bedtimes reinforce feelings of security.

◆ **When a sibling dies,** address the jealousies, the blame and the fights which happened between the living child and the dead in a gentle way. All children sometimes wish a sibling dead. To have that wish come true can be devastating.

◆ **Mourn the reality.** Missing someone's imperfections is, after all, a true sign of love and respect. Let each person grieve in his own way.

◆ **Share grief.** Explain that it is difficult for you to cope, and that you know it makes them sad to see you unhappy, just as you feel sad to see them unhappy.

Never make one child feel they must take the place of another

◆ **Give your children permission to be angry** and encourage them to express that anger, even if that means being angry with the person who has died. "Why did you have to run into the road?" is a legitimate question, and a legitimate reason to be angry with someone.

◆ **Missing the loved one.** In the first years after the death, family holidays, birthdays and celebrations can be very difficult. Don't shy away from this. Cope in your own family way. Some like to remember loved ones and past holidays. Some need to change routines.

◆ **Get as much help from friends and relatives** as you can. If you are not coping, get professional help for you and/or your children.

Stuttering

A child who stutters tries to say a word, hesitates, and tries to say the word again. Speech rhythm is disrupted and the child's words do not flow smoothly. Stuttering (which is sometimes called stammering) is speaking with involuntary disruptions, repetitions or prolonged vocal sounds. Stuttering is more common on 'voiced' sounds such as b, d and g, than on unvoiced or more breathy sounds such as p, t and k. Whether children or adults. there are from four to eight times more male stutterers than female stutterers.

Some facts about stuttering

◆ **Some stutterers do not stutter when alone or with their family.** They stutter when with strangers, especially people in authority. Clearly, anxiety plays a role.

◆ **Everyone occasionally stutters.** Children do so more often than others. One or two bouts of stuttering do not make a problem. Even if a child seems to be stuttering frequently, the problem may be only a temporary one. Most children grow out of it. Developmental stuttering usually begins between two and four years. It lasts a few months.

◆ **Benign stuttering begins at about six to eight years** and may last two to three years.

◆ **Persistent stuttering starts between three and eight years,** and in some, but not all, cases it persists into adulthood. In general, the later the onset, the more serious the problem.

◆ **Secondary stuttering needs immediate attention.** This can be recognized by a serious struggle to speak, facial grimacing, arm and leg movements and/or irregular breathing. If this is the pattern of your child's stuttering, consult your doctor at once.

◆ **Many people who stutter when speaking can sing without stuttering** or speak in time to a metronome.

◆ **Most stutterers are of average or above normal intelligence.**

◆ **Four per cent of children between two and five years stutter.**

◆ **One to 3 per cent of school-age children stutter.**

◆ **One per cent of the adult population stutters.**

◆ **Seventy-five per cent of ten-year-olds who stutter will stutter as adults.**

◆ **Eighty per cent of children who stutter will not stutter as adults.**

Stuttering often causes children to become shy and withdrawn. It saps all confidence and undermines social skills. The problems can out-live the stuttering. It is, of course, important to do everything you can to improve and maintain the stutterer's self-esteem.

Communicating with a child who stutters

You can encourage problems, or discourage them:

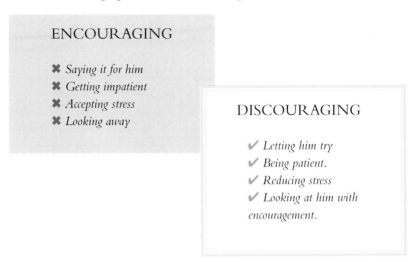

ENCOURAGING

✖ *Saying it for him*
✖ *Getting impatient*
✖ *Accepting stress*
✖ *Looking away*

DISCOURAGING

✔ *Letting him try*
✔ *Being patient.*
✔ *Reducing stress*
✔ *Looking at him with encouragement.*

Stuttering - some causes

A problem with auditory feedback. Everyone can hear themselves speak both 'in their heads' and through their ears. Most of us can put these sources of speech sounds together, even though there is in fact a short gap in time between the two. The gap arises because it takes a small amount of time for the sound wave to travel from the mouth to the eardrum.

One theory of why children stutter suggests that stutterers pay too much attention to the sound of their own speech. It is as if they are listening to themselves speaking with a slight echo. When normal speakers experience speech with this sort of echo, they also stutter.

Timing. Because speech requires very precise timing, any disruption in the ordering of the little sounds within a word, or to the length of any of these sounds, can cause a child to stutter. It is thought that some children stutter when (and while) these timing mechanisms are immature.

Cerebral dominance. Another explanation suggests that cerebral dominance may play a role. The brain is made up of two halves. Like our two arms or two legs, these halves are to a large extent independent, although they are in fact connected. Normally the left-hand side of the brain dominates while we are speaking.

The cerebral dominance theory suggests that children stutter if the

THE WRONG APPROACH TO A STUTTERING CHILD

✖ *Without meaning to, some parents pay more attention when a child stutters than they do when he is speaking fluently. This attention can take the form of criticism, sympathy, extra patience or time, or even extra privileges. If a child gains from his stuttering, he may persist. The best way to stop this is to do your best to ignore the stutter.*

✖ ***Apply pressure;*** *lose patience.*

✖ ***Worry too much.*** *Some parents react to the smallest hiccup of speech with exaggerated alarm. If you and your partner always say "Start again and speak more slowly this time," the child is bound to become anxious about speaking to adults.*

✖ ***Tell him he is a stutterer.*** *Labels never help children. If he expects to stutter, he will.*

✖ ***Expect too little*** *from a child with speech problems. Do not make his problems an excuse for lowered expectations. A child with a problem needs the tenacity to fight, not the passive resistance of one whose battles are fought for him by his parents.*

left-hand side of the brain does not achieved the level of dominance needed to ensure smooth speech. If this is achieved, stuttering stops.

Aggravating a stutter

While there may be a physical explanation for why some children stutter, there is also evidence for emotional causes. Tiredness, anxiety and emotional upset make matters worse for many stutterers.

Expecting too much. It is thought that developmental stuttering can result from parents expecting children to be able to speak fluently at a very early age. If talking to others is a source of anxiety rather than pleasure, stuttering can result. Once the child stutters, he becomes acutely aware that his listener sometimes lacks patience. This aggravates matters.

A HELPFUL APPROACH TO STUTTERING

✔ *Keep calm.* Anxiety makes matters worse. Provide a relatively peaceful, warm and emotionally supportive background, but don't over-protect. Over-protected children have enormous difficulties when parents are not there to protect them. Consciously aim for a happy medium between expecting too much and expecting too little.

✔ *Promote adequacy.* Emphasize the need to get along with other children and adults. Be especially vigilant about behaviour which will make him unpopular. Use role playing to bring this along: pretend to be another child and invite him to play a game. Set an example of relaxed interaction.

✔ *Adjust family style to suit the child.* Some families love excitement: they fight, scream and over-react. Not all children are robust enough to cope, and the stutterer is likely to be more fragile than most. Calm words and safe routines become essential. Make sure that he understands that the arguments and shouting are a natural part of your life together and that nothing terrible will happen. Be sure he is included when everyone makes up.

✔ *Accept that some stuttering is normal in children between two and five.* Remember that his speech will be smoother if he is not self-conscious. If a child starts to stutter, be as low-key, accepting and loving as possible.

✔ *Adapt professional methods for home use.* Speech therapy is always in demand. Even if you have been referred to a specialist, there may be a delay. While you wait (or before you are referred), try one of the following. Use one method for about a month. If your child's stuttering does not improve, move on. Start with whichever method you think will suit your child.

✔ *Slowing speech.* Encourage him to slow his rate of speech and to start each syllable in a whisper. Show him how to breathe from his abdomen, not his chest, and to use this deep breathing when speaking. Practice abdominal breathing by putting your hands on each other's diaphragms to check that the breathing is correct. You could try getting him to speak into a candle flame so that the flame bends, but does not blow out. Boys often find gentle speech more difficult than girls do. Encourage him to inhale and exhale once before he starts to speak and to do this again between each sentence. This will help slow him down, and calm him down.

✔ **Pacing speech** is the oldest method of helping stutterers. It still works. A metronome is the ideal aid to pacing speech. Simply get the child to speak in time to a slow beat of the metronome. Once he can do this without stuttering, increase the beat rate. Once the child is speaking at a normal rate, ask him to speak without the beat. If possible, make it a game. Take it steadily.

✔ **Reduce the child's anxiety**. First, identify those situations which make the child anxious. Then work out ways of exposing the child to those situations in a relaxing way. For example, if he is anxious about leaving home, you might sit him on your lap, cuddle him closely, and tell him a story about a child who goes out without his mummy. Later you might read him a book about a child who loses (and finds) his mother. He thinks 'dangerous thoughts,' but the anxiety does not actually occur. Always approach these sessions slowly and carefully. If he gets frightened, back off and approach even more gently.

✔ **If a child has a problem with speaking to strange adults,** you might start by talking with him as you cuddle on the sofa. Then encourage him to talk to relatives and friends while cuddled up to you. Gradually make it harder. He speaks while you watch, smiling, but not holding him. Then he speaks in shops while you hold his hand, and so on.

✔ **Reduce tension.** A common problem for this type of child is visiting other houses that are not child-friendly. He senses your tension and it reflects back on him. Ask friends to visit you instead.

✔ **Reward fluent speech.** Always ignore stuttering. While he speaks fluently, give him all your attention.

✔ **Set him targets.** At first you reward him when he manages a few words without stuttering; then a sentence, then two, three or four. As the frequency of stuttering decreases, the stutter-free time needed to earn smiles and attention should be increased.

✔ **If the child responds to these home treatments,** nothing more needs to be done. If the stuttering remains or gets worse, you will need professional advice. Ask to be referred to a qualified speech and language therapist, and/or a psychologist if you feel that the problems are primarily emotional.

Frequent quarrels and fights put children under stress and this can cause or aggravate stuttering in some children. It is thought that prolonged tensions can cause susceptible children to start stuttering.

Speaking too quickly. Sometimes a child tries to speak too quickly because adults look bored and uninterested when he speaks. When children speak quickly, mistakes are made. The adult then looks even more dissatisfied; the child goes faster - and makes more mistakes.

Forced changes, such as forcing a left-handed child to use his right hand, are also associated with stuttering.

Can an allergy cause bad behaviour?

When you think of a child with an allergic reaction your first thoughts are of runny noses, itching, sneezing, eczema or asthma. Or they used to be. Today, the definition of allergic reaction has spread far and wide. In some nursery schools, all children have some allergic reaction chalked up on the board. Allergy is not just seen as a digestive reaction to food, a skin reaction to touch or a breathing reaction to air-born substances, but as food-induced behavioural responses such as hyperactivity, irritability, poor attitude, aggression, social difficulties, poor peer integration, difficulties in control or the acceptance of discipline and so on. Name some piece of bad behaviour, and there's a food to blame. This seems nonsense to me.

There is evidence that a minute proportion of children may become irritable or hyperactive when they eat certain foods, but it would be simplistic to assume that even their bad behaviour is never encouraged or reinforced by parents. Which is not to say that allergic reactions never cause behavioural problems: just that such reactions are much less common than naughty children.

Some children and adults certainly have allergic reactions to common foods. Peanuts and wheat are common examples. Malt and yeast may be others.

But the widely-held view that foodstuffs cause hyperactivity, poor concentration and behavioural disorders is hard to prove. When tested using proper double-blind procedures (that is when patient, doctor and parent did not know which children were receiving certain foodstuffs in their diets) no evidence has been found for these claims.

There is some evidence that children diagnosed as hyperactive can be 'cured' by certain diets, but it is not very impressive. When tested with double-blind procedures, the activity of only about 5 per cent of those children diagnosed as having ADHD (that is, those with serious hyper-activity problems) could be controlled by diet. That means dietary effects on behaviour are found in less than one in 200 children.

Hyperactivity

Attention deficit hyperactivity disorder or ADHD, as hyperactivity is frequently now called, has not been well defined. In general, children diagnosed with this disorder (that is, about 5 to 10 per cent of the early school age and pre-school children in the USA, but a much lower pro-portion elsewhere) display inappropriate levels of activity. They race around, climb and rarely stay still. They lack, or appear to lack, the ability to concentrate and have short attention spans so that they do not stick with one activity but flit from one to another. They are also impulsive.

Such children require much supervision, and have difficulty waiting their turn. These symptoms describe the behaviour of most small to medium-size children some of the time. ADHD children do it more, and do it when much older. It is a matter of degree.

The underlying cause of ADHD is unknown, but many believe it is biological. Others think that the cause can be found in the modern diet. But research using proper blind procedures has found no evidence that diet plays any role whatsoever. Hyperactivity is more common in lower socio-economic groups, amongst boys, amongst the economically disadvantaged, among those overly nagged by adults, and among the highly intelligent. There is some suggestion that 'driven' adults were once 'driven' children, but no systematic studies of this.

Many of the things we know about the causes of disruptive and attention-seeking behaviours in children would suggest that hyperactiv-ity, if not entirely caused by parental reinforcement, is certainly aggra-vated by it. The fact that hyperactive behaviours can often be as effec-tively treated by behavioural modification (that is, teaching children how to behave) as by drugs, argues for this. But this is a minefield. In truth, no one really knows the extent of the problem or its causes.

Hyperactive children are often treated with stimulant drugs, particu-larly in the U.S.A., where alarmingly high numbers of children (1 per cent of all American children between the ages of four and 12) are now treated with daily doses of ritalin or amphetamines. While these drugs are clearly overused, they can, nonetheless, be beneficial. They should, however, be used in conjunction with a change in parental attitudes, expectations and behavioural treatment: not as an alternative to these. The long-term effects of giving children these drugs are unknown, which is worrying because there is evidence that regular use of amphetamines (in large doses) can cause a psychosis rather like schizophrenia in adults. In some cases, the drugs are known to cause seizures. Children who take the 'good pill' every day come to think of themselves as bad, and believe that they cannot control their own behaviour.

Symptoms of ADHD
Note that not all children have all these symptoms:

◆ **Poor attention.** He is a poor listener. He forgets or ignores instructions and is visually inattentive. He is easily distracted and blind to danger.

◆ **Impulsive.** Leaps before he looks. Speaks before he thinks. Aggressive. Easily led.

◆ **Over-active.** Irritable, driven, fidgety, disruptive, affected by noise (gets worse); tense when in crowds.

◆ **Clumsy.** Accident-prone.

◆ **Socially inept.** Low tolerance of failure. Acts silly in groups. Wants to mix, but does not always know how. Speaks without thinking and does not listen.

◆ **Disorganized.** Often messy, poor at dressing, finds it hard to string actions together. Poor sequencing.

◆ **Poor self-esteem.**

◆ **Specific learning problems** are more common amongst hyperactive children. So are sleep problems.

◆ **Aggressive.** Where aggression and ADHD are combined, the prognosis is poor. Problems (and aggression) tend to remain into adulthood.

◆ **Language.** The child may forget what he is saying in mid-sentence. Interrupts others. Gets confused.

Do hyperactive children really exist?
This is a question which has caused, and still causes, much debate, but the answer clearly is that they do.

It is more difficult to determine whether or not they are born hyperactive or whether they are made. On this the jury is still out. Common sense suggests that children's temperaments differ, and that so also will activity and ability to concentrate. Common sense also suggests that the way we treat children exacerbates these problems.

◆ **Turn off the TV**. If children find it hard to interact, they need more one-to-one interactions and less passive listening.

◆ **Turn off the radio.** All children tend to be distracted and hyperactive when noise levels are high.

◆ **Turn down the stimulation.** All children are distracted and hyperactive when stimulation is high. Hyperactive children are better when playing in one-to-one situations than in gangs. The fact that boys (who play in gangs and shout rather than talk to each other) are more often hyperactive may reflect this.

◆ **Practice a poker face.** It is hard to ignore hyperactivity, but studies show that time out and reinforcing children for appropriate behaviours works as well as drugs.

◆ **Improve self-esteem.** See pages 121-125.

◆ **Remove all labels.** A child who thinks he is hyperactive, and believes he cannot concentrate, will behave accordingly.

Start expecting good behaviour

◆ **Structure and organize.** Introduce routines, rules and expectations. Set firm limits and expect children to fit into them. Such children have difficulty organizing themselves, but they can do it.

◆ **Talking.** Get down to their level and look them in the eye when you speak to them. Speak softly, starting with a more breathy voice than usual and raising the volume slightly as you continue. Be economical. Make the message clear, short and to the point. Reinforce your words with clear body language. Listen to them. Show interest.

◆ **Watch out for low blood sugar.** Some believe that it helps if you feed at regular intervals and avoid making the child wait too long for meals. But the evidence is, to say the least, flimsy.

◆ **Reduce tension,** both in the home and in his life. Let him know when routines change. Hot baths, massage and relaxation help.

◆ **Don't over-punish.** Turn a blind eye. Praise his good behaviour and try to ignore all but the worst.

◆ **Use stickers, stars and stamps.** Good behaviour charts work with hyperactive children. Set a standard for the day (just a little better than yesterday) and reward him with a star when the goal is reached. Work on one or two specific behaviours rather than generally 'being good'.

◆ **Adapt the environment.** ADHD-proof the house. Do not make demands he cannot attain, like expecting him to sit quietly somewhere when he has nothing to do.

◆ **Medication is not advised for children under five.** After this, drug treatments are available.

◆ **The Feingold diet.** In 1973 Dr Ben Feingold claimed that there is a connection between diet and hyperactivity. He suggested that our diet contains up to 2,700 additives: not only artificial additives, but also substances that act as natural preservatives in traditional diets. He claimed that rapid improvements were found in 50 per cent of children who transferred to his special additive-free diet.

However, in spite of the fact that many parents swear by the diet, and state categorically that children on it improve, there is little evidence that dietary changes are the cause of these improvements. Studies which put children on to the diet, then secretly fed them additives in the form of drinks or sweets which were usually pure, but at unpredictable times contained additives, found that children did not behave badly or become hyperactive on 'additive' days.

A very small number of children may be affected by additives in their diet - at most about 1 in 500 children. Ten times as many are influenced by their parents' belief that they will be hyperactive. If you wish to try the diet, be warned that you will have to cut all natural salicylate (natural preservatives) found in oranges, apples, pineapples, pears (and their juices), berry fruits, tomatoes and Marmite. Nitrates as found in bacon, the preservatives found in packaged foods, artificial colouring as found in sweets, biscuits, many cakes, margarine, drinks, yoghurts and packaged custards and puddings, and the amines which are found in chocolate are all banned. Care also has to be taken with honey, toothpaste, dish washing agents, perfumed soaps, shampoos and conditioners. If you think it is worth a try (or even that it is easier to believe in the cure if you have to work so hard to achieve it), ask your doctor or a qualified dietitian for advice.

Expect good behaviour if trying a diet. Studies testing the Feingold diet suggest that 50 per cent of children improve when their parents put them on to special additive-free diets - in spite of the fact that the vast majority of studies show that the diet itself had absolutely no effect for the majority of these children. In nine out of ten cases, the improvement in the child's behaviour is caused by the parent's, and the child's, expectation that behaviour will improve. The stricter regimes that parents have to enforce in order to implement the diet may also play some role.

That parental expectations cause such differences is not surprising. There are many other examples in psychological

HOW NOT TO DEAL WITH A RUDE CHILD

✖ *Smack him and demand an apology.* A child treated like this does not learn politeness or good manners. He learns to be afraid.

✖ *Call him names.* Be rude to and about him. See how he feels. This only teaches him that being rude is acceptable.

✖ *Blame the person – maybe another child – who 'caused him to be rude'.* No one causes anyone else to be rude: they choose. By blaming others you excuse and encourage him.

HOW TO DEAL WITH A RUDE CHILD

✔ *State what you hear:*
"I hear a child who is being rude."

✔ *State what you feel:*
"I do not like that."

✔ *Accept the anger:*
"Having to stop playing makes you feel angry."

✔ *State the rules.*
"But rudeness is not allowed."

✔ *State your expectations.*
"I am sure that you will apologise to Grandma."

literature. Most clinical drug trials, which are carried out by pharmacologists and doctors, not psychologists, show that the expectation of cure plays a very large role in the efficacy of all known drugs. There are plenty of studies to show that patients taking little sugar pills which they believe to be some miracle drug do actually better, provided the doctor says that a cure is probable.
◆ **Get professional help**. Hyperactive children can be very wearing. It helps to have the advice and reassurance of a professional. But be careful not to use the professional endorsement of hyperactivity as either a label or an excuse. Children achieve control when we make demands and when they believe that control is possible. They do not improve when we tell them they cannot help but do what they do.

The shy child

Children need to be assertive, but they do not need to be forceful. You want them to have friends, but do not need them to be the life and soul of the party. Children who happen to need plenty of excitement tend to be extroverted. Those who need less excitement are more introverted. Although we cannot change a child's basic temperament, we can work within it to enable him to have as many choices as possible. Shy children can grow to be strong, competent adults, just like extrovert ones.

◆ **Let him know that he is important.** "You are so special."

◆ **Never let others label.** If someone calls him shy, find a positive way of correcting them. Say, for example, "Not shy, just very self-contained," and/or "Self-contained children like Jamie prefer to work things out before they rush in," and/or "He is often quiet at first. but once you know him better you will realize he is not shy but quietly competent."

◆ **Boost his ego.** "Jamie takes his time and considers what to do."

◆ **Don't push him into situations.** If he refuses, accept. Allow time.

◆ **Give permission to feel the way he does.** "If you do not feel ready to join in, you can stand with me and watch until you are."

◆ **Express his feelings and accept them.** "I understand you are afraid to go and play with the other children. I know you will go when you are ready."

◆ **Help him to gain courage.** "Shall we whisper the courage words? If you feel nervous, just say the special courage words and you will feel better."

◆ **Self-talk.** Encourage the power of a positive inner voice. If he says and hears positive things about himself often enough he will believe them. Show him how to use that voice. "Just keep saying I can." "When you say 'mazooma' it helps you to remember that Mummy and Daddy and Grandma and Grandad love you and know how hard you try." "If that 'no' voice starts shouting, tell it to be quiet. Just say 'Shut up, no voice; I'm not going to listen."

◆ **Think grey.** Children think in black and white. A single small mistake makes it wrong. Encourage him instead to think in shades of grey. He did not talk with other children today, but he did sit next to them. Sitting is a good grey.

◆ **It is not a catastrophe.** Respect feelings, but help him to get a grip on reality. "How shall we think of this? As a big mountain, a small hill or just like walking up Grove Avenue?"

◆ **Pretend.** When he says he cannot do something, say. "Let's pretend you can." Play some scenarios which give him in fantasy what he finds difficult in reality.

◆ **Model and teach social skills.** Let him hear you discussing the advantages of friendship, not the negatives.

◆ **Step by step.** Let him pay in shops. Have children around to play one at a time (and not for too long at first). Children who can manage in one-to-one situations can learn to survive in crowds.

◆ **Build confidence by engaging in formal activities he can do alone.** Music, swimming, trampolining, gymnastics. Later, consider activities he or she does with others which require little speech: karate, dancing.

◆ **The social isolate.** There is a degree of difference between being shy and being completely socially isolated. Social isolates have extremely disturbed peer relationships. Unlike shy children, social isolates do not want to interact with others, and take active steps to avoid doing so. Social isolation is very much linked with other problems such as learning difficulties, personality defects and emotional instability. Such children need professional help.

He is fearless

There is always one of our children who one way or another is lucky to have survived without injury. Sometimes the same child is lucky over and over again. If a child frightens you with a scrape, you feel like blaming, even smacking, because you've panicked. If you panic too easily, it can become a game. "How close can I get to the edge before Mum looses her cool?"

◆ **Put on a poker face.** Get him to safety, then say: "The cliffs are very crumbly. Look how those rocks have fallen down. Standing close to the edge was a dangerous thing to do."

◆ **Don't lecture.** Cool down. Ask questions that make him think, rather that dictate how he should feel and act. "What would happen if someone was sitting under the cliff and you made some rocks fall?"

◆ **Talk about common dangers:** traffic, heights, water, fire.

Feelings out of control; feelings under control
To feel is human. To feel a full range of emotions is to be complete; to

feel deeply no crime. Not to do so is abnormal, and to suppress emotion is harmful if you turn bad emotions in on yourself. But sometimes we must deceive, to protect ourselves from those who would use the expression of our emotions to hurt us further.

The dilemma for parents of highly-strung children is finding the right balance for their child. Do you try to teach him to control his feelings and perhaps turn bad feelings inward, or do you allow him to be 'himself' and make him prey to other's taunts and impatience? A child who fits the stereotypes is more acceptable than one who does not. Stereotypes differ from culture to culture; within societies certain feelings are acceptable for girls, but not for boys, and vice versa.

What you expect from an emotional child should always be a compromise between some ideal and reality. There are no ways to measure what to expect; anyway, very few children fit cultural norms.

HOW TO TREAT YOUR CHILD'S FEELINGS

✔ **Feelings are fine.** *Accept what he feels and acknowledge it. "That would make you angry."*

✔ **Feelings are personal.** *"But when you hit your sister she feels upset." "That makes me cross." Each of us has different feelings. Everyone's feelings are valid.*

✔ **Feelings do not have to be hidden.** *"Show me how you feel. Shout as angry as you feel."*

✔ **Feelings do not have to be understood.** *"Sometimes people just feel sad."*

✔ **Do not excuse actions.** *"I understand that you are angry, but that is no excuse for hitting Joe."*

✔ **Understanding your emotions can make you feel better.** *"You feel sad because Daddy is not here."*

HOW NOT TO TREAT YOUR CHILD'S FEELINGS

✖ **Suggest feelings need to be controlled.** *"Stop being angry."*
✖ **Try to control your child's feelings.** *"You don't really want an ice cream."*
✖ **Suggest feelings should be hidden.** *"Stop crying at once." "Big boys do not cry."*

A child who trusts adults can trust his feelings.

So:
◆ Treat him with respect; be caring.
◆ Accept him for who he is.
◆ Meet his needs.
◆ Make him safe and secure.
◆ Feel comfortable together.
◆ Be reliable.
◆ Say what you mean, and mean what you say.
◆ Keep promises.
◆ Be predictable.
◆ Be prepared, and make sure children are prepared.

Teaching proper control
◆ **Accept feelings.** "You want an ice cream."
◆ **Intervene at the thought level.** "But it's too close to dinner, it will spoil your appetite."
◆ **Intervene at the behaviour level.** "I'm sorry, but we cannot get one now."
◆ **Intervene with imagination.** "I wish I could buy you an ice cream as big as that car, but we are about to have lunch."

Teach coping skills
"When you feel angry with your sister, try imagining her with green hair. She would hate green hair, wouldn't she?"
"When I feel upset, I put on a record and dance. Sometimes it makes me feel better."
"When I can't do something, I find that I feel better if I think about all the things I can do."

He is stubborn

When a child digs in his heals and refuses too give ground, we call him stubborn and wilful. When we stand our ground and refuse to be bullied out of our rights, we call it assertiveness.

By stopping a child from ever being stubborn, we stop him being assertive. If we teach him to be assertive, we teach him to be stubborn. What we really want is a child who does as we ask, but holds his own elsewhere. Or do we?

I suspect not. When it comes down to it, we all want a child who can hold his own; a child whose self-esteem enables him to take control of what happens to himself.

Children can be stubborn for many reasons, some quite unfathomable. Who can tell why a certain jumper will not be worn, or why he will only eat potatoes if the gravy is poured on to the plate beside them?

Situation non-negotiable.

Identify his feelings.

You do not want to wear your raincoat

Give information:

Clothes get wet in the rain

Describe your feelings:

I worry that you will be ill if you wear wet clothes

Give a choice where a choice is possible:

You can wear your raincoat or stay at home: it's your choice

State what must be done:

We need to collect Ruth from school, please put your raincoat on

Situation negotiable.

Identify his feelings.

You want to wear your gumboots

Give information:

It is hot

Describe your feelings:

I worry that your feet will get all sweaty

Solve problem:

Perhaps we could take a wet flannel to wipe your feet

Perhaps you could carry your sandals in a bag

Maybe you could grin and bear it if you get hot

Can you think of anything else?

What do you think we should do?

Situation unimportant.

OK, if you want your gumboots, that's fine

He steals

There are very few children who get through childhood without taking something that belongs to another. Sometimes taking things is obviously harmless (like stealing a biscuit from the tin). At other times the behaviour seems much more serious. Most parents are shocked to discover that a child has taken money from their purse, or brought home a toy from another child's house. Before the age of four, children cannot put themselves in another person's shoes. Although they may seem to understand the concept of 'mine', what they usually mean is that the object in question is currently in their possession. So they cannot understand that other people might also feel 'that's mine.'

Small children grab what interests them. Even when they are old enough to realize what other people feel about their belongings, they still take things many times before understanding the difference between 'mine' and 'yours'.

- ◆ **Be patient. Keep faith and do not accuse him of stealing.**
- ◆ **Don't ask him if he took something when you know he did.** If he thinks you are angry, he will lie.
- ◆ **Explain what has to be done.** This car lives at play school. We must take it back to play school tomorrow.
- ◆ **Explain how others might feel.** Robert will be sad when he cannot find his car.
- ◆ **Pre-empt problems.** "Remember what we said yesterday. School toys have to stay at school."
- ◆ **Teach awareness of others.** Can he sort the washing into 'yours' and 'mine'? Can he lay the table for 'You' and 'Me'? "Whose plate is that?"

He spits

A common but annoying habit. It is also a wonderful way of becoming the centre of attention, especially in the classroom. A spitting child can make the most liberal parent wish the ground would open up and swallow them. This is the moment for your best poker face. Stay calm, lift him up and take him away.

- ◆ **Describe what happened and remind him of the rules.** "David, you spat at Hannah. We do not spit at people. That is the rule."
- ◆ **Accept his feelings and tell him how you expect him to behave.** "I understand Hannah made you cross, but you know how to use words to tell her you are angry. You will not spit at people again."
- ◆ **Intervene.** If he spits when he is frustrated, divert his attention

before he spits.

◆ **Plan.** Discuss the problem beforehand. "Jane is coming to play. Remember the rule about spitting? I know it is easy to forget. Shall I remind you with a secret word? What should we have as our secret word?" If he looks as if he is going to spit, remind him of the secret word. "Foxglove. Jamie, remember what we said."

◆ **Give choices.** "You can stay and play. If you spit, we will have to go home. It is your choice." Follow through. "I see you have chosen to go home".

◆ **Praise.** "No spitting today. That's great."

◆ **Let him spit where it's harmless.** "If you want to spit, why not gargle with this water and spit in the sink?"

Brushing teeth

In the battle against tooth decay, fluoride is your child's first defence. If he will not brush and it is not added to your water supply, you should give him tablets.

The second line of defence is tooth cleaning. Cleaning teeth can be largely managed without brushing. Most of the sugary substances that destroy teeth can be washed off with a glass of water. What is left can be wiped off with a cloth. If he objects to brushing his teeth after each meal, teach him to drink a glass of water and wipe with a napkin after meals. He should still use a toothbrush night and morning.

The third line of defence is to minimize the place of sweets and cola in the diet and to make the eating and drinking of sweet things conditional on tooth brushing. "Jamie, if you have cola you have to promise to brush your teeth afterwards. That is the rule. If you do not want to brush your teeth, have a drink of water. It is your choice." It is unreasonable to expect small children to remember to brush their teeth every night and morning. Ask them to do so and ensure that they do.

Eats too many sweets and snacks/drinks too much cola

Most children do not think they have enough sweets, snacks or cola, and most parents think they have too much. Forbidding their hearts' desire just makes it more attractive. You need to ration supplies, but in doing so will almost invariably increase the whining and nagging score for the week.

◆ **Ration.** Set aside a daily allowance. Put it in a special place. "When they have gone there are no more." Children will need separate boxes or bags for their daily booty.

◆ **Link the allowance to pocket money.** A set amount to spend on sweets each week. When the sweets are eaten, that is it.

◆ **Don't use sweet things as bribes.** This makes them even more special.

◆ **Special times.** Snacks, sweets and cola are only eaten when you are sitting together. They accompany your daily gossip. Alternatively, they are by the side of the bed when he awakes. This has the added advantage of giving you an extra ten minutes in the morning (no sweets in Mummy and Daddy's room). Of course, this precedes morning tooth cleaning.

◆ **Clean teeth after sweets.** If the child has to clean his teeth every time it takes a little of the shine away: as well as most of the problem. When out of the house, a glass of water washes away most of the sticky residue.

The impulsive child

Impulsive children act spontaneously in sudden, forceful ways. They tend to act first and think later, which can get them into trouble and puts them in danger. Such children rarely consider consequences, even though they know those consequences. In short they, like much younger children, are constantly at the mercy of their impulses. Impulse-led behaviour in late pre-schoolers and early school-age children is common. In children younger than this it is almost universal. Older impulsive children are also more likely to be aggressive and to argue and fight.

Impulsive behaviour, especially extreme behaviour, is probably caused by the slow maturity of the brain's inhibition mechanisms, or a failure to mature at all. Anxiety is another cause and anxious children often rush at things in a sense of panic. Because they are not calm, they cannot think things through. Some are impulsive because parents or elder siblings are impulsive, or because parents have never taught them how to delay gratification or plan activities.

◆ **Teach them to wait.** Learning how to wait is one of the most important lessons of early childhood. Parents should be firm but relaxed when asking a child to wait. They should say what they mean, and mean what they say. "I will help you with that as soon as I have finished peeling these carrots." Then do as you say.

◆ **Teach your child to listen to his inner voice.** Suggest he says to himself "I can wait my turn." Tell him: "It's good to learn to wait." Model such behaviour and show appreciation for his efforts. Try acting through pretend scenarios in which children have to wait.

◆ **Offer solutions.** Discuss ways in which he might learn to wait. "Perhaps you should touch all your fingers in turn, or take three deep breaths. What do you think?"

◆ **Prompt him.** Give him cues for good behaviour. Some children at this age find that making a C with their fingers and thumb helps keep control.

◆ **Get professional help.** A very impulsive child may need the help of a professional.

The clumsy child

Some children are clumsy because they are impatient and impulsive; some because they are hyperactive; others because they do not have good control over fine body movements, or find it hard to see themselves moving about in space. All children are clumsy to some extent, and there is no simple definition of clumsiness severe enough to need professional help - but see below.

◆ **A priority is to teach this type of child to be less impulsive.** See the suggestions above.

◆ **Structure and organize.** Sometimes clumsiness results from a lack of planning on the child's part.

◆ **Practise motor skills.** Children who use their hands regularly gain skill.

◆ **If dressing is difficult** go for ease rather than fashion. Dressing can be very frustrating for a clumsy child. It is a daily reminder that "I can't."

◆ **Encourage physical pastimes.** Children who rush about playing on bikes, climbing, and dodging others become more aware of their bodies in space.

◆ **Let him do things for himself.** Sometimes children lack skill because parents have always dressed them, never expected them to do things for themselves.

◆ **Get professional help** if you think he is exceptionally clumsy - for example, if he needs considerably more help with buttons or using crayons than other children of his age. It is recognized that some children have considerable problems controlling fine movement.

The spiteful child

Children learn to be spiteful. It may start when they become jealous of the attention you give to another child, or in retaliation for a teacher's preference for other children. Some children learn that spitefulness is a sure winner in battles with younger siblings. Others are goaded on by young siblings who see this as a sure way of getting an older sibling into trouble. It can be quite difficult to intervene because spiteful acts are often quick and sly. You may not see spiteful behaviour; you hear about it second hand. "Mum, Jamie knocked my castle down." "No I didn't, you knocked it down yourself." It will be easier to address the cause if you examine the context. Keep a record of the child's behaviour, recording the context of all spiteful acts. Is it a way of getting your attention. Is he only spiteful to his sister? Does she goad him? Does it only happen when he is tired?

HOW NOT TO TREAT A SPITEFUL CHILD

✖ *As ever, don't label. If he believes he is spiteful, that is how he will act.*

✖ *"I'm not going to discuss it. I don't want to hear your excuses." Children have reasons. Don't deny how he felt because you do not approve of what he did.*

✖ *Don't allow "Lucy's a meanie." Never approve of name calling: even when the cap fits.*

✖ *Don't compare. "I don't know why you always have to be so spiteful, Lucy. Jamie manages to behave." Comparisons undermine self-esteem. Low self-esteem often lies at the root of spiteful behaviour. Lowering it further worsens the problem.*

✖ *Don't say: "You can never be nice, can you?" And he might rightly answer: "I can, Dad, but you would never notice. I try, but you never see." Attack the behaviour, not the child.*

✖ *Don't say: "Oh, just shut up, I said just shut up, stop it, you two." If he needs attention, this is how to get it.*

✖ *Spite needs action, not words. Separate the spiteful one from playmates, impose a cooling-off period. Then discuss his feelings and talk through a solution to the problem.*

HOW TO TREAT A SPITEFUL CHILD

✔ *As usual, describe the behaviour, not the child.*
"I hear spiteful talk." "We don't want meanness. You know how to ask for what you want."

✔ *Acknowledge the anger.* *"Spoiling your game must make you angry." Describe the situation from each child's point of view. "You scratched your sister because she took the car you were playing with." Explain the rule. "But Lily, the rule is…"*

✔ *Never let others label.* *If he calls his sister a spiteful pig, say "You sound furious, but I expect you to cope with your sister without calling names." "No name calling, that's one of the house rules."*

✔ *Attend to the injured party.* *"Your castle's all broken up. Do you want me to help you rebuild it?"*

✔ *Teach the spiteful child that he can be pleasant.*
"But you can also be very nice."

✔ *Check for physical causes.* *A one-off period of spiteful behaviour can be caused by the child being in pain or under stress, insecure or uncertain. Children who are frustrated in social groups because of poor hearing are often spiteful or disruptive.*

✔ *Do not give spiteful behaviour your attention.* *Use time out and the poker face. Be careful not to reinforce the victim into egging on the aggressor into more spiteful behaviour. Children are canny. Watch the innocent party.*

The cruel child

For most children cruelty - whether to children or other animals - is a passing phase. Cruelty requires premeditation. A child can hurt another on impulse, but this would not be cruel. It is cruel when he intends to hurt and takes pleasure from doing so. Children who are cruel to animals and children tend to be boys, to have lower IQ and to be hyperactive and disruptive. They tend to have parents who bully or have been bullied. Parental style tends to be over-bearing or over-permissive.

Tackling cruelty

♦ **Reduce aggressive models.** If parents often hit each other, or always make aggressive demands, children will make such demands of others.

♦ **Set limits.** Of course, cruelty is not to be tolerated. As soon as you see the behaviour, act. Tell him that cruel behaviour is not allowed. Put on a poker face and remove him. "No cruelty. You know how to get what you want without hurting."

♦ **Raise expectations.** "I am confident that you can be kind to your sister."

♦ **Give choices.** "You know how to behave in a cruel way, but you also know how to be kind. If you want to act cruelly to other children at the playground today, I will have to take you home. If you want to act kindly, you can stay and play. It is your choice."

♦ **Encourage alternative expression.** Teach your child how to express his anger and his jealousy. Do not deny his feelings. "That must make you very cross." "You must be fed up with the baby interfering with your games." Show him how to express those feelings constructively. "Draw me a picture of how angry you are."

Such a worrier

Children worry. They worry what might happen to their parents. They worry about what they were before they were born. They worry when their big brother goes on the rollercoaster, or their little sister climbs up the steps to the slide. They worry about pets who do not come home, monsters in the landing cupboard and whether they will make friends. It is often a vicious circle. The more they worry, the more anxious they become, and the more they worry. They become tense. As they grow up they often deny unpleasant facts.

An infant's feeling of security is very tenuous, and he is easily frightened. By three, children show anxiety about physical injury, loss of parental love and approval, being different or being unable to cope.

The height of worry and anxiety occurs between three and six, when children are often beset with worries and fears. The real and the imaginary get rolled into one in the child's thoughts. They feel the same. Monsters in the cupboard and dogs in the playground are all the same.

Worry causes agitation, crying, screaming, pacing, obsessive thoughts, butterflies in the stomach, nausea, breathing difficulties, tics, nightmares and poor eating or over-eating. Some children seem generally anxious and almost seem to search out things to worry about. They often seem ill at ease and apprehensive. Highly anxious children are often less popular than their more easy-going peers; they may also be less creative and flexible. They are more rigid, cautious and indecisive.

How to help an anxious or worried child

♦ **Encourage a positive self-image.** Anxious children often have a poor self-image. Tell him he is special, and that you are glad he is yours; that you believe he can do it. Say this again tomorrow, and tomorrow and tomorrow.

♦ **Encourage independence.** Children who worry are often dependent. Let him make decisions. Give choices.

♦ **Help him to express anger.** Children who worry do not always express anger openly. Give him permission. "You must be angry." "Show me how angry you feel by kicking that pillow."

♦ **Acknowledge feelings.** "That must have felt scary." "That would make you worry."

♦ **Empathise.** "I remember when I was little I used to have a dress which had animals all around the hem. It really frightened me. I used to think the animals would bite me when I wasn't looking. But they didn't - here I am today."

♦ **Be consistent.** Inconsistency makes children very anxious. Make sure that all his carers give the same messages. Make a weekly plan so that he knows exactly what is going to happen every day. Consult it often. Tick off the things you do. Write any changes on the chart. It helps to have simple symbols that he understands. A child who can see what will happen until next Sunday has less cause to worry.

♦ **Expect imperfection.** Having unrealistically high expectations can cause anxiety. Let him achieve within his own limits. If children are anxious, they cannot learn. If they have low self-esteem, they cannot achieve.

♦ **Set limits.** Being too permissive and/or neglectful feeds the

child's insecurity.
- ◆ **Model.** Anxious parents frequently produce anxious children.
- ◆ **Accept fantasy.** Being told not to be silly, or that ghosts do not exist, makes him more anxious, not less.

Bossy

When he is small you may find his bossy ways endearing. As he gets older you will not. Nor will other children. Children are often bossy when they encounter other children at play school or in the park, especially when they are not used to playing together. Try not to embarrass the child in public. A quiet word - "Jamie, that's your bossy voice" - is often enough. When you get home you can discuss good and bad ways of asking people to do things. Model these with teddies and dolls. "Shall I ask this doll to wash up with a very bossy voice?" "Show me how that dolly would ask in a pleasant voice." Remember that he learns by example. If you boss him, he will boss others. Teach him to be assertive without being over-bearing. Shape the behaviour by attending to him when he gets it right and ignoring when he gets it wrong.

Handle persistent bossiness as you would any other attention-seeking behaviour.

Ignore it when possible
- ◆ **Describe his bossy behaviour** rather than label the child. "That is your bossy voice."
- ◆ **Encourage co-operation.** "Your sister knows how to share. Ask her with your polite voice if you can play with the bricks."
- ◆ **Set an example.** Encourage leadership rather than a demanding style. "Lucy, if you help me to clear the table, we can have lunch quickly. Then there will be time to stop at the swings on the way to collect Jamie."

Immature behaviour

Many children develop unevenly: mature in some respects, immature in others. Sometimes the immaturity is a reaction to stress or life events which undermine security (such as starting school, the illness of a parent or the birth of a sibling). Sometimes it has a more organic cause: illness may cause poor bladder control, for instance. Sometimes immaturity is actively encouraged by parents who do not want a child to grow up, or find it is quicker and easier to dress a child than wait for him to dress himself.

Sometimes parents label their child as immature: and the child simply obliges - as children (and adults) do when labelled in this way. Sometimes a particular stress can be coped with over a short period; but then the child loses stamina and will suddenly start to wet the bed or to whinge and complain. Or both: bad temper, tantrums and whining are more common on the day following a wet bed.

Regression - going back to immature behaviour - is commonplace when under stress, especially in younger children. Criticism intensifies the problem. If they are reverting to earlier attention-seeking strategy, comment and criticism merely prove their case.

Clowning; being silly

When a young child shows off, clowns or generally acts in silly ways, the natural reaction is to laugh. It is very endearing at first. But clowning and silliness can become wearing after the novelty wears off. By then the behaviour may be entrenched: a label you attach to him and he attaches to himself. For an insecure child who finds making friends difficult, clowning becomes a way of life. How and why it started gets lost in the mist of time and children continue to play the buffoon because this gets them the attention and the friends they need.

But long-term buffoonery is not always good for self-image or self-esteem. People want and need to be loved for themselves, not for the acts they put on for other people.

◆ **Children clown to seek attention.** It does not matter whether the attention is positive or negative.

WHAT NOT TO DO WHEN CHILDREN ARE SILLY

✖ *Always laugh. This reinforces silliness.*
✖ *Never laugh. Being funny is not a crime.*
✖ *Never invite a friend to play. Sometimes children use silliness as a way of being accepted into a gang, so encourage one-to-one friends. Silliness is less important in such contexts.*
✖ *Raise self-esteem. Silliness is often the outward sign of negative self-esteem.*
✖ *Reject him because he is not quite what you wanted. Expecting children to be things they cannot be drives them into attention-seeking and approval-strategies, of which clowning is one of the commoner. Therefore:*
✖ *Give the behaviour plenty of attention, whether positive or negative. If the child needs attention (and what child does not) he will continue to clown.*

WHAT TO DO WHEN CHILDREN ARE SILLY

✔ *Accept him.* *Pre-schoolers should be silly and light-hearted, especially when they are with other children. They should sometimes show off and blow their own trumpets and proudly tell us what they can do. They should collapse into giggles and push and shove their peers in obvious glee. However, the need to completely dominate all proceedings by silliness and clowning needs to be checked.*

✔ *Ignore.* *If silliness and clowning is going too far, or beginning to dominate, warn the child. If he takes no notice, put on your poker face and ignore. If it persists, remove him to his room.*

✔ *Show him how to get attention in other ways.* *"Jamie, my friend Mary is coming round. What would you like to show her?" If he does not know, suggest something. "Would you like to show her your new trainers and the pictures of what you did at school?" Find something interesting for him to do while you gossip. "Perhaps you would like to play at the sink while we have adult time?" Remember, small children need constant reassurance that you are still thinking about them. "I'm going to make tea for Mary and me: do you want any?"*

✔ *Do not expect a child to amuse himself while you entertain guests.*

✔ *Be consistent.* *Don't encourage him to dominate the nursery school, then to be a shrinking violet at home.*

✔ *Give all your children opportunities to be heard.* *Encourage discussion and gossip. Talk about feelings. The easiest way to do this is to have a regular gossip session at the end of each day, but family discussions and family meals are just as useful. Children need to be told: "It will be your turn in a minute." Remember that pre-schoolers' memories are short. He will forget what he wanted to say if he has to wait too long. This does not mean that what he wanted to say was not important. If possible, prompt him so he can remember what he was going to say.*

✔ *Other children are the best antidotes to showing off.* *They are less impressed, and less tolerant, than adults.*

✔ *If a child needs friends,* *discuss ways of making them.*

◆ **Sometimes children clown to hide the way they feel.**
◆ **Sometimes children clown because they are expected to be clowns:** the jolly, fat child being the classic example; the not very bright clown another.
◆ **Clowning is fun.** Sometimes children clown because they are children having fun: their birthright.

Belching and farting

Deliberate belching or passing wind are particularly irritating ways of showing off. If you are embarrassed into coaxing him to stop, this is a sure winner for the child. Remember, pre-schoolers love rude behaviour. Farting on cue is an absolute winner with other children. Belching is pretty good too.

HOW TO DISCOURAGE FARTING AND BELCHING

✔ *Say nothing. Just act. When he belches, leave the room. If you are with someone, suggest you both move. Or pick the child up and put him in his room. If he belches to get your attention at table, put on your poker face, get a tray and move to eat your meal elsewhere.*

✔ *In public. Quickly and calmly remove your child. Keep a poker face. When you get outside, tell him: "You can choose to go back, or you can choose to go home. If you belch, we go home. It is your choice." If he belches after you return, pick him up and walk out again. Say, "I see you have chosen to go home." If it is clear that he is belching because he wants to go home, then say: "You can go on belching now, but if you do I will put you in your room when we get home." In this case it is essential to be consistent: you must carry out the punishment, even if he does everything he can get back into favour on the way home.*

✔ *Bribery works with older children: a star for every day without belching; a small treat for seven stars.*

✔ *Identify his feelings, explain yours. "You seem to like belching." "It makes me feel embarrassed."*

Acting like a baby

HOW TO ENCOURAGE FARTING AND BELCHING

✖ *Pretend he never does it but look embarrassed.*

✖ *Give the child plenty of attention.*

✖ *Let him get his own way as a result.* If he knows this stops you talking to neighbours, he will continue.

Children often revert to whining babyish talk, especially if under stress, tired or in need of our attention. Sometimes this happens at certain times of the day. Sometimes children will suddenly revert to babyish talk after starting school or when a new baby is born. It usually stops as quickly as it began. Understand the message – "I need a little more attention" – but ignore the behaviour. Underlying the behaviour is probably a need to claw back some of the security the child felt at an earlier age, which now seems to be evaporating in the face of change.

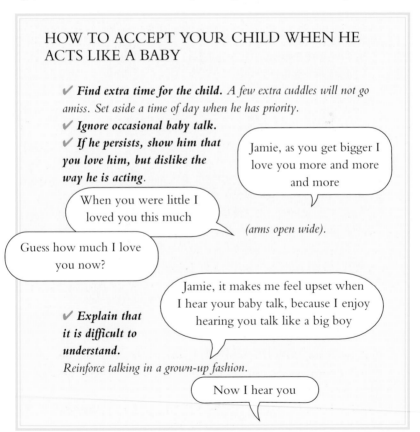

HOW TO ACCEPT YOUR CHILD WHEN HE ACTS LIKE A BABY

✔ *Find extra time for the child.* A few extra cuddles will not go amiss. Set aside a time of day when he has priority.

✔ *Ignore occasional baby talk.*

✔ *If he persists, show him that you love him, but dislike the way he is acting.*

Jamie, as you get bigger I love you more and more and more

When you were little I loved you this much

(arms open wide).

Guess how much I love you now?

Jamie, it makes me feel upset when I hear your baby talk, because I enjoy hearing you talk like a big boy

✔ *Explain that it is difficult to understand.*

Reinforce talking in a grown-up fashion.

Now I hear you

HOW TO REJECT YOUR CHILD WHEN HE ACTS LIKE A BABY

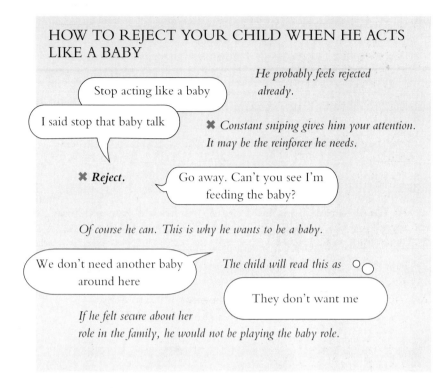

Stop acting like a baby

He probably feels rejected already.

I said stop that baby talk

✖ *Constant sniping gives him your attention. It may be the reinforcer he needs.*

✖ **Reject.**

Go away. Can't you see I'm feeding the baby?

Of course he can. This is why he wants to be a baby.

We don't need another baby around here

The child will read this as

They don't want me

If he felt secure about her role in the family, he would not be playing the baby role.

Messy, sloppy

Young children are normally messy. Some are messier than others. The more perfectionist the parents, the more the child's sloppiness shows. Realistic expectations are needed. Children can use their messy, sloppy behaviour as a way of attracting attention, especially where such behaviour is a major parental concern. Older children frequently use it to assert independence. Again, this is aggravated in families where independence is given reluctantly. How we look, and how our personal space looks, are two perennial, basic ways of expressing independence.

There are many reasons why some children are messier than others. Some, especially young children, simply lack organizational ability. Some live in disorganized homes: if you are messy, they may be too. Some have never been taught.

◆ **Pre-school children cannot organize a complex sequence of behaviours without help and guidance.** Teach them how to put away clothes and toys.
◆ **Pre-schoolers can be taught to keep a room *relatively* neat**, but not perfect. They should help to clear up their

177

playthings, although they will need encouragement, assistance and direction. Having toys organized so that those of one type (such as soft toys) live in one place and those of another (such as puzzles or construction toys) somewhere else helps the child to become organized. A general toy box or toy cupboard usually leads to disorganization. By three it is fair to expect that children will not leave toys out for days on end.

◆ **Teach children to do things in order**, checking off the items as they go. Instructions given as pictures on cards may help. A sequence might be: put puzzle pieces in box; put box on shelf; close door.

◆ **Doing simple household chores teaches children to carry tasks through to the end.** Let him mop the floor, wash the table or put away the shopping. Sorting the washing into piles prior to folding is another simple organizational task; or sorting the wash into different colours.

◆ **It is reasonable to expect three-year-olds: to keep themselves relatively clean for a short period of time** – although they should never be expected to stay clean all day or when playing in the garden or at play school; by school age to clean their teeth, wash and brush their hair; to check in the mirror, first thing each day, that clothes are tucked in, and that they are clean and neat. Passively having things done for them encourages messiness. If they never have to clear up, why bother?

◆ **It is reasonable to expect a five-year-old:** to put dirty clothes in the basket; to straighten his duvet and help to vacuum his room; to lay the table; to empty the wastepaper baskets into the rubbish bin.

Not yet potty-trained at three

It is difficult to deal with the screaming protests of a child who does not want to sit on his pot, and to keep calm about him still being in nappies after a year of trying to potty train. If it is not working, stop, calm down, and wait. After a month or two, try again.

Start with the potty in front of the TV or let him sit and watch his favourite video. If he shows any resistance, just leave his trainer pants on while he sits. Progress from here. At this age, the battle is getting him to sit: once he does so, he will be trained almost at once. If he does not like his pot, let him use the W.C. A special child seat and a set of steps may help. Not all children like seats, however. Some just like to perch. When children resist potty training into into their fourth year, there is usually a reason. It could be a cry for attention, underlying stress or possibly a persistent infection which makes control difficult. Children will not try if defecating or urinating is painful. Children with impacted bowels cannot learn control.

Bed wetting in older children

◆ **Most three- and four-year-olds produce the occasional wet bed.** One in ten five- to six-year-olds frequently wet the bed. As many as one in four children between the ages of four and 16 have occasional problems, and at any one time about one in eight children between six and eight years have a problem and about one in 20 ten- to 12-year-olds. More girls than boys have problems at all ages.

◆ **Some children wet themselves during the day,** especially when engrossed in play or when excited. This can often be avoided by suggesting that they go to the lavatory before they start to play, and by calling them to do so after they have been playing for a while. Such measures should stop embarrassment when they are with friends. But do not entirely take over responsibility.

◆ **There are two sorts of bed wetter.** Continuous bed wetters have never learned to control their bladders at night. Discontinuous bed wetters learn and then sometime later start to have problems.

◆ **Continuous bed wetters probably have slow maturation of the bladder control mechanisms.** Late control often runs in families. The parents of such children are about three times more likely to have had a similar problem when they were children. If you were still wetting the bed when you started school, there is an even chance your child will too. If your partner also had problems, there is a 70 per cent chance your child will, too. It's not worth being embarrassed about the problem.

◆ **Do not make a fuss.** Anxiety will exacerbate the problem. Shaming does not work, nor does punishment or criticism. The child is usually at least as anxious as you are about bed wetting. Relaxation is the key to success.

◆ **Reduce evening drinking.** Limited success can be achieved by not allowing the child to drink in the early evening, by ensuring he pees before going to bed and getting him up to pee again a couple of hours later.

◆ **Star charts work quite well with discontinuous bed wetters.** The child gets a star for every night he is dry. Wet nights are ignored.

◆ **Reduce stress.** Calm the child before bedtime. Set aside a short period before bedtime when he has the undivided attention of one parent.

◆ **Improve muscle control.** Sometimes continuous bed wetters have poor muscle control. Encourage him to stop and start the flow of urine. This strengthens the muscle. Put a ping pong ball in the loo and let him aim, stop, aim.

◆ **Train the child to retain urine.** Another system that sometimes works with continuous bed wetters is to train the child to retain urine by encouraging him to wait until his bladder is really full. Star charts help extend the period between peeing. Once the child can retain ten to 12 fluid ounces of urine - just over half a pint - the problem of night wetting usually disappears.

◆ **Waking in time.** If you know when he wets the bed, you can wake him up just beforehand. Use an alarm clock. If, for example, he wets the bed three hours after going to sleep, set the alarm for two and a half hours after bedtime. For the younger child, put a pot by the bed, or leave a light on in the bathroom so he is not frightened to get out of bed.

◆ **After a week of dry nights, set the alarm for two hours.** Then after another week of dry nights, set the alarm for one-and-a-half hours, and so on, until the alarm is not needed.

◆ **Progress in small steps.** If he cannot manage half an hour less between peeing, try 15 or even five minutes less.

◆ **Bell and pad method.** This works well, especially with older children. It trains the child to recognize when he is about to urinate. There is about a 70 per cent success rate after two to three months of use.

A special training pad is placed under the child in bed. When moistened, it makes a bell ring and a light go on. This wakes the child, who then stops urinating.

Soiling

Soiling, either by day or night, sometimes occurs in three- to eight-year-olds. It is rarer than bed wetting, affecting only about 3 per cent of children, mainly boys. Treatment is usually very effective.

◆ **Soiling is associated with stress.** It happens most often in children who deliberately retain stools. When children are severely constipated, they always have that full bowel feeling, so it is very difficult to tell that they are ready for a bowel movement.

◆ **Soiling in itself causes stress.** Children with this problem usually have or develop low self-esteem. Like bedwetting, soiling can be a continuous or a discontinuous process. Discontinuous soiling is usually associated with stress.

◆ **Soiling runs in families.** The parents of continuous soilers are likely to have been affected as children.

◆ **Psychological becomes physical.** Although the cause of soiling may initially be psychological (brought about by a family crisis, for example) it can become physical. When the child retains faeces, the bowel becomes distended and eventually, if retention continues, it becomes impacted. The anus then partly opens and seepage occurs. At this stage, even if the psychological problems cease, the colon cannot function correctly and the problem will persist.

◆ **It is usually necessary to get professional help.** This may mean an enema to empty the impacted colon; a change of diet will probably also be necessary to encourage regular bowel movements and avoid constipation. With the colon empty, signals that a bowel movement is imminent are easier to recognize.

◆ **Encourage the child to sit on the lavatory regularly.** Use a kitchen timer and make him sit for ten minutes twice per day. Directly after breakfast, lunch or dinner are convenient times. Star charts reward success.

Otherwise, follow advice given elsewhere in this book for raising the child's self-esteem (pages 121-125); reducing stress; avoiding labelling; and above all being patient - not easy.

Gender stereotypes

As soon as children can say the words, they tell you what gender they belong to, and once their language is good enough they tell us how men and women should behave. Stereotypes die hard. Small children think in black and white, not shades of grey, and their stereotypes are invariably sexist.

Don't worry. The current view will pass. In trying to understand the world, children smash and grab at ideas. They take on board simplistic views, then modify them when their environment encourages them to do so. Accept his views now, but hope to encourage, slowly, a fair-minded view of the differences between the sexes.

Gender identity describes the feelings we have about ourselves. It usually ties up with body shape: most people with female bodies think of themselves as female, even if that does not necessarily tie up with sexual preferences: gays are normally just as certain of their gender identity as straight people. Some people feel that they are trapped in the wrong body and feel this so strongly that they are prepared to undergo a sex change operation to make their body coincide with their identity. However, not everyone who undergoes such a change suffers from an identity crisis – at least, not a sex identity crisis. Sex change or partial sex change can increase earning power for male prostitutes, and can bring notoriety for individuals who desperately need it. This means that at least some aspects of gender identity can be unlearned – or learned.

Developmental psychologists divide the learning of gender roles into three phases: learning identity ('I am a girl'); continuity ('I always was and always will be female'); and permanence ('whatever I do, I will remain a woman'). Identity seems to be in place by two, continuity by four and permanence by six. This means that, as soon as children can tell us, they will know their gender. However, they will not, at that point, realize they were always the same gender or that they will grow up to be the same gender. So a boy of three might think he was once a baby girl (particularly if all the babies he knows are girl babies) and that he might grow up to be a 'Mummy'. By the time he is four, he no longer makes these mistakes – but may still think he will change into a girl if he puts on a dress or plays with a doll.

From the time they first show interest in other people, baby girls and baby boys show more interest in those of their own sex. It tends to stay this way until they reach adulthood. For many it is always so. Equality of opportunity may be possible, but creating a society which totally ignores gender is probably an impossibility.

Differences in behaviour

Parents tend to treat boys and girls differently. They are rougher with boys, throwing them higher, tickling them more forcefully and chasing them more often. When boys cry they find something to distract them. When girls cry, they show sympathy and cuddle them. Society's expectations for boys and girls mirror this treatment. We expect boys to be rougher and more physical; girls to be more gentle and emotional.

We expect girls to be more friendly, more conformist and easy; to be more nurturing, but also more manipulative. We expect boys to be more active, aggressive, pushy, competitive and dominant, and to get their way by demand rather than manipulation.

Sex-stereotyped toys

Since the 1960s, the role of women in many societies has changed a great deal. Many more women work, and many more men carry out household duties, cook and involve themselves in caring for children.

During the same period, parents have tried to treat children with greater sexual equality than before. The results of that equality of treatment can be seen in the higher educational achievement of women, the higher rates of female entry into the major professions and the greater independence of women. It has not, however, changed the way young children play, which remains sex-stereotyped.

In an attempt to wean girls away from traditional female roles, many parents have tried to encourage typical male play in daughters. Sometimes they succeed, usually they do not. The average British girl is said to have three glamour dolls, the average German girl rather more, and the average American girl between five and ten such dolls. Although glamour dolls have work clothes, including outfits suitable for overseeing the construction of roads, and join the army, it is the bridal outfits, pop stars' clothes and smart, pretty dresses that sell best. Nor have the dolls got flat-chested and androgynous over the years. On the contrary: they set a standard of female beauty that can only be achieved by a plastic surgeon and a large bank balance.

Meanwhile, boys play at doing those things that only real men do: gangs; fighting; conquering; protecting and saving the world: power rangers, action men, ghost busters. There may be the occasional female figure, the occasional black or Chinese figure, but on the whole the handsome white man conquers the world.

So what is this all about? There are no clear-cut answers, but I think it probably shows the need for small children to understand the unique roles of men and women: something which used to be so easy and now is becoming more and more difficult. There are no longer simple answers to the question 'What do women do that men do not?' At this age children need simple answers; the sex-stereotyped toys give them. So don't worry about your pre-schooler's apparently sexist approach to life. There is nothing wrong with a simple understanding now, which later can be developed into a broader picture.

He wants to wear high heels; she is a tomboy

Parents have always worried about whether their children play in ways appropriate to their sex, and this view is reflected by both society as a whole and by the child's peers. A daughter can go to the shops in a workman's hard hat and a tool bag. You are less enthusiastic about letting your son take his Barbie doll. 'Tomboy' is a form of endearment; 'sissy' is derogatory.

There is a justification of sorts for this inconsistency. Many more men than women grow up confused about their gender; which suggests that men's roles are more difficult to define than women's. Children learn by copying; when men are at home they seldom do what men alone can do - they do that away from home. Perhaps this reflects a central truth: that there is little that men do that women cannot sometimes do; but there is one major thing a woman can do that a man can never do: have a baby.

Can you hear yourself?

Don't shout like that, it's unladylike

Hannah, stop being so boisterous

Let's get you looking pretty

Don't get that dress dirty. Just look at your hair

The other boys will laugh

I think you'd rather have some Lego

You don't want a doll

No son of mine is playing with a doll

What really bothers you?

◆ **Gender problems.** There is no evidence that children who play with 'unsuitable' toys grow up to be either transsexuals nor homosexuals. The vast majority of boys who like girls' toys, and girls who like boys' toys, grow up to have gender identities which match their bodies and to prefer the opposite sex.

◆ **Homosexuality.** Some gay women always were, and still are, more masculine than feminine, but most gay women are not. Some gay men are and always were more feminine; most are not. There are studies to show that the effeminate boy who always thought of himself as girlish compared with other boys felt this way *before* he started to select toys that were 'inappropriate'; and vice versa for girls.

◆ **Transsexuals** also similarly report that they knew they were different from about six; they can remember being attracted to feminine things at this age; as are many boys who do not grow up to be transsexual or homosexual. So it is unlikely that boys playing with girls' toys (or vice versa) had any influence on the outcome.

◆ **Conforming.** Most children conform to the stereotypes they find around them. If they do not, other children laugh at them. Ridicule probably licks most boys into shape. If you find this harsh (which it is) you may wish to encourage or allow more feminine play in the privacy of your home. There is no evidence that this is harmful.

◆ **Cross dressing.** Many individuals get pleasure from cross dressing. It has little to do with sexual identity or sexual preferences. A few men and women who cross-dress are transsexuals. A few are homosexuals. Many are neither. A few of those who cross-dress remember enjoying doing so as children. Others who cross-dressed as children never do so as adults.

Found her in bed with the boy next door

Masturbation is normal, and the progression from exploring his own genitalia to exploring those of other children often occurs at about four. It is very common. In spite of Freud's insistence that children are sexual, most of us are shocked to find our children engaging in sex play. The idea that children get pleasure from sex is so shocking to most of us that we deny it. "They are just curious" is the most frequent comment:

HOW NOT TO DEAL WITH THE PROBLEM

✖ *Ignore it. Sex is powerful and everyone needs to know how to control and use this power.*

✖ *Scream in horror. Sex is not terrible, it is natural. It is quite OK to be sexual, but we have to learn to respect each other's bodies.*

✖ *Don't tell a soul. If it is kept secret, who is to monitor the children?*

✖ *Smack. Smacking in the context of sex is asking for trouble.*

✖ *Assume it has nothing to do with sex.. Are you blind? They are exploring and being curious. But it certainly feels good, too.*

✖ *Assume that they will never do it again. If it was fun and felt good, why shouldn't they do it again if they are bored?*

✖ *Assume they will always be at it. Busy children have got better things to do.*

HOW TO RESPOND HELPFULLY

✔ *Do not scold or lecture or send the playmate home. Let the children know it is quite normal and that you know why they like doing it. Avoid giving undue attention or causing undue embarrassment.*

✔ *Talk to the children. Make the distinction between self and others clear. It is OK to touch yourself, but not for you to touch other people. Children can touch their own genitalia, but have to wait until they are grown-up before they touch other people's or let other people touch theirs. Be firm and matter-of-fact. This is not, repeat not, a sin. It is just something adults do and children do not - like driving cars and going out to work. No sermon required: just a clear statement to both children. "I do not want you to do this again."*

✔ *Address his sexual curiosity. Provide him with sexual information. If you are unsure what to say, there are many excellent books available. Let these be the starting points for discussion. Children who have answers to sexual questions are less likely to engage in sexual play.*

✔ *Discuss the situation with the other child's parent. You each need to discuss this behaviour with your own child.*

✔ *Don't leave them for long periods behind closed doors.*

✔ *Don't be afraid to say no. If you find them again, describe what you see; tell them that you are upset and disappointed to find them with their pants off; ask them to put their pants back on, and arrange for the other child to be taken home. Next time the children play together, tell them that they can play all afternoon, but that if they play 'cuddling in bed games' the other child will have to go home. Say "It's your choice." If they persist, say "I see that you have both chosen for Jenny to go home." Saying no is not going to start a lifetime of sexual repression.*

✔ *Excessive sexual play and sexual precocity are worrying - a sign that a child may have been sexually abused. Most children who are abused are abused by relatives and family friends. Such people can seem normal, indeed engaging. They do not wear badges saying "I'm an abuser." Often they are pillars of the community, on the face of it thoroughly respectable. Talk about abuse to the child. Explain that he/she should always tell. If your child frequently takes the lead in sexual play, be especially vigilant. If he is led by one particular child, be cautious about letting your child spend time alone with the male members of that child's family, especially if that child shows signs of flirtatiousness and sexual precocity with adults.*

I think this is a cop-out, but of course ducking the issue is understandable when we don't really want to think about it.

And this is a dilemma. Will stopping sexual experimentation cause sexual repression? Will encouraging childhood sexuality open the way for those who might abuse them? This is a major worry for many people, but don't let it be for you. The answer to both questions is no.

If a family is open, respectful and candid about sex, it can set limits on childhood sexual experimentation without the slightest fear of harm. It is not what our grandfathers were told not to do that caused problems. It was what they were told not to feel, and how such feelings were used to undermine self-esteem that caused repression.

Many modern psychologists believe in any case that Freud was probably right first time around: that his patients were disturbed not by the repression of childhood sexuality, but by sexual abuse. Telling him not to climb into bed with the girl next door is not going to create later sexual problems. We should never be afraid to set limits on sexual behaviour, any more than we should be afraid to set other limits on any other behaviour. Sex, like any other behaviour, needs to be controlled. Sex is sex. It is fun. It is relaxing. But it is not the holy grail or the centre of the world. Nor is it the most important aspect of life. Nor is it something he cannot control. Everyone can control it, even at the moment of orgasm.

Walked in when we were making love

Children should learn to respect privacy. A closed door needs to be knocked on first. If your child walks in on you without knocking, tell him that this is a private time; that he must close the door and that you will be with him in a moment. Get dressed and go to him. Give him a hug. Keep to the rule: knock on his door if it is locked. This is obvious, but some people overlook the obvious: when there are things you do not wish children to see, it is best to get a lock for your door.

Sexually precocious children

A certain amount of sexual play should be expected. Children love to explore, and this sort of exploration feels good. A certain degree of flirtatiousness is to be expected, too. Girls look at men through their eyelashes be they three or 33. But what of more overt sexual behaviours?

A child will rub up against you in bed in the morning in ways which are clearly sexual. He may lie next to you and masturbate. At this point, 'normal' behaviour begins to move to towards the abnormal, and you may become uneasy and concerned. Such events are commonplace, but the unease is well founded. A small body rubbing against you can arouse sexual feelings unexpectedly and guiltily. His behaviour is not wrong because you have reacted in this way. Nor is does the stirring of desire make you a monster. Acting on that stirring does. Sexual abuse is always wrong, even when children appear to invite it.

Small children do not usually know what they are inviting. When they do, it is usually because they have been abused, and believe that this is the way people show love for children.

The ingredients for sexual abuse are always present in all families. That is why sexual abuse is as common as it is. Indeed, the ingredients for physical abuse are present, too.

Power is probably the key to both. Most of us have felt the urge to injure a child, and at your most powerless you may need to stamp very firmly on those urges to avoid doing so. The sad truth is that as many as one in ten adults were sexually abused as children, mostly, and most harmfully, by those they know and love. Now that people talk about such things, we probably all know someone who was abused.

One of the signs of sexual abuse in children is precocious sexual behaviour. A child who flirts overtly with men, and who frequently and persistently invites sex, may be the victim of abuse. A girl who is too knowing about sex or frequently climbs on to men's laps and rubs herself against them may have been taught to act this way. Small children who seek love and get sexual abuse are usually told that this is how adults and children show affection to each other. These are the ways they know.

Of course, all children are sexual; but if a child seems to be behaving in an overly sexual way, do not dismiss the behaviour. Be vigilant. Accusing your loved ones of abusing your child may be too terrible to contemplate. Refusing to believe and then discovering that it has happened will be worse.

How to protect children from abuse

The big problem is pinpointing sexual abuse. The vast majority of sexual assaults on children are committed by people known to the child. These are the most harmful, since they can persist over very many years, denying love and trust. Assaults by strangers are a tiny tip of a very large iceberg. We hear more about these because the papers make much of such stories. When a father abuses his daughter over many years, protection of the child's identity requires reporting restrictions to be enforced. These cases do not make good stories for the media.

Numerically, fathers are the most common offenders, although a higher percentage of stepfathers and mother's boyfriends are abusers. (The figures for these last two are lower because there are fewer step-fathers than fathers.) Older brothers also quite frequently abuse younger siblings.

Sexual abuse can start at any age. It rarely involves one episode or one act. Nor, if there are siblings, is it necessarily confined to one child. In most cases there is a gradual progression from appropriate to inap-propriate touching. Abusers often disguise what they are doing, from the child, from anyone who may observe them and even from them-selves. So abuse starts at bathtimes and bedtimes, as the child sits on their knee. Masturbation, penetration, and oral gratification follow on from this. Contrary to popular opinion, overt force is rarely used. Violent abuse occurs when strangers rape children. When relatives rape, they do not use violent force. They use statements of love "This is how daddies show they love children." "This is because you are special to me." They also use threats: "You will be taken away if you tell anyone." Since the abuser knows the child, he knows how to frighten, bribe and make the child feel that his behaviour is normal. That many children can be abused over very long periods shows how easily this can be done, Children are often told it is their fault, that they are bad, while the abuser is good.

The critical factors which lead to abuse are the presence of someone who has the motivation to abuse children, the overcoming of their own initial inhibition to abuse (often by drinking), lack of protection for the victim, and the child's own resistance.

Because child abusers are so often members of the family, it is little use telling children "Never take sweets from strangers" or otherwise implying that the dangers lurk outside the home. Nor is it easy to be vigilant against the abuser when that abuser is a loved one. We imagine that we would notice what is going on and that the signs would be obvious. They are not; and even if they were, few of us would want to see them. A curtain of self-protection descends and we do not see what is staring us in the face: because to see it is too terrible to bear.

Recognizing signs of abuse - under-fives

- ◆ **Abuse highly probable:** genital injuries; VD or other infection; disclosure; describing vivid details of, or knowledge of, sexual activities, such as oral sex, ejaculation or penetration; compulsive masturbation, especially in inappropriate contexts; acting out sexual activities, especially explicit sexual activities; sexual drawings.
- ◆ **Abuse likely/possible:** suddenly becoming afraid of a

particular person; showing intense fear of someone; frequent nightmares; chronic urinary/vaginal infection; soreness of genitals, bottom; specific fear of being bathed, changed or put to bed.

◆ **Abuse possible:** developmental regression; hostile and aggressive behaviour; psychosomatic illness.

Signs of abuse in five- to 12-year-olds

◆ **Abuse highly probable:** as for the younger age group, plus exposing himself; precocious sexual behaviour; inviting or initiating explicit sexual activities; promiscuity; running away; suicide attempts; drug and sex abuse.

◆ **Abuse likely/possible:** chronic urinary/vaginal infection; soreness of genitals, and bottom; obsessive washing; criminal behaviour such as arson; depression; hysteria; bed wetting and soiling, daytime wetting and soiling; anorexia; frequent nightmares; playing truant; unexplained money or gifts; taking drugs.

◆ **Abuse possible:** developmental regression; hostile and aggressive behaviour; psychosomatic illness; problems with peers; abdominal pains; poor progress at school; frequent poor behaviour at school.

Signs of abuse: over 12

◆ **Abuse highly probable:** genital injuries; disclosure; self-mutilation of breasts and genitals; VD or other infection; pregnancy when under 14; prostitution.

◆ **Abuse likely/possible:** sexual boasting; chronic urinary/vaginal infection; VD in 14-year-olds and above; pregnancy in 14-year-olds and above; sexual offences; self-abuse; suicide attempts; hysteria; obsessive behaviours; rebelliousness against men; abuse of drugs and other substances; continual and compulsive lying; playing truant; running away; unexplained money or gifts.

◆ **Abuse possible:** depression; anorexia; refusing to go to school; delinquency; psychosomatic illness; problems with peers; problems with authority.

Why children do not tell of sexual abuse

◆ They feel no one will believe them.
◆ They think it is their fault.
◆ There is no one they can tell.
◆ There is no one they can trust.
◆ They are afraid that they will be harmed if they tell.

◆ They are afraid of what will happen if they do tell.

◆ They are afraid it will turn their parent(s) against them.

◆ They are afraid that they and their brothers and sisters will be separated by the authorities.

◆ They feel dirty, that no one will want to know them, and are worried what friends will say.

◆ They are too young to realize what is going on.

◆ They do not that know that it is wrong.

◆ They have tried, and people did not believe them.

◆ They do not believe that it would make any difference if they did tell.

What to tell a child about abuse

Sexual abuse is common enough to be on guard against. About one in ten of the population say they were sexually abused as children. In the vast majority of those cases, at least one of the child's parents wished to protect them from abuse and believed that they were doing so. Unfortunately, it is impossible to put a tight cordon around your children. Most children are sexually abused in their homes by relatives or friends who they (and you) think can be trusted: fathers; stepfathers; boyfriends of their mother's; grandfathers; uncles; elder brothers and friends of the family. Most abusers are male, but some are female. Make sure your child understands that:

◆ **Nudity** is natural and normal if taking a bath, swimming, playing on the beach or in the paddling pool. On these occasions tell him that it is OK to let other people see his bottom or genitals; but not OK for people to ask to see him naked or to tell her to pull down her knickers. "You should always tell someone else if they do, even if the person asks you to keep it a secret."

◆ **Looking at nude people.** It is OK to look at people on the beach or to go into the bathroom when members of the family are bathing or taking a shower. It OK to see his brother's penis. It is not right for a man to ask him to look at his penis, even if he is someone the child knows. "You must always tell someone, even if the man asks you not to do this."

◆ **Make the distinction between self and other clear.** It is OK for children to touch their own genitals, but not for other people to touch them in those places, even if they know those people. This message is clearer if you always ask the child to wash his own genital area. "Even if the person who asks is someone you know, you must always tell, even if the person asks you not to."

DANGEROUS PLACES

◆ **The home; the homes of friends and family.**
◆ **Lifts and stairwells.** These are common places for
strangers and neighbours to molest children. If you live in a
block of flats, your children will obviously go up and down
between floors or between the flat and a garden. Tell small
children that they should never get in a lift with just one other
person in it.

   Tell children to go up and down stairs together, or to wait
until there are a group of people coming up.
◆ Tell children to ring your bell before they come upstairs so
that you are waiting for them.
◆ Tell children to yell or to bang on the door of the nearest
flat if someone approaches them. But tell them not to go into
a strange flat.
◆ **Public lavatories.** W.C.s in motorway cafés and fast food
restaurants can be happy hunting grounds for the see-me-
touch-me paedophile. The main danger is to boys, but girls
are sometimes at risk. Accompany small children to the W.C.
Send older children in pairs.
◆ Tell children to leave immediately if someone tries to touch
them, or chat them up. Tell them to inform someone in
authority.
◆ Tell them never to go into a cubicle with anyone, no
matter what they say. Explain that people try to trick children
by saying there is a kitten stuck, or that they have dropped
their watch and need someone with a small arm to reach it;
say that these are always lies.
◆ Stress that they should not be afraid to make a fuss if there
is a chance that someone will hear; but not to do so if
threatened.
◆ Tell older children that they should never go into isolated
public loos by themselves.
◆ **Dirty talk and flashing.** Explain to children that they do
not have to listen to obscenities or to look at anyone who
shows them their penis. Tell them to look away and/or put
their fingers in their ears. In public places, tell someone.
◆ **If someone approaches.** Always move towards shops or
houses, or any place where other people are to be found.

◆ **Sitting on people's laps.** "It is all right to sit on people's laps, but you do not have to do so if you do not want to. If you are frightened to sit on someone's lap, you should tell. If someone keeps asking you to sit on their lap, and you do not want to do so, you should tell."

◆ **Explain to grandparents** that you have told your child this is a rule, and ask them to respect it.

◆ **People getting into your bed.** "Adults should never get under your quilt. If someone asks to get under your quilt, tell another person, even if you know that person and they say it is all right."

◆ **Getting into other people's beds.** "It is all right to come into our bed; maybe into Grandma and Grandpa's. It is all right to get into other small children's beds. But it is not all right to get into big children's beds or into grown-up children's beds if you are spending the night at their house. If someone asks you to do this, tell."

◆ **Even if something feels good it can be wrong.** Abuse sounds as if it should feel terrible, but often it does not. The progression from cuddles to abuse can be very gradual. A child may think it is not right, but because it does not feel bad either, he may fail to tell anyone.

◆ **Telling tales.** "It is all right to tell tales. If things frighten you, tell your parents, even if someone else has told you it is a secret."

◆ **"Nothing bad will happen if you tell."** "Telling tales does not mean you will be taken away from home."

◆ **Not making too much fuss at the time.** Being abused by a stranger is frightening and horrible, and can hurt. "If someone threatens you and says they will kill you if you are not quiet, it is OK to keep quiet. It is best to do as they ask. But you must always tell someone what has happened to you. Once you are safe and back with your family, nothing terrible will happen."

◆ **Not all men are bad.** Explain that most people like children and are good to them. A few people have problems.

◆ **Abused children need professional help.** The police will advise you where to find counselling.

Holidays

Small children like things to remain the way they always were. A change may be as good as a holiday for an adults; children hate them both. If the three- to five-year-old had his choice, it would be for the

HOW TO MAKE HOLIDAYS A DISASTER

✖ *Wind the children up to a fever of anticipation.*
✖ *Expect them to keep quiet, even though you did not bring toys.*
✖ *Stay out in the sun.*
Children burn easily.
✖ *Tell them that they should be enjoying themselves.*

same favourite T-shirt, beans on toast for supper, the same old video and the same old story every day. They feel secure with routine and familiarity. Although they are excited by house moves or holidays, the excitement mimics yours; they do not know, and you do not tell them, all the implications. In reality children are often unhappy and disturbed by house moves and holidays. In truth, many adults are, too. Such events commonly precede bouts of mental illness and depression.

Moving house

Moving house is doubly destructive if it also takes him away from his play school, park and friends. Expect your child to be clingy, to sleep badly and need plenty of attention and cuddling.

Don't be a whirlwind. If it takes an extra day or two to get straight, does it really matter? If parents are happy and relaxed about the new house, children will be more likely to take the move in their stride.

◆ **Prepare the child.** Show him his new house and school; how you will walk to the new park; where he can spend his pocket money. Show him in words and deeds that much of his daily routine will remain the same after you have moved. It may be worth making a chart to show the week's routine.

◆ **Say goodbye.** A four-year-old rarely understands that change is permanent. He may expect to return to the old house after a few days. Give him in fantasy what he cannot have in reality. "You wish you could go back to your old house? Shall we pretend we have a magic carpet to whisk us back? Now we are back. What shall we do first?"

◆ **"Someone else will live here."** Children are often shocked at the thought that someone else will sleep in their room or eat in their kitchen. Reassure him that all your furniture (and in particular his bed) will be moving to your new house. Tell him how pleasant it will be to have new curtains and covers for his new bedroom.

HOW TO ENJOY A HOLIDAY WITH CHILDREN

✔ *Keep calm,* and don't strive for perfect organization. If you forget the sun tan lotion, you can buy it when you get there.

✔ *Keep preparation* and packing for the day before, and do it when the children are in bed.

✔ *Maintain a few home routines* if you can. It's a holiday. Relax. Don't spend every minute doing things. For this reason, city breaks are usually unsuitable for younger children. Children are usually happiest if you establish a base and take side trips.

✔ *Sleep late.* If they stay up late, let them sleep in next day.

✔ *Take some of their favourite snacks.* Hunger adds an extra notch of irritation to tiredness, and few children like unfamiliar food.

✔ *Don't expect too much.* Accept that they may not be happy on holiday. Don't get angry because of 'ingratitude'.

✔ *Choose an appropriate holiday.* Hotels have very little personal space for a child, and large rooms can seem intimidating. Trying to keep them quiet in public places puts everyone in a bad mood. Camping or self-catering may be a better choice with pre-schoolers.

✔ *Give choices.* Monday we all do what Dad wants to do. Tuesday is Lucy's turn, Wednesday we just relax, Thursday is Jamie's choice. On Friday Mum chooses.

✔ *Go with another couple* to give you the odd day or evening free of children.

✔ *Prepare your child.* Explain what will be happening; how routines will change. He may not remember last year's holiday.

✔ *Let him eat what he prefers.* A fortnight of eating junk food is not a disaster.

✔ *Prepare for the journey.* Children are often surprisingly good on long flights and on long car journeys. Story tapes, colouring books, and games help pass the time. Talk about the landmarks you pass; sing songs.

◆ **"The pets are coming too."** Reassure him that his pets and soft toys will be living in the new house.

◆ **Don't tell him he will love it.** He may not. Accept his worries. "It will seem a bit strange for all of us when we move."

◆ **Talk about the old house.** Because his memory is made up of more pictures than words, when he moves house his cues are left behind. With little to jog his memory, he feels disoriented. Try to compensate by keeping the past alive. Talk about things that used to happen, people he knew, places he visited. Keep the connection between then and now alive, at least until he has some new yesterdays.

The adopted child

In the past, adoption was something to be hushed up by both the birth mother and the adoptive mother. Many children did not know that they were adopted until they were adults. Some probably never knew. Today, most people involved in adoption recommend that a child should know he is adopted long before he can understand what adoption means. The easiest way to do this is for parents to talk about wanting and choosing him. As he grows up, he will need to explore what this means, who his birth parents were and why he was adopted. Answer such questions in a straightforward loving way: always emphasising that he is very much loved, wanted and chosen by you; and that his birth parents could not look after him - not that they did not want to do so.

Make a photo album which shows the story of his adoption. "This is us bringing you into our house. Look how happy we are."

In a large comparative study of adopted children, no differences were found in adjustment between adopted children and those living with natural parents.

The only child; the elder child; the younger child

Common sense tells us that only children grow up to be perfectly sane and well balanced individuals. In fact, research tells us that only children grow up to be very successful individuals. Take any list of great men - be it scientists, politicians or writers - and more of them turn out to be only children than one would expect.

It is generally accepted that first-born children are achievement oriented. They tend to be capable, strong-willed, responsible and secure. They are also conformist, do the right thing and are more likely to get on well with their parents.

Second children are much less driven. They are more spontaneous and easy-going, more tactful, adaptable, patient and relaxed. On the whole they are better balanced, perhaps because their social skills are well honed by a lifetime of practice with equals (or almost equals). The baby rapidly learns how to get his elder brother into trouble, irritate, manipulate and manoeuvre. They are also more likely to be loved for themselves: not for our dreams. Maybe the fact that they do not win academically or physically when up against their older sibling (at least in the short term), is why middle and younger children are less competitive and adaptable. When they do succeed it is often with crazy notions. Galileo and Darwin were both younger sons, and although Freud was the eldest, he had two young uncles who lived in the same house when he was growing up. Because younger children have to learn ways to come out on top and to attract the attention of adults, they are sometimes manipulative, at other times more democratic. (Which does not predispose them to be politicians: most political figures are elder children.) They are also more likely to protest and rebel. The youngest child has a special role in families of more than two. They may occasionally feel inadequate or inferior. More often they learn to use charm to get their way.

Siblings

No tricks succeed. No deception works. They know each other much too well. Nothing slides so easily back into your life as a sibling you have not seen for a while. Siblings cannot hide from each other because in their most formative years they shared many secrets (and gave away most of the rest). What skills you have in expressing yourself, hiding your feelings, understanding others, deceiving, cajoling and manipulating you were honed within that relationship.

In some societies, sibling relationships are considered the most important in life. As the eldest of five, I understand that. They are usually the longest-lasting relationships we have, stretching in many instances from cradle to grave. Siblings provide each other with the company of other children, and move the focus of a family away from the world of adults and into the world of children. Although siblings play power games with each other, they do so as near-equals. Siblings often understand each other rather better than their parents understand them.

Having siblings creates the sorts of stresses and strains, competition and co-operation which are best practised and overcome in childhood. If you are one of several siblings, you see parents dealing with your brothers and sisters, losing their tempers, getting on edge: you see them in a more complete and human light than the only child. Adults are less godlike when you have seen them being twisted around a two-year-old's finger. Children who grow up with siblings tend to have a rounded view of other people compared with only children and a more natural self-confidence in superficial relationships.

Few children who have siblings would choose to be only children, although not all families are close, caring or mutually supportive. It is a topic I find it impossible to be neutral about. I find it impossible to imagine being an only child, or to see any advantages.

Sibling relationships, good and bad

There are times when children get on with each other and times when they do not; age gaps which work, and those which don't. There are no guarantees as to whether children will get on. Nor is the picture fixed for all time. Sometimes a particular age gap between children will seem quite small and children will get along well. Sometimes the same gap will seem very large and children will fight and quarrel. Or the reverse can be true.

That they are getting on well at the moment is no guarantee of what will happen next year. Nor, fortunately, does present conflict mean conflict always. All children have easy and difficult phases, which roughly correlate with their stage of development. See below and page 199.

The relatively easy threes correspond to a period of stability and steady consolidation of skills. They are followed by a turbulent fourth year in which children begin to think and feel differently about other people. Then there is an easy year at five before children rush into the very turbulent and quarrelling sixes. The relationship between children can thus see-saw from easy to impossible in a matter of months. If, for example, you have the traditional two-year gap between siblings, you might find the combination of two/four and four/six pretty deadly, while three/five is remarkably easy.

At three

Three-year-olds tend to be easy-going and peaceable. If he is the youngest child (especially when older siblings are considerably older) he will probably get on well with them. If siblings are just a little older or just a little younger, the behaviour is less predictable. He can be very equable, even when provoked, or he can hit out without warning.

The three-year-old probably has most difficulty with others aged two and four. One three-year-old may be delighted by the arrival of a baby, another may protest alarmingly and get in a few rabbit punches whenever parents look the other way. But in general, the average three-year-old left to himself is a sociable soul. His problems arise from smash-and-grab younger siblings who spoil his peaceful games; and his bossy, wilder, older siblings who exert power over him in ways he rightly dislikes.

At four

Children are wild and wonderful, more independent, more social, and more concerned with what other people say, think and do. At four children are often extremely loving and giving to baby siblings, but are not necessarily trustworthy. A spate of jealousy may cause sudden meanness. His relationships with siblings between three and six are often very stormy. He can be bossy, overbearing, mean and violent. He can bully and manipulate; and he can be very unpleasant - all sweetness one moment and all venom the next. He is not necessarily overawed by older siblings, and can be aggressive and disruptive with them, spoiling games for spoiling's sake. He can make quite unrealistic demands of his siblings, complaining that they are looking through his car window or that they touched one of his books, even though he was neither looking at the book nor wanting to do so.

At five

By five children are calmer and easier. He is less bossy and demanding. This is the lull before the stormy sixes. Five-year-olds can be particularly good with younger siblings, full of small kindnesses and loving gestures. He is less selfish and exacting than he was a year ago, better able to take turns and share. He likes adult approval and knows how to manipulate it. But beware: when backs are turned he may be less of a model child. The willingness to please means, however, that he often gets on extremely well with older siblings.

Boys and girls

Although there are exceptions, it is probably true to say that families of girls are more peaceable than families of boys. But both are less peaceable than mixed pairs.

Boys come to blows. Girls have their own ways of hurting one another. They snipe, they tease, they manipulate and call names. They argue and generally bitch. They may also have major histrionics.

Although they scratch and pull hair, they are less likely to fight physically than brothers. These are, of course, generalities.

All families have personalities of their own. When parents and children were asked in a recent study about how siblings got on together, all combinations of brothers and/or sisters reported good and bad relationships: pinching, hair pulling, punching, sitting on, chasing and a host of other aggressive behaviours. They reported meanness, such as not sharing, hiding toys, locking them out of rooms and telling tales, bossing, bribing and tricking. They get angry, scream, yell and frighten each other. But asked if they would rather be an only child, all said no.

Combinations, good and bad

The relationships which tend to cause most violence are boys with older brothers, and girls with both older and younger sisters. Most verbal quarrels and threats come from boys and younger brothers; they are less frequent from girls with older sisters. Girls get most upset with older and younger sisters, and boys with elder brothers. All combinations use emotional blackmail and make demands. The easiest combination, and the one which leads to fewest quarrels and fights throughout childhood, is a boy with his younger sister. Same-sex children usually quarrel more than opposite-sex pairs: but this is of course just a statistic, to which there are many exceptions.

A family's temperament

Within these general groupings, there are of course many differences. The temperaments of the children play a role, as does the temperament of the family. Emotional families probably fight and quarrel, probably because the model provided by the parents sets the pattern. If you quietly and rationally discuss your differences, so might they, at least some of the time.

When a child always has to win

It's his party and he'll win if he wants to – and if he does not, he will simply sulk. It can be embarrassing and frustrating when your child shows you up by refusing to play the game. It is even worse when they have to win family games. If he has to win, someone else has to lose, and if that child is not prepared to give way he or she cries; you try to smooth it over, but the others shout, "It's not fair," and storm off in huffs. The scene is all too familiar in most families. Sometimes the parents are not much better. Get out the Happy Family cards and Dad sets out to win while Mum feeds the youngest with winning cards. "How will the children learn give and take if you let him win like that?" "How can you be so childish, it's only a game." Happy Families turns into a Family Crisis.

Most children under five only find it possible to play games of chance. They also find it easier to play with adults.

◆ **Co-operative games, or team games** are often the easiest to play with small children. Rules can be changed and most games adapted so that you play them in pairs.

◆ **When competition is a problem,** identify his feelings and empathize. "I understand. I remember I used to feel like that when I played with my sister". Find solutions. "Nobody *has* to play. Games are for fun. If this game does not feel like fun to you, it is best not to play."

◆ **Don't compare.** It is tempting to say, "Look, Jessie is playing well," but don't.

◆ **If he loses control,** remove him. Let him take time out to cool off.

◆ **Play down competition.** Laugh when you get a low score. Say, "You did well," even when he loses.

◆ **Cultural influences.** Competitive parents have competitive children. Competitive cultures produce competitive children. If you want him to claw his way to the top of the pile, you will have to grin and bear the practice games.

How not to be a referee when children quarrel

Children quarrel first and foremost because they enjoy a good fight. They do not quarrel all the time, although it may seem as if they do. Parents tend to have a rather selective view of things. In fact, their quarrels are often about sensible things - matters of principle; belongings - and they also quarrel about things which, to any reasonable person, would not be worthy of a cross word. This is the behaviour to which you are attuned, because it causes you most trouble. Quiet, happy spells cause you no waves and you tend to ignore them. But all children have quiet, loving, supportive spells; periods of pulling together and of mutual concern. These are less noisy and less stressful, so often we ignore them.

If it's a minor squabble:
Ignore it.

If it is more serious:
Start by acknowledging the children's anger towards each other.

> You two sound very angry

Listen to each child with respect.

> He took my Lego bit

> I needed it for my wall

Show that you understand that it is a difficult problem.

> One bit of Lego that you both need. That is a difficult one

Reflect each child's point of view.

> You wanted that Lego bit to make your car: you needed to finish your wall

Express faith in their ability to solve the problem.

> I am sure that you can work this one out

Leave.

This may not actually solve the quarrel, but it can stop a quarrel getting any worse. If it does not work, and if the quarrel is getting out of hand:

Describe what you see and separate the children.

> I see two very angry children. You both need to cool off. Jamie, go to your room, and Lucy, go to yours. Come back when you feel you have calmed down.

KEEPING QUARRELLING CHILDREN FROM ALWAYS QUARRELLING

Rule 1: Places we do not quarrel: the car; no quarrels in the sitting-room after lunch; no quarrels at meal times.

Rule 2: Everyone has their own territory. Each child has a place to keep his things, and a box with a lock for special things.

Rule 3: People are allowed to say who uses their things.

Rule 4: If children cannot sort things out, the toy is confiscated. They have ten minutes to sort it out. Set the kitchen timer. If the quarrel is over which video is to be watched, or which TV programme, switch off.

If it's been a morning of squabbles, offer alternatives. "OK, you two get your coats on, we are going out." Especially on rainy days, plan ahead for this eventuality.

Notice when fights occur. Keep a record. If there is a pattern, try to break it. Maybe they fight when they are hungry, If so, a biscuit might help. Maybe they fight when they are tired. Sitting watching a video might help. Maybe they fight when they are cooped up in the house. Take them out. Maybe they fight when they have surplus energy. Let them have a session of dancing wild and screaming loud.

Rule 5: We do not call each other names. "Say what you mean – 'I don't think that is true', not 'You little liar.'"

HOW NOT TO BE A CHEERLEADER WHEN CHILDREN QUARREL

✔ **Don't label.** Children have a
habit of living up to their labels.
Avoid the constant refrain:

> You are always fighting

Remember:

> Why can't you get on like
> other children?

...suggests they can't, so why try?

✔ **Don't compare.** Everybody's children fight. They do. Like
most children, they fight
most at home, where
outsiders do not see or hear
them.

> Lisa and Mark don't fight
> like you two do

> No fighting in the dining
> room

✔ **Try defining a quarrel-free
zone** in the house and retreat to
it. If they follow, remind them
of the rules.

✔ **Accept what they say.**
Nobody has to like anyone
else all the time.

> Lily took your car
> without asking first

> I'm not surprised you
> feel like that. It would
> make you mad

✔ **Accept what they feel.** At
this moment they do hate their
brother.

✔ *Allow them to be angry,* but insist they find ways of showing anger without hurting others.

> Show me how angry you are. Draw me a picture

> Lucy to the kitchen. Lily to the dining room

✔ *Prevent injury.* Separate them. Impose a cooling-off period.

✔ *Listen to each side.* Be neutral. Just reflect what they say, do not judge.

> Lily, you wanted the dress for your Barbie. But the dress belongs to your Barbie, Lucy

✔ *Notice them when they are good.*

> I'm going to make a cup of tea; would you like juice?

> When I get very angry with someone I think of them wearing a silly hat and slippers

✔ *Make them laugh.*

205

Behind every quarrel there is a battle of wills, the urge to assert self, a desire for attention and respect and love. Children quarrel most with those who matter to them most, just as adults do. Many children who battle throughout childhood are close as adults. Parents are drawn into battle as referee, judge and jury. They are asked simultaneously to play counsel for the prosecution and counsel for the defence. Try to avoid this role. When the children want to draw you in, simply say "I have confidence you two can sort this out without my help."

The bully and the victim: family roles

Families frequently cast children in roles. The roles may be good: "He's the clever one" - or bad: "He's always so argumentative." But good or bad, roles are limiting, not just to the child but also to his siblings. If one child is the clever one, another child has to be less clever. A negative role for one child can give a positive glow to another: but also teach her how to manipulate the situation to her advantage.

No more bullies

◆ **Do not call one child a bully.** A child who believes he is a bully will act like a bully. Look for opportunities to show the child a different picture of himself.

◆ **Put him into situations where he can see himself differently.** "Jamie knows how to do that. Jamie, could you show your sister?"

◆ **Let him see he is capable of getting what he wants without bullying.** "You also know how to *ask* your sister for what you want, rather than just taking it."

◆ **Let the child overhear you saying good things about him.** "Jamie was so patient with Lucy today. You should have seen him teaching her how to put her gumboots on."

◆ **Let other children overhear you saying good things.** "He knows how to be pleasant."

No more victims

◆ **Calling one child a bully** encourages the other to play victim. Not only does he get his parents' sympathy, he gets his sibling into trouble - almost certainly worth a thump. Look for opportunities to show the victim a different picture of himself. "Lucy, if you do not want your brother to play, I know you can tell him so."

♦ **By always giving comfort to the victim** you encourage a child to play this role.

♦ **Raise the victim's self-esteem.** Find 50 ways to tell her "You can; you are capable."

♦ **Let her know she is capable of being assertive.** "I expect you to ask for what you need; I know you won't disappoint me."

Rotten deals

Children are always trading property. My two youngest spent three months in California at the height of a certain card collection craze. They came home with a series of cards which had not yet been published in Britain. The cards were like gold dust. As far as six- and seven- year-olds were concerned they were worth a great deal. The value of the toys brought in to swap must have averaged about £10 or US$15. I had to ban the cards from going to school, and the toys from coming home.

Most swaps are not fair. Even if they seem fair at the time, they rarely do five minutes later. But the winner is bound to say a swap is a swap and there is no going back on it.

♦ **Children have to learn that they have power.** Tell them that they can refuse to do things they do not want to do, and that they should assert themselves when they think things are unfair. No one can buy friends. Talk about examples of things that are fair swaps and things which are unfair swaps. If they have a firm grasp of what is fair, they can deal with things which are not fair.

♦ **Children have to learn how to be fair.** The easiest way to do this is to expect them to be fair, to have faith in their ability to sort things out and to let them do so without undue interference.

♦ **When in doubt, fall back on a house rule.** "Swaps in this house are temporary. Everyone has the right to reclaim their property unless the swap has the family seal of approval." Get a notebook. Write in family-approved swaps and initial them. Now the property belongs to the other child. He has the same rights over it as if it had always been his.

overruns
by 1 line

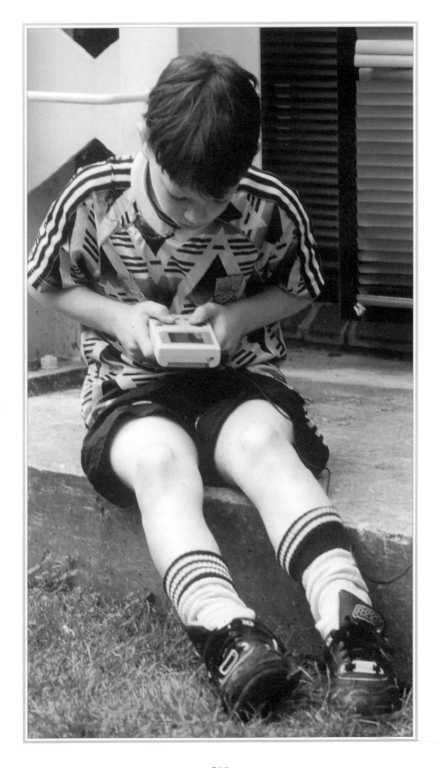

Five to eight

Milestones: your child at five

After the turmoil of four, the five-year-old child is easy, eager to learn, helpful, and openly affectionate. Savour it. There may be difficult years to come. When you reach the far side of those years, the open child who shared everything with you will have gone for ever.

By five, most children can run and dodge, stopping and starting each trajectory with ease. They can hop, skip and jump, go up and down stairs using alternate legs, and can manage the pedals on a tricycle. Some children can even ski, swim, ride a bike without stabilizers or a horse. Don't worry if your child cannot. These skills need the confidence only ample practice can give.

The hands of a five-year-old are more controlled. She will be able to build with small bricks, placing things carefully so she does not topple the tower she is building. She can build you a model with boxes and yoghurt pots, glue the parts into place (with only occasional bad temper) and paint it. She can do puzzles with interlocking pieces, hold a pencil, draw, and maybe write her name. She will recognize a few letters and possibly a word or two. Some children may even be able to read. She can count, say nursery rhymes and sing, although perhaps not very tunefully: her range of notes is limited. She can use a knife and fork but will probably still need to have her meat cut up. She can spread a piece of bread with soft butter or margarine, but will still have difficulty peeling oranges. She can dress herself, although she may still have difficulty with shoe laces and small buttons in awkward places. She can wash her hands and face, clean her teeth and brush her own hair if it is short. She may not always brush the back hair and will not be able to make a parting or tie her hair up.

A five-year-old will extend her capabilities to match your expectations. If you are still doing up the buttons on her blouse, she may stand there passively expecting you to do so, but if you expect her to butter her own toast she will. It is always wise to remember that, in the 19th Century, children of this age were expected to put in a day's work in the mine or factory. In some parts of the world they still are.

The five-year-old has very definite likes and dislikes. There is little obvious logic to them. She may eat carrots sliced into rounds but not carrots cut into strips, raw vegetables with a dip but not the same vegetables without one. She loves butterflies but is afraid of moths; loves ladybirds but hates other beetles.

By five, most children can sustain attention long enough to carry out simple tasks with care and absorption. They are frequently busy, able to amuse themselves and happy to look at a book or watch a video by themselves. She will play in the garden while you stay in the house, or in her bedroom while you are downstairs. When she has company she will disappear into her bedroom or out into the garden. These things happen gradually and it is hard to say on what day you feel that there is no longer the need to watch her constantly. But by five or six the need has gone. You can now read the newspaper or drink a cup of coffee without interruption. Life is a good deal easier.

She talks in a more adult fashion. Gone is the running commentary of her thoughts, actions and feelings, and in its place are requests, questions and something more akin to gossip. Her language is sophisticated and adult. She uses different tenses and makes fewer grammatical errors, although she may still have difficulty with the pronunciation of certain words. She is able to express her thoughts and feelings and is able take your feelings and viewpoint into account. She does not assume you see what she sees or feel what she feels. She talks to the baby, dog or her dolls rather as you do, raising her voice, explaining carefully. When she wants to tell us what happened at school she will fill in the necessary details. Not "naughty Sam" but "A boy called Sam in my class at school was very naughty today."

Because she knows she can hide her thoughts and feelings from you, she begins to have secrets. Between the ages of five and seven these will become more and more important. At five she is still the unself-conscious child you have come to know. By seven you will find she is probably too self-conscious to do her party piece for your guests.

By five, most children are able to follow a story without pictures, and can listen to a conversation without constant interruptions. They tell themselves stories and carry out conversations with and for their toys. At five, a child's days are filled with imagination and fantasy, on which you may still be able to eavesdrop; by seven she will have withdrawn into a much more private world. When she returns from school at seven she will no longer babble joyfully about her day but is likely to grunt in a monosyllabic fashion when you ask what she did. "Oh, things," she will say, or "Nothing much." Boys are often worse than girls when it comes to letting parents into their world in mid-childhood: but the difference is not absolute.

At six children begin to wrench power from you whether you like it or not. They no longer do what you ask but argue the toss and use delaying tactics. A five-year-old who was pliant and gentle with younger siblings can become wilful and quarrelsome at six. This is the age of the fight, when children complain that a sibling touched their chair or looked out of their window just to annoy them, and when an eye for an eye becomes the underlying ethos. While it is almost invariably true that her brother did look out of her window in the car with the express intention of annoying her, it is hard not to be angry with a child who screams and shouts over such trivia. To a seven-year-old such things matter. She uses them to assert authority and independence. She needs to think for herself, do for herself, make demands and deal with refusals. She also needs to know you are on her side.

Parenting between five and eight: letting them go

Once a child understands that her thoughts and feelings are separate from those of other people, she will want her privacy. This is hard to accept, especially if the child has always shared everything with you. Start in small ways. By five parents should not be commenting on every action, intervening in every fight or expecting a child to explain her every thought and feeling. On every front, you have to begin the long process of letting go.

Someone once said that the measure of a good parent is what she does not do for her children. At no age is this more true than now. If you do not acknowledge and accept the child's need to make at least some of her own decisions, she will become resentful, and may grab at independence without responsibility. Children are safer and happier if you encourage and expect them to be both responsible and independent. A child will not 'look out for herself' unless she is given autonomy. If her mother always buttons up her coat, she will expect her to continue. If she runs after her with her gym kit, the child will never remember it herself. If a parent always tells her "that's high enough", she will wait for that shout and go on climbing until it comes.

You help a child to grow up by not helping and not dictating. A seven-year-old needs firm limits, but does not need every action to be regulated and controlled by his parents. All children should be allowed enough freedom of action and thought to develop self-confidence and self-control. This may be particularly hard for parents of only or handicapped children. But a child who grows up a compliant subject of dictatorial parents is in great danger of moving on from parental rule to the rule of much less benign dictators. So are those children who grow up without limits. It is a difficult path to tread.

Formal ways to improve family relationships

◆ **House rules.** These should clearly set out how family members should treat each other. They may, for example, include statements about name calling, hurting people's feelings and doing physical harm. They should state clearly how each person should treat their own and other people's property, and what to do about rudeness, stealing, or borrowing without permission. They may dictate when and where noise can be made, which property and space is communal and which private. Rules should also state what members of the family have to do to compensate each other for damage to property or to feelings. If a rule is frequently broken by one or all family members, it may do no harm to write it down and stick it on the wall. "Jamie, look at the car rules. What do they say about quarrelling in the car?"

◆ **The family contract.** A family contract is a formal, signed agreement between two children or an adult and a child. Research suggests that contracts can teach siblings consideration for one another and reduce rivalry. A contract might for instance say something like: 'Jamie agrees to ask Lucy before he borrows her Lego. When he has finished using it he will put it back in her box. Lucy agrees to lend Jamie her Lego if she is not using it. In exchange for borrowing Lego Jamie agrees to let Lucy ride his bike when he is not using it'.

A contract should be clear and specific, and cover only one piece of behaviour. It should be discussed and agreed between the children (or parents and children) before being put into writing and signed. (A scribble will do.) Like any contract it should have a date, and a renewal date. Contracts should be put on a notice board in full view. Failure of one party to keep to their side of the contract voids that contract.

◆ **Family meetings.** These are discussion forums in which every family member meets as an equal. Each has the right to state their case and the family group then arrives at a consensus. Although these are popular with many parenting 'experts', they are, I feel, a trifle idealistic; dare I even say rather 'twee' and a touch patronising. Family meetings are depicted as having formal agendas, minutes and public praise for jobs well done. They assume open reasoned discussion of problems between all family members. Families who can easily achieve this sort of open, democratic discussion of problems probably do not need to wait for formal meetings. Families who cannot do so probably would not consider them. It is, however, worth taking some of these ideas on board. Families should discuss problems, and where an issue concerns more than one member of the family, each member should be given the opportunity and responsibility of stating their case. Public praise is something all families should engage in, but be careful that public praise of one child is never used as back-handed criticism or condemnation of another.

◆ **Stars and charts.** Praising a desired behaviour and ignoring an undesired one is the best way to shape the behaviour of children. This can work even for the most difficult children and the most entrenched behaviours. 'Token economies' (as such regimes are called when they are used in hospitals and hostels for difficult and disturbed children or adults) have been very successfully used in many institutions for many years. Remember that you should deal with one behaviour (or group of behaviours) at a time. Stars are gained when the child behaves in the desired way, 'bad behaviour' is not given any attention. Stars can be (but do not always need to be) exchanged for certain privileges.

◆ **Family therapy**. Sometimes problems get out of control and families need professional help. Never be too proud to ask. The school psychologist and/or your doctor or health centre should be able to put you in touch with a therapist. It is also worth consulting a self-help parenting group. If you have a problem associated with a child who has behavioural or physical problems, contact a related charity group.

How to listen to what children say

◆ **Listen with full attention**. Instead of saying "I'm listening, Lucy" while you keep half an eye on the TV, give your full attention. Look at the child when she speaks to you and lean towards her. You do not have to say anything. Sometimes she just needs to see your head nodding or hear you say "Uh-uh."

◆ **Never deny what children say**. "You think you saw something in the cupboard" not, "Don't be silly" or even "Let's have a cuddle and forget about that." Naming a feeling makes it better, not worse.

HOW TO TALK TO SCHOOL-AGE CHILDREN

That needs mopping up: come and get a cloth

✔ *Describe how you expect her to act.*

✔ *You do not have to hide your anger. But you do not need to use it to belittle or hurt.*

Looking at this mess makes me angry

Oh

Oh dear

I see

✔ *tells the child you are sympathetic and understand her feelings—even if you do not agree.*

What a shame!

✔ *Express what the child must feel. Clarify her feelings:*

You must be sad about that

you wish...

you feel...

you want...

I know you can...

I expect you to...

I have confidence that you will...

it would be helpful if...

Jenny I have to go and get supper now

✔ *Children have to know we have rights, too.*

Don't give up

✔ *However you say it or imply it, this is one message which should be writ large.*

I trust you

✔ *A child who knows she is trusted has the confidence to become independent.*

We all make mistakes

✔ *Let children know that parents make mistakes too. A confession session where everyone tells about the silly things they have done that week, and the family laughs with (not at) the person telling the tale, lets children know that they do not need to be perfect to be loved and respected. A child who is prepared to make mistakes will try until she succeeds.*

HOW NOT TO TALK TO SCHOOL-AGE CHILDREN

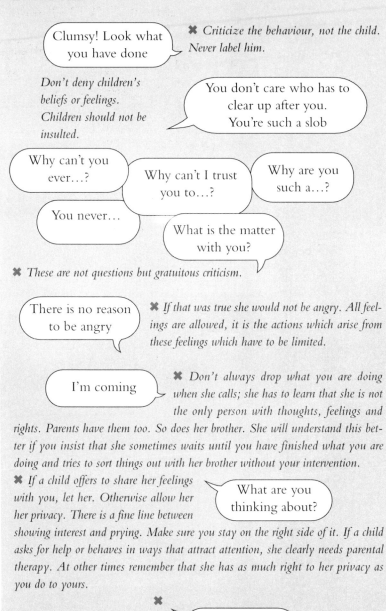

Clumsy! Look what you have done

✖ *Criticize the behaviour, not the child. Never label him.*

Don't deny children's beliefs or feelings. Children should not be insulted.

You don't care who has to clear up after you. You're such a slob

Why can't you ever…?

Why can't I trust you to…?

Why are you such a…?

You never…

What is the matter with you?

✖ *These are not questions but gratuitous criticism.*

There is no reason to be angry

✖ *If that was true she would not be angry. All feelings are allowed, it is the actions which arise from these feelings which have to be limited.*

I'm coming

✖ *Don't always drop what you are doing when she calls; she has to learn that she is not the only person with thoughts, feelings and rights. Parents have them too. So does her brother. She will understand this better if you insist that she sometimes waits until you have finished what you are doing and tries to sort things out with her brother without your intervention.*

✖ *If a child offers to share her feelings with you, let her. Otherwise allow her her privacy. There is a fine line between*

What are you thinking about?

showing interest and prying. Make sure you stay on the right side of it. If a child asks for help or behaves in ways that attract attention, she clearly needs parental therapy. At other times remember that she has as much right to her privacy as you do to yours.

✖

Here, let me do that for you

215

HOW TO TREAT A SEVEN-YEAR-OLD

> Lucy, we have to leave for school in ten minutes

✔ *She can assemble the things she needs and get her coat on for herself. If you always do her thinking for her, she will let you.*

> Mum, I forgot my gym kit again

> I think we'd better get you a calendar and put it on your wall. If we write in everything you need each day, you can check before you set of to school

✔ *A seven-year-old can take responsibility for remembering even if she is scatter-brained. If she checks the calendar, she will not forget her things. At first remind her to do this rather than what has to be remembered. Later expect her to consult it automatically. If she does not read, drawings will help.*

> Mum can I have a drink?

> There is juice in the fridge. Careful, it is rather full!

✔ *A seven-year-old can pour herself juice if the carton is open. Let her try, but be sure she understands it is possible to ask for help if she feels it is too difficult.*

> It's coming up to 8.30, Lucy

✔ *Within a time frame, children should be responsible for getting themselves to bed. They have to be in bed by 9.15 pm, so they need to be stopping what they're doing soon after 8.30 if they are to have a wash, get into their pyjamas and have a story.*

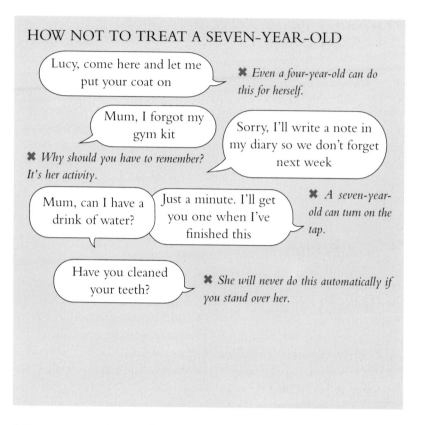

HOW NOT TO TREAT A SEVEN-YEAR-OLD

Lucy, come here and let me put your coat on

✖ *Even a four-year-old can do this for herself.*

Mum, I forgot my gym kit

Sorry, I'll write a note in my diary so we don't forget next week

✖ *Why should you have to remember? It's her activity.*

Mum, can I have a drink of water?

Just a minute. I'll get you one when I've finished this

✖ *A seven-year-old can turn on the tap.*

Have you cleaned your teeth?

✖ *She will never do this automatically if you stand over her.*

Trust your intuition

◆ **When in doubt, put yourself in the child's place**. Think in terms of your own relationships. "How would I feel if someone kept telling me what to do? How would I feel if the person I loved most had found a new love? How would I feel if people always talked to me with one eye on another task? (How do I feel?) How would I feel if people always assumed I could not do things rather than that I could?"

◆ **When in doubt, do what feels right with confidence**.

◆ When in doubt, remember that, if the child has high self-esteem, she can cope. You love her, cherish her, support her, and allow her space to grow, you can occasionally lose your temper, make mistakes, and in general fall off your pedestal without doing any damage. It is good for children to know that adults cannot always cope. It gives them a realistic model to emulate.

Why can't she be clever, why can't she be pretty?

Cleverness and prettiness are largely the luck of the draw. While not entirely endowed at conception, there is probably a fair degree of pre-disposition for such things fixed in our genes. Children build on their initial endowments, and what they build depends upon their experiences and circumstances, personality, confidence and self-esteem. It also depends on the love, teaching and support of those who influence and guide them. A beloved child may not become a great cathedral, but she will almost always make a make pretty good church.

Typecast children

Although, thankfully, most teachers have a professional attitude towards the children in their care, they cannot help showing a little favouritism. Some children are more endearing and do have more attractive person-alities than others. You have not failed your child if she is not the pretti-est, most clever or most endearing child in the class. You will have failed her if you lead her to believe that this matters to you and that you are dis-appointed in her failure.

Research carried out in the United States many years ago suggested that children tend to rise up to meet their teachers' expectations of them. If expectations are low they do not rise very far. So a child wrongly labelled as 'not very bright' in one experiment ended up doing about as well as a not very bright child would do, even though IQ tests suggested she was in fact very intelligent. The reverse was also true. An average child labelled 'clever' was a great success. Although such results have not been replicated in all experiments, it is worth keeping them in mind. Always believe your children can do things. Do not believe the impossi-ble. Most children will run to catch the child one step ahead of them in the race, but if the leader is already lapping them, they will slacken off and coast home.

 ◆ **Remember that, however old they are, children need to be told they are special.** They need to be loved for who they are, not what they do.

 ◆ **Children should be rewarded for effort,** even if they do not always succeed. Be realistic about expectations. Never be dismissive. Children invariably surprise us if we allow them to.

◆ **Don't be a groupie.** Living through your children is pathetic and unfair. It is not a small child's job to boost his parents' flagging self-esteem, especially when she has to do this at the expense of her own. If you always wanted to play the piano, have lessons yourself. A child's ambition has to come from within.

◆ **Don't make your children the epicentre of the world.** Living for your children invariably means you expect too much from them. Of course children must know how special they are to you, but they also need to know that you are special, too - not just in your role as parent, but as an individual. If you stop living for yourself, how are children to grow up respecting you?

◆ **Don't take over.** She should be having not the music lessons you missed as a child, but the lessons she wants to have. If she refuses to do the necessary practice, stop the lessons. More children are put off music by being forced while too young than ever succeed.

◆ **Let go.** It is hard for a child to live up to a parent's ideals without also becoming deeply resentful.

Starting school

These days, starting school is rarely the landmark it was in the past, because schools are a good deal more welcoming than they used to be. For most children, the first day at school is not the first day away from home. Most children will have been to nursery, playgroup or day care before, and will have spent time with childminders or babysitters. Those with working parents will know they have little choice about being left all day, every day. Those who have only been at play school will need to be told that going to school is no longer voluntary.

Reading problems

In order to learn to read, a child must first know what reading means. That is, she must know that information can be gained from marks made on the page. Children go through three basic steps when they learn to read. At first, children substitute words they think should be there for the actual words on the paper, usually using the illustrations as a guide. This 'guess-read' strategy gives confidence.

In the second stage the child realizes that what she 'reads' must have some connection with the squiggles on the paper. She will stop short when she comes to a word which she does not know, or may simply jump to the next word she can read.

Finally, she recognizes words she does not know. She will try to figure out what the word is by looking at its general shape, by decoding the letters one by one and spelling out the sounds, or by analogy with a similar word she can read. The sorts of errors children make will depend on the stage they have reached.

Most of the time we read by recognizing words or even phrases within a context. So, for example, if we are reading about someone who is sad, we are not surprised to read, "Mary shed a tear." On the other hand, when reading about someone climbing a tree, we are not surprised to read, "Peter was worried he would tear his coat." We do not think about the alternative pronunciation or meanings of the word 'tear'. Spelling out the word in this case would not help us to distinguish the two meanings. In other cases, of course, spelling out a word does help us to read it, especially a word we have not seen written before (obvious examples are chemical names which we might read in a text book, or the names of drugs which the doctor has prescribed for us). We guess at new words by analogy with known words when the unknown word is short, and spell it out if there are more than one or two syllables or no obviously analogous words. So the nonsense word 'falm' might be read by analogy with 'calm' but a longer nonsense word like 'caperoximitationer' would need spelling out.

Over the years there has been much controversy about how we set about teaching children to read. Do we combine the context with a look-and-say method of teaching whole words, or do we use the spelling-out method of building up word sounds? Most studies suggest that some element of look-and-say gets children started more quickly, but that their peers trained with the spelling-out method catch them up within a year or so. The reading scheme your child's school uses will almost certainly combine both methods. The most common combination starts with look-and-say and context, and introduces spelling-out methods as the child builds up confidence.

Typical dyslexic reading mistakes

A dyslexic child may show some or most of these, but before suspecting a learning problem, see also the symptoms listed on pages 225-227.

◆ Making up a story based on the book illustrations which bears no relation to the words on the page.

◆ Hesitating before words and in general reading very slowly.

◆ Using a finger to follow text.

◆ Losing her place, missing out chunks, skipping lines and reading some passages more than once.

◆ Reading word by word, and without expression or changes in intonation.

◆ Demonstrating inability to put sounds together. She can say how each letter sounds but cannot put the sounds together to make a word. She can say l-e-g without being able to say they make 'leg'.

◆ Mispronouncing words, for example ferry instead of fairy.

◆ Putting the stress in the wrong place, for example photogra'phy instead of photo'graphy.

◆ Misreading tenses. Reading in the present tense, although the written words are the past tense.

◆ Making wild guesses.

◆ Reading words backwards. 'Saw' for 'was' is a typical example.

◆ Putting letters or syllables in the wrong order, so 'cat' for 'act'.

◆ Confusing vowels, so 'dog' for 'dig'.

◆ Misreading initial letters. Especially letter reversals like 'dog' for 'bog' and inversions like 'pig' for 'big'. She may also confuse similar letters and read 'not' for 'rot' or 'hot'.

◆ Putting syllables in the wrong order, so 'hospalit' for 'hospital'.

◆ Reversing short words, so 'is it' for 'it is'.

◆ Shortening words, so 'phography' for 'photography'.

◆ Adding to words, so 'returned around' for 'turned around'.

◆ Omitting endings like 'ing', or 'ed' on the ends of verbs.

◆ Ignoring punctuation.

◆ Adding words that are not in the text, for example reading 'goes to' when only 'goes' is written.

◆ Omitting little words like 'the', 'that', 'are' or 'there'.

◆ Adding little words like 'the', 'that', 'are', 'not' or 'there'.

◆ Misreading common words and confusing them – 'here' for 'there', and so on.

◆ Misreading words which look similar, such as 'convert' for 'convince'.

◆ Misspelling by writing letters in the wrong order.

◆ Using mirror writing.

◆ Reversing or inverting letters when writing; using b for d or p.

◆ Spelling words as they sound.

◆ Omitting letters and syllables from written words.

◆ Inability to write the letter when given the sound.

◆ Inability to write the letter when given the name.

◆ Inability to pick a letter from a display, or match up letters when asked to do so.

Dyslexia/specific learning disability

The phrases 'dyslexia' and 'specific learning disability' are used inter-changeably to describe otherwise intelligent children who have reading and/or spelling problems. As many as 5 to 10 per cent of all children of school age have difficulty in learning to read and spell. Children are called dyslexic if they show essentially normal development, yet are still having substantial difficulty in reading two to three years after starting school. Children who learn to read at about the right time, but later have seri-

222

ous spelling problems, are also considered to be dyslexic although they are clearly not as seriously affected.

Children with dyslexia find it difficult to process certain information. They are often unsure in which direction to write, and commonly confuse b and d or other similar letter pairs. This confusion in the direction things are facing may be more general. For example, children may have difficulty knowing their left hand from their right. Dyslexic children also have difficulty in finding the right word and often substitute words or phrases such as 'thingy' or 'you know what I mean'. Sometimes they summon up the wrong word and misuse it without apparently realizing that they are doing so. They may have difficulty hearing the little sounds which make up words and may find spelling out those sounds extremely difficult. The sequence of sounds within long words can also produce problems, and sometimes a dyslexic child may even have difficulty saying long words. When writing a long word, the child may get the sequencing of the sounds wrong. So, for example, they might write 'invegistation' for 'investigation'.

Some of these problems are not unique to dyslexic children. Most children have problems with d's and b's and many write in the wrong direction before they can read well. Indeed there are those who feel that such problems are a result of dyslexia rather than the cause: the dyslexic child's confusion simply reflects the relative immaturity of her reading skills. Most people sometimes have problems finding a word. The 'tip of the tongue' phenomenon — where one knows the word needed and may even know the first letter but simply cannot find it — is common to all of us. Usually the word comes to us as soon as we stop trying to remember it. In dyslexic individuals this just happens more often.

Dyslexia, like all language problems, is more common amongst boys than girls. There are about three boys affected for every girl. It also tends to run in families, although not all members of a family are affected in the same way. One may be very late reading and spelling, another may read at the normal time but have poor spelling. Yet others may have difficulty learning rhymes and tables. These are some of the major problem areas:

◆ **Seeing the words.** Very few children have difficulty decoding visual information. The written word itself does not seem to be the problem for dyslexic children. It is the translation of the 'shapes seen' into the 'sounds heard' that dyslexic children find difficult. The problem seems to lie in integrating the two sources of information.

◆ **Hearing the parts of words.** Some children have a genuine difficulty hearing the parts of words. Those pre-school children who have difficulty making rhymes or playing games such as I Spy are more likely to have reading problems. Practice can help, but not if it produces too much pressure.

◆ **Broader language problems.** Many dyslexic children have broader language problems, such as difficulties with the sequencing of sounds, or recognizing words. The old name for dyslexia — word blindness — may not be entirely incorrect.

Dyslexia runs in families

Dyslexia runs in my family. I am dyslexic and all three of my children are affected in some way. One had difficulties with spelling and pronunciation, one with spelling and rhythmic rote-learning tasks such as learning tables and nursery rhymes. My youngest child, like me, had difficulties with both reading and spelling. I started to read at eight, and although I was a 'whiz' at maths, I always had difficulty knowing which side to start when adding or multiplying. In fact it does not matter, and I early discovered that adding and subtracting from left to right is much faster and easier to do 'in one's head'. It does matter where one starts a division, and this always gave me problems.

Although I can now read (rather slowly), I still have problems with spelling. I write on a word processor with a spell checker. When I run the spell checker through a page of writing, I typically have about eight to ten spelling mistakes. Some of them are so bad that the checker cannot work out what the word is that I am trying to spell. Sometimes in this case I am at a loss to find the correct spelling. So, for example, I know that a word like 'tube' does not start with 'ch' but cannot think what letter could be used.

The dyslexia comes from my mother's family and I have uncles, cousins, nephews and nieces who are affected. I do not know about my grandparents, but my great-grandfather could not read. He tried to learn as an adult, and family history reports that he was extremely frustrated by his own inability. Mine is not the only family with many dyslexic individuals. A London clinic which sees dyslexic children claims that 88 per cent of them have a family history. Some researchers have suggested that dyslexia is carried by a dominant gene. That means that, if you are dyslexic, your children have a 50 per cent chance of being dyslexic, and that, if both parents are affected, all their children will be dyslexic. This pattern does not seem to fit the distribution in my family, where unaffected individuals seem to have children who are seriously affected. Nor does the idea of a dominant gene explain the uneven distribution between the sexes.

The reason why dyslexia occurs is still uncertain, although growing evidence from PET scans and autopsies suggests that a particular area of the brain may be damaged. Autopsies suggest a jumbling of brain neurons in certain language areas as well as the presence of neurons without myelin sheaths. (This means that the neurons in this area are a bit like electrical wires without their plastic coats.) Nerves which have no myelination are slow to transmit messages. Since language information must be very precisely timed, getting the sounds in the wrong order can completely change the meaning of a word. Incomplete myelination is obviously problematic.

The fact that dyslexia may be fixed in one's genes does not mean it cannot be overcome. At eight I could not read the word 'moon' — I know, because I remember other children laughing at me — but I went on to get a good degree, a Cambridge Ph.D. and a job as a university lecturer. There are many more dyslexic individuals like me, and others who achieve a great deal more. In my own case the desire to prove that I was not as stupid as some teachers thought me to be eventually led me into doing the one thing they all believed impossible: writing books.

Recognizing dyslexia

Children can be given tests to assess their reading age, and the results of these can then be compared with the child's IQ. Children of average IQ (that is, children with an IQ of 100) are expected to have a reading age which matches their chronological age. For each 10 IQ points above 100, a child should gain one year of reading age. For each 10 points below the average, she should lose one year. Obviously opportunity and general maturity must be taken into account: a child with an IQ of 140 will not read at three if she has not been taught. It is impossible to get a very clear picture of reading problems until the child has been at school for a year or two. However, even in the early stages, it is possible to say that, if a child seems much brighter than her reading and written work suggests, she may have a problem.

We do not need an IQ test to say whether or not a child is intelligent. A child who thinks about things and asks penetrating questions, who is socially aware and quick to solve everyday problems, is intelligent. But there are reasons why an intelligent child might not do any of these things. There may be family problems. She may be bullied at home. She may never have been encouraged to think or discuss her thoughts. For these and other reasons it is difficult for the non-specialist to recognize dyslexia, or even for a teacher to notice it in the first years.

Parents can make an informed guess about their child's intelligence, but are not always particularly good judges. In fact, most parents say that their sons are more intelligent than their daughters, although the average intelligence of boys and girls does not differ, and in tests parents (particularly fathers) invariably overestimated the intelligence of sons. Men overestimate their own intelligence, too. On the other hand, both mothers and fathers make fairly accurate estimates of their daughters' IQ.

If you suspect that your child is falling behind with reading and writing skills, it is best to get advice as early as possible, and especially if you have a family history of dyslexia. Remember that the list given below applies to all children in the initial stages of reading. It is the persistence of these problems which is symptomatic. Even if a child is dyslexic, not all the signs given below will be present. Dyslexia is not a straightforward problem with clear unambiguous symptoms, and can show itself in a confusing number of ways. Many children will have one or two of the symptoms listed below: If they have more than one or two, and if these persist, discuss it with the school.

◆ Is she bright in most ways, but with particular difficulties reading or spelling? This is the defining characteristic of dyslexia.

◆ One of the best ways to test whether your child may have dyslexia is to ask her and a group of friends each to stand on one leg with their eyes closed. If she can't stay upright as long as the others, you should be alert to the possibility of dyslexia, and make some further tests as suggested below.

◆ Does she have difficulty finding a rhyme for words like 'bar' or 'tat' or hearing the little sounds that make up words like in-vest-i-ga-tio-n?

◆ Is punctuation a closed book?

◆ Can she read a word once and then fail to recognize it further down the page? Does she seem to guess at many words?

◆ Is she thrown by the language of mathematics? Not realizing subtraction and taking away mean the same thing or that adding and finding the total are the same? Does she confuse plus and minus? (Or, as in my case, find it impossible to learn the difference between < and >?) About 60 per cent of dyslexics have difficulties with basic arithmetic, but many find higher level mathematics much easier.

◆ Does she have a family history of late reading or poor spelling? About 85 per cent of dyslexics have a family history.

◆ Does she find it difficult to follow body movements when she has to translate them? For example, does she move the wrong leg when copying a dancing teacher who is facing the class?

◆ Does she confuse her left and right?

◆ Does she have difficulty learning to tell the time? About 90 per cent of dyslexics do.

◆ Was she late learning to tie her shoelaces? About 90 per cent of dyslexics are.

◆ Does she confuse tenses?

◆ Does she have difficulties concentrating when she reads or writes?

◆ Does she spell words in many different ways?

◆ Does she have difficulty putting names to things, remembering authors or the names of books?

◆ Does she, or did she, find it difficult to learn the days of the week in the correct order?

◆ Is she left-handed, or slow deciding which hand to use? About 25 per cent of dyslexics are left-handed.

◆ Is there left-handedness in the family? About 90 per cent of dyslexics have close family members who are left-handed.

◆ Was she late talking? About 60 per cent of dyslexics are.

◆ Was she unco-ordinated as a toddler or late walking? About 20 per cent of dyslexics are late walkers.

See also the list of typical dyslexic reading mistakes on pages 220-222.

Hidden dyslexia

These days bright children with very obvious reading problems are usually spotted by teachers and parents. It is those with more marginal problems who pass through the net. Signs of the hidden dyslexic include poor spelling, poor concentration, poor copying from the board or from rough, and being badly organized. My eldest son was such a child. Although he read very early, was bright and fluent in class and clearly had mathematical abilities, his written work was always poor. Three schools put this down to laziness and poor concentration. The general opinion was that he was too busy sharpening up his social skills to get down to work (and in part this was true). Having had serious reading problems myself, I was so relieved that he could read early that I failed to notice the other signs. When people told me that he guessed a large number of words when he read, I dismissed it. It was only when he was about nine that I began to accept that he had problems.

Helping school-age children with dyslexia

If you suspect your child is dyslexic:

◆ **Ask for the child to be referred to the educational psychologist for an assessment,** or arrange for an assessment to be done privately. Your doctor may be able to help. Alternatively, look up the local dyslexia association in the telephone book or get the national association from directory enquiries, the library or the school.

◆ **Arrange for specialist teaching to supplement his normal school teaching.** Some schools can provide this; in other cases parents have to provide it themselves. If you are approaching a private teacher, ensure that they have a specialist training in teaching dyslexic children. Not all tutors supplied by tutorial colleges are trained in this way. Check with your dyslexia association if you are unsure.

◆ **Do not expect your child to co-operate with you.** Many will not. Sometimes it is easier to get help from outside the immediate family.

◆ **Try to motivate without pressurizing,** and always keep your temper. If you are on edge, you will transmit this to the child. Stress is not helpful. Praise every achievement, however small. Remember that the child is almost certainly critical enough of herself: try not to add to the chorus.

◆ **Help to maintain her self-esteem.** Reading is the cornerstone of early education. Failure can undermine the child's feelings of self-worth.

◆ **Take off the pressure.** Motivate her by playing educational games rather than teaching directly. If she is working at school and having tutorials at home, she is working hard enough. If she wants to relax and forget the pressures when she is home, allow this. Don't keep harping on her mistakes. Build on her strengths.

◆ **Do not expect quick results.** Progress is always slow.

◆ **If the child becomes angry, accept her anger.** Sympathize and show her ways of letting anger out. Allow her to have in fantasy what she cannot have in reality: the ability to read overnight. "Lucy, let me sprinkle some magic reading powder, and we can pretend you can read!"

◆ **Keep in touch** with her teachers and schools. Ask their advice. You should be working together. Keep the school and the tutor informed about what each is doing with the child: the last thing a dyslexic child needs is inconsistent teaching or expectations. Your child is one of a class full of children and all of them have needs. You cannot expect the teacher to hear your child read every day.

◆ **Get in touch with other parents.** Swapping information and advice can be every helpful. It is also reassuring to find that children's problems can be overcome.

◆ **Read to her**. Do not try and make her read to you every day unless she wants to. Demanding that she reads puts too much pressure on a tired child. My children were greatly helped by comics books such as Tintin. The pictures carry the story, even when the child cannot read all the words, and the comic format teaches the correct order of written English: left to right along the line, top to the bottom on the page. This order is sometimes confused by children with dyslexia.

◆ **Find things she is good at.** Excelling in something can help her feel she can succeed. But do not go in for too many activities.

She also needs to wind down, flop and feel no pressure to achieve anything at all.

◆ **Help her with homework, but do not take over.** Be available to help if asked. Check her work, praising the good bits. Ask her if she thinks certain things might be improved, or whether she is sure of certain spellings: let the positive things you say outweigh the negative.

◆ **Help with spelling.** Games such as I Spy and those that require rhythm and rhyme help children with spelling. Good toy shops have many spelling games and puzzles - but avoid very complex games such as Scrabble; they are much to difficult. There are also plenty of helpful computer games which assist spelling. Again, your local dyslexia association can advise. A spell checker is advisable for older children.

◆ **Help with sequences.** Dot-to-dot games using letters or numbers are useful. Saying the letters of the alphabet in turn also helps. Teach her songs and rhymes—especially those that help children learn the alphabet, months of the year or days of the week. (Ask at your local library for suitable books if you do not know any of these rhymes.)

◆ **Help her with word direction.** Comics are excellent for this. Lay her clothes out from left to right so that she picks them up in order. Teach her that her right hand is the one she writes with (if she does) and help her to use it to locate her right eye and right foot. When she is clear about her right, can she do your right? Hokey-cokey and 'Simon Says' can also be used. Perhaps the easiest method is to write L and R on the back of her hands.

◆ **Telling the time.** I found clock puzzles a great help with this. We also used a diary with a clock drawn on each section showing the time for breakfast, school and bed. The best way to learn is to buy her a watch and suggest that she consults it a frequent intervals.

◆ **Have confidence.** The most important message is: "You will conquer this. It will take time, but you will get there. This is not a judgement of you. It is not something that anyone can help."

Famous dyslexic people and problem children

Books on dyslexia always start with a list of famous dyslexics. It is reassuring to know that Albert Einstein did not begin to read until he was nine; that Thomas Edison, the inventor, could not spell; that the artists Rodin and Leonardo da Vinci and the writer Hans Christian Andersen were probably dyslexic. It is reassuring to know that there are dyslexic children who have grown up to become eminent brain surgeons, architects, generals and politicians.

But books which list such people do not always point out that up to 10 per cent of children have such problems and that in 2 per cent of children the problems are severe. Andersen does not constitute 10 per cent or even 2 per cent of famous writers, nor do Rodin and da Vinci account for 2 per cent of great artists. Most famous people are not dyslexic and do not have spelling problems. In fact, dyslexic individuals are grossly under-represented amongst the rich and famous, as one might expect.

While the existence of successful dyslexic individuals proves that reading and spelling problems do not make children stupid, the under-representation of dyslexic people amongst the successful underlines the reality. Reading problems are a severe handicap for anyone trying to succeed - not least because they undermine self-esteem. For every child who says to herself, "Just wait, I'll show you I'm not stupid", there are probably at least ten who say, "If you cannot understand that I am trying, I won't bother." I remember both feelings. That in my case the first has prevailed is, I think, a matter of luck and chance.

Recent research shows that dyslexic children are over-represented amongst schoolchildren with behavioural problems. The research also suggests that in many cases reading problems predate behavioural problems. It is known, for example, that, although signs of ADHD (hyperactivity) are usually spotted in children before they reach school age, there is a sub-group of children who are diagnosed as having ADHD after they start school. These children also have reading problems. Studies which follow such children from school into adulthood suggest that they are more likely to drop out of school, and if they do, that they are likely to become juvenile offenders. Poor readers are over-represented in the prison population.

Helping in the house

You can nag, or you can insist. You can bribe, or you can do it all for them. But whether children help or not, the chores have to be done. Even in a home with a professional mother or a regular housekeeper, children should do some chores. Very few of us can raise children with the expectation of servants, and although many men are still largely cared for by women (if surveys of male involvement in household chores are truthful), few men in the near future will be entirely cared for by others - unless perhaps their mothers remain spry and outlive them.

Everyone needs to know how to care for him or herself: to cook, clean, wash and shop. They also need to understand what it is that others do for them if they are to appreciate the care given. A man who has never ironed a shirt is in no position to understand the gift of a freshly ironed shirt. A child who has never tidied her room does not appreciate the efforts which go into her care. There are ideological as well as practical reasons why children should help with the chores.

By the time a child is ten she should be able to shop locally and catch a bus into town to buy selected items - assuming buses are frequent and both bus stop and town are relatively close. She should be able to purchase, prepare and cook a simple meal, and wash up afterwards. She should be able to clean a room without anyone standing over her, wash her clothes, iron them, hang them up, and carry out simple repairs such as sewing on a button or mending a tear. She should be able to care for younger siblings (dressing, feeding, bathing), run errands, and handle money. Many children can do a good deal more.

◆ **At five** a child should be able to put away groceries; wipe the table; pick up toys; tidy away newspapers and books; set the table; sweep floors; vacuum; empty waste baskets; help cook lunch (or make a simple sandwich lunch for herself); prepare breakfast (put toast in toaster, cereal and milk in dish, spread butter and jam on bread); clear the table; help serve food; help cook; get the post; help with weeding; feed pets; polish silver; help plan meals; pour her own drinks; tear lettuce and prepare salad; chop vegetables (with supervision); clean mirrors; polish tables; separate white and coloured laundry; make her bed after sleeping in it; wipe tables and counters; answer the phone and call a few friends.

◆ **By six** a child should also be able to deal with minor cuts and bruises; peel vegetables; water plants; cook simple food; hang up clothes; straighten and tidy the contents of drawers.

◆ **By seven** a child should be able to go to the local shop; answer the phone and write down a number and/or a simple message; get up and go to bed without being asked; iron simple items; clean the bathroom; fold washing; help make the bed with clean bedclothes.

◆ **By eight** she should be able to mop the floor; run her own bath or shower; sew on buttons; mend small tears in clothes; clean out pets; help paint walls; help bath and dress a younger sibling (but not a tiny baby). The responsibility for water and bottle temperatures must remain with parents.

◆ **By nine** she should be able to cross streets and deal with shopping lists, money and change; prepare her own packed lunch; prepare a family meal (and cook it if not too complex); make coffee and tea.

Chores without tears (or very few)

Many parents do not expect much of young children because they assume they are incapable of carrying out household chores. This is a mistake. Children need to experience team work, not least because schools and modern working practices demand it. In most modern households help from the children is not a luxury: it is essential.

◆ **Let children do the chores.** If asked to do something, most children will try the 'go-slow' or 'let's do it badly' routine. It is frustrating, and you will almost certainly feel like stepping in. Don't. Next time they will go even slower and do an even worse job. If they go slow, so should you, especially when it comes to their pile of washing, or their supper.

◆ **They are not fun**. Most three-year-olds think chores are fun. By the age of eight children have no such illusions. Chores are boring and keep one from doing all sorts of interesting things. Don't expect smiling faces, just a job well done.

◆ **Let each child select their own household chores.** Some families do this at a meeting. Others put up a rota. An alternative is to ask each child to choose their responsibility for the next month. Don't be rigid. Let them exchange chores. Beware of weaker, younger family members being conned by the older, stronger ones.

◆ **Put up a chart or rota of things to be done.** Attach a pen so they can be ticked off as completed. Put the rota in a prominent position (we put ours on the fridge). Say when things have to be done — but be flexible. If their favourite TV programme is on immediately after tea, let them watch before they clear away.

◆ **You can expect five-year-olds to carry out certain tasks,** but not to organize their time to make this possible. Even at the age of seven they will probably need reminding. Tell the children what has to be fitted in that day and suggest times when chores could be carried out.

◆ **Show children how.** Do not assume a young child knows how to vacuum or put the plates in the dish washer.

◆ **Put on music.** Noise makes us 'go'. A simple repetitive task is best carried out against a noisy background. But noise makes it difficult to stop and think, so a difficult task - like measuring the ingredients for a cake - is best carried out against a quiet background.

◆ **Don't nag.** Just insist quietly and calmly. Give a warning that the TV is going to be turned off at the end of the programme, and follow though.

◆ **Give positive labels.** Call them good workers, competent, independent, self-sufficient.

◆ **Make tasks a precondition for something preferable.** "We'll go to the park when we've finished this."

◆ **Agree what happens if chores are not done.** Whoever does the chore for them has to be paid in kind (they take on another equivalent chore); in money (deducted from pocket money at an agreed rate); or in privileges (such as not watching a TV programme). Alternatively, the child gets up early and does the chore before breakfast.

◆ **Don't wait to praise her** until she has finished.

◆ **Praise her for her efforts.** Words work, so do gold stars. There are those who think that housework should never be rewarded. While I do not think that children should always be paid for what they do, I see no harm in putting gold stars on the rota, especially with younger children, or in allowing an extra half-hour of TV if the job is done at the parent's convenience. We award silver stars for competence, gold for excellence.

HOW TO ENCOURAGE HOUSEWORK WARS

✖ ***Tell her to do something five times.*** *Then say, "You never help me when I ask you, you are so lazy. Go to your room." Set the table yourself and remain in a bad temper. If the child plays in her room and then comes down to eat, she has escaped the chores very easily.*

✖ ***Do it yourself with a bad grace.*** *Who cares about a bad grace if she can carry on doing what she wants to do? Mum often sulks. It does not mean anything.*

✖ ***Expect her to enjoy helping.***

✖ ***Dish out tasks without consultation or choice.***

✖ ***Expect nothing from certain children*** *"because they need to practise their music, do their homework …" and much from others.*

HOW TO AVOID HOUSEWORK WARS

✔ ***Develop a plan of action.*** *Make lists of responsibilities for all household members and ensure that they are carried out.*

✔ ***Don't let sanctions for bad behaviour lead to avoidance.*** *"You will need to make amends for your rudeness, but first lay the table for me. After dinner I expect you to stack to compensate me for your rudeness."*

✔ ***Explain.*** *"We are all busy people in this family. When you are busy at school Daddy and I are busy at work. We all take something from each other and that means we should all give something. Love is not just about cuddles. It is about helping each other and looking after each other. Anyone who is old enough to go to nursery or school is old enough to do something to help."*

✔ ***Give choices,*** *but do not include the choice of doing nothing. "You can stack the dishes or lay the table. It is your choice."*

✔ ***Co-operation works better than the expectation of obedience.***

◆ **If possible, make tasks interesting.** It's more fun to pick up the toys if they are all in the box before the music stops. Remember, though, that they are not called chores without reason.

◆ **Work as a team.** "Lucy and Dad do the living room and Jamie and Mum do the kitchen."

◆ **Don't give them the choice not to do what has to be done.** If they can watch TV without clearing up the living room first, they will. Who wouldn't? Make watching conditional on clearing up first. No clean living room, no TV. The way to phrase this is of course: "I see you have decided not to watch TV to night."

◆ **Do not engage in power struggles.** When she prevaricates, do not nag. Give her a choice. "Lisa, we agreed that clearing the dishes is your chore. You can pay me or Mark to do it for you, or you can do it yourself. The cost is £2. I can take the payment from your pocket money if that is your choice. Either way, it must be done by six. Let me know by 4.50 pm what you have decided to do." Then offer the chore and the payment to another child.

Giving children independence

In the early years, a child needs to be able to look to you for love, care and control. She does not know what to do, so looks to you for guidance. A child growing up in a household with unconditional love and firm control is secure and happy. As children grow up they must make a gradual shift from depending on your external authority to becoming dependent on their own internal authority — from doing what they are told, to doing what they believe it is right to do.

By the age of five, children should be taking their first steps on the road to self-control — but only steps. They still need limits and control. We empower children by gradually letting go of the reins so that they are able to assume control of their lives. We further empower them by expecting them to be capable and competent. If we do not have this trust in our children, they may grow up more dependent on others than they should be. A child we trust is a child who can trust her own feelings and beliefs.

THE RIGHT WAY TO GIVE INDEPENDENCE

✔ *Let go gradually*. *Today she can post a letter. Tomorrow she can buy a stamp. In a few months time he can walk to the post box while you stand at the corner. Independence should be built on firm foundations. Holding on for too long, then letting go when forced to do so, is likely to tip children into an orgy of freedoms they cannot control. We cannot remain in charge of their lives for ever.*

✔ *Trust*. *Do not stand over children while they carry out tasks. Trust them. "Linda, I expect you to clear up the toys before supper." Sometimes trust is hard. The first time they let a child cross the road alone or catch a bus, all parents sit at the window until they return. Explain this to your child. "Sometimes it is hard not to worry, even though I know that you are very grown-up and responsible."*

✔ *Nurture*. *Base your responses on respect, love and support. Encourage her to take responsibility for herself and for his actions: "I know you can …" "I trust you to …" Invite her to express her needs: "Ask me for a hug if you need one," and offer help: "Let's both clear up together, then you can go to the park for a game before it gets dark."*

Believe in her. Expect him to be a winner, to blossom and succeed. Give your permission for this success and for her independence. Be open, affectionate and demonstrative. Do not make your love a secret.

✔ *Structure*. *A child gains respect from knowing and abiding by limits, from knowing that things are expected of her, and by reaching those expectations. Children who are expected to be capable are capable. "William, I know you want to finish that drawing. But I expect you to leave time to get into your pyjamas before nine o'clock." Children who are expected to ask if they need help will ask.*

✔ *Value*. *The best message a child can read between the lines is 'You are a valuable person who is growing and developing in ways I admire and respect. I am proud to be associated with you'.*

THE WRONG WAY TO INDEPENDENCE

✖ **Control and restrict, then suddenly let go.** *Take and collect the child from a local school until she is 11, then suddenly let her cross town to senior school. Always clear up after her then suddenly set draconian standards of neatness for her room when she reaches the age of 13.*

✖ **Stand over her.** *Keep on telling her when to go to bed and asking him if she has washed and cleaned her teeth. Expect her to wash up, but stand over her to see it is done properly. Imagine that she is fit to go to university, but not do her washing.*

✖ **Fail to trust.** *Assume that she cannot be trusted. Tell her (and anyone else who will listen) that she is unreliable.*

✖ **Reinforce her ruse of doing all chores badly.** *"Oh, just give it to me, I'll do it."*

✖ **Grant freedoms without responsibility.** *"Now you have eaten half your sister's share you might as well finish." "I wish you would ring and let me know where you are."*

✖ **Criticize.** *"Why can't you do it properly?" "You are so stupid."*

✖ **Undervalue.** *"Why can't you behave like a normal child?" "Look at those saucepans: do you call that clean?"*

Going to bed

Keep the bedtime ritual of a story, a cuddle and a one-to-one discussion for as long as the child wishes you to do so. As children get older they may prefer the discussion sessions to take place outside their bedroom door: their bedroom is becoming their own private space. If this is the case, you should respect it.

Even when a child can read for herself, she still enjoys listening to her parents reading bedtime books. Take the opportunity to read more adult books. My children enjoyed *The Hobbit*, *White Fang* and *Black Beauty* at times when they could not quite manage to read them for themselves. It is easy to think that once they can read they can manage the 'good-night story' for themselves, when in fact it will be some time before their skill catches up with their sophistication. The promise of a story is a useful bribe for getting to bed before the time limit.

As children grow up, time limits should become loose, and you need to allow them more freedoms within those limits. I found that allowing an upper limit for bedtime (adult time starts at 9.30) worked quite well. Before 9.30 the children decided when to go to bed, have a shower, get into their pyjamas. They decided when to turn off their lights.

By eight children are able to organize their personal time to fit in any school work, bathing, plans for the morning, and getting to bed at the correct time. But they will not choose to do any of these things for themselves if you do not allow them to do so. Tiny children need you to take total care of them. School-age children do not.

Routines do not come naturally to most six- to ten-year-olds. They need to be taught how to structure their time, and control over the planning of routines has to be handed over gradually. Make lists of things that have to be done, but give the child responsibility for doing them all. You should not need to check tooth cleaning and face washing in ten-year-olds. Nor should you be getting them up in the morning or dictating when they turn off their light.

Discuss with your children when they should retire to their room, how much TV they should watch, what time they need to arrive at breakfast. Suggest sensible times for organizing their clothes for the next day, getting together their PE kit, reading books, homework and so on. Give them an alarm clock. Show older children how to make lists.

What children need to know when they become independent

Although our perception is that the world 'out there' is now 'a very dangerous place for children', the reality is that it is barely more dangerous than it was when I was a child or my mother was a child. There is of course a good deal more traffic, and children cannot ride bikes or play street games with the freedom they once enjoyed. Children know this. They do not run into the streets as carelessly as their parents once did.

Other dangers have disappeared. I can remember playing in factory effluent; pouring petrol into drains and setting fire to it; throwing fireworks; playing on building sites, railway lines and canal locks, where I doubt many children play today. When my mother was a child, she and her friends used to put their legs through the railings of the bridge and hang down as steam trains approached.

What most of us mean when we say the streets are not safe for our children is that children might be snatched from their bike, pushed into a strange car or lured away by child abusers. In truth, the number of cases of children being abused by strangers has not increased over the years. What has changed is the amount of media attention. Abuse by strangers is, and always has been, rare. Unfortunately, not all abuse is rare. About one in ten adults now claim they were abused as children, almost always by close relatives and family friends. The danger comes not from a stranger hiding behind a bush in the park, but from fathers, stepfathers, uncles and grandfathers who have free access to the child's bedroom. Missing children – especially missing teenagers – are more likely to have run away because of abuse from family than to have been abducted and abused by strangers.

You need to keep things in proportion when children want to play away from home. Deny this freedom, and you rob your children of magic years. I hope that my children and grandchildren never do many of the silly things I did as a child, but I want them to have the joy of belonging to the world of children; to enjoy the freedom of a world which is entirely separate from that of parents: dens, gangs, secret codes, scrumping apples; above all, the freedom to roam. If children do not try out freedom at seven they will demand it later. The 'freedom' desired by a 13-year-old can be an altogether more dangerous thing: drugs, drink, glue-sniffing, sex, fast cars, fast older men. They are all more real and more common than the 'nasty' man behind the bush.

As parents we need to warn children of dangers, but to balance these warnings and our fears against their need for independence. They should be made aware of the dangers without becoming so cautious that they miss out on the joys of childhood. In the past, few parents felt that they had to warn children about sexual abuse. The price for this was that children rarely spoke out, and if they did, were not believed. By implying that abuse and danger are out on the street, we also fail to protect.

How to warn a child about danger outside the home

◆ Never accept lifts, sweets, presents or an invitation to come and play from an adult or older child without consulting Mum or Dad – even if you know the person inviting you.

◆ Do not stop and talk to people you do not know, especially if you are by yourself.

◆ If someone follows you, go to the nearest house and tell the person who answers the door what has happened. But do not go into strange houses.

◆ Never answer the phone and say "No one is in," even if this is true. Say "Mummy is in the bath, she will ring you back later".

◆ Always try and come home with other children.

◆ See also telling a child about sexual abuse, pages 191-193.

It is important to remember that a child who is cautious yet confident is less vulnerable than one who is over-fearful. We do not always behave sensibly when we are frightened and upset.

When should children go out alone?

The vast majority of children who go out alone do so in complete safety. In Britain the chances of being sexually abused by a stranger are minute, but the chances of being sexually abused at home somewhere in the region of one in 20 to one in 50, with the figure for girls almost twice as high.

But the anguish of parents on the news begging for the return of their child affects us more than these statistics. We do not register the fact that missing children are frequently taken by neighbours, or that sometimes one of those anguished parents turns out to be the murderer. The abduction and murder of young children is a horrific crime. But so is the abduction and murder of 12-year-olds, 16-year-olds and 18-year-olds. We cannot keep children in the back yard for the rest of their lives.

How soon you start letting a child play away from home depends upon your child, where you live, and what attitudes other parents in your neighbourhood take:

◆ Two children playing outside the house act as a safeguard for each other. A gang of children playing together are not at risk (unless one of them falls out with the others and goes off in a sulk).

◆ Children who know the dangers are usually safe from them. They are more likely to learn caution when young, certainly before they reach the age of bravado and gang silliness at the age of eight or nine.

◆ **Teach them to be responsible:** to take care of their own needs; to report back at intervals; to ring if they are going to be late; to let you know where they are and who they are with.

◆ **Teach them to be independent:** use a public phone; know what to do in an emergency. Let them have their own opinions. Encourage them to think for themselves and express their thoughts and feelings. Respect them as independent individuals. Allow privacy.

◆ **Teach them to be confident.** Let them know they are special, that you trust them and that they can trust themselves. Talk through potential problems and come up with model solutions.

◆ **Teach them when to scream and shout.** Practise what the child should do if approached by a stranger. Define stranger. Tell them who is allowed to touch them and when. If people are nearby, ensure they tell them if strange men approach. Encourage them to scream and shout if people can hear, but tell them that they should never threaten to tell or make a fuss if there is no one who could hear. If the choice is rape or murder, rape is preferable.

◆ **Teach them that they can say no.** If you have always expected compliance, your child may find this difficult. As children grow up, they should be encouraged to put their point of view and to question limits.

◆ **Teach them that they can tell.** Some tales must always be told.

Hates the dentist; afraid of hospitals

No one likes going into hospital, or having treatment from a dentist. Children today have less reason to fear these places than they did in the past. Sometimes it is your fears that are expressed by the child.

◆ **Never belittle a child's fears.** Accept them.

◆ **Talk about your own fears.** "I remember going into hospital when I was small. I was very frightened."

◆ **Do not say it will not hurt if you know it will.** Be direct and honest.

◆ **Never threaten.**

◆ **If a child needs to go into hospital, explain what is to happen.** Take her to the hospital. Stay with her. Most hospitals now let parents stay with children in hospital, and many allow parents to go into the preparation room while the child is given anaesthetic. Most will encourage you to be there when the child wakes from the anaesthetic.

◆ **Take your child with you** when you go to the dentist/hospital. What the child understands is not frightening.

◆ **Play games.** Ideas she has played with are less frightening. There are a number of doctor and hospital toys on the market.

◆ **Read books.** Thinking about her fears when she is cuddled up with you reduces their power to frighten her. Your local library, children's book shop or book club will help. If you have difficulty, the school may be able to offer suggestions.

◆ **Role play.** It is hard for a child to act out the unknown. So an adult needs to play the doctor/dentist in the initial games. Let a doll play the patient. This way you can show the child exactly what will happen to her.

Teeth grinding

This is very common in children as well as adults. It is particularly common just before and during the process of losing milk teeth and gaining adult dentition.

◆ Teeth that are losing support feel strange, and grinding is a way of investigating these feelings. Such grinding stops once the new teeth have erupted.

◆ Sometimes teeth grinding is a sign of tension and stress. It is often temporary and will disappear when the stress (such as starting school or family tensions) subsides. If your child shows persistent tooth grinding, try to teach her to relax: calming music, warm baths with aromatic oils, taking deep breaths and learning to relax muscles one by one, starting from the head and working downwards, all help. So does foot massage.

◆ See your dentist. He can fit a guard which stops grinding.

Picky eater

Most children go all through the school years with a long list of dislikes and a limited menu of foods they will eat, refusing to eat more than the smallest portions. This can be infuriating, especially when you have more than one child and more than one set of dislikes. In many families there are only one or two meals the whole family can eat together. They are rarely the sorts of meals most parents would choose.

◆ **Set rules.** Tell the child you will provide one meal. If she does not wish to eat this, she must provide something for herself. Insist you sit down together. A five-year-old can make a cheese or peanut-butter sandwich if you have sliced bread and if you slice the cheese for her. She can put a potato in the microwave and get out the butter. She can get a small pizza out of the freezer and put it on a baking tray. At the age of six she can open a tin of beans and put them into a dish to warm in the microwave while she makes toast. All children can get a bowl of cereal or a yoghurt. Since getting her own supper is likely to mean she misses her TV programme, it may put her in mind to try your food.

◆ **Try to serve something she will eat at each meal,** even if it is only garlic bread or peas. Warming a small dish of frozen peas in the microwave is not a problem. I have found the bamboo steamers one can buy at chinese supermarkets a godsend for fussy vegetable eaters. Each child makes their selection, seasons as they wish and puts the selection in their own basket. This is then piled up on top of a saucepan.

◆ **One bite.** Let the child select the day of the week when she will try 'one bite' of a new food. One bite does not mean one swallow. Put a small cup beside her so she can spit out things she does not like. Define a bite. A flat teaspoonful is reasonable if she is allowed to spit it out. Never insist on more than one bite. Next time you are serving the food, ask if she would like 'a bite' on her plate. The time after that, offer her one bite or two. Remember there are inbuilt mechanisms which dictate that children try new foods one bite at a time. It is a hangover from our days as hunter gatherers. The 'one-bite' rule was there to stop us being poisoned by new and harmful foods.

◆ **Raw vegetables are better for children and also more acceptable to them.** Try starting meals with raw vegetables and a dip. By seven the children should be able to prepare this.

◆ **Remember that healthy active children are well nourished, even if they seem to eat very little.**

◆ **Don't label or nag.** The correct message is: "Lucy is a selective eater who is still deciding what he likes and dislikes," and that Lucy knows what she likes and how much she needs.

◆ **Pushing food around on her plate.** Set a time limit on dinner. What is not eaten by a certain time is put away or thrown away (the child chooses). Put-away food is eaten in preference to other snacks. It is thrown out next morning.

◆ **Fidgety children.** Children should sit down with the family to eat. But they should not have to stay until everyone has finished. Let them go off and play until pudding is served.

◆ **Try to be positive.** Not "You are so fussy," but "Many children are more sensitive to taste and texture than grown-up people are. I think you are one of those children with sensitive taste buds. As you grow up you will probably find you start to like new things".

Table manners

◆ **Family mealtimes are not the times for adults** exclusively to discuss adult topics, or for children to have to listen to conversations which do not concern them. It is a time for everyone to discuss their day. Each member of the family should have their say, select a topic of conversation and be heard. Exclusively adult conversations can wait for the coffee. Let the children get down when they have finished. It is perfectly reasonable to let children get down between courses.

◆ **Simple rules.** The table rule book says we are polite to each other, we ask for things to be passed, we ask to leave the table, we eat with our mouths closed, we do not slurp, we do not touch every piece of bread before choosing one, we do not belch or pass wind, and so on. If children transgress we remind them. "Lucy, we do not belch at table, that is the rule." If she does it again: "Lucy, hearing belching is very unpleasant when people are eating their meals. Please go to the kitchen and get a glass of water. You can come back when the belching is under control."

◆ **Family mealtimes are public times.** Invite their friends and yours. Public behaviour is always polite and considerate of others. Don't shame a child in front of his friends. After they have gone, say, "Lucy, I realize you were excited, but I expect you to remember that we are thoughtful to other people when they are our guests. It is hard, but you must. Next time we should have a secret word so I can remind you." What should you say? When things are getting out of hand, say "Lucy, remember our secret". Or simply say the word.

◆ **Family meals are for all the family.** The younger they sit up to table, the sooner they imbibe the culture and rules of the table.

◆ **Mealtimes are teaching times.** These are the times you discuss manners and mealtime concerns. Each person can say what he does not like, and the accused can defend his position.

◆ **Be reasonable.** Children should not be expected to sit quietly through a long meal, nor always to swallow what goes into their mouths. If meat is tough, or, having tried something new, they find that they do not like the taste, let them spit it out discreetly.

◆ **Don't compare.** Never say "Lucy, Mark has managed to clean his plate." Instead say, "Lucy, have you had enough to eat?" and if you wish to compliment Mark do so directly: "Mark, I am pleased you have eaten all your food." Never say, "Jamie, look how good Lily is." Instead say, "Jamie, you are free to get down if you wish, but if you want to stay you need to stop fidgeting. It is your choice." And if you wish to compliment, Lily do so directly: "Lily, you are behaving very well. That makes me very pleased."

Manners: thank-you notes

I did not grow up with the tyranny of thank-you letters. My family lived close by and I saw them all over Christmas, so I thanked them in person. But I had friends who had to write thank-you letters, even when they had said "Thank you." In the normal course of events, this seems to me to be rather silly, but sometimes, if the relationship with the giver is formal, or they themselves set particular value on thank-you notes, then you will want your children to write as well as say "Thank you" on the spot.

◆ In any case, it is fair to remind your children before they receive presents that they must be polite and enthusiastic about the present. It is understandable that, in the excitement of opening a gift, manners are forgotten.

◆ If the present is opened later, a telephone call, fax, e-mail, or a postcard saying thank you will be gratefully received. A drawing of the child with the present may be even more special.

◆ Special people such as grandparents will be delighted to receive a drawing, call or card from the child, even if they said "Thank you" at the time. But it seems to me that children should not have to wait for presents before they ring or send pictures to such people.

Being polite

Greeting rules vary from family to family. Some say "Hello", others hug. When one type of family meets another, children can get engulfed in unfamiliar rituals.

◆ Children should never be made to hug and kiss people if they do not wish to, saying "Hello" should suffice, especially when they do not know the person. (If the would-be hugger looks upset, tell her you have told the child never to hug strangers.)

◆ Children should not be rude unless people try to make them do things that are wrong. Make sure they know that safety comes before manners.

◆ Children should not be expected to be better mannered than their parents.

◆ Children can be assertive without being rude. "Grandma, that was a lovely lunch but I don't want any more pudding: I am really full to the brim." "Aunty Susan, I don't think I should be hearing this, can you wait until I have left the room?" "The cover of this comic is ripped. Could you please let me have another one?"

◆ It is difficult to remember. Notice when they do.

◆ Discuss with children why manners are important. Good manners are about being considerate and kind. Good manners are about asking and asserting without hurting or belittling. Good manners are about keeping family conventions.

◆ Let children know that what is considered polite can change. "We let children get down from table without asking. At Grandma's house we have to ask." "Our family think it's all right to talk about wees and poohs, but Auntie Susan's family don't. When we are visitors we have to keep their house rules, not ours."

◆ Work out manners which suit your family members.

Swearing

Children swear. These days, most children swear even if their parents do not. If your child has not yet started to swear it is probably only a matter of time before she does. By the time they reach secondary school, many children's language is liberally peppered with swear words. Sometimes it seems that this is their only source of emphasis. I freely admit to swearing once in a while. Sometimes there is no other word which quite has the emphasis that is needed. But I find sentences which contain two or three swear words, or use f– as the only adjective, dull and tedious to listen to.

◆ Children swear in order to shock or embarrass. It usually gets them plenty of attention. Ignore them and they will say it louder. Turn an even deafer ear and they may even ask if you heard what they said. Turn a totally deaf ear and put on a poker face and they will probably stop. If no one is paying attention, there is little point.

◆ **Set a good example.** Children always mimic you. The only way around this is to clean up your language.

◆ **Explain.** Children do not know what the words mean. Explain them. When children know what they are saying, they are often more embarrassed about using the words.

Wants a Newcastle football strip and some Nike trainers

The function of advertising is to tempt you into buying. If advertising did not make us want things, it would have died out long ago. Which is all very good, but as children jostle for popularity and friendship, 'objects of desire' can put a more sinister gloss on advertised goods. Certain things become badges of friendship, 'must have' items, especially for less popular children. If 'everyone' has something, it is hard to say no.

In our possession-centred society, the badge of gang membership is likely to be the ownership of the right football strip or trainers. This is a particular problem for boys. While girls form friendships with one or two others, young boys often go around in gangs of sixes and sevens. His insistent "Please, Mum" sounds desperate because it is desperate. A child who finds it hard to make friends does not just want those trainers: he may need them. Without the right football strip he may not be able to play. Without playing video games he may have nothing he can talk to his friends about.

Children have to know the value of money: what can and cannot be afforded; how to budget and how to save. But parents also need to be aware that manufacturers and football clubs target young boys unmercifully. Most big football clubs make a good deal more from the sale of strips than they do from people paying to watch football matches. However much we abhor this, we have to accept that it can matter desperately to our children. Although of course we can't necessarily afford all the 'gear' he says he needs to have.

◆ Christmas and birthdays do not have to be times for orgies of presents. Some of the money which is given can be spread through the year. Sit down with your children and decide on what can be afforded. If his 'must have' football strip costs three times what you would pay for a similar outfit, the money can be taken from the treat and present fund. But it is taken. He cannot also ask for an expensive item for Christmas. A football strip now and a second-hand bike for Christmas, or a new bike for Christmas. It is his choice. Ordinary trainers and a football shirt, or special trainers and a normal sweat shirt. Again, it is his choice.

◆ Getting a step ahead. One up on owning the strip and the trainers is of course going to see the team play. It may be cheaper.

How to explain family finances

◆ Sit down with the children and explain in simple terms how much you earn each week/month. The easiest way to do this with a small child is to sit down with a pot of sweets. The sweets represent your weekly income. Now take away the 'cost' of rent, heating, electricity, telephone, food, clothing and car expenses, putting the 'spent' sweets in another pot. Using another pot, put in the savings for Christmas toys, birthday parties, outings, holidays and emergencies. A third pot is savings for long-term projects such as new cars, education, old age. What is left over is what all the family have to share for treats. Don't paint too gloomy a picture. Give information, but do not worry the child.

◆ **Explain that this is private.** This is for our family to know and to discuss. It is not to tell other people.

◆ **Explain rich and poor.** Not all parents have the same amount of money. Some have their cars given by companies. Some have rich grandfathers. Sometimes people lose their jobs and have very little money. People earn different amounts.

◆ **Explain what you can afford and/or what you think is normal.** Even if there is plenty of money to spare, giving a large sum in pocket money would make the child different.

What to do about pocket money

◆ **Set up an allowance.** I pay a small standing order into the children's bank accounts. This is meant to cover holiday spending and the purchase of Christmas and birthday presents for family. I also include a modest monthly sum for small treats and a sum which, if saved, would provide enough money for one bigger purchase (such as a team football kit, or a pair of skates) each year. As children grow up, this can (but does not have to) be expanded to include a clothing allowance, a tape/disc allowance, monthly lunch money, subs for clubs, travel and so on. In addition I give pocket money in hand each week which covers sweets, magazines, small toys, and so on. Obviously, presents for birthday and

Christmas are additional. My children also choose one book or story tape each month.

◆ **Don't give more.** Allowance and pocket money should be fixed. Do not bail out the children if they spend it all in one go. If they spend their pocket money on Saturday and need something on Wednesday, too bad. It does not hurt to learn to wait. There are a few exceptions to this rule. Personally, I always top up holiday spending money by an agreed amount, and on holiday do not expect the children to buy every can of drink or ice cream. If you are having one, too, it would be fair to pay for the child's.

◆ **Be fair.** The amounts may need adjusting in line with inflation, and also need to increase as children get older. Within reason, children should receive approximately the same amount that other children receive.

◆ **Be realistic.** There will always be occasions when she wants to join in a group activity which she could not realistically have budgeted for, such as a school outing. It is realistic to give her a little extra on such occasions. As she grows up, these will be more frequent and you will need to judge each request. A simple rule might be that, if she can contribute some of the cost of a cinema trip or the entrance to the ice rink, you will top this up.

◆ **Talk about advertising.** A little cynicism helps here. Talk about exaggeration, tall stories, temptation and realism. I find comparing the cake on the box with the real cake inside a useful tool for this lesson. Talk about how big the cake looks, then open the box and find out how big it really is.

◆ **Earn extra money.** Certain chores should be expected from all children, such as tidying up toys, making beds or clearing the table after supper. As they grow up, children should also take on a general household chore such as vacuuming the living-room or cleaning the bath once a week. Extra money can be earned if they do extra jobs or take on some of your jobs.

Why do siblings fight?

Children fight because they enjoy fighting. It gets them attention and it's exciting. They fight because they believe something is unfair, because

WHAT NOT TO DO WHEN SIBLINGS ARGUE

✖ *Shout "Stop it this minute." It is a waste of breath. Obviously they are not going to obey.*

✖ *Ask who started it. There is only one answer to this question: "He did!"*

✖ *Accuse them of always fighting. It's not true, even though it may seem this way.*

✖ *Say they are giving you a headache. They will not believe you. You said it yesterday and the day before, and on neither occasion did you take an aspirin.*

✖ *Ask why. Would it help anyone if you knew?*

✖ *Always intervene. This just heats up the argument.*

their territory or belongings have been violated and because they think something, or everything, is unfair. They fight because they feel unloved; in order to take control; and to hurt. All siblings sometimes fight. Most siblings often fight. A few persistently fight. Same-sex children are the worst, boys being worse than girls.

Children cause fights. They deliberately irritate and annoy one another, much as they deliberately irritate and annoy their parents. They do this even though it upsets them, and even if they have experience of it all getting out of control. Children deliberately induce tantrums in much the same way. Like tantrums, most fights take place in the home, and are conducted with those they love best. They happen more often when children are tired. Most arguments are best left to the children.

How not to be piggy in the middle

◆ **Don't judge.** If your judgement seems unfair (as it is bound to do to one or both children) you simply increase the anger and prolong the fight.

◆ **Don't interfere.** Unless the fighting is getting out of hand (when you should separate children) this will just aggravate matters.

◆ **Don't protect the younger.** This will only encourage him to goad the elder child so he gets him into trouble.

◆ **Don't blame the elder.** A child who is labelled a bully often becomes one.

252

WHAT TO DO WHEN SIBLINGS ARGUE

✔ **Ignore.** *If you can leave the room, do so. Do not say a word. Put on a poker face and go.*

✔ **Acknowledge their anger.**

> You two sound angry

Listen to any explanations.

> OK. Jamie, you say Lily is sitting too close; Lily, you say you always sit there

✔ **Describe the problem without judging or taking sides.**

✔ **Express confidence.**

> I see that is a problem for you both, but I am sure you can sort it out

✔ **Withdraw.**

✔ **If the same situation arises again and again,** *talk to each child separately about the problem.*

✔ **Without taking sides, suggest strategies** *each might use to get a fair outcome. Don't impose the solution: let them work it out for themselves.*

> Why not play with your back to the chair? Then you cannot see Lily

✔ **Suggest that the children sort it out without fighting.** *Withdraw.*

> Lily could gather up the cushions and make a comfy nest over by the fire

✔ **If quarrels flare up persistently, it helps to organize an activity.**

> Would anyone like to help me make a chocolate cake?

WHAT NOT TO DO WHEN SIBLINGS FIGHT

✖ *Shout. This just raises the tempo. Remember that noise makes children do what they were already doing with more vigour!*

✖ *Hit. Research evidence suggests that this simply teaches children that violence is the only way to solve arguments. It is likely to increase the level of fighting rather than decrease it.*

✖ *Blame one child. It takes two. If one child is usually blamed, the other has a motive for starting fights.*

✖ *Comfort one child. If fights lead to one child being comforted, that child has a motive to annoy his sibling.*

WHAT TO DO WHEN SIBLINGS FIGHT

✔ *Describe. Without judging, say what you see.*
✔ *Ask. Is this a real fight or a pretend one?*
✔ *Remind them of house rules. "In this house we do not hurt each other. That's the rule. I think you'd both better cool down."*
✔ *Separate them. "To your rooms, both of you. Come back when you have calmed down."*

Falling out with school friends

There is not a parent born who does not want his child to be popular, or, failing that, simply to get on with his friends. And there is not a child born who does not occasionally fall out with his friends. In these early school years, parents are probably rather too ready to jump in to solve problems between children when they should be standing back and letting them sort their own problems out.

If children come around to play, try to avoid playing competitive games, since these encourage bad feeling. Children love to win and hate to lose. The more competitive their culture, the more this feeling grows: and the more fighting occurs.

◆ **Ignore squabbling.** Just because your child has a guest does not mean that your child has to give way. Remind your child before his friend arrives that he will have to share his things. Let him put away any toys he does not want his friend to use. Remind him that he should not fight with guests. Then leave them to it. If things seem to be getting out of hand, or the children are coming to blows, intervene. Otherwise, let them be.

◆ **Show faith.** If the quarrelling is getting worse, intervene. Ask each child to tell you their side. Listen respectfully. Then restate each child's case without judgement. Say, "This is a difficult one," but add that you have confidence they can sort it out without hitting each other. If you think blows are imminent, suggest another activity. Most friends are less likely to hit each other than siblings.

   If the children are really unhappy, ask the visiting child if he would like you to ring his mother. Tell him to ask when he is ready to go home. "You two don't sound very happy. Sam, tell me when you are ready to go home."

◆ **If one or both of them are very angry, describe their feelings.** Suggest they separate and play in separate halves of the room until they have calmed down.

◆ **If they start to fight, intervene. Don't take sides.** Ask them to sit in separate chairs. Say they can get up when they have calmed down.

◆ **Give choices.** "Fighting is against the rules. You can stop now or I can take Sam home. It is your choice." If your child wants the guest to stay, suggest they sit on the sofa and decide how to solve the problem. Go and get them a drink while they are doing this.

◆ **Children get over-excited.** Keep play sessions short.

◆ **Bored children fight.** Keep them occupied.

◆ **Let off steam.** Boisterous games can sometimes let off steam which would otherwise fuel aggression.

◆ **Find a quiet activity.** If the child cannot go home yet, find the children something engrossing to do while you wait. Watering the garden works quite well; TV, videos and books are other useful fall-back activities.

Bullies: who and why

The stereotype of the big, mean, nasty male bully does not quite fit the bill. The more accurate stereotype is the child who feels inadequate, has low self-esteem, does not know how, and/or has never been allowed, to show his feelings. A bully has often been bullied himself, usually by a member of his own family. He is often a victim of physical abuse. Children who bully have in common a need to humiliate and harm their victims. He may even be encouraged by his family to get his way by bullying, or sees within his family that bullying gives the weak power. Such children are rarely successful on any other front.

The child who succeeds at school, has plenty of friends, is generally popular or always makes the football team, rarely needs to bully. A few do. Spoilt, over-indulged and self-confident children, who expect to get their own way as a matter of right, often insist that other children fall in with their needs. This can extend to bullying, bossing and belittling other children. This sort of insensitivity (in its mildest form) is particularly common amongst over-indulged girls. Such girls may extend their power base to lead gangs of mean-mouthed individuals, who do not stand up to their leader for fear of victimization. Such individuals are usually very successful bullies.

Because bullies are likely to have been bullied themselves, they know exactly how their victims feel, and how to make them suffer. Many model their behaviour on their parents or siblings. Bullying rewards them: it makes them feel in control.

◆ Research suggests that children who are aggressive towards other children are often the victims of harsh disciplinary procedures and physical and verbal abuse. They are frequently bullied by members of their own families.

◆ Research suggests that children who are rejected and unwanted are likely to be aggressive towards other children.

◆ Permissive but unloving families also produce aggressive children.

◆ Children who bully often do badly at school and feel inadequate.

◆ Children who bully have learned a pattern of making aggressive demands and expecting compliance, which makes them unpopular amongst peers.

What is bullying?

Bullying takes many forms. It is not just hitting or punching, but includes any form of aggression which intends to hurt or harm another person. I suppose that most of us think of it in terms of the persistent victimization of certain children which causes pain and distress. But bullying is bullying even if it only occurs once. Most children we consider bullies are persistent bullies. Many of their victims are singled out for persistent abuse. Sometimes bullies run protection rackets. A child is immune as long as he pays his dues, hands over his lunch or does homework for the bully.

◆ Physical bullying. Punching, kicking, hitting, pushing or any other sort of violence.

◆ Verbal bullying. Name-calling, taunts, sarcasm, spreading rumours, teasing, rude gestures. Calling attention to physical handicaps or blemishes.

◆ Emotional bullying. Threatening, excluding, making fun of, tormenting, racial taunts, taunts about family. Calling attention to things the child cannot do. Making public the very things the child wants to keep private.

Recognizing a child who is bullied

Small children usually tell you when they are being bullied. Older children rarely do. To help children who are being bullied, you have to recognize that it is happening. If your child shows any of the following signs, tell him that you think bullying is the problem. If you say, "Are you being bullied?" he will almost certainly say no. If you tell him you believe he is, he may admit it. If not, wait. Tell him you are there for him whenever he feels like talking about it. A child who is being bullied may behave in some of the following ways:

◆ He may be frightened to walk to and from school alone, or may come home or go to school by a different route to the others. If asked why, he will probably come up with some improbable reason, such as saying it is shorter when it clearly is not.

◆ He may want you to take him to school, complain his legs hurt too much to walk, or that he does not like the school bus.

◆ He may say he is ill in the morning, but show no obvious symptoms.

◆ He may play truant.

◆ He may begin to bully other children, especially his siblings and their friends.

◆ He may become aggressive, rude and disobedient.

◆ He often has unexplained bruising or scratching.

◆ He may come home with his books or clothes ripped.

◆ He may start taking toys into school which never return.

◆ He may come home hungry because his dinner money (or lunch) has been taken.

◆ He may start stealing to pay the bully, or ask for pocket money mid-week and never seem to spend it.

◆ He may cry himself to sleep, wet his bed or have nightmares but refuse to say what is wrong.

◆ He may seem unhappy but refuse to say what is wrong.

◆ He may start to do badly at school.

◆ He may start to stammer, become withdrawn, suddenly lack confidence.

◆ He may become distressed and anxious.

◆ He may stop eating.

◆ He may threaten suicide. Do not ignore such threats. Every year a number of bullied children do commit suicide.

Bullies at school

Some children remain quiet and rather timid in crowds. If, beneath the quietness, there rests a self-assurance and self-confidence, such children rarely become the victims of bullying. Bullies do not prey on children at random. They prey on those it is most fun to hurt: it is those children who are unsure, have low self-worth, desperately want to be liked and/or wear their feelings on their sleeve who are prey to the bully. The child who is 'different' is also at risk. However confident and self-assured a child is amongst 'his own kind', it is impossible for him to stand up to the taunts and prejudices of a class of children who are in some way different from him. Even if he is well liked by classmates, friends are not always strong enough to stand at his side against a victimizing gang.

Thus the only Afro-Caribbean child in the class, or the only middle-class child in a working-class school (or vice versa) can find himself isolated against a gang of bullies. His self-confidence and self-worth are undermined in the playground by the sheer weight of numbers on the other side.

Bullying is endemic, part of our everyday life. From the petty official to the boss who sexually harasses women (or men) at work, there will always be men and women who misuse power and try to get their way by aggression and victimization. To survive, children do not just need to be protected, they also need to learn how to cope. If your child is often bullied, he needs help to gain the confidence to stand up to and ignore bullies. If he does not allow himself to be bullied, he will eventually find that it stops. Parents should enlist the help of the school in solving the problem, since most bullying takes place here.

◆ Tell him to try and stay with other children. Bullies pick on children who are alone.

◆ Tell him he can walk away. Teach your child how to keep a poker face. If bullies cannot see how much it hurts, they do not get their fun.

◆ It is right to tell if he is being bullied. "Never keep bullying secret. That means the bully wins. Tell a teacher. Tell your friends. Tell your parents."

◆ Practise saying no. Timid children often find this difficult. Teach him how to look someone in the eye, say no, and walk away.

◆ Act out threatening situations. Ask the children to show you how they were bullied. With young children the easiest way is for him to play the bully and you the victim. Show him how to respond calmly but firmly. Then switch roles.

◆ Remind him how to diffuse anger. Find a teddy who can be the bully. Show the child how to hit the teddy or kick him across the room. Undiffused anger makes a child more vulnerable.

◆ Think green. Imagination can transport the child away from the taunts and jibes. If he isn't there he is not upset. If he is not upset there is no pleasure for the bully. Teach him how to imagine himself in a bluebell wood on a sunny day, looking up into the green leaves. Tell him to take a deep breath and feel calm. If the child practises this often enough, he will be able to stay calm and in control. Which is the last thing a controlling bully needs.

Another ploy which a friend of mine found effective is to visualize a large red spot on the end of the bully's nose. Concentrating hard on that meant that she wasn't concentrating on what the bully had to say - which the bully found disconcerting.

Or try thinking about pimples on the bully's bottom - or, better still, large festering boils which are spreading all over his back and up on to his neck. Think about his family laughing at his boils, calling him names: opening the door and laughing when he is having a bath.

◆ Teach him how to respond in ways that give no pleasure - for example by answering "Yes" or "Thank you" to each taunt. This may initially cause more taunts: but if there is no response, there is no fun and the bullying may wane.

◆ It goes without saying that he needs love, acceptance and the rebuilding of his self-confidence, self-love and self-esteem.

◆ Assure him that the bullying is not his fault. That the names he is called are untrue. Tell him and show him you are on his side. Tell him you are proud of him for speaking out, and that you know how difficult this must be.

◆ If he has difficulty making friends, encourage him to join groups or activities which will give him confidence in social situations, such as martial arts classes, cubs, mini-football or rugby classes, swimming clubs. Invite children from these clubs round to play.

◆ Teach him how to relax. Tense children are easy to pick out and to pick on. Teach him the relaxation techniques you learned when pregnant. Show him how to breath deeply and stand tall.

◆ Help him to rid himself of irritating habits: tics and nervous mannerisms, or bragging.

◆ If none of this works, think of getting professional help.

Schools should:

◆ **Make it clear that bullying is not tolerated** and that it is every child's duty to report bullying when they see it or experience it for themselves.

◆ **Make certain they act on information given.** Children should be believed. They should be given a supportive and sympathetic response.

◆ **Adopt a buddy system for new pupils.** It is children who are alone who are picked on. Having a buddy protects children at vulnerable times.

◆ **Adopt a system of monitors.** A nervous, bullied child may find it easier to approach a 'bully monitor' than a teacher. The monitor informs the teacher, or acts as a supporter to the child when she goes to inform. In senior schools, monitors or counsellors may listen to other children without necessarily passing the information on. Such monitors should be elected rather than selected.

◆ **Set up bully courts.** where bully, victim and teacher are brought together initially to discuss the problem. Later, one or both sets of parents may be involved.

◆ **Call in professional help if necessary.**

Helping the bully

Sometimes it helps to recognize that the bully is also a victim. Occasionally, by ensuring that the child can gather self-esteem in some other fashion, the bullying can be eradicated. But this is difficult, because many bullies come from unloving, abusive and unco-operative families which the bully cannot escape. The needs which the child fulfils by bullying remain. If you are yourself the parents of a bully, but do not recognize this scenario, it is worth trying to help your child.

◆ **When told of the bullying, remain calm,** do not counter-accuse. Find out the facts.

◆ **Do not defend your child.** Bullying is inexcusable.

◆ **Talk to your child.** Find out why he has started to bully.

◆ **Seek out causes for his behaviour.** Is he worried by problems at home? Is he having trouble with school work? Does he find it very difficult to make friends? Explain that bullying is no excuse and no solution.

◆ **Individual children may be weak.** They fall in with a bully and act as his helpmate and instigator. They may do it from fear, inadequacy or boredom. Later they do it because the new-found power gives them pleasure or because they need the friendship of the instigator. Remember that children, however weak, are responsible for their own actions. Telling him he has been led astray lets him off the hook. The fault remains his. Don't make excuses for him. There are none.

◆ **Examine whether the child understands about bullying.** Sometimes the child is very immature rather than very aggressive.

◆ **Try to talk to the victim's parents;** work with the school to put things right.

◆ **Ask if your child can be referred** to the educational psychologist.

◆ **Give your child love, teach him self-love and enhance his self-esteem.**

◆ **Make a good behaviour chart.** Mark his achievements with stars. Ignore failures.

Bragging

Few of us are immune from the occasional tall story. Nor do we mind being on the receiving end of one. The ability to judge just how tall a story might be is part of the art of good conversation. Life would be dull if everyone always stuck strictly to the facts. But there is a wealth of dif- ference between a funny story or an exaggerated view of an individual's role in events, and a constant stream of bragging. Bragging is a symptom that the child needs attention in order to feel important. Low self-esteem underlies that need. See also pages 121 to 125.

Here again, I have to repeat that one of the most important functions of a parent – perhaps the most important – is to build their self-love and self-esteem. Children should always be made to believe the glass is half full, not half empty. Never criticize him unless you can also say something good. If he has tried, he deserves praise.

◆ **Show him how to think positively about himself.** "Pat yourself on the back, Jamie." "I think you should say at least three times 'Jamie I'm wonderful' for that."

◆ **Teach him to say, "That's not like me,"** not, "I've messed up again."

◆ **Teach him to think "I almost came first"** not "I only came fifth."

◆ **Love her for herself alone.** "I love my Lily," not "I love my little ballerina."

◆ **Have confidence.** "That's difficult but I'm sure you can do it. Let's think how to start." and give suggestions leading to him finding the solution. Never, "Don't be silly Jamie: you can if you try."

◆ **Never do for children what they can do for themselves.**

◆ **Give independence.** Trust. Let him spend his pocket money as he wishes.

◆ **Stop nagging.**

◆ **Give him jobs** to do about the house and garden. Let an older child go to the corner shop for the paper. Let him know you appreciate his contribution.

◆ **Buy him a dog or a hamster.** Caring for a pet can increase an insecure child's self-love.

Bossiness in older children

Bossiness rarely amounts to bullying, but if it goes unchecked it can come very close. Few children enjoy being constantly bossed about by another child, so bossy children rarely have bosom pals.

◆ **Do not embarrass your child by telling her off in front of her friends**. Her friends' opinions are vital at this age, especially if she is not that popular. Talk to her in private after her friends have gone home. Discuss how she might ask for co-operation from friends in a less dictatorial way.

◆ **Encourage discussion.** If you always lay down the law, so will she.

◆ **Carry out role play** if your child needs help. How do you ask for help? How do you express what you want? Most of all, how do you listen to the needs of others?

◆ **Discuss the difference between asserting her wishes and dictating to others.**

◆ **Discuss her feelings** and how others feel when they are bossed. Take time. Do it gently. Being a bossy parent is not going to help a child to be less bossy.

◆ **Family meetings** are good places to air problems of bossiness between siblings.

◆ Team sports are useful training games for being both assertive and co-operative. So are brownies, cubs and woodcraft folk.

She does not make friends

No one wants their child to be lonely. It is distressing to find that your child is obviously not being invited to other children's birthday parties and never seems to be invited to tea. Especially when this is backed up by claims that other children will not play with her. No parent wants their child excluded in this way. Before you panic, check what your child means by not having friends. Some children believe that everyone in the school should be their friend, and that they should go to all the parties. She may have plenty of friends. Some surveys suggest as many as one in ten children do not have a close friend at school.

Friendship problems are very normal in the early school years. Take heart from the fact that few friendships are fixed at this stage. Children frequently start and stop being 'best friend' at this age. Just because she does not have a friend today does not mean she will not have one by next week. Be patient and help her to gain the skills necessary to be a good friend, and to eliminate habits and interactional styles which may be making her unpopular.

◆ **Being alone and being lonely are not the same thing.** Some children just enjoy their own company. They may have friends they can play with when they want to, but choose to play by themselves at other times. If they seem happy and contented with this situation, there is no problem.

◆ **Check with a teacher if** you think there is a problem. She will know what happens in the classroom and can find out what happens in the playground. Ask if she feels the child is troubled in school.

◆ **Check with the child.** She may be quite happy. Do not interfere unless she is distressed.

◆ **Deal with any bossiness.** Bossy children are rarely popular.

◆ **Encourage her to make friends with younger children.** This can allow her to build up the confidence and skills to make friends of her own age.

◆ **Invite other children home to play.**

◆ **Show her how to take a deep breath and calm herself** before interacting with others. Tense children do not seem attractive to others.

◆ **Do not try to make friends for her.** You cannot force children to be friendly with her.

Socially isolated

There is a difference between not having many friends and being socially isolated. Social isolation is an extreme form of social disturbance.

Socially isolated children do not simply have few friends: they spend virtually no time interacting with others. Shy children constantly want and desire friends. The social isolate actively avoids other children. Social isolation is highly correlated with other problem behaviours such as school difficulties, personality problems, delinquency and conduct disorders.

Most isolated people feel fearful, rejected and alone. Some children are isolated from everyone. Others can interact with much younger or much older children although they have difficulty with children of their own age. Sometimes playing with older and younger children enables them to develop the skills they need to interact with their peers, in which case isolation is only a temporary problem. However, if the problem persists, or if the child seems to make no friends at nursery and later at school, you should seek professional advice.

◆ **Parents sometimes reject a child's friends.** Do you have too high an expectation of his friends? Do you discourage him from playing with certain children? Children may not like the children who please you, and may be too fearful of your displeasure to choose other friends.

◆ **Children may not have the social skills to make friends.** Helping them to develop these skills can avert the problem. Expose the child to other children by joining groups such as cubs or junior football teams. Invite children to play. Actively encourage any group participation.

◆ **Model social skills with the child.** Play interactive games.

◆ **Teach and coach him in skills that others value.** Athletic skills tend to make boys more popular. So does knowledge about football. Take him to a few football games. Then practise talking about the match.

◆ **Promote risk taking.** A child who makes friends takes chances.

◆ **Promote self-confidence.** Love uniquely. Praise often. Make him feel he belongs in your family and that you accept him for who he is. A child who feels secure and confident can be more outgoing.

◆ **Reward any social interaction.** See also pages 305–307.

Tries to buy friends

Finding that your child has been buying friendship is of course horrifying, but be reassured that it is surprisingly common. One in ten children in primary school are not selected as a friend by other children. The temptation to bribe their way into favour is huge. Some children simply do not know how to make friends. Others irritate by their manner or mannerisms, so they are not selected. Bossy, aggressive children tend to be left out.

◆ **Check that she is not being bullied.** She may be buying protection, not friends.

◆ **Talk to the school about the problem.** It may be quite widespread or it may be very specific. Schools will almost certainly monitor the situation if you inform them. Talk to the child's teacher about her interaction with other children. Teachers may be able to give an insight into the child's problem. Don't get angry or upset and don't feel defensive. An honest assessment may be hurtful, but it is necessary if a solution is to be found.

◆ **Talk to the child about the problem.** If she does not have friends, are there children she would like to make friends with, or whom she feels she could make friends with? Get her to make a list of these people.

◆ **Talk to the child about what she likes in friends** and what she thinks friends might like in her.

◆ **Role play with the child.** Practise approaching other children, talking and asking if they would like to play. Teach her to say no to children who try to buy her friendship.

◆ **Invite a child to play.** When your child has located a child she might like as a friend, invite that child over to play.

◆ **Enlist the teacher's help.** Could she alter the seating arrangements so that your child could make friends with another child? Are there other lonely children in the class, or a child who is good-natured and easy and might include her?

◆ **Children like happy children,** who join in, are not bossy, are helpful, share, make them laugh, are fun to be with, listen when they talk and are kind. Read though this list with your child: and role-play each of these characteristics.

◆ **Children who make friends easily are self-confident,** well-organized, good at sports; they shrug off disappointments, communicate and listen, know how to sort out conflicts, do not criticize others, and have supportive parents.

◆ **Observe your child with other children.** This may give you insight into her needs and her unpopularity. Work on changing behaviours which are making her unpopular.

Taken over by an older child

When children first start school, it is quite common to find them taken over by an older child. This is especially likely to be a child who is otherwise rather lonely and isolated.

◆ **Check on the child.** Sometimes a younger child is taken over because older children think he is especially cute. Such relationships are likely to enhance your child's esteem. There is little to worry about. A child selected for his popularity will later be selected by his peers.

◆ **Check with the school.** When a child is taken over by a rather lonely older child, ask the school's advice. The child may be manipulative and may isolate your child from others, or she may just need a friend.

◆ **Review the situation.** If one child is completely dominating your child's friendships, invite children of her own age round to play. If you think she is having difficulty making friends with her peers, talk this through with her. Consider what she wants from friends and how she might make friends in her class. Role-play with her.

Answering awkward questions

Just because children start school does not mean they stop asking awkward questions. On the contrary, now that they are mixing with other children they become more 'street-wise'.

Between the ages of five and seven children love rudeness. They think it is silly and funny and rather grown up. So they say 'rude' words to each other and ask questions which have 'rude' answers. Some of these questions spill over into family life, because the child is repeating a game he played at school or with a sibling; because he does not realize what he is asking; or because he only half-realizes.

Other sources of 'awkward' questions are more sinister. If your child talks about sexual practices with more knowledge than he should have, find the source. Someone may be trying to abuse him or abuse the child who is his source. If this sex talk can be located to one child, inform the school. That child may need protection.

Whatever your child asks you, do not show shock or surprise. This will only alert him to something 'really rude' and encourage him to use the words again. It will also make it harder for you to strike a balance between answering the question honestly and answering it too fully. Remember that, if you do not answer his question, he will probably ask someone else. That person may not give such well-judged replies.

◆ What is sex? Children usually start asking this question long before they start school. At first they need a simple explanation. If you are embarrassed about this, there are many excellent books which will help you. Children find it easier to understand sex if you provide them with illustrations. By the time they reach school age, they will probably be asking more searching questions.

◆ What is a condom? They may have seen the advertisements, heard the word in the context of safe sex, or seen a used one in the park. Start by explaining sex, then by explaining that people sometimes like to have sex without making babies. Explain safe sex with reference to a virus that can pass from one person to another during sex. Explain how a condom can stop this. Reference to rubber gloves might be a help here.

◆ What are tampons? Again this needs a simple and straightforward answer. Books can help if you are embarrassed. "The place where babies grow inside women is called the womb. Every month the womb gets ready for a baby to live there. It makes a nice soft lining: a bit like a carpet all ready for babies to snuggle into while they grow. Women do not want babies every month. (We wouldn't want one every year, would we?) When a baby does not start to grow, the womb gets rid of all the things it had prepared. A bit like letting the plug out of the bath when you don't need the water any more. Tampons mop up. It stops Mummies having wet knickers!"

◆ What is that? This can range from the string hanging out from a tampon, a used condom in the park, a cap or even sex toys. Obviously the motto here is to keep things you do not wish to explain to your children out of sight. Don't be afraid to duck this one. We do not always have to be absolutely straight with six-year-olds. Use your ingenuity.

◆ What is AIDS? Children cannot avoid knowing about AIDS. Explain what it is, what it does and how people catch it. Then reassure the child that for it to be passed on, people have to have sex with someone who already has AIDS. A six-year-old needs to be reassured, that when his parents have sex, this is not dangerous.

◆ What are gays? "Some men fall in love with women and marry them and live with them. Some men fall in love with other men and 'marry' them and live with them. They are called gays or sometimes homosexuals. Some women fall in love with men and marry them and live with them. Some fall in love with other women and 'marry' them and live with them. They are called lesbians."

◆ What is oral sex? The easiest answer is "When people have sex with another person's mouth." Small children do not need more detail. Find out where he has heard this.

◆ What is anal sex? The easiest answer is to say "When people have sex with another person's bottom." They do not need more detail at this age. Find out where he has heard this.

◆ Why do some children not have dads? "Everyone has a dad. But sometimes dads do not live with their children. Sometimes they go away and do not have anything to do with their children. But that does not happen when dads want to be with their children. Your dad really wants to be with you."

◆ What is rape/abuse/incest? Find out where he has heard this. Give him just enough information to satisfy his curiosity. "Rape is when someone touches your genitals when you don't want them to."

"Abuse is when a grown-up person touches a child's genitals, asks the child to touch their genitals or tries to have sex with the child. People who abuse usually ask the child not to tell anyone else."

"Incest is when one relative touches another relative's genitals, or when a relative tries to abuse a child. Some dads or grandads try to abuse their children. They usually say the child should not tell and that bad things will happen if they do. This is not true. Children should always tell, even if the relative says bad things will happen."

◆ Why do people hurt children? "Some people have very sick minds. They think it is fun to hurt children. There are not very many of these bad people about, but it is not easy to tell if a person has a very sick mind. It is best not to talk to strangers when you are by yourself."

What to do when a child cheats

Most children are not good losers. Even if they are winning at Snakes and Ladders, they may 'miscount' the squares to climb another ladder. They hide cards, start before anyone shouts go, and cut off corners when no one is looking. If there is a way to cheat, small children know it. If sleight of hand or subtle change of rules does not bring success, they will knock the board, spoil the game or go off in a huff. In this they are not unlike many adults.

All normal children cheat when they are young; just as all children tell lies. We cannot set up a competitive society where winning matters more than playing the game, then expect children to be egalitarian. We cannot tell children they should win, encourage them to claw their way to the top and expect them always to do this fairly. The old adage, "It's not winning that matters, but taking part in the game," was only ever true (if it was true) for a small class of people with so many advantages that they did not need to bother to win something as unimportant as a game.

◆ **Always explain that cheating is wrong.** Encourage children to 'walk in each other's shoes'. How would they feel if others cheated? Give examples. For children who find it very hard not to cheat, act through a situation in which they are the ones cheated against.

◆ **Expect co-operation and mutual help.** If families expect

271

every child to do their share of tasks, and to help and take responsibility for one another, children will be more co-operative and less competitive. It will reduce the problem.

◆ **Don't give equal shares.** If children always look at things in terms of who has the most, they are more likely to cheat in order to get the upper hand.

◆ **Treat uniquely.** Treating each child as special in their own way gives the message to children that winning every game is not so important.

◆ **Explain the rules.** Sometimes children 'cheat' because they are not certain how to play a game. Say you expect them to play fair. If one is caught cheating, discuss what you should do about it with all players. Insist that there is no namecalling.

◆ **Expect children not to cheat.** "I know you can play fairly."

◆ **Stop children cheating when you see them doing so.** If young children need to be given an advantage in a family game, make this clear by setting up the handicaps before you start playing.

◆ **Ask for an apology,** but never humiliate.

◆ **If your child cheats at school,** make sure that she apologizes and accepts whatever sanctions are set. This should not include public humiliation. Challenge the school if they impose this. Let the child know that people make mistakes and sometimes behave badly, but that this does not make them a bad or unlovable person.

◆ **If your child cheats at school, find out why.** She may be cheating because this is the only way she can keep up. Children need to be taught how to do things for themselves, not for someone else. Beware of any tendency to live 'through' your children.

◆ **Comment on good behaviour.**

◆ **Get help if you cannot cope,** or if you feel that your child's cheating has become endemic.

◆ **Model being a good sport.**

◆ **Don't always play games** which result in winners and losers.

◆ **Socialize with other children.** Playing with peers is often the cure.

◆ **Remember to criticize and praise the behaviour, not the child.**

◆ **Team sports** such as rugby or football may help persistent cheaters.

Telling tall stories

Young children do not necessarily know the difference between fact and fantasy. Nor do most of us want that distinction kept strictly in place. It's a dull companion who never embellishes the truth, and an unsympathetic friend who never tells a white lie to avoid hurting or deflating someone he cares about. There are good reasons for telling lies. A good story makes us laugh. A good friend does not tell us before the interview that we do not have a chance of getting the job, or say we look awful when there is no opportunity to change a dress.

A lie is an untruthful statement, but so is a story. We tell her acceptable 'lies' every night with her bedtime book. She hears us telling tall stories that make people laugh. We laugh at her jokes. So who is to say that a lie is an untruth that gives us advantage? The distinction may be clear to you, but it's a fine one for a small child whose days are enmeshed in fantasy.

Story telling is one of the basic elements of all human cultures: indeed, the feeling of belonging to a society is very much tied to a set of shared cultural stories and myths. For generations, these stories were passed by word of mouth; now they mostly come via books, education, newspapers and television. Family stories remain, and if we are lucky, so do the family story tellers. One of the things that bind us to our family is a set of shared experiences reiterated and embellished by the retelling. I am fortunate to have heard and to be able to pass on to my children the stories my grandmother told about her family. I know they are exaggerated, but it is the embellishment that delighted me as a child. That is why I remember the stories and can pass them on.

How does a child learn the difference between acceptable and unacceptable lies when language is so peppered with untruths; advertising

273

with exaggeration; politics, newspapers and TV with manipulation?

The only way a child learns which lies (and truths) are acceptable and which are unacceptable is by telling a few and awaiting your reaction. You shape a child's behaviour by approval and disapproval. The line most of us draw is between amusement and harm, advantage and disadvantage, covering up something which would hurt others' feelings, and covering up something which would reflect badly on you. It is a difficult line to draw, and a difficult one to learn. One thing most of us are clear on is that we do not like lies which are used to manipulate us, and we do not like myths which always get in the way of the truth.

Good lies

Puffing someone up by praise is a good lie. Enhancement of their virtues is the right of all children.

◆ Talking ourselves into believing we can is a good lie, because, if we believe, there is a better chance of making it come true. A lie which brings something within our reach should be told. "I'm going to be a footballer when I grow up." "That was beautiful." "That was delicious." We gauge our expectations to fit what we believe we can do.

◆ Words can enhance our self-esteem whether they are the truth or a tall story.

◆ Laughter is the best tonic. Trite but true. Embellishing a story to create laughter is a good lie.

◆ Empathy is a social virtue. Putting yourself in someone's shoes and walking a mile as them is fantasy, but good fantasy. If caring, sympathising, and considering others is based on a lie, it's a good lie.

◆ If white lies stop people hurting when they do not need to be hurt, they too are good lies.

Sometimes it is better to say nothing, even when you know the answer to the question.

Bad truths

◆ **"I want you to ..." "I expect you to ..." "When you are ..."** Expectations are powerful ways of controlling children. Impossibly high expectations mean that the child can never measure up. A child does not see his parents' standards as unrealistic; she sees herself as inadequate. Her only option is not to try. That way she has an excuse which does not deflate her. "I could have done it if I had tried harder." The statement can become a way of life.

◆ **Truth can damage our self-esteem.** "You are not as pretty as Lily." "Jamie, you are stupid." Judgements based on gender and race - even if they are based on historical fact - are bad truths. "Men don't know how to look after children." "Black people cannot get good jobs." Anyway, these are very partial truths.

◆ Telling people the truth when the truth hurts and the hurt serves no purpose is a bad truth.

◆ Telling selected truths which manipulate to your advantage and another's disadvantage are bad truths.

◆ Personal remarks which are unflattering are bad truths. "Your head is a funny shape."

Story telling and fantasy

Some children always tell fantastic stories. Because we laugh and show interest in them, we reward the child. At nursery the child who creates the fantasy leads the game. Sometimes this story telling can get out of hand. It might, for example, be used to escape blame. A child who habitually makes up a tall story to get out of trouble, or uses an imaginary friend to take the blame for his wrongdoing, needs gentle correction. It is natural for a child who is frightened of the consequences to say that someone else did it.

◆ **Accept the child's explanation** and seek clarification. "Tell me why you think this naughty boy did this?" "Tell me what Gilla did when you were on the toilet."

◆ **Tell her it is safe to tell.** "I know I was cross, but I'm not cross now. I know you think Gilla did this. But did Gilla do all of it? You can tell me if you helped a bit. I will not be cross with you. You do not have to pretend any more."

◆ **Never call a child who is frightened to tell the truth a liar.** She is telling lies because she is afraid. You increase her fear by calling her names: this is likely to make her tell more lies.

HOW TO ENCOURAGE CHILDREN TO TELL LIES

✖ *Label the child: Children become what they are labelled.*

You liar!

✖ *Lie often and blatantly and within earshot of your children.*

I called you yesterday, you must have been out

✖ *Ask the child to lie for you.*

Tell him I'm not in

✖ *Never admit your mistakes. Lies are a means of covering up error. The best way to discourage them is to set a good example.*

✖ *Fail to let the child face the consequences of her lies. If she forgets to do her homework do not send in a note with a false excuse.*

✖ *Fail to follow through. Don't let the child off the hook because she lied. If a lie has enabled her to avoid doing what was asked of her, letting the matter slide encourages lies. She should do as she was originally asked, or if this is not possible make amends.*

It is too late to post that card today. If you had told me you had forgotten when I first asked about it we could have caught the collection at the post office. You will have to ring Grandma after breakfast tomorrow to wish her a happy birthday; we'll post the card on the way to school

How to recognize a child who tells lies

Young children may be lying if:

- ◆ They do not look you in the eye, and shift their gaze away.

- ◆ They shift around and look uncomfortable.

- ◆ They change their story several times.

✖ *Blame. This increases fear and makes another lie more probable. Avoiding shame and humiliation is one of the major reasons for telling lies.*

✖ *Ridicule. This just increases her bad feelings and lowers her self-esteem. If low self-esteem is one of the root causes of her telling lies, this makes things worse.*

✖ *Fail to let the child face the consequences of her lies. If when she forgets to do her homework you send in a note with a false excuse, she will 'forget' again. What has she to lose?*

✖ *Be totally unreasonable. If, after you have said a child cannot go out until she has finished her music practice, her friend invites her to go with her family to the cinema, saying she cannot go unless she has finished his practice encourages him to lie.*
Instead say

> It's OK to go swimming but I expect you to find time to finish your music practice when you get back

This encourages both honesty and self-reliance.

✖ *Going overboard about small things encourages him to lie about big things. A child's life would be filled with criticism if we jumped on every misdemeanour. Remember that your praise should always outweigh the criticism.*

277

HOW TO DISCOURAGE CHILDREN FROM TELLING LIES

✔ *Praise and compliment* her *for telling the truth.*

> I'm proud of you. It was hard to own up

> Do you need any help with that?

✔ *Give her attention* before she *demands it.*

✔ *Do not expect too much.* *Praise her for being herself and trying her best.*

> You tried your very best and that is important

> Lily, you are wonderful

✔ *Be a good listener.* *Even if the truth is not immediately forthcoming.*

> That sort of thing would make anyone a bit nervous. They are bound to think the other person would be too cross to listen

> I bet they wish they could tell their side of it

> I know you were afraid to tell me when I was angry. But blaming your sister is not good. How do you think Lily would feel if I had accused her of breaking the vase? Would she have thought it was fair?

✔ *Be ready to sympathize.* *Listen to their side. Then state yours (or the other person's) view.*

✔ *Love her for herself alone* and not for what she can do.

✔ *Stay calm.* *Don't over-react to a young child's lies.*

✔ *Question,* find out the facts without laying blame. Bite your tongue when you want to berate her. Never call her names, even if the names are true.

✔ **Let her know she can be honest.**

> Lily, you can also tell the truth

✔ **Tell her in a matter-of-fact way that you know she told lies.**

> Lily, I know Jamie was out in the garden, so he could not have broken the clock

✔ **Find out why children are afraid to tell the truth.**

> What do you think would happen to the person who did this? What do you think would happen if this was true?

✔ **Give good labels.**

> I also know you can tell the truth

✔ **As ever, label the behaviour, not the child.**

The child may not believe this if she has just been telling lies.

> I know you can tell the truth

not

> I know you are an honest person inside

> I know that what you have just said is untrue

not

> You are a liar

✔ **Let it end.** *Put a line under things. Do not keep playing the same old record. She told a lie. So what. We all do.*

✔ **Let the child both know and face the consequences of her lies.** *Sometimes one of the consequences is owning up and telling another person you lied.*

✔ **Admit your mistakes** *and make amends if you accuse the child wrongly.*

✔ **Get professional help.** *If a child of school age is a persistent and compulsive liar she probably needs help. This is usually a symptom of some underlying problem.*

◆ They are very vague.

◆ They are inconsistent

◆ You think they are lying.

◆ They seem nervous or afraid.

Self-centred children

Self-centred people act as if they should have everything they want without putting in any effort. They are overly or exclusively concerned with themselves, and think of their needs without regard for other people. They always place their own desires first on any list. If this description sounds like a small person you know, do not be alarmed. All children start life self-centred.

Until she is four, a child only has one point of view, and that is her own. she cannot put herself into someone else's shoes, or imagine how they might feel. By the age of five these skills are coming on line. She can take other people's views into account, be more sympathetic and imagine how they feel, but she is not entirely skilled in these matters. She practices as she plays through imaginary roles, listens to stories, or watches videos and TV. By seven, most children are still rather absorbed in themselves but are beginning to be a little less self-centred. As imaginary play declines, the skills should be more or less in place, but this is not inevitable. As we all know, some people remain self-centred and self-absorbed throughout life.

An individual who is totally unconcerned about other people makes a poor companion. Often other children are as uninterested in her as she is (or acts as if she is) in them. Self-centred children rarely feel as if they belong to the group, or have close friendships.

Encouraging selfishness

◆ **Label her**. "You are so selfish."

◆ **Agree with the child's poor view of herself.** "I'm not surprised children do not want to play with you.""No one wants to play with selfish children like you."

◆ **Agree with the child's poor view of others.** "They are not worth bothering with." "They don't have half a brain between them."

◆ **Discourage her interaction with others.** "No, he cannot play here now, this is my busiest time." "I don't care what all the other parents allow, you are not playing out, and that's that." Self-centred children often find difficulty relating to their peers: they find it difficult to take part as 'we' rather than 'I'. Without practice, this cannot improve.

◆ **Spoil her.** A child can have lots of toys without being spoiled. She can have few material things and still be over-indulged. Parents also spoil children by being over-protective, and by not asking anything from the child. A self-sacrificing parent invariably spoils the child. Spoiling is often fuelled by guilt. A parent may spoil a child she has little time for or did not want, or whom she finds unattractive. She may spoil the child because she wants to compensate for her own difficult or deprived childhood.

◆ **Don't let her grow up.** Selfish children remain stuck in a more infantile way of interacting with the world. Parents encourage this if they make no demands on the child, and if they do not allow or expect independence and self-reliance. "Let me do that." "OK, OK, I'll get it for you."

◆ **Sometimes children are selfish because they are frightened of rejection, or are frightened of being close to other people.** This can happen when children are excluded by self-centred parents, or those who do not know how to give or express love. "Can't you see I'm busy?" "You know I have an important meeting tomorrow." "Go and play."

◆ **Sometimes children are selfish because they are immature.**

How to help selfish children

◆ Prevent selfishness by helping the child feel worthwhile. "Lucy, you are such a good helper." Love her uniquely and for herself, not for what she does. "Who's my mint julep?" "What a poppet! You have been a great help." Display love and encourage the child to love herself. "Give yourself a pat on the back and then let me give you a hug." A child with high self-esteem can afford to consider other people. She does not need to be tied up in herself.

◆ **Respect and accept the child's weaknesses as well as her**

strengths. A child who is loved for herself does not need to act selfishly. "Lucy, sometimes it is hard not to blow a fuse. Sometimes everyone needs to kick a cushion." "I know you find this very difficult and I really appreciate how much you are trying."

◆ **Let the child know you value her.** "Lucy, you make me so proud."

◆ **Model and teach children to be concerned about others.** Showing a real interest in your children is the first step. Showing concern and being involved in the welfare of others is the second step. Children copy what we do. If we do not seem to be concerned with individuals in the outside world, nor will they.

◆ **Teach the child to role-play.** Acting out the role of another person is the best way to think and feel about them. Play with soft toys and puppets. This works best if you switch roles as you play. The idea is that she starts with one puppet while you have the other. Halfway through the game, you change over the puppets. She now has to play your role while you play hers.

◆ **Play real-life roles.** Let her play the caring father and you play the selfish child.

◆ **Tape-record her interactions with you.** She may be surprised how she sounds. This works particularly well with older children. After listening, act out the role of dealing with such a selfish individual.

◆ **Tell stories.** Let the child tell a story. Then the parent tells a similar story, emphasising all the caring and unselfish behaviour of the child. After doing this a few times, you tell a story and let the child give the second version.

◆ **Always reinforce any changes the child makes,** however small. "You were really thoughtful today."

◆ **Gold stars** on a chart can mark the really caring responses of the day, and silver ones the unselfish actions.

◆ **Talk about why people do not like selfishness.**

She is so destructive

Why children are destructive:

◆ **Some children are clumsy.** They do not intend to break things.

◆ **Some are over-inquisitive.** They do not think until after they have taken things apart and cannot get them back together again.

◆ **Some children do intend to break things.** Children are rarely deliberately destructive without reason. This is probably a cry for help. If you cannot give that help, you need to call in a professional.

◆ **Sometimes it is just a prank,** or a joke that goes wrong. Older children are particularly prone to pranks, especially when with other children in a gang. A group of children can egg one another on to do things they would not do if they were alone.

◆ **Frustration.** Anger is a natural response to frustration. Sometimes an angry child will be destructive.

◆ **Malice.** Some children damage things deliberately – out of hostility. This is by far the most difficult behaviour to deal with.

What to do if a child is destructive

◆ **Confront the child.** Interrupt her and describe what you see and feel. "Stop. You are breaking your brother's toys. The rule of this house is that we do not break each other's things. I want you to stop." Then remove the child. After a short period out, ask the child how she could make amends. Praise her for doing this. Discuss alternative ways in which she could show her anger and frustration.

◆ **Look for causes.** A child who suddenly starts being wilfully destructive is probably under stress. A child who is often destructive may be seeking attention. A child who destroys a sibling's toys may be jealous. Step outside the situation and look with an open mind. Treat the causes. Teach a tense child how to relax. If she is having a difficult time at school, take off the pressure at home. Stop the extra lessons until she is coping better. Children do not need to

HOW NOT TO TREAT A CARELESS CHILD

✖ *Label her.* *"Lily you are so careless!" "How can you be so stupid?" "Any fool could see it would get knocked over."*

✖ *Make a big production.* *"That juice has ruined the carpet and I do not know where I am supposed to find the money for a new one."* If it is true that the carpet is ruined, why did you allow her to have juice in the room in the first place?

✖ *Say nothing and just clean up after her.* How is the child to learn if her mistakes are never acknowledged? How is she to learn if she never has to take the consequences?

✖ *Never expect her to make amends.* Why be careful if carelessness has no consequences?

✖ *Make threats you do not carry out.* *"That cost a lot of money. I will stop your pocket money until you have paid for it."* If you threaten but do not act, she will learn to ignore you.

✖ *Pretend that it did not matter when it did.* *"It was only an old plate grandma left me."* How is she to learn to be careful with other people's property if you imply that your things have no value?

✖ *Stress her.* Carelessness is often caused by stress. Increasing her stressors is likely to make things worse. *"It's difficult enough, Lucy, without your constant carelessness."*

start dancing or music lessons early in order to succeed. (Some very famous dancers did not begin lessons until they were teenagers.) Give attention before it is demanded by bad behaviour. Show love equally, for no other reason than that the child is there. Do not make comparisons. Ignore bad behaviour and the demands which this makes. Address jealousy by giving individual attention.

◆ **Show children how to release anger.** Let them kick a pillow

HOW TO TREAT A CARELESS CHILD

✔ *Describe the behaviour.* *"I see the cup has been knocked over."*

✔ *Express your feelings.* *"It makes me cross when you leave things where they can so easily be knocked over."*

✔ *State your expectations.* *"I expect you to be careful when you take drinks into your room."*

✔ *Show the child how to make amends.* *"That needs mopping up. Get a cloth from the bathroom. It will need rinsing out when you have finished."*

✔ *Express confidence in her.* *"I know that you can be careful."*

✔ *Give choices* *to those who are persistently careless, to emphasize responsibility. "You can make sure that you put drinks on your bedside table, or you can come downstairs to have your drink: you decide."*

✔ *Carry through.* *"Lily you will have to drink that here."*

✔ *Build self-esteem.* *"Lily you are very special." "Lily I know how hard you try and I'm very proud of you."*

✔ *Talk about prevention.* *Instead of constantly coaxing, reminding and taking responsibility for seeing she is careful, work with her to see what she can do to organize this for herself.*

or shout very loud.

◆ **Reward.** Carefully record how often she is destructive, every day. Reward her with a gold star if she is less destructive than she was the day before. She gets another star for keeping up this level for the next two days. Now she has to be less destructive to gain a star.

They say she is disruptive in school

There is usually a reason why a child is persistently disruptive at school.

◆ **ADHD.** Children who are persistently disruptive at home and school may be hyperactive (see page 154). Hyperactive children find it difficult to focus attention, so the atmosphere of the classroom is very difficult for them. Children with ADHD will show symptoms of hyperactivity and poor attention outside the classroom as well as in it. If you are surprised to be told your child is disruptive, this is almost certainly not the problem.

◆ **Dyslexia.** Children with reading difficulties are often disruptive. Some show all the symptoms of ADHD, except that the problems only start after the reading problems begin. Sympathy and understanding are essential. Professional help with reading may be needed. Children with reading problems do not always want to be reminded of them at home. If this is the only environment in which she does not feel judged, do not disrupt this by trying to help her to read. Ask your school to assess the child, and ask the educational psychologist to recommend a special teacher. (See also dyslexia, pages 220-231.)

◆ **Exceptional ability.** Sometimes children with exceptional ability are disruptive in school because they are bored, or because they have difficulty making friends. This is another situation which may need professional advice. Do not treat an exceptional child as one whose abilities condone her bad behaviour. That she finds school work easy is no excuse for making learning more difficult for other children. Excuses should never be made for anti-social behaviour. Teach your child to pause and take a few deep breaths before she acts.

◆ **Need for friends.** About 10 per cent of all young children do not have a close friend at school. If silliness and bad behaviour bring her the attention and admiration of other children, there is an enormous temptation to disrupt. Talk to her teachers about this. Can you invite friends round? Can she join a club so that she can learn how to make friends? (See also social isolate page 265; no friends page 264.)

◆ **Home problems.** Children who are hurting and/or afraid of loss often behave badly at school. Sometimes the unhappiness leads to withdrawal, sometimes to attention-seeking behaviour. If you feel this may be the cause of her disruptiveness, have a word with her teacher. However much you are hurting yourself, try to find time each day when you can give her some extra special attention. Show her how to express anger by kicking at cushions or drawing angry pictures. Reassure her (and get her father to reassure her) that she is loved and that what is happening is not her fault.

She won't listen

Not listening or doing what is asked of them is a common problem for many children in the early school years. Children switch off because we nag them repeatedly. Remember that, if you always repeat things half a dozen times before you yell at her or expect her to comply, she will wait until the seventh time before she acts. Why not?

Make sure that she has heard

◆ **Always make eye contact with your child.** Sometimes children do not respond because they are engrossed in a game and genuinely do not hear. Touch her to attract her attention before you speak. Young children do seem to have difficulty doing two things - such as listening and doing - at the same time.

◆ **Ask once.** Make it clear that you mean what you say the first time you say it. "Lucy, I expect you to pack up your game now. I am only going to say this once."

◆ **Give warnings.** "Lily, we are going to pick up Jamie in ten minutes. That is when the big hand of the clock is here. Here is your coat. I expect you to have it on by then."

◆ **Check that she understands.** "Lucy, what did I ask you to do?"

Rather than nag

◆ **Set a good example.** If you want her to listen to you, make sure you listen to her.

◆ **Be sure that she can hear.** Get a hearing test if you think there may be problems. Sometimes children have particular problems in certain ranges. Children who have frequent ear infections often do have problems.

◆ **Praise.** Tell her that she is a good listener. Show her how much you appreciate her doing what is asked of her.

◆ **Be consistent.** Don't go back on what you have said. Don't nag.

◆ **Love her to bits.** Sometimes children feel that interaction with parents is unimportant. This is less likely to arise in families in which parents and children mutually respect each other.

◆ **Turn down the noise.** Children sometimes find it hard to hear above the noise of the TV, or to pay attention when watching a TV programme because it is difficult for them to divide their attention between two things. Remember that for the young, noise means 'Go'. A small child who is in a noisy place is likely to carry on doing what he started to do, rather than change to a new task. If you want her to change tack it is wise to turn the volume down.

She always interrupts me

Children are often so full of their own ideas that they cannot wait to get them across. Children of all ages pester and interrupt us when we are on the phone or talking to friends. It is when we are involved in a lengthy conversation which does not include them that interruptions occur most often. All children need to be taught not to interrupt. On the other hand, they don't need to be nagged about this. Nagging disturbs you more than it influences her. If your child cannot wait for five minutes, try pausing after three minutes and asking what she wants. It can work wonders.

HOW TO DISCOURAGE INTERRUPTIONS

✔ *Give her opportunities to be heard.* *Always acknowledge small children who try to talk to you. Tell them that they need to say "Excuse me" before they interrupt.*

✔ *Teach her to wait and listen.* *"Lily, if I put my hand up like this it means I have seen you and will come to you as quickly as I can." Then make sure you do not break your promise. "My daughter needs me. Can I call you back in half an hour."*

✔ *Locate the situations that produce most interruptions.* *Talk about them to the child. Try to find solutions that are fair to both of you.*

✔ *Suggest what she might do rather than interrupt.*

✔ *Be reasonable.* *Keep conversations with adults short. Learn to talk to friends or work with frequent breaks. Children do not always need your full attention. They need attention. Do not have long telephone calls when they are alone with you.*

✔ *Teach.* *Act out scenes where he interrupts you, and you interrupt him.*

✔ *Be a good model.* *If you need to interrupt her, wait then say, "Excuse me Lucy …"*

✔ *Praise effort.* *"You tried very hard. It must have been rather boring listening to all that grown up talk."*

HOW TO ENCOURAGE A CHILD TO INTERRUPT

✖ *Never let her come between you and a friend.* *If interrupting is the only thing that gets your undivided attention, she will interrupt. What else can she do?*

✖ *Say it can't have been important if she has forgotten.* *Children find it hard to think about more than one thing at a time. If she has been concentrating on being cross with you, she will have forgotten what she wanted in the first place, however important it was.*

✖ *Expect her to wait:* *however long you take.*

✖ *Ignore effort.* *If she has waited, she needs praise.*

✖ *Put what you want to do and say above what she wants to do and say at all times.* *With such an example how is she to be anything but self-centred?*

Eight to 13
Milestones: your child at eight

And then they grow up. The innocence of that first school nativity play is by now long gone. It is replaced by an awkward self-consciousness in public. At eight a boy will probably speak his line with a rather bland monotone, as he does on most public occasions, while a girl uses that bright, slightly bossy tone of the early broadcasters. Without the innocence of five-year-olds or the competence of teenagers, the school play can be pretty dire when your child is not speaking.

It is not that he cannot modulate his voice. Away from the stage he produces a constant stream of silly voices: whatever he thinks is needed to play the game. In the back of the car he talks incessantly, but in more formal public settings he will tend to become mute in front of adults, or play the comedian. The humour is crude and repetitive at eight, somewhat more sophisticated by ten. The laughter potential of making a belt into a 'six-foot willy' is lost on most parents; but, since it amuses his friends and his brother, he laughs. An eight-year-old always laughs at his own jokes. Every time he tells them.

There is a serious purpose behind the jokes and silly voices. Until they are about seven, children are not able to understand most jokes. They think saying something rude is naughty, and therefore funny, but since they are not able to hold two views in their mind at any time, or see two meanings, they cannot understand why most jokes are funny. Seeing two sides of the question is an essential skill, required as much for understanding jokes as it is for reasoning. Holding two views at the same time is essential if a child is to understand irony, democracy, strategy or reason. In the years between eight and 12, children are developing and practising these skills. Jokes are one way of doing this. Playing different parts and using different voices is another.

The middle years of childhood are more hidden from parents than those that precede or follow them. In the early years a child is rarely out of the sight or hearing of his carers, and parents take a keen interest in almost everything he does. Parents know what their child likes doing – when they walk into a toy shop they say with confidence, "That is exactly what he would like." Now they are less certain. We do not know him as we did at three. The appeal of computer games, the cartoons he loves or the games he plays are less familiar.

Rudolf Steiner described the middle years as "the heart of childhood", and for most of us they are the years we look back on when we think of being a child. Others have called this the 'angular age' on account of the coltish movements of many children. It is the age of gangs, freedom and the earliest real taste of independence. According to Freud this is also the latency period between the development of early childhood sexuality and the adult sexuality of puberty: an age of knowing innocence.

Eight marks a pre-pubital growth spurt. Children suddenly shoot up, and their shoulders broaden, and for the first time a small difference in size appears between the sexes, the average boy being very slightly taller and broader in the shoulders. There is an improvement in balance and coordination, including hand-eye coordination. This means that the child can climb, skip, race and dodge. By 12 a girl will be able to juggle, or run in and out of a skipping rope. A boy will be a competent footballer and will shoot the ball through the basketball ring with skill.

Eye-hand coordination also improves, and the child begins to write and draw neatly. Gone are the pin men and the wonderful naivety of their drawings, and in its place we find rather neat and formal drawings of people. Children also tend to draw less often, and with less obvious pleasure in their work. This is the time of games of strategy: they begin to enjoy board games and street games.

At this age children hide many things from their parents. It is a time of secret societies, codes and camps. Some of the warmth of the early years has gone. Between fierce cuddles there is often something akin to indifference. A typical conversation may go something like this:

"Where did you go?"
"Out."
"What did you do?"
"Nothing much."
"Who were you with?"
"Oh, friends – you know."
"Was Jamie with you?"
"What can I eat?"

By eight, children's affiliation and loyalty change, and it seems they live only for the moment when they can tear out of the house or off to their room. A child may pester you to get him to school an hour early so he can be with his mates. Where once they were talkative, now they are reticent. Where they were affectionate, they are cool. A suggestion that the chores should come before playing with friends leads to a long session of pleading "But Mum...." on good days, and insolence and rudeness on not such good days.

Above all, these are the playing years, when adults are shadowy figures on the edge of 'real life': the life with his friends. We remember these years with affection. The child has just enough independence to play without supervision, and is still far enough away from adulthood not to have to worry about coming responsibilities. Until they are about seven, children's friendships are rather inconsistent. Best friends today, acquaintances next week. Girls and boys often play together in nursery school, and this pattern is carried over into the first years of school. But by the time they are eight, the sexes are almost entirely segregated in the school playground, although mixed groups of children will sometimes form a gang at home.

Boys are almost always in the majority in such gangs. In the

HOW TO GET YOUR CHILD'S APPROVAL AT THIS AGE

✔ **Keep a respectful but affectionate distance.** *Be there if needed, but don't try to intrude.*
✔ **Allow them their privacy.** *If a child does not want to tell you, he does not have to.*
✔ **Allow them independence:** *the world out there is dangerous, but sooner or later he has to go out into it.*
✔ **Behave like an adult in an Enid Blyton story:** *a shadowy figure who supplies food and drink while children enjoy themselves.*

HOW NOT TO GET YOUR CHILD'S APPROVAL

✖ **Expect to be included.** *He does not want you at table when his friends come to tea.*
✖ **Keep asking him what he has been doing.** *If it's legal and safe, it is his business. If it's not, would he tell you?*
✖ **Draw attention to yourself.** *Parents should be in the background when his friends are around.*
✖ **Speak as if he was not there.** *Tiny children may tolerate this: middle-stage children hate it.*

playground, boys tend to congregate around a leader. That leader is surrounded by an inner circle, and a loose pack of members. At school there will always be one or two unpopular boys who are left out. Being fat makes a child a likely candidate for this treatment.

Girls tend to go around in much smaller gangs and spend much of their time together in twos and threes. Even when they play in bigger groups, there is not usually an obvious leader. Because gangs are smaller, girls are also less likely to be left out, and unpopular girls can often club together.

Getting middle-stage children to talk to you

Where once we were enchanted by their excitement, now we find ourselves irritated by the silly voices and endless monologues on advertisements, TV superheroes or computer games. Had we experienced these things first-hand, we might have found them pretty dull. Regaled in a false accent, they are dire. How can you have a conversation? What can be said about a computer game you have not played, or an advertisement you have discussed 20 times already? Suddenly that enchanting child is becoming a bore. Now children can pick their own topics of conversation they rarely choose to talk about things you want to hear. Their interest is in their mates and how to get to the third level of the computer game. We want to know what they are doing, feeling, achieving. We want to feel needed and wanted. In short, we want to be boring, too.

Middle-stage children do not want to tell their parents everything. Why should they? Now that they can fully understand their separateness, they want to maintain some of the barriers. It is easier to get children to talk if you do not invade their space: so allow them privacy on those things that are important to them, but unimportant to you. Avoid questions like "Who else was at the party?" and don't ask what games they were playing.

If you are just passing the time of day, steer clear of anything very personal. If you need information from them, explain why you want to know. In other words, start talking to children as you would anyone else. You might get more than a monosyllabic answer in a natural voice if you have a conventional daughter. The chances are lower if you have conventional sons. But there are no guarantees. It helps if you ask a question that requires more than a one-word answer.

Remarks that stop conversations dead

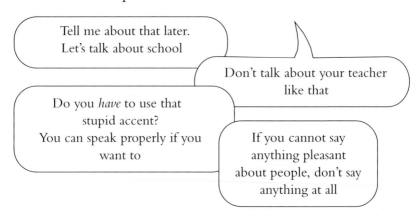

Tell me about that later.
Let's talk about school

Don't talk about your teacher like that

Do you *have* to use that stupid accent?
You can speak properly if you want to

If you cannot say anything pleasant about people, don't say anything at all

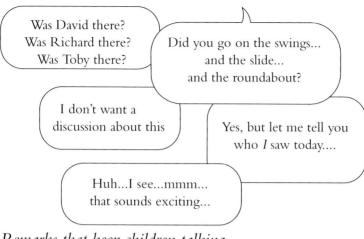

Remarks that keep children talking

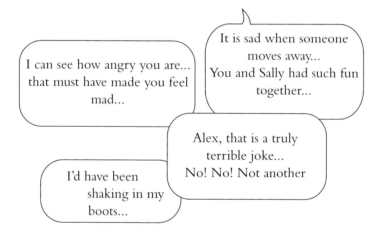

Ways of getting them to talk

◆ **Don't contradict.** Contradiction ends the sentence. If he says his sister is stupid, ask why and he will explain. If you say "Don't call your sister names" he will shut up or defend himself. If he says his teacher is stupid, ask him why he thinks so, don't just tell him he is cheeky. There will be time to defend the teacher after you hear the story.

◆ **Allow him to hold his own opinions.** A child will not be able to stand up and argue the case as well as you can, but equally, he will never learn to do so unless you let him. Shout children down, and they will not try next time.

◆ **Compliment.**

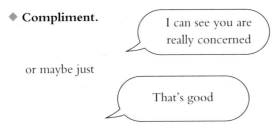

or maybe just

◆ **Acknowledge without interrupting.** Words such as

Mm....
Oh...
I see

...are invitations for the child to continue.

◆ **Draw them out.** Ask questions which need more than a monosyllabic answer, but don't turn it into an inquisition. A conversation should include encouragement, comments and answers too.

◆ **Listen.** Why should a child bother to talk to you if you don't listen? Don't half-listen. Listen properly and make it obvious. Turn off the TV, put down the paper. Turn and look him in the eye. It is much easier to talk to someone who seems interested in what you have to say.

◆ **Don't be so serious.** A sense of humour is essential for good conversation.

◆ **Allow them the best jokes.** Don't cap every story or joke. Don't win every argument.

◆ **Don't lecture. Pause and hand over the conversation.**

◆ **Find the time and the place.** The dinner table is good. In front of the TV when his favourite programme is on is not.

◆ **Share your feelings.** Revealing your feelings encourages him to reveal his.

◆ **Respect his silence.** Don't pry if he is effectively saying "No comment."

Questions which may get more than monosyllabic answers

"Did you hear any good jokes today?"

**"How's your team doing?
Did they win yesterday?"**

"What problems are you doing in maths?"

**"Are you OK? Do you want to talk?
We could make a drink and sit
in the kitchen where it's quiet."**

**"I've had a bad day today.
I'd only give it two out of ten.
How would you rate school today?"**

A question of independence

If nothing else, child rearing has to be about enabling a child to become a separate and competent adult. The only way to do that is to let him do things for themselves. Who wants to be told what to do, feel, and eat? To have every problem solved for them before they have had a chance to try? Parents are constantly saying "Eat your cabbage... Brush your hair... Give me that and I'll undo it..." Such comments will, in time, make a child feel helpless, worthless, incompetent, frustrated and resentful.

There are no hard and fast rules about giving children independence, except that the process should have started by now, and that it should be increasing year on year. Exactly what you allow an individual child to do outside the home will depend, to some extent, on where you live, and on the child himself. Children of this age want to go to the corner shop and to play with their friends. I'm inclined to feel it is their right to do so.

I can think of few situations where a ten-year-old should be confined to the house and garden, except perhaps when they are temporarily grounded for poor behaviour. The print and broadcast media have encouraged us to believe that the world outside the home is much more dangerous than it really is, and that the world inside our own four walls much safer. Most accidents to children occur when they are inside cars, not outside them. And most accidents, attacks, murders, rapes and sexual abuse of young children occur within our own house and garden. The thought that it is more likely that we (or one of our loved ones) will physically or sexually abuse our children than that a strange man in the park will do so is unacceptable. But true. Children are more likely to be injured by a house fire than to be burned by a fire they light in the woods, to fall down stairs than down a tree and to die when inside a car than if hit by one on the street.

◆ **Children only become responsible if you let them.** Ask yourself what new freedoms you have given your child in the last three months. If it is only extending the boundary of their play space from "Down as far as number 58", to "Down as far as number 72", then something is lacking.

◆ **Children need to build responsibility on a firm base.** If you do everything for a child, then suddenly let go because the child has reached a certain age, that child will be lost and unsure. Such a child is in danger.

◆ **People make foolish mistakes when they panic.** A child who is gradually introduced to the world outside the home is less likely to panic.

◆ **Children will sometimes prefer to face danger than an angry parent.** Ensure that your child knows that whatever he has done, if he is in real danger you will rescue him without being angry.

◆ **Judge each request for more independence on its merit.** Is it reasonable? Are other children of his age doing this? Can I trust him? Have I allowed him to be trustworthy? Could we move towards this sort of independence by the end of the summer?

◆ **Start trusting.** It is hard to let go, but it must happen sometime, and you may as well have some control of the process rather than none at all – which is what may well happen if you leave this too late.

◆ **Don't expect independence to move at the same pace in all areas.** He may be able to put his washing in the machine before he can make tea: or vice versa. He may be able to go to school by himself before he can go to the corner shop for you. It will depend on where you live.

HOW TO LET GO GRACEFULLY

✔ *Give them pocket money. At first the money should include no more than the cost of a few sweets and maybe a comic. Once they are managing this, the money should include an element of saving towards a bigger item. By the time they are ten, they should be able to manage a simple budget. This is much better than handing over money every time they ask for it. If a child spends all his pocket money in one week and than cannot go to the cinema, he will learn this lesson – but he won't if you pay up.*

✔ *Give them domestic chores. Independence demands responsibility.*

✔ *Let them make some of their own decisions. Tell them what has to be done: not the order in which it has to be done. Tell them they have to be in bed by 9 pm. Not that they have to go to bed this minute.*

✔ *Show respect. It is often hard. Respect their efforts, don't ask too many questions, or rush in with answers.*

✔ *Be available. If they cannot ask advice from you, who can they ask?*

✔ *Show an interest in what they do, but do not expect to be told everything.*

✔ *Encourage them to do things outside the home.*

✔ *Don't take hope away. Whatever they are doing, if they make an effort, give them hope that they will succeed. Praise the little steps in between, even if progress is painfully slow.*

HOW TO HANG ON DESPERATELY

✖ *Interfere first, think second. Never ask if it is really necessary.*

✖ *Think of him as an extension of you.*

✖ *Choose his friends. Dictate who he is allowed to bring home.*

✖ *Resent him talking to his friends. Friends should be providing emotional support.*

✖ *Have fixed rules. If you find yourself completely out of step with other parents, you need to start letting go.*

✖ *Play groupie. Your child should not be everything to you.*

✖ *Play hurt parent.*

◆ **Listen.** If you are constantly arguing about what he is or is not allowed to do, you are probably too slow at letting go.

Peer pressure

Children want to be like their friends, but it is not just peer pressure that makes them join a gang. We are all more careless and carefree in a group. Being with others makes us feel more relaxed. We do not watch our backs in the same way we do when alone. Children can get into trouble because skateboarding down the middle of the road feels safe when everyone else is doing it. Peers have other influences, especially young male peers. The loose gang structure of young boys' friendships at this age cries out for chance taking.

Most gangs have a leader: a good all-rounder. Next in line come the henchmen, often valued for specific skills. Then there is the ever-changing rabble. It is the henchmen and rabble who are most under pressure from peers. A boy valued for his climbing skill may get the kite out of the tree even though he knows it is dangerous. A boy valued for his ability to nick a sweet from the 'pick and mix' at the corner shop may then start to take chocolate bars or videos in order to impress even more.

Helping children avoid peer pressure

◆ **Make him feel secure.** A child who feels loved has less need to be loved by others.

◆ **Make them feel self-confident.** A child who knows "I can", does not need to challenge himself to feel good.

◆ **Give them encouragement.** A child with high self-esteem is more likely to feel he will be accepted for himself. He will be less reliant on showing others what he can do.

◆ **Help him to make decisions.** A child who has a history of deciding things for himself is more likely to find a way of escaping from a situation which is getting out of control.

◆ **Tell him how to detach himself.** Suggest ways he can escape from gang activities without losing face. He can pretend to be ill, say he has to find a loo, pretend he has diarrhoea.

◆ **Have a code.** Work out a code which your child can use to escape from other children's houses if things get difficult. For instance, he could ring you and ask: "Has Aunt Jill has arrived yet?" This gives the parent the opportunity of ringing back later to say yes; or of coming round to collect him immediately.

Spending too much time with friends

By the time they reach seven or eight, children would sometimes rather be with their friends than with their family. From now on, year on year, they will want to spend more and more time doing things with their peer group, and less and less time doing family-oriented activities. At eight he may still be happy to come out on a family walk (just); by nine he will ask to bring a friend. By ten he will suggest he could stay at home. Friends are important. Because families tend to make allowances for children, it is through their friends that children learn to get on with other people. Without friends, a child is unlikely to learn how to be flexible in social situations or how to hold his ground in a dispute.

Friends share a child's obsessions, serve their needs, understand their jokes. They are part of the secret, private world of childhood in a way that parents can never be. None of which alters the irritation you will often feel about your children's friends and friendships.

As you give more and more freedom to choose where they play and who they are with, they will spend more and more time out of sight and earshot with their friends. It may seem like the beginning of the end. It is not – it's just another phase.

How not to get upset when he starts spending all his time with his friends

◆ **Don't take it personally.** This is not a rejection, just a natural and healthy step into the wider world. The family is still important, still the secure base; but it is no longer the be-all and end-all of his existence.

◆ **Make use of your freedom.** Now you can read, cook, do the garden, have your friends round.

◆ **Don't be a groupie.** It is sad when parents have so little going for them that they need to live through their children. Your child will love and respect you more if you depend on him less.

◆ **If it hurts, don't show it.** The time to worry is when children do not have close friends. It is more worrying when he always spends his time productively and prefers the company of adults, than when he fritters his time away laughing and joking with his friends.

◆ **Let your home be the base.** It may be noisy but you will know who your child is with, and where he is going.

◆ **Don't let them lose face.** Never criticize or embarrass them in front of friends.

Falling out with friends

All children sometimes fall out with their friends and find themselves temporarily without anyone to play with and therefore unhappy and with nothing to do. If this happens at school they can find themselves sitting on the sidelines watching everyone having a good time. Even at home they may sit in the window watching soulfully as the gang plays outside the house. The cruelty is intentional. He would do the same if someone else was 'out' and he was in.

It will not last long. The gang says that they will never play with him again, and although they have said this before and not meant it, he clearly believes them. Be sympathetic. It does matter. It is the end of the world. But don't interfere. Asking his friends why, or their parents to intervene, makes him lose face.

Find something for him to do. An outing to the cinema or swimming pool; a visit to cousins or friends across town.

If he has always had friends he will make it up with them sooner rather than later.

Don't like his friends

Just because you like someone it does not mean that you will like all their friends. Not all of our friends necessarily get along with each other. The same will go for your children's friends: some are a delight, others we do not like. Sometimes we feel they are a bad influence.

◆ **Encourage your child to bring friends home.** You will, at least, know the worst. Make them welcome even if you do not like them very much. If the friendship is unsuitable, he is more likely to break it off if you do not nag.

◆ **Trust.** If you have no worries about your child, it is most unlikely he will be led astray by bad company.

◆ **Remember:** almost all delinquent children have delinquent friends, and if a child is not a delinquent, he is very unlikely to have a delinquent friend.

◆ **Help them to stick to limits.** "My mum won't let me... my mum's so mean" are useful excuses when needing to escape from the rule of the gang.

◆ **Encourage interests which will help them meet different friends.** If a child becomes too reliant on a fast-living gang, help him make new friends by going to judo, swimming, dancing, horse riding, or computer groups.

◆ **Give it time.** Sometimes simply standing back and allowing an unsuitable friendship to pass its sell-by date is all that is needed to kill it. Kids come and go from most gangs.

◆ **Get tough.** Know the signs of drug involvement. Check with the school if you think he is playing truant. Believe friends who tell you that they have seen him hanging around in the wrong places. This is not a situation which you can let run its course. If you think the child's present gang are involved in drugs, stealing or playing truant, separate him from them. Ground him, deliver and collect him from school, whatever it takes. He may even be grateful.

Why children choose bad friends

At eleven, one reason may be to shock parents and question values. How can a child be sure that your values are right if you never test them? Other reasons:

◆ **To find out about being grown-up.** A child who finds it

WHAT CHILDREN LIKE ABOUT FRIENDS

I have spent much time asking children of this age what they like (and don't like - see below) about other children. Here is the consensus:

✔ *That they are usually smiling and happy.*
✔ *That they are kind and sympathetic.*
✔ *That they listen.*
✔ *That they share.*
✔ *That they are helpful.*
✔ *That they are fun.*
✔ *That they are confident and good at organizing games and activities.*
✔ *That they have a sense of humour and can shrug off setbacks.*
✔ *That they stick up for other children.*
✔ *That they have good social skills, are not critical and compliment others.*
✔ *That they can sort out conflicts.*

hard to get along with other children sometimes pals up with a younger child. Children on the verge of puberty are particularly vulnerable. Unsure where they are going, the sudden appearance of an older guide seems wonderful.

◆ **To act grown-up.** On the verge of adolescence, smoking, drinking and sniffing glue are ways some children taste the more adult world ahead of them. No longer a small child, not yet a teenager, some of the problems of adolescence can arrive very early in some communities. Most individuals try alcohol and cigarettes during their teens, about half of them try illegal substances. A few do so before they reach their teens. Be especially alert for these problems if your child is skipping school.

◆ **To meet an individual need.** Some children need to take people under their wing, just as some adults do. Maybe having a friend who is less adequate than they are makes them feel more secure. Sometimes a loner gains strength by joining a gang of bullies.

◆ **To maintain their excitement level.** On the cusp of adolescence the need for excitement begins to rise. Children choose dangerous friends in order to keep their arousal up.

◆ **To attract attention.** Sometimes an unsuitable friendship is like a cry for help. A child wants to demonstrate to parents who are engrossed in their own worries that they have problems too. He is asking them to demonstrate that they still care.

◆ **To be accepted.** At ten or 12, children will do almost anything to be accepted into the group. At the beginning of puberty, children need friends who understand what is happening to them in a way only children of their own age can understand.

Lack of friends

Some people seem to have a natural ability to attract other people and make friends. Others always seem to be on the outskirts. As life centres more and more around friendships, a child without friends becomes more and more isolated.

WHAT CHILDREN DON'T LIKE ABOUT OTHER CHILDREN

✖ *That they are bossy.*
✖ *That they are sometimes nice, sometimes nasty.*
✖ *That their moods are unpredictable.*
✖ *That they are spiteful.*
✖ *That they are moody and bear grudges.*
✖ *That they are mean.*
✖ *That they always talk about themselves and never listen.*

◆ **What is the problem?** Does your child know how to begin to make friends? Does he rely on other people to make the effort? Is he being deliberately excluded at someone else's behest? Does he irritate other children? Does he fail to listen when they talk? Is it because he is not allowed to play out? Is he aggressive or does he pick on others? If you know the problem, you can begin to find the solution. Talk to the child and to his teacher.

◆ **Let the child decide what sort of friend would suit him.** Select such a person and both make an effort to make that person a friend. Invite him over.

◆ **Talk to the school and enlist their help.** Most friendships are formed in school. If some children are excluded, it can help if the teacher sits them together. It can also help if the children move around so that they are not always sitting with the same children.

◆ **Talk to the playground supervisor.** Sometimes he or she can help to ease the path for a child trying to enter a group.

Things to tell a child with few friends

◆ **"Start liking yourself more."**

◆ **"Don't put yourself down."** Saying critical things about yourself is habit-forming. They start to sound like the truth. A child should never say things to himself he would not say to a friend.

◆ **"Praise yourself for your efforts,** not just when you succeed." It helps if parents praise too.

◆ **"Don't compare.** Pay attention to your own strengths and weaknesses. There is always someone who is prettier, stronger, cleverer. Forget them. It is too depressing. If you catch yourself thinking like this, say 'He is better at maths than me, but I am....' Keep the plus register higher than the minus."

◆ **"Try not to be shy."**

◆ **"Start conversations by saying something about yourself.** 'I just don't understand this maths problem.'"

◆ **"Fall back on a standard conversation opener.** 'Just look at that rain.'"

◆ **"Compliment the person you want to talk to.** 'I really like that dress. Is it new?'"

◆ **"Ask for help.** 'Any idea where these are supposed to go?'"

◆ **"Follow up conversation openers by asking questions** and getting people to talk about themselves. React to what people tell you."

◆ **"Listen** if you find it hard to talk." See also pages 264-268.

Bitchiness

There is nothing like children in their middle years for reinforcing sexual stereotypes. While boys of this age brag, boast and fight, girls are more likely to be unkind, bitchy and manipulative. The classic view of a bully is a boy who beats up other children. In recent years it has been accepted that girls are just as likely to be bullies. Girls' name-calling, belittling, and mental cruelty are just as harmful as boys' physical violence. Maybe more so.

◆ **Nine- and ten-year-old girls can be very unkind to each other.** It may only be a phase, but a year is a long time for those who are the butt of other girls' unpleasantness. Of course, you have to talk to the school.

◆ **Check the facts.** A certain amount of give and take is normal at this age. Children do fall out, make up and fall out again. Making a fuss every time there is a squabble will not help your child. Keep a sense of proportion.

◆ **Being left out hurts.** Girls tend to go around in smaller groups than boys, and in time many of those who are excluded find other friends. They do not always manage this straight away. Be supportive and sympathetic. Build up your child's self-esteem. Make her feel important.

◆ **Bitchiness is a form of bullying.** Inform the school if your child is called names, or victimized by other girls. (See also pages 256-262 for more on bullying.)

Teaching children values

Children sometimes behave badly because they crave attention, or because they are angry, frustrated or stressed. Mostly they behave badly because the people who interact with them show them bad behaviour works better than good. There is now a mountain of evidence which shows that if parents behave aggressively towards children, those children tend to be behave aggressively towards others. If parents are considerate and kind, their children often behave in this way too. At this stage in their development, children are looking to see how the world works, and trying out the modes of behaviour they see around them.

If we do not respect our children, and help them abide by the limits we set for them, we leave them floundering. If we do not let them take the consequences of their actions, they will not respect us or what we tell them. It is always easier to leave the toys on the floor and the bike out in the rain. If the only consequence of doing this is that you moan and nag, why should they bother to do anything else? Why should a child respect you if you always threaten and never act?

Children grow up to be reasonable and well-rounded individuals if they take responsibility for their own and other people's possessions. They take responsibility if we expect and insist that they are responsible. Of course there will be times when it seems as if all the good parenting work we have put in over the years is for nothing, but if the child has a fundamental respect for himself and others, he will eventually come through such patches.

◆ **Teach your child to respect you.** Insist that he considers your needs as well as his own. Respect yourself and act as if respect is your due. Don't threaten and nag. Act. If children expect action, they will start listening to what you say.

◆ **Teach children that they must accept the consequences of their own actions.** Discuss with them how people feel when their goods are stolen or their belongings are broken. Discuss the consequences of not letting people know where you are, or what you are doing. If they break a rule, steal, lose their coat or dinner money they should pay something towards the lost or broken goods and return stolen goods to their owners.

◆ **It would be foolish to suppose that honesty is still always the best policy.** But that is no excuse for not instilling the value of honesty into children. Talk about why it is wrong to tell lies, cheat or steal and who gets hurt.

◆ **Explain and discuss your values.** If you disapprove of something, say why. If you approve, explain that too. Encourage children to express their opinions. Accept that they can be different from yours.

◆ **TV, books and plays are great teachers of values.** Select videos, books and TV programmes which reinforce your values. If a programme or book gives a different view, discuss this with the child. A child who learns to question is less likely to be led astray. He is also more likely to live by his principles.

How to encourage respect from children

◆ **Say what you mean.** Ask for what you want. Say how it is to be.

◆ **Insist persistently.** Say it again. Don't be critical, just be firm.

◆ **Trust.** Assume and trust children to do as you have asked, and as you expect.

◆ **Explain the consequences.** If they do not do as you ask, they must accept the consequences. If the washing is not in the basket, it does not get done. If they do not come straight home from school, they cannot play out.

◆ **Act.** If they do not take responsibility, they cannot have the privileges of independence.

◆ **Go on limited strike.** If they treat you like a servant, assert your rights.

Dealing with common problems in the middle childhood years

As children become more and more engrossed in their own world, they present parents with new problems. Almost all of them are concerned with the child's claims to independence and the need for parents to renegotiate their role.

The fact that children now know for certain that we do not know what they are thinking, and cannot see them when they are out of our sight, makes it ever more easy to deceive us. Their memory span improves, and by the time they are eight they have the capacity to hold two views in mind and make comparisons, which of course fuels any tendency to dispute our view or that of their siblings and friends. Children of this age can be argumentative and petty just because they can now hold on to their view while listening to yours. In younger years it was 'No!' followed by a tantrum. Now it is more likely to be 'But mum.....' followed by defiance. If they have younger siblings who as yet lack their negotiating skills, they may well play dictator.

Unless parents begin to respect the child's need for independence there will inevitably be problems at this stage. If the parents get it right, it can be a comparatively easy phase. The underlying message of these years must be mutual respect for each other and a growing sense of responsibility on the child's part.

It is not difficult to instil if you go about it in the right way. But unless you respect your child and expect him to be responsible, he will not develop the self-respect and self-control which enable him to negotiate his growing independence.

PROBLEM OWNERSHIP

Does your child fail to treat you with the respect you deserve? Sometimes this is a problem that affects your child more than it affects you; sometimes it is the other way round. Once a child reaches eight, you need to look at his problems carefully and to decide who owns the problem.

Then you should try to apply this simple rule: deal with your problems, and with those aspects of the child's problems that affect you; and, increasingly, leave the child's problems for him to sort out for himself.

Problem: not coming straight home from school

Whose problem? Yours - the parent. You are the one who is worried and upset. The child is out having fun.

Underlying message: independence entails responsibility.

What to do: Explain to the child why he needs to come straight home from school. Discuss any reasons for being late, and make allowances. Some schools allow children to use the sports facilities after school. Discuss with him which days he can stay behind, and what time he needs to be home by on these days.

◆ **Give him a chart.** Let him fill in the times of football practice or any other reason for being late. Set a time by which he should report back each day.

◆ **Give him a watch with a bleeper.** Set the bleeper for ten minutes before the last possible time for setting off home. If he cannot make it on time, he must phone home. Agree with all his friends' parents that he must either come home directly or ring you if he stops at a friend's house on the way home.

◆ **Agree on the consequences** of being late. Abide by them.

Problem: won't say where he is going

Whose problem? As for not coming straight home from school, this is your problem because it makes you worry.

Underlying message: independence entails responsibility.

What to do: As above.

- ◆ **Remind him of the rules before he goes out to play.**

- ◆ **Trust him.**

- ◆ **Give choices.** "You can go to the park to play and come home at the agreed time; or you can play in the house and garden. It is your choice."

- ◆ **Buy him a watch with a bleeper** to remind him when to call home.

- ◆ **Buy him a phonecard,** and teach him how to use a payphone. Tell him that in emergencies he can reverse the call charges. Insist that he reports home at regular intervals.

- ◆ **Agree on the consequences** of being late. Abide by them. Ground him if he does not play by the rules.

Problem: missing meals

Whose problem? The parents'. It is they who slaved over the hot stove while the child was having fun.

Underlying message to instil: the child has to learn to respect the parent who works to service his needs.

What to do: Explain to the child that it is family policy to serve meals at certain times. Make it clear that meals do not wait for anyone who has not called home to explain their delay. If he arrives late he has the option of eating his food cold or having a bowl of cereal. If the choice of alternative food is too wide or too interesting, he may simply choose this option.

◆ Make sure that his bleeper is set so he has 15 minutes to get home for his meal.

◆ **Serve meals at specific times, and keep to them.**

◆ **Remind the child of the agreement.**

◆ **Be flexible on occasions when he has special activities.**

◆ **Do not pander to persistent offenders.** Ground them: don't let them go out.

◆ **Agree on the consequences.** If he is more than an hour late he will be grounded for two days.

Problem: the child who always answers back

Whose problem? Part, if not all, of it belongs to the parent. It is you who suffers the insolence. However, some of the problem may also belong to the child. If you don't allow him any freedom of action, or to have his say, or if you do not listen to him, he may see such rudeness as his only course of action.

Underlying message to instil: even if provoked, the child has to learn to respect others. There are ways to make demands, and ways not to make them.

What to do: All children are sometimes cheeky and rude – how else would he forge his independence? This does not mean that you have to enjoy, understand or condone rudeness.

When faced with aggression from your children, the simplest rule is to act rather than react. Show children how to practise emotional control and to develop ways of communicating their needs in a less aggressive manner. Tell your child you didn't hear his first remarks and that he should come back later and try a different approach.

Questions to ask yourself if your child is constantly angry and disrespectful

◆ Is he is under stress?

◆ Am I being too restrictive?

◆ Am I setting the wrong example? If you constantly shout, threaten, scold and punish, he will not learn how to ask, only how to demand.

How to respond before a child answers back

◆ **Listen with full attention,** and acknowledge his feelings with one word – "Mmm..."

◆ **Voice his feelings.** "You are upset because..." "You feel that..."

◆ **Don't constantly question, blame or advise.** It is hard for a child to listen to you and to think through his problems at the same time.

◆ **Invite the child to explore his own thoughts and feelings.** Don't suggest that he turns away from bad feelings. By encouraging the child to talk about emotional pain, you make rude outbursts less necessary. By showing you understand, you make it easier for him to cope.

◆ **Don't always be logical.** There is nothing more irritating than being constantly told what you know has to be true. Give the child what she wants in fantasy if you cannot give it in fact. "I wish I could win the lottery. Then we could have a season ticket to all the matches."

How to respond to answering back

◆ **State what you require.** "I expect you to treat me with respect. I am not rude to you and I expect you to be polite to me."

◆ **Insist – and persist.** "I expect to be treated with respect. I will not discuss this while you are being rude to me."

◆ **Explain the consequences.** "I have asked you to speak to me with more respect and consideration. You have ignored me. Please go to your room. Come down when you have cooled off and are able to behave in a more civilized manner."

◆ **If the behaviour persists.** "You rely on me to cook, wash and care for you. If you cannot show me some respect, I do not see why I should continue to do these things for you. If I do not see an improvement in your behaviour over the next two days I will stop making meals for you. Every time you answer back, I will withdraw one meal."

◆ **Act.** If he is rude, let him make himself a peanut butter sandwich, while you sit down to his favourite meal. Be firm. Once he understands that you mean what you say, he will start to take notice.

Problem: disagreeing about clothes for school

Whose problem? Both the parents' and child's. The parents have to pay and may not be able to afford the clothes the child wants. The child may need to wear the right things if he is to be one of the gang.

Underlying message to instil: the child has to learn the value of money and the need to compromise. The parents have to learn that from now on how the child looks is increasingly the child's responsibility. These are just the first forays into a long battle.

What to do: Understand. At eight, he wants to look exactly like his friends. "I understand that you want to wear the same clothes as your friends."

♦ **Explain if this is not possible.** "Mark, I cannot afford to buy the football strip for you."

♦ **Give a choice.** "Mark, I can buy one strip and that means you cannot wear it every day. If I buy it for you, will you promise me not to argue about wearing it when it is dirty?"

♦ **Ask the child for solutions.** "You want to wear your football strip every day. It gets dirty. I cannot wash and dry it every night. What do you think we could do?"

♦ **Suggest solutions.** "We could use some of your birthday money to buy another strip, but you could only have a very small birthday present if we did that. I could teach you how to wash the strip. You could wear it every day if you washed it."

♦ **Make advance agreements.** "Florence, if I choose what you wear for school, you can choose clothes to wear at other times."

Problem: pets

Every parent who has ever bought a pet for a child finds that after the initial days of devoted care, interest wanes and the pet becomes yet another parental responsibility.

Whose problem? Part of it belongs to the parent. You have given in to the child's request, even though in your heart of hearts you knew that the child was not old enough to take on the responsibility. Part of it belongs to the child. He has to learn that a responsibility for another living thing has to be taken seriously.

Underlying message to instil: the child's desire for a pet outweighs his understanding of the responsibility - but he is not alone. Most new parents are much the same.

What to do:

◆ **Don't be naive.** What children say *before* they have a pet does not have much value *after* they've had their way. All parents have to remind children to care for their pets, or do it themselves, to some extent. Accept this, or do without the pet. Eight-year-olds are not responsible.

◆ **Make it clear why the hamster must be cleaned out.** "Hamsters in cages cannot keep their own beds clean. When an animal depends on you, it is unfair to let it down. I expect you to take care of your pet. I am sure that you will not let Harry Hamster suffer any longer."

◆ **Remind them.** Point to the dirty cage. Leave a note about it. 'Please clean me.' Make a simple statement: "The hamster needs cleaning."

◆ **Let them work out a solution.** Ask them to decide when the hamster is to be cleaned, describe what will happen if it is not cleaned.

◆ **If they still do not do it,** tell them that you are angry. "I am annoyed and disappointed." "Jamie, you agreed to look after your hamster. I am upset to find the cage is still dirty."

◆ **Offer a choice.** "The hamster must be cleaned out now. Jamie, I can cook dinner while you clean the hamster, or I can clean out the hamster. It is your choice."

◆ **If that has no effect.** "The hamster must be cleaned by Sunday lunchtime every week. After that there will be no TV until the cage is cleaned."

◆ **If the hamster is still not being cared for,** cut your losses. Take care of it yourself. Offer it to the school, or advertise it "Free with cage". Agree to no more pets.

Problem: not looking after his possessions
Whose problem is it? It belongs to the child.

Underlying message to instil: the child has to learn that he must take responsibility for his possessions.

What to do: It is extremely irritating when your child's carelessness leads to broken toys and lost possessions. When he leaves a brand new coat in the park, or his bike is stolen because he forgot to lock it up, you are understandably angry. If we always gave in to our feelings, the nagging, scolding and lecturing would be unending. It is difficult in a world of plenty to teach a child that caring for things matters.

  ◆ **A sense of order gives a sense of value.** If possessions are allowed to be left scattered all over the floor, he'll never feel that they deserve care. Also, give toys in an orderly way: one toy is precious. A hundred toys are not.

  ◆ **One at a time.** Possessions have added value if they are not always available. When you run out of space to put regularly used toys away, consider finding a new home for the ones he does not use.

  ◆ **Make the rules together.** "I expect you to put your new bike away under cover every night. When I see it left out at the end of the day, I will tell you once to put it away. If you do not put it away, I will confiscate it for two days." Act on what you say. Get a padlock and lock up the bike next time he fails to put it away after the first warning.

  ◆ **Do not keep blaming.** Concentrate on finding solutions. If he forgets to bring his coat home, don't nag him – having said your bit, find him another coat for the next day. Work through the possibilities. He should look for the coat. Ask the teacher whether it has been handed in. If it is lost, he may have to make do with a second-hand coat, or wear his old coat. If you have to buy a new coat, insist that he pays for part of it out of his savings, or has it for Christmas or his birthday.

◆ **If something is lost or broken, do not always replace it.** Help the child to decide what contribution he should make. Teach him that there are natural and logical consequences to his actions.

◆ **Praise him when he takes care of possessions.** "You have had that bike for two years and it looks almost as good as new."

Problem: complaining neighbours

Whose problem is it? It's your problem, since you have to deal with the neighbours. But: the child has to learn to respect others and take responsibility for his actions.

Pranks are part of the middle-stage years: sitting or walking on someone else's garden wall, ringing doorbells and running away, making joke telephone calls, breaking the windows in someone's shed; it's a familiar list for most parents. Most reasonable people accept a few pranks from the neighbouring children; but not everyone is reasonable.

Most people rightly get thoroughly fed up of being the constant target of local mischief, and/or of having a constant stream of boys asking for their football back.

HOW NOT TO DEAL WITH NEIGHBOURS COMPLAINING ABOUT YOUR CHILDREN

✖ *Accept the neighbours' word without question.* There may be another side. Wait until you have heard it before making any concessions. Do not make promises on behalf of your children before checking the facts.

✖ *Assume that the child is lying.* Children do make excuses and certainly bend the truth when they are afraid, but even a child who often behaves in this way may be telling the truth this time.

✖ *Assume the neighbour is lying.* He may be exaggerating, but it is much more likely that he is not.

✖ *Humiliate the child.* He will feel resentful and possibly vindictive.

✖ *Assume he has been led astray* and blame his 'so-called friends'. If a child does wrong, he is responsible. There may be mitigating circumstances, but that does not mean he is blameless.

HOW TO DEAL WITH A NEIGHBOUR COMPLAINING ABOUT YOUR CHILDREN

✔ *Keep calm.* *You cannot respond to accusations about your children if you are upset. Take a deep breath and play for time. "I am sorry to hear the children have annoyed you. Can you just wait while I turn off the stove?" Walk away and calm down. Then go back and say "Tell me exactly what happened." If you think it will take longer to calm down, say you are on the point of making an urgent phone call and that you will get back to them in ten minutes.*

✔ *Get your neighbour's side of the story.* *Be apologetic but neutral. Tell him you will talk to the child at once and then get back to him.*

✔ *Get your child's side of the story.* *Don't assume that he is in the wrong. If the football was confiscated the first time it went into a garden it sounds as if the neighbour, not the child, was being unreasonable.*

✔ *Get other opinions.* *If more than one child was involved and a serious accusation is being made against your child, talk to the other parents. What do their children say?*

✔ *Reflect.*

✔ *Act decisively.* *You must talk to your neighbour. The child should apologize, and you may feel like apologizing again too. If damage has been done, it should be paid for and the child should do extra chores in order to contribute to the cost.*

✔ *Trust* *your child not to do it again and tell him so.*

✔ *Criticize the behaviour, not the child.* *The message should be: "I don't like what you have done, but I still love you."*

✔ *Do not agree when others criticize your child.* *Calmly agree that the behaviour was bad, and then say something positive about the child too. Then make your exit. If they persist, say "I know my son. What he did was wrong; I will ensure that he apologizes and that he pays for the damage. I agree his behaviour was bad, but he is not a bad child." Again, don't allow further discussion; leave the scene.*

✔ *Make sure that your child understands what will happen if he behaves like this again.*

When he really screws up

Give children a little freedom and they can get into plenty of extra trouble. It's easier to play truant when you go to school alone, or to shoplift when you go to shops alone. You may be lucky enough to avoid the mega-crisis, but it is a rare parent who never has to face at least one major crisis.

Caught stealing

Stealing is so common among six to ten-year olds that some teachers check pockets routinely at the end of each day. Sometimes children are tempted by the goods. More often they steal just for the thrill of trying not to get caught.

◆ **Don't invite lies.** If you know he had no money, he could not have paid for the sweets. So don't ask him how he got them.

◆ **Tell him what has to be done.** "Tom, sweets have to be paid for. You must come back to the shop and pay for them now." Make it clear that he must take responsibility. "Luke, we have to take that back to Sam now. Do you want me to come with you, or will you go by yourself?"

◆ **Don't embarrass him.** Give him the opportunity to talk and to say he is sorry. Accept that this is difficult and don't force him, or make a big scene. Go with the child to the shop. Wait until it is quiet. Call the shop assistant over and say: "We would like to pay for this... Tom took it today. We are very sorry. It will not happen again."

◆ **Try to determine what is causing him to steal.** Stealing is very common attention-seeking behaviour, and a common response to stress. Have a talk about his worries.

◆ **Give him time.** If he is crying for help, you need to give him your time.

If he is guilty of a crime:
◆ **Accept that he is guilty.**

◆ **Don't withdraw love, but make sure he understands you hate his behaviour.**

HOW TO MOTIVATE A WINNER

Parents tend to believe that these years lay the groundwork for life. This, they think, is when future academics begin to shine at school; when dancers start to stand out from the crowd; when musicians show their inherent musicality.

In fact, most great dancers and musicians were not child prodigies. Some of the most outstanding male ballet dancers did not start to dance until they were teenagers. Future academics are not usually spotted at this stage either. Something of that future skill may be evident: intelligence, delight in movement, athleticism, tunefulness. The perseverance and hard work needed to reach the top may still be sorely lacking. In many cases this is no bad thing: a single-minded child may be ideal for the groupie-parent, but sane parents want their children to lead fulfilled and happy lives – no more, no less.

✔ **Share your interests and skills.** *A child who grows up knowing that music, reading or science gives pleasure is more likely to pursue these goals than one who has not seen what pleasure they can give.*

✔ **Give time.** *A child who has sat and talked with a grown-up finds it easier to ask an adult for help.*

✔ **Pile on the praise.** *Praise effort, not just success. Build self-esteem. Without this, he cannot have confidence.*

✔ **Make learning fun.** *If it is fun, a child will be motivated to learn more, independently of parents and teachers.*

✔ **Point out his strengths.** *"How did you manage that? I'd never of thought of doing it like that. That's terrific."*

✔ **Encourage a variety of interests, outings and activities: reading, theatre, cinema, TV, computers.** *The more, the better. A child needs to know that there is more than one way to learn.*

✔ **Encourage questions,** *and answer them as fully as you can. If you don't know the answer, say so. Then suggest how you can both find out.*

HOW TO MAKE HIM A LOOSER

✖ *Leave teaching to the school.*
At school he is one of 20 to 30.
At home he is one in two to three.

✖ *Never sit down and talk.*
You can throw money at learning,
but unless you give children time
and encouragement, finding the
pleasures of success will be a matter
of chance.

✖ *Pile on the pressure.*
Compare him unfavourably with
others.

✖ *Criticize him and expect*
him to cope with
disappointment without any
practice or support. Tell him to
try harder next time.

✖ *Undermine his abilities.*
Make fun of failed efforts. Say it
could be better if only he had…

✖ *Discourage him from asking*
questions. Suggest he accepts
what you say.

✖ *Suggest that his interests are*
a waste of time or money.

✖ *Place no value on the things*
he likes or loves.

✖ *Never question anything that*
keeps him quiet.

Daydreaming

Once children reach double figures, daydreaming is common. The most obvious reason for this is that it is now possible. Until they are about ten, children act things through rather than thinking them through. It is the development of abstract reasoning that makes daydreaming possible. This does not mean that they are daydreaming about anything very serious. They daydream because they can generate and explore ideas, look at alternatives, make deductions and generally ponder things in an abstract way that was impossible a year or two earlier. At every stage in their development, children practise the skills they have recently mastered. This includes staring into space, just as much as it earlier applied to jumping off the sofa again and again.

In the early stages of daydreaming your child may not even be thinking things through in a logical way, or following a single train of thought. At first, daydreams are disjointed and vague: escapes into romance, vengeance, heroics or the reworking of recent quarrels. Practice, however, makes perfect.

Daydreaming means children can play things through in their minds without having to do anything. It enables them to plan ahead, and is an escape.

It only becomes problematic if it starts to replace living; if a child spends most of his time in daydreams, it is worth asking why.

Success at school

There is not, and probably never will be, full employment. This naturally puts pressures on children to do well at school. You want your child to be among the percentage of school leavers that get jobs. So does he. Surveys invariably show that children do not want to spend the rest of their life doing nothing.

In the past, wanting children to do well meant parents concerning themselves with the last stages of a child's education. As the pressures to succeed have increased, parents have become concerned about success in younger and younger children. 'Hothousing' tiny children has become a problem. In some cases, baby burn-out is a problem.

For most children, however, the pressure does not begin to tell until they reach about nine or ten, when secondary school is in sight. Pressure is applied by both parents and school; and, don't forget, by the children themselves.

There are those who compete and win – but not always without cost. Sometimes they are ostracized by their peers. Sometimes they have been encouraged by parents not to waste time with other children. Social isolation rarely makes people happy or well rounded. They may succeed academically, but this does not mean that their lives will be happy or fulfilled. A healthy bank balance is not everything.

There are those who are single-minded – who make an enormous effort and win, but do so at the expense of their emotional and mental health. Stress has always been common among high achievers.

There are those who compete and fail. They try hard, but their best is not good enough. Not everyone is a brainbox. For every child of above-average ability there must be one of below-average ability. That is what average ability means. Struggling to do one's best, and finding it is not good enough, can undermine a child's self-esteem. A child who is under pressure from home as well as school, may well add feelings of guilt to poor self-esteem. This can be particularly acute for the younger sibling of a highly successful child. Or for the older child with a successful younger sibling. Young people who constantly fall short of expectations may become depressed.

There are those who refuse to compete. One way of hanging on to your self-esteem is to opt out. If you do not try, you can always say to yourself "I could have succeeded. I'm not stupid. I just don't care about it."

There are those who see no point in competing – because they know they cannot win, or that no one will notice if they do. If hard work moves them up from 26th to 22nd in class, there is not much incentive to compete. Those who opt out may become disruptive, bored and rest-less. Some play truant. A few lucky ones find another area of achievement such as sport.

It seems a dismal picture, viewed like this, but there is no need for it to be, because I have left out one crucial factor. Academic success at school helps to get a child a good start in the job market, but is no guarantee of success in the world of work. That will depend on many other factors. Indeed there are surveys to show that by their thirties, children who succeeded well in the education system and went to university are no further ahead than those who did not have higher education.

The message should be: "You should work hard at school in order give yourself the best chance of getting a job, or of going to university, to get you started in life. It's not the end of the world if you don't succeed at school, but it may make things more difficult for you." You might add that employers are looking for convincing achievers, not Einsteins.

Tell them that *most people are average* and that being average, or a little better than average, can be an advantage because employers are looking for people who can be good team members. As long as they play to their strengths and always translate thought into action, they can succeed, even if they are not top of the class.

Above all, be realistic: most children have no areas of excellence. This is not worth a moment's loss of self-esteem.

Encourage and support them to learn what there is to learn, achieve what can be achieved, and cope with school as best they can.

Does not want to go to school

Of course, there are many reasons why this should happen. Before insist-ing he attends, check out the possibilities. Is he genuinely ill? Is he wor-ried about family upset or illness? Is he being bullied? Is he rejected and unhappy? Do the obvious before doing anything else – take it up with your doctor, and with the school, as appropriate.

◆ **Explain.** There is no choice. He has to go to school. It is the law.

◆ **Don't play along.** If he claims he is hot, feel his forehead and say "Seems OK".

◆ **Offer choices which do not include taking the day off.** Will you walk to school, or shall I give you a lift?

◆ **Insist.** "I can hear what you say Jamie, but you must go to school."

◆ **Persist.** "I understand you do not like your teacher, and I wish you were in another class. But these are temporary problems. Everything will change next year. You must go to school."

◆ **Get help.** If he refuses school every morning, and there are no obvious problems at school or home, call in a counsellor.

Hobbies

As children are confined more and more to the house and garden, the market in classes and activities increases. Tennis, rugby and gymnastic lessons replace the scratch game in the park and the traditional games of childhood. While children gain by the discipline of lessons, they also lose. Scaled-down versions of adult activities place more emphasis on winning and losing than on cooperation and skill: fine for those at the top of the heap, not so good for the average boy or girl.

There is nothing wrong with swimming and football lessons, or with learning the trampoline or martial arts; there *is* something wrong with a schedule that rushes the child from one activity to another without time for relaxation or play.

◆ **One activity at a time** is enough for younger children.

◆ **Make sure a child signs up with friends** so that the activities have a playful, social element.

◆ **Sit in on a class.** Avoid dictatorial and short-tempered instructors and those who make fun of weaker children.

◆ **Let your child try one class.** Don't push him if he is not enthusiastic. After the starter class, sign up for the minimum number of lessons possible, even if the price per lesson is higher than for a longer course.

◆ **If he wants to drop out after a couple of lessons,** point out that you have paid for the next six and that he agreed to go. Discuss why he does not want to carry on and encourage him to persevere. But never force him kicking and screaming into the class. Nor should you make a habit of letting him start, then stop.

When to start dancing/music lessons

Recent research suggests that children who have outside activities often do better at school, probably because *any* sort of achievement gives children confidence.

Music certainly helps children to listen, and listening can increase reading and spelling ability, as well as the ability to hear the sounds of a new language. But while doing something well can increase confidence, the opposite is also true.

Outside activities can also become one more area in which parents attempt to control their children. You should ask yourself "Who wants the child to have the lessons?" If you always wanted to learn the piano but never had the opportunity, you shouldn't be trying to fulfil your ambitions through your child. Do it yourself, instead. The same is true of dancing lessons. The groupie parent is a familiar figure in the entertainment world.

Dancing lessons

Although a high proportion of children start dancing lessons, the majority give them up after a year or two. Often this is because the lessons are too formal, or because children start them too early. Until children show signs of responding to music, they are too young. Eight is early enough to start.

Shop around for a dance teacher who you feel will be sympathetic to your child. A very competitive teacher with tough demands may be fine for the enthusiast but is rarely any good for the beginner. Dancing should be fun. The teacher needs to be as enthusiastic about her pupils as she is about her dance. There is time enough for a demanding and critical regime when the child has the skill to gain from it.

◆ **There is more to dance than ballet.** The child may prefer the less formal approach of Irish dancing or tap.

◆ **Start with movement to music.** Formal steps are fine once the enthusiasm is there.

◆ Don't buy all the gear until you are sure this is what the child really wants.

Music lessons

Some parents take it for granted that their children are musical. Others feel that music is something that is restricted to an elite. Most know that a high proportion of those who start music lessons ultimately fail. For everyone who still plays the piano, there must be at least ten who had lessons as children but no longer play.

Musicality is not something you have or have not got. Most people can learn to play an instrument if they really want to, and some who gave up as children learn as adults. Studies suggest that those who give up on music lessons are probably no less musical than those who continue. In fact, those who reach music college are, on the whole, no more musical than those studying any other subject at university.

Most people drop out of music lessons because they choose the wrong instrument. The biggest drop-out rates are found with two of the most popular instruments: the piano and the violin. Both instruments make much greater mental demands on a child than, say, a trumpet or a flute. They demand work rather than relaxation, and this can be too much after a hard day at school. Only a child with surplus mental energy should consider them.

For many children, the pleasure of making music comes from doing it with others. A child who would love a brass band may hate sitting at home at the piano. For others it is the solitary relaxation of playing the piano or flute which gives the pleasure.

Most music teachers agree that there are more problems caused by starting too early than by starting too late.

Instruments can be divided into five groups. There are woodwind instruments such as the flute; brass instruments such as the trumpet; strings such as the violin; percussion such as the drums; and the self-contained instruments such as the guitar or piano. Only violins, cellos and guitars come in small sizes. The rest are designed for adults. Some instruments are therefore too heavy or too large for small children to play easily and comfortably.

Almost all children can gain by starting with the recorder. It is cheap to buy, and many schools give lessons (and provide instruments). Although group lessons are not necessarily suitable for the slower and less musical child, or for the more advanced, they introduce the child to the pleasures of playing music with other children.

One of the easiest ways to begin music lessons is to buy or borrow a recorder from school, and if the child shows enthusiasm to look into the possibility of extra, individual recorder lessons. Even if the child does not get any extra lessons, school recorder lessons can be a reliable indicator of a child's readiness for a more complex instrument. When he asks for a more advanced instrument, you can be fairly sure he is ready.

A child has the ability to learn an instrument if he:
♦ **can recognize theme tunes from radio or TV.**

◆ **can tell a high note from a low note** when you sing a simple song such as *Ba ba black sheep*. Does the tune go up or down?

◆ **can clap a simple rhythm** to a familiar song.

◆ **can tell with eyes closed whether you are tapping a glass or a cup.**

◆ **can sing a song,** and finish off one you have started.

◆ **shows an interest** in music; so can, for example, name three musical instruments or name a musician.

◆ **enjoys** listening to music.

◆ **responds physically** to music.

◆ **can read and write fluently.**

◆ **does not have problems with spelling, writing or reading.**

◆ **does not have problems with maths,** and has reached a stage where he can add, subtract, multiply and divide.

◆ **shows evidence that he can sustain an interest,** such as going to brownies, dancing or gymnastics for more than six months.

◆ **understands music is a pleasure that has to be worked at;** that music lessons also mean music practice.

Will not do music practice

Practising between music lessons is tedious for most children. Agree on a routine. Parents often find that a chart is helpful. Refuse to battle over practice. Lessons at this stage are not essential. No practice, no lessons.

◆ **Consider whether the child is playing the correct instrument.** If it is no fun, there is little point.

◆ **Look around for a brass band.** A child who practises music with other children gets extra pleasure from playing.

Instruments with special physical requirements

◆ **Flute.** Difficult for most children under ten, or who are left handed, and those with thick lips or large front teeth.

◆ **Clarinet.** Difficult for most children under nine or ten, or those with small hands or narrow fingers. The range of finger movements required make it hard for a clumsy child.

◆ **Saxophone.** Few children under 12 can cope with the size.

◆ **Oboe.** Unsuitable for children until at least 12. The breath control is much too hard for a young or frail child. It is no good for asthmatics whose wheeziness is poorly controlled; on the other hand, it can help develop the long capacity of an asthmatic whose breathing is more or less normal as a result of successful medication. The child ideally needs thin, tight lips.

◆ **Bassoon.** Too large for a child under 13.

◆ **Trumpet.** Children under ten are better with the cornet. Even for those over ten, learning the cornet first will make life easier.

◆ **Trombone.** The length makes this impossible to play before the child is about 11.

◆ **French horn.** Not a first instrument for anyone – child or adult.

◆ **Piano.** A child who cannot sit still cannot learn the piano. Because it requires the player to read double-clef music, reasonable eyesight is needed. It is not suitable for the impatient or highly social child.

Instruments for social children

◆ **Flute and clarinet.** Because they can be part of an orchestra.

◆ **All brass instruments.** Because they are always played in bands, and are often learned this way.

◆ **Percussion.** Especially for marching bands.

◆ **Violin.** If played in an orchestra.

◆ **Viola.** If played in an orchestra.

Instruments for solitary children

◆ **Flute and harp.** Because they make such a wistful sound.

◆ **Piano.** The very mode of playing means the child cannot look at others.

◆ **Drum kit.** A way of getting rid of anger.

◆ **Cello**. Comparatively easy string instrument with a soothing sound.

◆ **Violin/viola.** Because a child learning a string instrument needs a good rapport with the teacher, a solitary child, who gets on well with adults, generally enjoys the lessons. A child who likes to please adults is more likely to put in the practice.

Instruments for aggressive, dominant, restless children

◆ **Clarinet.** Although most children can produce enough notes for a simple tune quite quickly, the range of music, and the degree of finger skills necessary for advanced playing is a worthwhile challenge for this type of child.

◆ **Trumpet.** Most children progress to the trumpet from the cornet. Trumpets are for playing with others, not alone. Not for children who are mortified by their mistakes. Bad notes are extremely public.

◆ **Percussion.** The child who enjoys percussion is one who is constantly drumming, even before he gets the kit.

Instruments which require mental agility

◆ **Violin/viola.** The child must not only produce an acceptable tone but also play accurate notes: compared with other instruments, you do much more work.

◆ **Piano.** Just reading the music is difficult.

◆ **Classical guitar.** Needs good hand control; and, because the hands work in such different ways, it also needs of mental agility.

Always watching TV

TV is a valuable resource, both for learning and recreation. Kept in proportion, it is a force for the good. Those who watch TV have a much broader outlook on the world than those who don't. But like all good things, there can be too much of it.

If you are worried about how much your children they are watching, set a reasonable weekly limit, in hours.

Look at the TV listings each week with the children and discuss what they want to watch. If too much of one particular type of programme dominates the choice, agree a limit to that too.

But: be flexible. Watching their football team play an essential match should be considered a bonus. A child mad about running should be able to watch a little extra in weeks when there is a major athletics meet. If it rains all week, and he cannot go out to play, he may need to watch rather more TV than was on his schedule, especially if all his friends are on holiday.

◆ **When they are about to exceed the allowance, offer a choice and ask the child to make a decision.** "Hannah, we agreed you could watch ten hours of TV this week. If you watch this now, you will not be able to watch *Superman* tomorrow. It is up to you."

◆ **Set an example.** Plan your viewing, rather than flicking though the channels for something to watch.

◆ **If your child constantly abuses the agreement, use action not words.** Unplug the TV.

Video games

It is sometimes hard to remember what eight-year-old boys did before the advent of video games. You may admit they are fun, and even that they improve hand-eye coordination and visual memory. But how much do these things need practising? What is he losing along the way?

When he says for the fifth time that he will come to lunch at the end of the game, it can be hard not to yell. Who wants to wait for supper until he has finished the fourth level?

There is only one way to deal with video games, and that is to have rules about when they can be played, and for how long – just as with TV (above). Set firm limits and stick to them.

◆ **Give him mealtime warnings.** "Dinner will be ready in ten minutes." Then, three minutes beforehand, insist that he pauses the game and comes to table on time. Video games are a secondary, not a primary, activity.

◆ **Don't nag.** Say what you mean and mean what you say.

◆ **Make reasonable rules** about how much, and when, he can play. If rules are broken, confiscate the game player.

◆ **Make playing conditional** on homework, housework and other activities you expect the child to undertake.

◆ **If he does not obey the rules give him a choice.** "Mark, you can stop playing now, or I will confiscate that game."

◆ **Do not assume that nothing good will come of it.** Show an interest in his skills. In their place, there is nothing wrong with video games, as long as they do not exclude all other activities.

Nail biting

Nail biting often starts as a tension-relieving exercise – sometimes to offset nerves frayed by parental nagging.

◆ **Find other ways to reduce stress.** Exercise often helps.

◆ **Observe the situations in which your child bites his nails.** Ask him when he thinks he does it; watch him when he is at home. Discuss it with him. Ask him if he wants to stop biting his nails. If he does, agree a cooperative campaign. If he doesn't, don't insist. Instead:

◆ **Consider ways of keeping his hands busy.** Music lessons? Video games? – But see above.

◆ **Touch him on the shoulder when you see him biting his nails.**

◆ **Suggest he keeps his hands in his pockets.**

◆ **Try a star chart with a prize for a full-grown nail.**

Puberty

Milestones: changes at puberty

Most people do not remember the early stages of puberty. Even university students, who have passed this way quite recently, remember their childhood rather better than they remember the early teenage years. Maybe forgetting the awkward times helps one to adapt. But the fact that we do not remember puberty well does not help us to understand our children at this stage of their lives.

One incident I do remember illustrates the gulf. I was about 13 and on a family picnic by the river. My aunt suggested that my cousin and I swam in the river wearing our knickers. This was at the stage when both my cousin and I had little more than breast buds. There was, my aunt said, no one about. No one about! Exposing my chest to anything but my bedroom walls was completely unthinkable. I recalled this incident because years later I had to stop myself saying the same thing to my nieces.

The changes that occur at puberty are embarrassing and confusing. If they always started at exactly the same age for each child and progressed at exactly the same rate, they might be easier to cope with. But they don't, and children, emerging from the conformity of middle childhood, can find the disorderly, untimed changes of puberty very disturbing.

One child may be fully developed before another has even started. A child who has been amongst the tallest in the class finds her friends shooting past her while she remains resolutely child-like. A girl can find herself coping with periods while still in junior school. Puberty can start as early as nine, or as late as 17. It separates friends; it makes some envious, others embarrassed and alarmed.

What happens at puberty

Parents are in a better position to understand their children's behaviour at this stage if they have a basic knowledge of the changes that come with puberty, physical and psychological. One can hardly appreciate the second without going into the first.

Always keep in mind the social context in which all this happens – your child will be constantly making comparisons with peers: not just comparing height, but comparing breast or penis size, hip width of and belly fat.

The term puberty describes the first phase of adolescence when sexual maturity starts to become evident. Strictly speaking, it begins with the release of hormones from the pituitary gland of the brain. These hormones cause the growth of the testes or ovary and this in turn causes an increase in the production of the steroid hormones testosterone and oestrogen.

In practice, however, we mark puberty by the consequences of these hormonal changes: the gradual development of an adult masculine body (controlled mainly by the higher levels of testosterone produced by the testes) or the adult feminine body (controlled mainly by the higher levels of oestrogen produced by the ovary). In boys there is a broadening of the shoulders, increased strength of the muscles, a reduction in body fat and the growth of the genitalia. The voice also lowers and, somewhat later, the Adam's apple develops.

In women there is a broadening of the hips, development of the breasts, the growth of the genitalia and uterus, the beginning of menstruation, and the consequent production of a second female hormone, progesterone.

The development of pubic and axillary hair is controlled by testosterone and other androgens in both men and women. (Which is partly why men have more of it.)

As a result of these physical changes there are also psychological and emotional changes. Children do not just look more like adults when they reach puberty, they feel more like them too. Testosterone and oestrogen awaken adult sexual emotions. Whereas in the past masturbation has felt good and acted to soothe and to calm, now such experimentation is more driven, more serious.

Sexual desires are now more likely to be associated with people other than themselves. Testosterone also increases the level of aggression in boys. When boys get angry, they now have an extra engine feeding their fury.

When do changes take place?

Exactly when puberty occurs depends upon genetic, nutritional and racial factors. If parents developed late it is likely that their children will do so too. Girls of Chinese origin begin menstruation earlier than those of European origin. Girls with more than 17 per cent body fat tend to reach menarche (the onset of first menstruation) 'on time'. If body fat falls below this level, menarche is delayed. Boys typically mature later than girls.

This pattern ensures that the first individuals in the class to reach puberty are the girls, and the last are boys. Because of the deep-seated desire for conformity amongst children and teenagers, early puberty tends to be problematic for girls and late puberty for boys. These children are out on a limb, and they feel it.

In both girls and boys, puberty coincides with an adolescent growth spurt. The spurt lasts about four-and-a-half years. The peak rate of growth for the average girl is at 11, and for the average boy at 13. Most girls are more or less fully grown by 13, most boys by 15. However, this average can be very misleading. Some girls begin menstruation and growth at nine. Some boys do not start to grow until about 16 or 17.

The fact that puberty occurs alongside marked physical growth makes it impossible for children at the extremes to hide. Not only is his penis half the size, but he is head and shoulders shorter than his friends.

There is *nothing abnormal* about the individuals at these extremes – but it is no help telling your child that. In most cases, a child's height before the onset of the growth spurt correlates with adult height. But again this is not absolute. Small children sometimes grow into tall adults and vice versa. This tendency may run in your family, as it does in mine. As a child I was in the bottom 5 per cent for height (as was my daughter). We have both ended up taller than average.

The parts of the child's body which reach adult size first are the head, hands and feet. These are followed by the arms and legs, then the shoulders and hips widen, and lastly the trunk lengthens. However, since trunk length accounts for the greatest proportion of the total increase in height, most children continue to grow a further inch or so after the main spurt is complete. Most adults are rather taller than they were at 16.

There are more subtle changes in structure that happen at the same time. The forehead becomes higher, the mouth widens, lips become fuller, the chin juts out more, the nose becomes prominent. The childish face becomes more craggy and angular. Fine for boys, but not always welcome for girls, given that what is accepted as pretty in magazines and on the cinema screen tends to be doll-like, small features rather than real women's faces.

Before puberty, girls have wider shoulders and narrower hips than boys. By the end of puberty, the reverse is true. After puberty, the variation in hip and shoulder width is greater for women than men. Again, these extremes are not always welcome. You can be sure that children of this age notice their physical imperfections; you can be certain that they think they matter.

The changes, in order

In boys, sexual maturity begins with the growth of the testes and scrotum, which typically happens at about eleven-and-a-half. This is followed about a year later by the growth of the penis. The development of axillary (body) and facial hair follows about two years later. However, both the onset and the ordering of these things can be quite variable. The lowering of the voice usually occurs fairly late in puberty. In some boys it is quite gradual. In others rather dramatic. Dramatic is best: long-drawn-out squeaking is embarrassing and a cause for teasing.

In girls, the first sign of sexual maturity is the development of downy pubic hair and the gradual elevation of the breast (so-called 'breast buds'). In most, but not all, girls the first pubic hairs precede breast buds. About a year later the uterus and vagina begin to grow and the labia and clitoris enlarge. Pubic hair increases and vaginal secretions begin. By 12, the majority of girls have pigmented nipples and breast development is clearly under way. On average, menstruation begins at twelve-and-a-half.

For about a year after the onset of menstruation, an adolescent girl is physiologically incapable of conception, and for some time her fertility remains low. Similarly, boys are capable of ejaculation and intercourse for some time before they produce live spermatozoa in sufficient numbers for conception to occur.

Psychological effects of early and late puberty

Once it is over, most of us suppress the memory of the anxiety, the needs, desires and fears associated with puberty. Even when development is 'on time', the child's sense of herself as a certain sort of individual is challenged by the changes in her own body.

Among boys, those who mature early or 'on time' have the highest self-esteem and describe themselves as self-assured. Such boys find themselves popular with peers in the adolescent years. Studies have shown that late-maturing boys are less poised, more talkative, more likely to be self-conscious, restless, overeager and attention seeking. They were also less popular. In psychological tests these boys show more feelings of inadequacy than their peers, poorer self image, and claim that they feel rejected, dominated and dependent. A boy who develops late is at the bottom of the pile; one who develops early is simply keeping up with the girls.

A boy's anxiety is very much tied up to the size and development of his penis. This anxiety often continues into adulthood. When standing at the urinal, it is often possible to check out the competition; and the late developer has ample occasion to prove his 'inferiority' to his peers in the changing room or shower.

Among girls it is those who mature earliest who tend to have the worst self- and body-image. Perhaps this is because early maturity in a girl happens when all her friends, boys and girls, are still children. Having the body of a 13-year-old does not make a nine-year-old more independent and intellectually advanced. It makes her different, insecure, and the subject of whispering in class. Girls in middle-class homes seem to cope better with early maturity than working-class girls, perhaps because they have the chance to maintain greater privacy.

Average ages for development: girls

◆ **Normal age for the growth spurt is ten to 11.** You should be concerned if it occurs before nine. Early and late maturation runs in families. Unless you have a family history of late development, see a doctor if growth is delayed beyond 13.

◆ **The normal age for breast development is ten to 11.** Consult a doctor if the buds have not appeared by 15.

◆ **Pubic hair:** downy hair is often the first sign of puberty in girls. Full growth occurs by about 12 to 13, but it is quite variable.

◆ **Vaginal discharge:** usually starts between ten and 13. This will decrease when periods begin.

◆ **Underarm sweat: usual onset, 12 to 13.** Adult body odour depends upon apocrine glands which do not develop until sexual maturity. There are also glands in the genital region which produce a characteristic female smell. Generally this is thought to be a pleasant smell by men, and an unpleasant one by women.

◆ **Menstruation usually starts at 11 to 14** - but periods may start as early as nine. Consult your doctor if they have not begun by 16.

Some worries for developing girls

◆ **Odd breasts.** Breasts do not always develop evenly. Even when fully developed, they may not be quite the same size.

◆ **Late menstruation.** There is often a family tendency for a late or early start. Body fat also plays a role. Few girls menstruate unless they weigh more than 99 lbs. Early periods are variable in length and girls do not settle down to a monthly pattern at first.

Average ages for development: boys

◆ **Normal age for growth spurt: 12 to 13.** You should be concerned if this occurs before 11. Late maturation runs in families. Unless you have a family history of it, you should be concerned if growth is delayed beyond 15.

◆ **Normal age for growth of testes and scrotum: 11 to 12.** The skin of the scrotum darkens and the testes begin to grow. Consult a doctor if there is no enlargement by 14.

◆ **Normal age for enlargement of penis: 12 to 13.** The penis lengthens and then thickens. The average length of an adult erect penis is 5 to 7 inches.

◆ **Normal age for appearance of pubic hair:** about 12 to 13; underarm hair 13 to 15; facial hair 13 to 15, but this is very variable.

◆ **Normal age for underarm sweat: 13 to 15.** Adult body odour depends upon apocrine glands which develop at about this age. There are also glands in the genital region which produce a characteristic male smell, generally pleasant to the females, unpleasant to the other males.

◆ **Normal age for ejaculation: 13 to 14.** Starts about a year after the penis starts to enlarge. Initially there are no sperm in the ejaculate.

◆ **Normal age for the voice to break: 14 to 15.** About a year after the voice begins to change, the Adam's apple develops.

Some worries for developing boys

◆ **Embarrassing erections.** Almost anything can give a young boy an erection. It is normal and natural, but potentially embarrassing. Thinking very hard about something else can make it subside.

◆ **Morning erections.** Erections occur automatically when dreaming (not only when dreams are sexual). Most men wake from dreaming sleep. So they wake with an erection.

◆ **Wet dreams.** Sometimes ejaculation occurs during dreaming. It does not depend on having a sexy dream.

◆ **Breast development.** It is not unusual for boys to have quite marked changes in alveoli size, and to have quite pronounced

WHAT TO DO IF YOUR CHILD IS DIFFERENT

✔ *Sympathize. It is important. Do not deny what your child knows to be true.*

✔ *Enable. Gather positive forces to build up her strengths Make her feel more able. The more she can counteract feelings of inferiority, the less she will be affected in the long term. Keep her in touch with her successes.*

✔ *Never undermine. If a child's self-esteem is low, it is cruel to make it lower.*

✔ *Disclose. Being short/tall is a genetic trait, which means that she probably takes after one of you. Explain how you feel/felt about your size. Don't preach. Make a sincere attempt to bridge the gap between the generations. Be honest about how you felt at his age. Admit that you didn't always cope, but that it worked out in the end because once past adolescence, the changes will be less important to him – and his peers.*

WHAT NOT TO DO IF YOUR CHILD IS DIFFERENT

✖ *Say it does not matter.*

✖ *Keep telling her not to worry, that she will grow.*

✖ *Say it never bothered you.*

nipple and breast development in the early stages of puberty. This is brought about by the release of oestrogen by the testes. This is quite normal. The testes always produce a little oestrogen, and the ovaries a little testosterone. The alveoli changes remain, but the breast changes disappear.

◆ **Squeaky voice.** Voice changes can be quite sudden or quite gradual. When the voice-change is gradual, the range often changes within a sentence.

Too short, too tall

The teenage years are more difficult if you are short, especially if you are a short male in a society that values height. Short teenagers are extremely sensitive to stares, and to rude comments. Short boys find it harder to attract girls (who at this age are often very sensitive to the view that men should be taller), and tend to have low self-esteem and to feel inadequate. It takes a big personality to cope.

Often it is the shortest boy and the fattest girl who are left out when the gang pairs off. The vast majority of short boys have short parents, but knowing it is in the genes is not much compensation. Being too tall used to be considered rather a problem for a girl. But in recent years the advance of supermodels as icons and role models has rather lessened the stigma of being six feet tall.

Acne

These years bring adult concerns about the importance of beauty. Even one spot is a disaster. You may not notice it: you can be sure your child will. It's not much help to say "All teenagers have spots at some time." For her the only concern is how many of her friends *have spots this morning*, and how many photographs she's seen recently of girls without a single spot.

◆ **Acne is not an infection.** Nor is it infectious. The pus in the spots is sterile. Until the child starts picking at and fiddling with the spots, they are not infected. Obviously, since acne spots are sterile, medicated preparations cannot prevent acne (see below). They can stop the spread of any secondary infection, but may also cause irritation.

◆ **Acne is not caused by dirt or pollution.** Too much cleansing or washing is more likely to cause problems than not washing. Twice daily washing with neutral soap or cleanser is sufficient.

◆ **Thoughts, habits and sexual activity** have nothing whatsoever to do with spots.

◆ **Diet is less important than people used to think.** Fat is not excreted through the skin. It is excreted via the bowel. Nor is chocolate problematic. A double blind study of the effects of chocolate on acne (that is, a study in which neither the patients nor the doctors knew who was getting the most chocolate) showed it had no effect on the number of spots.

◆ **There is no way of ensuring that you will be spot-free by**

Saturday night. Alas.

◆ **Lotions, creams, gels and antibiotics to treat acne can improve, but not prevent.** It is best to find one that works for you and stick with it.

Sleeping forever

People grow in their sleep, and since teenagers grow so much it is not surprising that they sleep for so long. Physical growth is a tiring business. Remember how they slept as babies? It is also painful, which probably makes adolescent sleep restless. Growing up is a time of anxiety and change. Relationships need to be shifted on to a rather different footing, independence has to be negotiated, sexual feelings have to be addressed. Change is inclined to make people down and a little depressed. So the sleep of adolescence is probably also an escape.

THE WRONG WAY TO DEAL WITH ADOLESCENT SLEEP PATTERNS

✖ *Wake them up at eight regardless. As long as they get to school on time, and do their homework and chores, it is their business when they get up. Does it really matter if they stay in bed until three on Sunday? At least the house is music-free.*

✖ *Call and call until they get up. Call twice, and they wait for the second call. Call five times and they wait for the fifth. "I'm not going to call you again," you say. But you always do. So it is safe to ignore you.*

✖ *Insist that if they cannot get up in time, they must be in bed by nine. They are old enough to work this out for themselves. They will – if you stop nagging.*

✖ *Rant and rave, nag and moan. What better reason for going back to sleep than avoiding parental put-downs?*

THE RIGHT WAY TO DEAL WITH ADOLESCENT SLEEP PATTERNS

✔ ***Set out what has to be done at the weekend and leave them to it.*** *"Alex, don't forget it is your turn to mow the lawn this weekend and remember we are going to Gran's for lunch." As long as they do what has to be done, sleeping the weekend away is their business.*

✔ ***Buy them an alarm clock.*** *If getting up for school is their responsibility, they must see to it. If it is yours, they won't. Make some allowance for error. If they haven't surfaced twenty minutes after the alarm usually goes off, call them. But don't do it every morning.*

✔ ***If they are late for school, don't make excuses for them.*** *Give them the responsibility, and they will become responsible. If they get a detention, that is up to them.*

✔ ***Wait for them.*** *If you give them a lift to school, give a warning of impending departure and then go. The train would not wait. Why should you? If they have to walk or use public transport one morning, they will get up in time the next day. "Alice, the car's leaving in ten minutes if you want a lift, otherwise there is money for your bus fare in the tin."*

✔ ***Cook breakfast at a certain time.*** *If they are late, they must feed themselves, or do without.*

✔ ***On weekdays, take them a cup of tea or coffee.*** *Why not if you are making it anyway?*

Should parents dictate a teenager's bedtime?

When should a teenager go to bed? Getting to bed is her responsibility, as is getting up in the morning. Don't make staying up late a form of rebellion. Her sleep patterns are entirely her responsibility.

◆ **"But her records keep me awake."** Your sleep patterns are your responsibility and so you should do something about this.

> Alice, when you sleep is up to you. I want to sleep between 11 and eight and I need the house to be quiet at that time. You can play your music and computer games whenever you like, but between 11 and eight, would you please use your personal stereo/headphones/turn off the sound on the computer

◆ **Should her friends stay so late?** No, not if it disturbs the rest of the family.

> Alice, I like your friends to come around, but during the week I need my sleep. Could we make some rules? Everyone out by ten during the week and 11 at weekends

◆ **If they do not go.** Ten minutes before they are due to leave, offer a drink for the road.

> Alice, I'm making a cup of tea. Do you and your friends want one before they go?

Then if they are still there 15 minutes later, just say

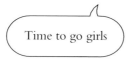

> Time to go girls

◆ **If the parents who are collecting the child have not turned up.** Ring them and remind them. "Rob, would you mind picking Joanna up? I need to get to bed early". Don't apologize. Don't say "It normally would not matter". He may take you at your word. Let the other parent do the grovelling.

Eating you out of house and home

At puberty children can grow at a phenomenal rate. The average male may only grow nine inches in height between 12 and 17, but he does not do this at a steady rate of an inch a year (or even 1/10 of an inch per month). He grows in leaps and bounds, upwards and outwards; first the bone, then the muscle. Growth needs fuel, protein, fat and carbohydrate. Growth can also be a painful process. The aches and pains of growth are real and almost certainly contribute to restless sleep and short temper. Hunger makes people irritable. It has been estimated that six times as many arguments occur before dinner as after it.

The way to deal with constant hunger

♦ **Provide easily prepared food and snacks.** Make these as healthy as possible, especially if the child has a tendency to put on weight. A toasted-sandwich maker can be very useful.

♦ **Teach them to cook.** Their snack diet will feature less junk food if they can cook a simple meal for themselves and their friends.

♦ **Have some basic rules about replacing food.** If milk or bread are finished, they should be replaced. This is obviously easier if money for this purpose is left in a special place and if you live near to late-night shops. Extra bread and milk can be kept in the freezer.

♦ **Expect them to clear up after themselves.** One can always hope.

♦ **All eating to be done in the kitchen/dining area.** Again, you can hope. This may be more realistic if there is a TV in the kitchen/dining area.

What is healthy eating for a teenager?

No different from a healthy diet for anyone else. About 55 per cent of daily calories should come from complex carbohydrates such as cereals, root and leaf vegetables, and about 30 to 35 per cent of calories should come from fats. The fats should derive from plant sources (olives, nuts), animal sources (chicken, meat, oily fish) or dairy goods (milk products, eggs).

Fats have a bad name among teenagers, but some fat is essential for

GOOD FOR TEENAGERS

✔ *All fresh fruit and vegetables.*
✔ *Grains, especially whole grains.*
✔ *Bread, especially brown bread.*
✔ *Potatoes, boiled or baked. If making chips, keep them chunky: they will be less fatty.*
✔ *Fish, especially baked, grilled or steamed.*
✔ *Poultry.*
✔ *Skimmed milk and skimmed-milk products such as low-fat yoghurt.*

BAD FOR TEENAGERS

✖ *Chocolate bars.*
✖ *Too much ice-cream.*
✖ *Cakes and biscuits.*
✖ *Too many chips and crisps.*
✖ *Too many hot dogs and hamburgers.*
✖ *Too many fried foods.*
✖ *Carbonated drinks.*
✖ *Fat meats.*
✖ *Tinned fruits in syrup.*

Recommended daily calories for growing teenagers

	Age	Average weight	Height	Calories
Boys	11-14	97 lbs	63 inches	2,800
Boys	15-18	134 lbs	69 inches	3,000
Girls	11-14	97 lbs	62 inches	2,400
Girls	15-18	119 lbs	65 inches	2,100

growth. The body's cell walls are made up of fats. Without fat to build cell walls, growth is impossible. This is not to say that growing teenagers need a fat-rich diet. The fats contained in meat, oily fish, eggs, and nuts are quite adequate in themselves. Proteins such as those found in meat, pulses, grains, dairy goods, together with fibre provide the rest of the diet.

Wants to be a vegetarian

Millions of people live very healthy lives on a vegetarian diet. Beans, peas, lentils, grains and nuts are sources of protein and perfectly adequate as long as a full range is eaten. Dairy products are also excellent protein sources, but too heavy a reliance on full-cream milk and cheese is likely to make the diet rather high in fat. Those who do not eat dairy goods need to find a source for vitamin B 12. A vitamin pill is probably the easiest way.

If your teenager insists on being a vegetarian, don't maker it an issue, just be practical:

◆ **Select meals which are easily adapted.** A vegetarian burger can replace hamburgers or lamb chops, for example. Tacos can contain meat or cheese. A baked potato can be served with steak or kidney beans and sour cream. Stir-fry vegetables can be made with and without chicken.

◆ **Adapt the family diet so that the whole family eats vegetarian meals some days.**

◆ **Have a few standbys** - eggs, baked potatoes with cheese, baked beans - for days when meat is eaten by the rest of the family.

◆ **Cook special vegetarian meals and freeze in small portions** for days when family meals cannot be easily adapted.

◆ **Teach the vegetarian to cook.**

Worried about being overweight

Teenagers worry about being fat even when they are not fat. With reason. Being overweight may not be as harmful to one's physical health as most people believe it to be, but it is certainly harmful to one's mental, psychological and social health. 'Fatism' is probably the only actively encouraged and socially acceptable form of prejudice left.

The prospect of poor health is not what makes people unhappy about being overweight. It is the social isolation, and the prejudice that cause the unhappiness. Plump people are less likely to find themselves in well-paid jobs. Fat women do not get into the best colleges and are more likely to be secretaries than office managers; teachers than head mistresses; radio presenters than TV presenters. Even doctors are more sympathetic when patients are slim. In a well-known study, actresses were sent to different doctors with the same list of symptoms. If they wore padding (and thus looked overweight), doctors tended to think the illnesses were their own fault and to describe them as lazy and malingering. When slim, they thought them genuinely ill.

There is little evidence that being overweight is unhealthy for women, but overweight men are more prone to heart disease. In fact, the main dangers for women come from repetitive dieting. Radio, TV and magazines tell a rather different story. Persuading women to stay slim is big business. There are diet foods and pills, dieting magazines and dieting classes, exercise machines, exercise classes, beauty parlour slimming treatments, books by the shelf load and now a growing market in fat-reducing cosmetic surgery. It is a business with a built-in obsolescence. Of all those who diet, 95 per cent put every ounce of the weight back on again. Many of the customers for all these treatments are young teenagers.

Over the last twenty years, models have got slimmer (even Playboy centrefolds are a different shape these days). The in shape is like a Barbie doll. And since this is unobtainable, models tend to have surgically enhanced breasts on naturally thin frames. As models get slimmer, the rest of us get fatter. Some think the increased weight is the direct result of all that dieting. If we tell the body that times are lean (as we do when we diet) it will go into storage mode and lay down more fat.

No one knows with certainty why some people are fatter than others. Certainly there is a genetic component. If you have two fat parents, there is a high probability you will be fat. One fat parent, and you are less likely to be fat. Two slim parents and you will almost certainly be slim. It used to be thought that fat children always grew up to be fat adults, but current evidence casts some doubt on this. Children, adolescents and adults who are less active are more likely to be plump.

Not infrequently, weight gain is associated with stress, depression and unhappiness. Stress is often eased by eating high-energy food, but such foods also cause weight gain. Being plump increases stress, and so an upward spiral of stress and weight gain can occur.

Another cause of obesity (and a component of anorexia and bulimia in some girls) is sexual abuse in childhood. On a simplistic level it is as if the child eats to intentionally make themselves less desirable.

Recognizing a child is overweight and giving help

Sometimes it is not just puppy fat. Children are often vulnerable to weight gain because they eat more food than their bodies need. Sometimes the problem is a temporary one. Sometimes it is more persistent. Stress-induced eating is common in women and the teenage years are stressful.

◆ **It may be puppy fat.** Some children put on weight in the early stages of puberty. Whether this is a direct result of hormonal imbalances or a result of comfort eating is unclear. Fat accumulates slowly and steadily, and the longer it goes unchecked, the harder it is to shift.

◆ **Children cannot lose weight unless they are highly motivated.**

◆ **Sensible diet (rather than dieting) and ample exercise are the best way to lose weight.**

◆ **Fad diets and meal replacements** are not recommended for growing teenagers. They cause a loss of body fluid and glycogen, but are unlikely to affect body fat.

◆ **Slimming with a group** is more successful than slimming alone.

◆ **Appetite suppressants** are not suitable for adolescents.

◆ **Anorexia and bulimia** (see pages 351-353) are far more dangerous than being overweight. A high proportion of anorexics start off as chubby adolescents. Prolonged dieting is not recommended for any adolescent.

◆ **A high percentage of all food advertisements are for high-fat and sugar-rich foods.** Many are specifically targeted at teenagers. Keep the snack cupboard healthy.

◆ **Role models are often abnormally thin.** Magazines aimed at teenagers are often prone to use extremely thin models. Talk to teenage girls about this.

◆ **If your teenager shows any tendency to put on weight** it will make her life easier if you try to keep temptation (biscuits, cakes, sweets, crisps, cheese) out of the cupboard and use the savings to buy a microwave. A baked potato with a spoonful of low-fat yoghurt takes six minutes to prepare.

Anorexia

Anorexia nervosa is most common in teenage girls (90 per cent of all sufferers). Sufferers believe themselves to be fatter than they really are. Even when painfully thin, they go on dieting. No one knows for certain why anorexia occurs.

Girls who become anorexic have often been exceptionally good, quiet, hard-working and eager to please their parents. They were very dependable, did well at school and in all ways were the pride and joy of their families.

Closer examination often suggests a lack of autonomy and individual initiative. They are, perhaps, too good, too ready to please. They are sometimes described as being enslaved to parental ambition; not having a life of their own. They often have an obsessive need to control.

Cultural expectations clearly play a part. For example, anorexia is more common in Caucasian groups than amongst Afro-Caribbeans, who prize slimness less.

Role models could well play a part. Anorexia is very common amongst dancers and models. It has become more common among teenagers as models have become teenage icons.

One third of girls who develop anorexia have been overweight.

Anorexic girls are more likely to have been sexually abused.

Middle-class girls with ambitious parents have an increased chance of becoming anorexic. Many attend schools with a high academic standard.

What happens in anorexia

Typically, anorexia begins in the early or mid teens. The girl decides she is overweight and begins to diet. But the dieting continues long after a normal or average body weight has been achieved. The girl becomes very thin and, in spite of family pressure to stop, continues to lose weight. At this, or at a later stage, she may also try methods other than dieting to further weight loss. Frantic exercise is a common sign - take note if you see her exercising obsessively for a long period each day. Taking laxatives is another sign. Sometimes anorexic girls take so many that they causes kidney damage.

The lack of nutrients eventually make the anorexic depressed, irritable and unable to concentrate. Her skin will become dry and she may grow downy hair on her face, arms and legs. Her weight may fall so low that her periods cease. If a girl becomes anorexic before puberty, its onset will be delayed.

Anorexia is a very serious disorder. About 5 per cent of sufferers die, either because of infection, damage caused by laxative use, or suicide. Of the rest, about 20 per cent remain anorexic for much of their lives, about 25 per cent recover somewhat and the other 50 per cent eventually recover. For most, however, it is a long haul. Typically, the problem lasts at least two to three years.

DIAGNOSIS OF ANOREXIA

As well as the other characteristics of anorexia described here, doctors will diagnose the problem with certainty only if they can see:

♦ **Intense fear of becoming obese** which does not diminish as weight loss progresses. A preoccupation with body size and a relentless pursuit of thinness.

♦ **Disturbance of body image.** Anorexics see themselves as fatter than they really are, and continue to complain about fat tummies and thighs when in reality they are painfully thin.

♦ **No known physical illness.** That is, no reason for being thin.

♦ **Weight loss of at least 25 per cent** of original body weight.

♦ **Refusal to maintain normal body weight.**

All anorexics need professional help. This is a life-threatening condition. It is not something parents can deal with alone.

How is bulimia different from anorexia?

Bulimia is a variant of anorexia that tends to occur in rather older women. Some who start off as anorexics will later become bulimic. Bulimia is characterized by a cycle of starvation, binge eating, and purging. Sufferers may also be obsessive about exercise and take laxatives.

Because bulimic girls are not necessarily thin, it is sometimes difficult to spot that they have serious problems. Vomiting and laxative abuse can be extremely dangerous. Laxative abuse causes kidney damage and infection. Repeated vomiting harms the teeth.

Are teenagers confused about sex?

In recent years there have been a number of surveys of sexual behaviour amongst adults in Western developed countries. Each one of them looked at a large cross-section of people. They were carried out, in part, so that governments could assess the likely spread of the AIDS virus. Whether conducted in the U.S.A., Britain or France, each survey came up with the same answer: men have sex more often with women than women have sex with men; men have sex with a larger number of female partners than women have male partners.

Now, quite obviously, one and one should make two. For every man who has sex with a woman there must be a woman having sex with a man. The sums should add up, but they never do. They are not just out by 'a bit'. The average woman in each of these countries says she has about three partners. The average man says he has 11. It looks as if women look for a figure which sounds respectable without being prudish, and men decide that they ought to make it into double figures.

If adults who are interviewed anonymously as part of a scientific survey feel a need to conform to society's expectations (men should be experienced, women should not) then what about teenagers? Surely we should expect that they will be confused about sex?

In truth, we are all confused. Old morals and old expectations run deep. The old double standard in sexual behaviour could never have existed in reality, but the fiction lives on. Men still brag about their conquests. Women still brag about their purity. How are teenagers to steer a course through this minefield? Magazines, films, pop songs and TV broadcast that sex is fun, natural, automatic, something men and women do when they spend time together. Conventional morality still says women should be cautious, men should grab every passing opportunity. How are teenagers to appreciate that things are not as simple as this?

The double standard

The double standard is alive and kicking, especially amongst men. Parents – and especially fathers – are still likely to be more suspicious and more protective of their daughters. Boys should 'score'; girls should take care.

Teenage attitudes towards sex are culturally determined. Only in Western countries do more than 65 per cent of adolescents claim that

UPDATING SEXUAL STEREOTYPES

As soon as children can name the two genders, boy and girl, they know that there is some kind of difference between the sexes. But it is not until a child reaches three or four years that she realizes that because she is now a girl, she will one day grow up to be a woman; not until six does she realize that there is no way that this can change.

As they try to understand themselves, so children try to understand just what it is to be a woman or a man. They tend to be rather stereotyped about this, as is clearly demonstrated by girls' devotion to Barbie dolls and boys' to war games.

As children reach adolescence, girls are bombarded with two new themes. The old romantic view that happiness is boy-shaped, and that success is making oneself pretty enough to get boys. This last has been joined in the last 30 years by a new view: that there is more to life than men and babies.

Men are also bombarded by two confused views. There is the old macho action-man image, somewhat weakened by the knowledge of poor employment prospects and successful women; and there is the romantic image, which although never fully stated, has always been part of the male psyche, where women are treated as sacred objects to honour and adore,

sexual experiences give them pleasure. Less than half of the girls made such claims, and the younger they were, the less likely they were to find sex pleasurable.

The standard Western story about sexual activity during the teenage years goes like this:

◆ Boys should score – all their mates claim that they have. Who wants to be the last? So boys give boys pressure and boys give girls pressure, and occasionally girls give way.

◆ Girls should score. Isn't that what all the magazines say? Girls should talk, dress and act sexually. If they don't, they are probably frigid. If they are not interested, there is something wrong. But sex should only take place with the right boy. Otherwise they will be branded a slut.

◆ Boys should have sex as much as possible, and with as many girls as possible.

◆ Girls should stick to one boy at a time, and leave a respectable interval between one and the next.

◆ Consequently: boys are almost always less experienced than they say, and girls more experienced than they say – perhaps sometimes more experienced than they want to be.

Being the parent of a sexually active teenager

It can be hard to come to terms with your offspring's developing sexuality: to think about them as someone who dreams of sex, thinks of sex, wants sex and even has sex. More than any other aspect of their growing up, developing sexuality divides them from us.

Crushes

First infatuations occur at about 11 or 12. Often they involve a member of the same sex. The common feature of crushes is that the feelings are new and intense, and the loved one invariably unobtainable. Pop stars, schoolteachers, or perhaps an older boy or girl at school are the most common objects. They are, in short, the stuff of daydreams. Having a crush on someone of the same sex does not indicate homosexuality. Having a crush on someone of the opposite sex does not confirm heterosexuality.

Although crushes are commonest in the early stages of puberty, they do not entirely disappear as people get older. Daydreams are always pleasant, and for many they remain a harmless escape.

Is my child gay?

In the early teens, intense friendships are often formed with members of the same sex. In fact, these friendships can be so intense that parents often wonder if the relationship is sexual.

While it is true that these relationships occasionally hover around the edges of sexual involvement and experimentation, for most teenagers strong sexual feelings towards a member of their own sex are a passing phase. Exploring sex with someone who is like you feels safe. It is exploration with someone who understands. Few people are entirely fixed about what turns them on. If we imagine all possible sexual partners

UNHELPFUL PARENTAL ADVICE ABOUT SEX

✖ ***Don't have sex unless you are in love.*** *What's love got to do with it? We all know that love can deceive. This is a rule that is likely to make lovers blind and encourage the sexually needy (or curious) to talk themselves into love.*

Readiness is more important than love. The time to start a sexual relationship is when it feels right to do so. The important message is that love and lust do not always coexist, and that no one should be tempted into sex in the name of lust ***or*** *love unless they are certain that it feels right for them.*

✖ ***Don't do it unless you are married.*** *The advice will be unneeded, or unheeded.*

✖ **Don't talk to me about it.** *This is either judgemental, threatening or suggests that you cannot cope with the answer. Parental ignorance may be bliss, but who then should give advice? Someone in the playground? The fact that they cannot approach you with sexual problems means they cannot be helped. Not wanting to know is also not caring enough to find out what is happening. Putting your head in the sand will not stop your child taking risks*

✖ **Tell me all.** *How can she? Could you tell her all about your sex life?*

arranged in a continuum from the most macho man to the most feminine of women, the majority of us would position ourselves as having tastes which are reflected by people at or near one end of the continuum or the other. But even those of us who consider ourselves entirely heterosexual will recognize the attraction of members of our own sex.

Many boys, and some girls, have sex together without being gay. If they really are gay, they usually know this by late adolescence, if not earlier. However, although they may be fairly sure by 14, they may not be certain until they are 19 or 20. For some women, the realization comes very much later, often not until their mid-30s.

Although some men and rather more women are bisexual, for others there is no choice: it can only be a member of their own sex. It is not clear why this happens. Some believe there is a genetic predisposition

HELPFUL PARENTAL ADVICE ABOUT SEX

✔ **Don't rush.** *It is difficult to return to a sex-free life once you have had sex. Each new relationship tends to become sexual, even if you feel unsure of its importance. Each time, sex sooner than before. Sex too early may lead to a committed sexual relationship too early. Try to give your child the confidence to wait. The inevitable pattern for most of us is dating for a while, a committed relationship or two, then settling down. Starting early does not seem to alter the pattern. It just means that we settle down sooner.*

✔ **Do what you feel is right.** *Set your own pace. Most teenagers are capable of deciding when they are ready for sex. If they ask your advice, you can be pretty sure that someone is putting them under pressure. The answer to "Should I?" is invariably "No – not until you are sure you are ready." If sexuality and their independence are accepted, teenagers can make up their own minds. Most are sensible if you allow them to be.*

✔ **Accept your child's sexuality.** *But not necessarily his or her decisions. Adolescents quickly discover that sex and the flaunting of sexuality is an excellent means of provocation. Accepting their sexuality does not mean that you should allow your 12-year-old daughter to spend the night with her 20-year-old boyfriend.*

✔ **Be well informed.** *When she asks for information and advice, she does not want vague or embarrassed mumbling. Make sure that adolescents are well informed about the mechanics and the risks of sex. Talk to them about how people feel and respond to each other, and about the realities of sex. It is not always good. Love does not necessarily make sex a moving experience. The giving and taking of pleasure is something we have to learn.*

✔ **Talk to them** *about your teenage years. They may not be that different.*

✔ **Trust them.** *And stand by them if they make mistakes.*

for men to be gay which passes in the female line (so boys inherit the tendency from their mother's family); others that it is caused by early foetal hormones. There are those who claim men are more likely to be gay if they mature early, and those that feel gay men have a certain sort of mother. No one story entirely fits the facts. One thing is certain. People are not free to choose. Nor is it always easy to come to terms with homosexuality. When all the talk is of the opposite sex who can share his or her dreams of their own sex?

An adolescent who realizes that he or she is gay needs extra support. Society still has strong homophobic tendencies, and even if family and friends are accepting and supportive, feeling different can cause unhappiness. The path is rarely as smooth as it is for a heterosexual.

Not all adolescents have the strength or the courage to 'come out'. Not all families have the strength or courage to support them if they do. The decision to tell the family is a personal one, as is the reaction of parents and siblings. We cannot always help the way we feel. Knowing that life is likely to be more difficult for the individual is bound to cause anxiety. "Be happy for me" is easily said, but it is unrealistic to suppose all parents can feel this way immediately. But in time most loving families come to accept their children's sexuality.

If she tells you she is gay

◆ **Believe what she says.** She would not have told you unless she was sure.

◆ **Accept her.** She is no different today than she was yesterday. She still needs your love and support.

◆ **Be honest.** Say something along the following lines. "Lucy, I can't pretend this isn't a shock. It will take me a little while to accept. But you are my child, and I know I must accept what is right for you. I can't be happy for you today. Give me a few weeks and I will come to terms with it." Let her know she has your love and support, but do not hide your worries and your fears.

◆ **Acceptance means accepting her friends and girlfriends.** Let her know they are welcome. Judge them as you would her sister's boyfriends – for themselves, not for their sexuality.

◆ **Let her be the judge.** Whether she 'comes out' or keeps her sexuality secret is her decision. Respect it either way.

358

Dating

Couples usually start to split off from the gang at 14 to 16. Girls start from about 14, boys a year or two later. There is a class pattern here, with middle-class girls and boys starting to date rather later than those of lower social classes. Early dating is a reassuring sign of popularity for the parent, but also worrying. Dating is distracting, and interferes with school and homework. Sometimes dating becomes too exclusive too fast, and old friends are dropped in favour of the boyfriend or girlfriend.

Although it is rarely in the nature of these first relationships to be anything but fleeting, it would be wrong to think that they are unimportant. They are often deeply felt and deeply mourned when they fail. Just being in a relationship teaches adolescents about themselves and about the opposite sex.

Teenage sex

In the early stages, sex usually means kissing, cuddling and petting. But by the age of 17, about half of all boys and girls will have experienced sexual intercourse. By 18 about three quarters will have done so.

Most teenagers are not promiscuous, and early sex usually occurs within committed relationships. However, since sex is often opportunistic, many of these early encounters take place without contraception. It is fortunate that teenagers are so infertile. If they were not, there would be many more teenage pregnancies.

Sex too soon

Children mature at different rates, and a girl who matures early in a community in which early sex is the norm may start having intercourse before the age of consent. Although discovering your 13- or 14-year-old is having intercourse is obviously both alarming and worrying, this behaviour is not necessarily either deviant or abnormal.

If the teenager presents no other problems:

◆ **Don't let the shock and disappointment blind you.** If this
child has a good relationship with you and her behaviour does not
otherwise cause concern, (ie if she has plenty of friends, and is
getting on well at school) early sex is not necessarily a catastrophe.
It may simply be the case that your daughter is mature beyond her
years.

   If the relationship has been going on for some time there is little
you can do about it. To intervene may be more disruptive to her

than the relationship itself.

◆ **Ensure that her boyfriend is neither controlling nor possessive.** Early sexual relationships are sometimes formed between two addictive personalities. This can be very restricting and is ultimately harmful.

◆ **Ensure that she is using, and understands the need for, contraception.**

◆ **Ensure this is her choice** and that she has not been pressurized into sex by an older boyfriend, or a need to show off to her friends.

◆ **Emphasize the need for her to maintain other friendships and spend time with friends.** If you are worried that the relationship is becoming too exclusive, make your acceptance of her relationship contingent upon this. Equally, ensure that she is working at school.

If the child is rebellious

Sometimes sexual experimentation is part of a wider pattern of disruptive and deviant behaviour. Angry girls sometimes use sex in the way that angry boys use aggression. If you suspect that this is the case, you may need to get outside help in dealing with the problem.

Make sure that the child is absolutely certain of your love and your acceptance. Try to build up her self-esteem. If she can feel that you give her strength, she will have less need to look for it outside. Show her a better way to express her anger.

If you feel that she is being lead into sex by an older man, intervene. Allowing a relationship between a child and an adult is likely to lead to problems. Stop it before the younger one is hurt. Ask yourself why this man wants this relationship. Does he need to control women? Does he find it easier to control children? Does he have a sexual obsession with young children?

Tell him to back off. If he refuses, remind him that sex between an adult and a girl under sixteen is illegal and that you will not hesitate to inform the police if you find he is breaking the law. Don't hesitate. Once your daughter reaches 16 or 17, she can legally make up her own mind. She can also leave home if she wishes.

Birth control

All teenagers should be informed about birth control and safe sex before the need arises. However, information on sex is rarely the problem. Most adolescents are well aware of the various methods. Their problem is that for them sex is so opportunistic. The opportunity arises before contraception has been organized.

Make sure that your daughter understands that men can wait. They are not express trains. They do have brakes and, contrary to what they say, they do not come to any harm if they apply them. Opportunity and temptation should lead to making plans, not taking action. Plans should include contraception.

◆ **Make sure that she understands she can get pregnant first time.** The chances may be very small, but they are real.

◆ **Make sure she understands that a young baby means total commitment** and will destroy her freedom and halt her development.

◆ **Make sure she understands that abortion is never easily undertaken.**

◆ **Go with her to the doctor if she is embarrassed**. Suggest that she can get condoms from a machine in an emergency.

◆ **Do not put her on the pill in readiness.** Sex is her decision. Contraception her responsibility.

Pregnancy

If your daughter tells you that she is pregnant, it is almost certainly true. Few girls make mistakes about this, or tell their parents before they are certain.

She is bound to be frightened. However angry and upset you feel, your first duty is to be as supportive as possible. It is no use shouting or screaming, nor in asking why. It has happened and all that remains is to deal with the consequences. Whatever you feel about termination, you cannot dictate to her. It is her body and her baby and, ultimately, her choice.

Sometimes pregnancy is the result of failed contraception, sometimes of a foolish chance. Occasionally it is a deliberate act on the part of a troubled teenager who wants to find someone to love; or a way of demanding love and attention either from you or her errant boyfriend. If this is the case, you should realize that it will be almost impossible for you to help and advice her. Get professional help as quickly as possible.

Dealing with an accidental pregnancy calls for patience, calm and love. Whatever the ultimate decision, the future has to be considered as objectively as possible. There are, of course, only three options and she has to give each one a fair hearing: abortion; birth and adoption; or bringing up the child either by herself or with the baby's father.

Questions that need to be addressed

Will the baby's father stand by her? Do you want him to? Does she? Can the relationship survive? Although young marriages do not have a very high survival rate, they are not necessarily a disaster. The prognosis for any marriage is little more than 50/50.

How would having the baby affect her future plans? Children do not put an end to a career or to the possibility of university, but they do delay things. A career started at 30 can progress without interruptions.

Ask her how she would feel about bringing up a child on her own. Could she cope with the responsibility and the commitment? Would she miss out on youth?

Point out that the baby is the easy part. How would she cope with a seven-year-old? A teenager?

How would she support herself? Could she live in a bedsit? Could she live without a telephone? Would she be unhappy if she could not afford clothes and outings?

How would she feel about having the baby adopted? What would be the fairest thing to do for the child? Evidence suggests that adopted children do better and are happier than those who stay with very young single mothers.

What does she feel about termination?

Tell her that there is never an ideal or easy solution.

Sexual problems at a glance

◆ **Sex games with younger children.** These are always wrong. If you find your adolescent child playing sex games with siblings or their friends, stop them immediately. Make your disapproval and horror very clear. Talk to both children (and the parents of the other younger child). If it persists, you will need to call in professional help.

◆ **Masturbation.** Virtually all boys masturbate. By the age of 16, two thirds of girls masturbate. This could well be a fairly accurate reflection of their respective sex drives at this age. While the view that women need love and men need sex does not accurately reflect the needs of adults, it may be a fairly accurate comment on teenage feelings. In the past, masturbation was shameful and children were afraid of what might happen to them if they did it too much. Thankfully this is no longer the case, and most teenagers accept that it is quite normal.

◆ **Porn in a boy's bedroom.** This is no more than a sign he is growing up. If in doubt, ask his father. Almost all boys look at pictures of nudes. Older men and boys often use these as images for masturbation. Young boys often do not need such images to arouse them. It may be curiosity, it may be arousal. Either way, it's his business.

◆ **A boyfriend or girlfriend staying the night.** If you accept your children's sexuality, and know they are sexually active, it seems to me that you should accept that they have to do it somewhere. I have always felt that I would rather know who they were with, and have thus given limited approval to girlfriends and boyfriends staying overnight. My simple rules are: not before 16; not unless I have met their partner first; and no casual partners.

◆ **Sleeping away from home.** When I was growing up 'staying with a friend' was our way of arranging sexual encounters. It still is. The duplicity can be quite dangerous. It means no one knows where your child is staying. Always insist on a telephone number if she is spending the night with a friend, and check that she is staying where she claims to be staying.

Teenagers behaving badly

There, of course, times when we feel low, moody and upset; and there are times when we feel happy, energetic and enthusiastic. Such extremes are more commonplace when we undergo change. New parents feel this way. So do the middle-aged and the newly retired.

Change often leads to inertia, and studies invariably show that change predisposes people to depression. Even good changes such as new friends, jobs or a new house can have this effect. Given the enormous changes of puberty, it is not surprising that adolescents sometimes feel depressed.

Just add them up: a change of body; a change of status; a change in the nature of the central relationships in their lives; a change of school, of friends, of responsibility. You should allow teenagers to be moody, depressed and easily upset. There is rarely any cause for alarm.

Tell your adolescent that accepting the occasional 'down' is the price to pay for growing up; that if you have a really good wallow you you'll probably end up laughing at yourself; and that, if possible, depression should be fought by going out and doing something.

However, it can be dangerous to assume that a teenager who threatens suicide does not mean it, or that one who seems to be seriously unbalanced is just in a particularly bad mood. Remember, too, that rapid mood change can be a sign of drug problems.

What is 'normal' adolescent behaviour?

If a behaviour pattern interferes with life, start worrying.

If her behaviour makes her extremely difficult to live with, take note. Similarly if a youngster is socially withdrawn and unhappy. If she seems unable to find the energy for action, seems depressed and unhappy, you should seek help. If she consistently acts in order to attract attention, ask why.

As you would expect, some prickly children grow into even more prickly teenagers. A sudden onset of difficult behaviour is, however, a cause for concern.

As ever, low self-esteem is a potent cause of bad behaviour during the teenage years. A person who feels bad may act bad.

Remember that when things go seriously wrong, it is rarely one person's fault. Some of the fault almost certainly belongs to the child, some to the child's peers, some to society, some to the family. Blaming helps no one. Problems need to be accepted and dealt with.

As a child, your adolescent probably played monster games. They were a useful way of coming to terms with fear: pretend there were monsters under the table, feel terrified, then shriek with laughter as you poke them with a stick. Adolescent sadness and depression could well serve the same purpose. As the blues come and go, you learn a necessary lesson for adulthood – how to cope with them. Tell her that you have discovered:

◆ **Sadness *always* has a beginning, a middle and an end.** If it is allowed to take its course, it will evaporate.

◆ **Sadness should be shared.** Sometimes it is not possible to find your way out of sadness unless it is shared.

◆ **Bottoming out can help.** Crying is therapeutic.

When depression is an illness

Clinical depression is quite rare in children, but relatively common in adults and adolescents. There is quite a strong familial tendency. It can occur quite suddenly or creep up gradually. Although life events such as changing school, the break-up of relationships or friendships, can aggravate depression, they probably do not cause it. Sometimes clinical depression arrives without obvious rhyme or reason.

Some people seem to be prone to depression on dark days, and for them depression is most common in winter. For anyone who is more sad in winter it is worth seeing whether exposure to bright light helps. Consult your doctor.

Clinically depressed individuals find it hard to do things. They are not just sad; they are temporarily inactive and incapable of organizing their lives. Treating them is a job for the professional.

The classic symptoms are:

◆ **Not feeling 'yourself'**; putting yourself down; feeling that you are a bad or useless person.

◆ **Feeling numb and empty.** Not being able to feel any emotions except sadness.

◆ **Feeling unable to change how you feel,** or any aspect of your life; not knowing how to snap out of it any more. Seeing the future as unutterably bleak.

◆ **Disturbed sleep.** Finding it hard to get to sleep. Waking up in the night.

◆ **Often feeling nervous and on edge.**

◆ **Disturbed eating patterns.** Either overeating, or not feeling like eating at all.

◆ **Unable to concentrate** or to organize time.

◆ **Feeling tired and inert.** Wanting to sleep during the day; watching TV all the time.

◆ **Avoiding people.** Wanting to be alone.

◆ **Not caring how you look.**

Helping someone with depression

Getting through the day is an effort for someone who is depressed, *but* simply getting out of bed alleviates depression. Emphasize that even small achievements are worthwhile. Go to school, even if it is hard. She may not achieve much, but simply getting there is a plus. Praise her for going. Get her to praise herself.

◆ **Help her to stay busy.** Talk, even if she does not always feel like it.

◆ **Encourage her to write down her feelings.**

◆ **Find things to look forward to.** Plan holidays and outings, accept invitations, even if you know she may opt out.

Suicide

The slide from depression to suicide can be gradual or abrupt. In the depth of depression people rarely kill themselves. Depression happens in cycles. Suicide is more likely to happen on the way down or on the way back up, perhaps because it needs anger as well as despair to kill yourself. In the pits of depression the inertia is too great.

In the early teens the slide from depression to suicide can be particularly rapid. The turning point is often an event which not only makes her unhappy but angry, too, such as being dumped by a boyfriend; family discord; failing exams; or being the victim of bullying.

Warning signs include: deep depression; lashing out; preoccupation with death and suicide; talking about suicide; planning how and when to kill oneself; saying that death is romantic; seeing killing yourself for love as noble. Almost half of all suicide victims have talked about killing themselves in the previous 24 hours.

Gathering the means, such as hoarding pills; withdrawal from friends and family; giving away valued possessions; crying and not being able to stop; taking more drugs or drinking more than usual.

If you fear your child is suicidal

The obvious steps are:

◆ **Get professional help immediately.** Ring the Samaritans. See your doctor. Make sure that she carries the number of the Samaritans and that she can contact you at all times

◆ **Talk.** Get her friends to talk. It may well be a cry for help and attention, but it is a desperate one. She may not mean to commit suicide, but that will not necessarily stop her doing so. Many of those who succeed have made previous attempts to kill themselves. Some of those who succeed may also be asking for help; it is a chance you cannot take.

◆ **Openly discuss the importance of avoiding the final slide.** If she feels desperate, she has to pick up the phone and keep talking, or to ask someone to come around. If there's no one available, then she must get out of the house and away from the means of death. Even delaying suicide by ten minutes will almost certainly save her life.

This is because for most people the temptation is fleeting. Make sure that she understands this; that if she can hang on for half an hour she is probably safe.

Are you an embarrassment?

It is perfectly normal to be embarrassed by teenagers and for them to be embarrassed by their parents, especially when we fail to act like the middle-aged bores we really are. It is not a parent's job to stand out from the background, especially at a school function. All teenagers want average and invisible parents.

I can remember thinking my mother was too friendly and too ready to talk to my friends. My sister remembers being embarrassed because she discussed poetry. My son once refused to stay at school on parents' evening because his father was wearing a purple jacket.

The very qualities that will be valued in later years – empathy, sympathy, gregariousness, support – are the ones which now embarrass them most. This is because they are the most likely to bring you into contact with their friends. Never mind that their friends say you are terrific. That is not the point.

You will be less of an embarrassment if:

◆ **You let them check out (or better still) choose your clothing for parents evenings and school functions.** Never wear anything loud, out of fashion, overly grand or that draws attention to you. Jeans and a dark jumper, a black skirt and sweater hit the right note. Never wear a pink shell suit, mirrored sunglasses or a wedding hat.

◆ **Greet her friends, then recede into the background**. Do not share your opinions with her friends. Never try to act their age. Never think you are their friend's friend.

◆ **Never whistle or sing in public.**

◆ **Never express your fondness for ageing rock stars.**

◆ **It helps if your home looks how she and her friends think homes should look.** That is, like those of all of her friends.

◆ **It helps if your car is suitably impressive.** If it is not, it helps if you park it around the corner.

Teenager – parent relationship

It's bound to be a confused relationship because one moment she may feel and act very grown-up, the next just like a child. It is unavoidable that sometimes you treat the 'adult' as a child, and the 'child' as an adult.

Rest assured that the teenager who has never given her parents a moment's worry is either very secretive or unusually quiet. Parents have always felt that young people are more rootless, troubled, promiscuous and less idealistic than their peers in earlier generations. Like our parents, we point to increased drug use, teenage suicide, delinquency, teenage pregnancy and the growing preoccupation with self-fulfilment. It is perfectly normal for teenagers to take the opposite view.

After all, most of them are better informed at this age, less foolishly idealistic and sentimental, more open, pragmatic, tolerant, and honest than their parents. The differences between our children and our young selves (or our great grandparents when young) are largely illusory. Flapper girls of the 1920s did not dress like their mothers. Hooligan was a term coined in the 19th century. If today's youth are more troubled, promiscuous, and self-involved than yesterday's youth, in being so they do little more than reflect the rest of society. Today's mid-lifers are also more promiscuous, self-absorbed, and dependent on (legal) drugs, than their parents' generation.

Over the past 40 years there have been many surveys of teenagers' opinions, beliefs and actions. They are in general agreement that the vast majority of teenage and pre-teenage kids are well behaved, law abiding, hopeful, hard-working and realistic. In fact, there is no evidence to suggest that most do not cope well with adolescence. Anorexia, drug addiction, teenage prostitution, unwanted pregnancy, petty and violent crime give teenagers a bad press. But those involved are a minute proportion of all teenagers. Adults are involved in similar problem behaviours.

Most adolescents succeed. When they fail, they try to find out what they can do to avoid another failure. When facing a new situation they make plans and try to find out everything they can about it. Most teenagers report that they can become independent of their families without bitterness. Most also report that they enjoy life, and keep their temper most of the time. About a third of them say that they often feel sad, unsure and tense, and that their feelings are easily hurt. About 20 per cent are sometimes depressed. Few admit to taking criticism without resentment.

Most teenagers do not give their parents any major problems. They may irritate us at times. But what adult sharing our homes and our lives would not?

How different are teenagers from adults?

◆ They are likely to be more concerned about their appearance.

◆ They are likely to be moodier. Boys may be more aggressive.

◆ They are likely to assert independence by dressing and speaking differently, by having different beliefs and values. They may be rebellious and occasionally rude.

◆ Their friends are important, in fact they may seem to value their friends' good opinion more than they value yours.

◆ They need to wear the 'right' clothes, listen to the 'right' music.

◆ They need to feel they belong to a peer group.

◆ They can have a strong sense of justice and a need to fight for their rights.

◆ They often need to take risks

◆ They want increasing independence; they no longer want to join family outings or family holidays.

Changing your attitudes

It is difficult to give independence of thought and action to your teenage child, more difficult still to a pre-teenager, but it must be done. Remember, independence which is not freely given will be hacked away from you. The harder you hold on, the more violent the break needed. Sometimes the act of claiming independence is too violent for the wounds ever to heal completely and the scars made in the relationship will always remain.

When children are tiny, they see their parents as perfect, even when in reality they are clearly flawed. What they want from them is love and attention, and if these are forthcoming, they are willing to overlook most of the parents' faults. As children grow up they realize that love and attention are not enough. They also want acceptance. The gift of acceptance is sometimes hard to give to a moody, self-absorbed and selfish pre-teenager who questions her parents' dearest beliefs. Equally, that gift of acceptance is hard for a teenager to give to a controlling, fallible parent who wears the wrong sort of clothes, drives the wrong sort of car and has values which she thinks were out of date in Victorian times.

Stay with discipline that works

The pre-teen years are not a time for throwing out a system that works. If your child has not become a seething mass of belligerence, you are probably hitting the right note for this child. Stick to it. If, however, you are beginning to find that the controls which worked in the past now lead to desertion, it may be time to start looking at how to change things.

Methods of discipline that sometimes work

◆ **Bribery/rewards.**

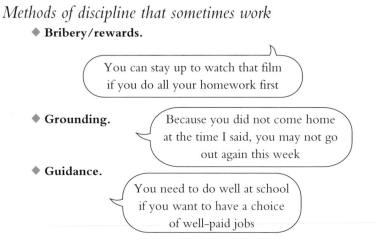

> You can stay up to watch that film if you do all your homework first

◆ **Grounding.**

> Because you did not come home at the time I said, you may not go out again this week

◆ **Guidance.**

> You need to do well at school if you want to have a choice of well-paid jobs

◆ **Understanding.**

> I understand that you find the work difficult, but copying Alice's homework will not help you

◆ **Threats.**

> If you are rude one more time, I am stopping your pocket money

(But threats only work if it is known that you always carry them out.) Better to say

> You can be rude to me again, or you can have pocket money this week: it is your choice

◆ **Pleading.**

> I've been so worried. Please try to think about how I feel sometimes

Better still:

> Here is a phonecard. I expect you to call me if you are going to be later than ten thirty

Equally, let her know if you are going to be out late. If you play by the same rules, they are no big deal.

◆ **Orders.**

> I expect the table to be cleared and laid for supper by seven

Orders are pointless unless you see to it that they are obeyed.

◆ **Supervision.**

> The school say you have not been going in. I am going to deliver you to the door each morning

◆ **Explanation.**

If you leave food to dry on to the plate, the dishwasher cannot cope. You will have to wash the dishes from your room by hand. If this happens again I am going to buy paper plates. I will take the cost from your pocket money

◆ **Withdrawing privileges.**

If you are not back in time for tea, you will not be allowed out at the weekend. If you continue to be rude, I will not cook any meals for you

Teenagers are not there to make you happy

And nor are children. To deal with a teenage child you need to be strong, happy and self-sufficient. All too often, parents replace feelings of strength and happiness with guilt, worry and frustration. Instead of being happy for themselves, they make their happiness dependent on their teenagers' behaviour. There is a strong tendency for parents who think like this to put their own wishes, thoughts and feelings to one side and respond only to what the child demands. They end up sacrificing both their own happiness and the child's respect.

Instead of feeling:

"I'm here to wait on her."
"I'm going to have to cook another meal for her."
"I don't like her friends."
"She is too young to be sensible."
"What will other people think?"
"I have to mould her into the paths of righteousness."

Ask yourself:

"Why do I always make her the focus of attention?"
"Why am I trying to control her behaviour rather than doing what I want to do?"
"Why am I trying to convince her to change, but ultimately fitting in with her demands instead of concentrating on what I can do?"

HOW NOT TO MAKE THE TEENAGER JUST ANOTHER WORKER BEE

✔ *"I expect you to keep your room tidy."*

✔ *"I expect you to take the dirty dishes out of the living room and put them in the dishwasher."*

✔ *"I do not have time to take care of that. You will have to do it yourself."*

✔ *"I wash at the weekend. If you need clean clothes at other times, wash them yourself."*

✔ *"I only wash the things in the laundry basket."*

✔ *"I see a lot of long-distance calls on this bill. I expect you to pay for them. We can deduct them from your pocket money or you can do some extra work about the house."*

✔ *"I am afraid your Christmas present this year will be these bills in a pretty card."*

✔ *"There are probably some potatoes you could put in the microwave."*

STATEMENTS THAT MAKE YOUR TEENAGER FEEL LIKE THE QUEEN BEE

✖ *"Why can't you keep your room tidy?"*

✖ *"Why must you play music so loud?"*

✖ *"Why didn't you tell me you needed your football kit this afternoon?"*

✖ *"Have you been ringing up chatlines again?"*

✖ *"I told you we were eating at 7 pm. Now the meal is ruined."*

✖ *"Why do you leave dirty dishes in the lounge?"*

✖ *"I shouldn't have to collect up your dirty underwear."*

The need for privacy

If she wants to put up a 'Keep Out' sign on her door, that's her business. Don't read her letters, or her diary. Don't tell her secrets to your family or friends. Don't expect to be her best friend, or her confidant.

Letting go of their problems

Teenage problems come in two varieties. There are those things that primarily affect her behaviour; and those that primarily affect yours. 'Mistreats my property'; 'does not do household chores'; 'lies to me'; primarily affect you. 'Uses drugs'; 'skips school'; 'does not do her homework;' 'won't clean her room' primarily affect her.

You can deal with the problems that primarily affect you, but when it comes to the problems that primarily affect her, she is in control. You can try to cling on to these problems, believing they are your fault or that it is your responsibility to protect her from hardship that she brings upon herself. But taking responsibility for policing her behaviour is likely to lead to even greater irresponsibility on her part. If a parent picks up the pieces why should a teenager bother about what gets dropped?

You cannot be responsible for another adult. You can advise and you can lay the ground rules. Sooner or later you have to turn the responsibility for all problems which affect your child's life over to her. I am not suggesting this is easy. Whether she does her homework, or makes an effort at school can affect the child's entire future. But it is not your job to ensure that she does her homework. The whole point of homework is that children learn the responsibility of working by and for themselves. If teenagers can leave all the worrying to parents, they will. In the short term, being irresponsible is fun.

A child who makes her own decisions can feel pride. One who learns by her mistakes really learns.

Problems that belong to her
- How she looks.
- Her room.
- When she gets up.
- What she tells you.
- What music she likes.
- Whether or not she works at school.
- Whether she takes drugs.

Problems that belong to you

◆ Her radio playing loudly in the living room and kitchen.
◆ Her mess all over the house.
◆ Never being able to find a dry towel in the bathroom.
◆ Rudeness.
◆ Mistreats my property.
◆ Does not help in the house.

Problems that concern you both

◆ What she wears when we visit Aunt Maud.
◆ Whether she has her boyfriend to stay.
◆ Whether she goes to school.
◆ Whether she smokes marijuana in her bedroom.

THE WRONG WAY TO DEAL WITH TEENAGE PROBLEMS

✖ *Pretend they do not exist. Pouring a stiff drink and watching the TV is fine if it helps you summon up the energy to tackle the problem; not if it helps you avoid facing it.*
✖ *Store them up. Hoarding problems only brings more pain.*
✖ *Blame. Laying blame does not help you find a solution.*
✖ *Rejecting the child. Cutting yourself off produces a temporary solution, not a long-term one.*
✖ *Aggression. You can use your aggression constructively but fighting entraps you.*
✖ *Passivity. You can ask for help but passively waiting for it entraps you.*
✖ *Defeatism. Assuming that you cannot solve problems stops you seeing that you can.*

THE RIGHT WAY TO DEAL WITH TEENAGE PROBLEMS

✔ **Accept.** *The first step to a solution is admitting a problem exists.*

✔ **Believe that the problem can be solved.**

✔ **Don't try to find out whose fault it is:** *judgement is best left to judges. It gets in the way of understanding.*

✔ **Talk.** *Bottling things up often gets them out of proportion. Talking it through can help you see solutions. Getting external help (from councillors or parents' networks) can empower you and make you feel less isolated.*

✔ **Determine who owns the problem.** *See pages 374-375. Let everyone solve their own problems. You cannot make a teenager do something she has no intention of doing. You can only deal with that part of her problem that belongs to you.*

✔ **Break it down.** *Sometimes a problem is too big to handle. So try to solve parts of it. In doing so you may well find, incidentally, that you can tackle the whole problem.*

✔ **Say what you want and what you feel rather than make accusations.** *"I want the dishes taken into the kitchen." or "I feel hurt that you did not discuss this with me first." Avoid "You are always leaving dirty dishes about." and "You never let me know what you are doing."*

✔ **Express your beliefs, values and opinions for what they are: your opinions.** *Do not pretend or believe these are the only truth.*

✔ **Give permission to tell you how she feels.** *"If you want me to listen, ask. If you do not think I am being fair, tell me. If you need my support, ask me directly."*

✔ **Read between the lines.** *People never say entirely what they mean, or mean entirely what they say. Is that fear or anger talking? Is she asking for something you are not giving? Is she seeking attention? Protection?*

Power? A return to the safety of childhood?

✔ **Time it right.** *Judge when to talk. Ask if you are unsure. Always allow the time and the privacy for a full discussion. Discussion on a full stomach is always best. Families fight more often before dinner than after.*

✔ **Respond rather than react.** *If faced with an inflammatory statement stay calm, count to ten and express what you feel. "It upsets me when you are offensive, and I am sorry you feel it is necessary. I expect you to take responsibility for putting your dirty cups into the dishwasher. I want it done right away. You can do it yourself or pay me or your brother to do it. If this is your choice I will deduct the money from this week's pocket money."*

✔ **Ask for what you want.** *It sounds obvious, but this is far more effective than you may realize. "I want you to listen quietly while I tell you how I feel."*

✔ **Be willing to make changes.** *Negotiation is not possible with a dictator. If you insist you are always in the right, she will fight you to the bitter end. Conflicts are resolved more quickly if each person's priorities are understood.*

✔ **Accept that you make mistakes and learn by them.** *If you always insist on being right, so will she. Apologize and figure out a better way to do it next time.*

✔ **Keep focused on the here and now.** *Of course problems have a history, but the history is never helpful. It is the dirty cups that are the problem – not the mess he left last week or the fact that he did not work in primary school.*

✔ **Check that you are not getting the wrong end of the stick.** *"Do you mean…?" "Are you saying…?" But don't be snide or sarcastic; play it straight. This is a useful delaying tactic – a way of responding, rather than reacting.*

✔ **Don't be afraid to ask for professional help.** *Ask the school to refer you to school counsellors or educational psychologists. Ask your doctor.*

HOW TO ASSERT YOUR RIGHTS

When it comes to dealing with lifestyle clashes there are some very basic rules which seem to work in most situations.

Select the most irritating habit or the one you think is most easily handled.

◆ **Start with a clear statement of intent and your willingness to negotiate.**

> I want to come to an agreement about the volume of the music played in the house. I think we could work something out together

◆ **State what you think would be a fair agreement.**

> I want you to leave your ghetto blaster in your room and to keep the door closed. You can take it into the bathroom, but use your Walkman if you want to listen to music in another part of the house

◆ **Let her state her case.** She might, for example, say that she and her friends like music when they are together in the kitchen, or that she needs music when she is clearing up. Negotiate a reasonable compromise.

◆ **Then, insist** – and do so with utmost persistence.

> We made a deal, turn that down

Don't get into fights about it; don't put yourself in a bad light. Don't give her the opportunity to play the victim. Just firmly insist that the music is turned down until the end of the song, and that she then returns the ghetto blaster to her bedroom and uses her Walkman if she wants to continue to listen.

◆ **If you are ignored or further discussion ensues, assert your rights.** Start by summarizing her excuses:

> I know you are listening to that song

Then give your side.

> **AND** I don't want that loud music in the kitchen, especially when I am trying to prepare dinner

The use of 'AND' implies some accommodation – it reiterates the agreement you made.

◆ **Take action.** You may never have to make a stand, but some teenagers do push parents to the limit. If this happens, keep calm. State what you want using a relaxed statement which keeps the issue in focus.

> Susan, we are all getting hungry and I need to be in the kitchen. I am not prepared to make supper with that music playing

If this gives no result, say what you are going to do. Choose something that is clearly related to the request, so the focus is on him doing what is asked, rather than punishment.

> I'm sorry, I don't want to be in the room with that music playing. If you want to prepare supper for us all that is fine, if not please switch it off. If supper is not under way by 6.45 I will order a pizza and take the payment from your pocket money and your school lunch money

If this still has no effect, move into action. Remember this is not about punishment or teaching her a lesson. It is about your credibility. She has to learn to take you at your word. Order the pizza, present her with the bill, and don't give her pocket money or school lunch money until you have recouped the cost.

◆ **Go on strike.** If after systematically following these steps she still plays loud music, does not help to bring the shopping in, or persists with any other ungrateful or thoughtless behaviour, go on strike.

> My time is limited. I have decided that I am not going to cook for the next week

Don't be afraid to do something which will affect other members of the family, even if they are innocent. The overriding aim now is to show you that will not be taken for granted. It will not hurt the rest of the family to take note of this.

In between

Children do not always know what they want: just that they want something. They do not always want their parents' attention, but they certainly do not want their inattention. They want parents who place them at the centre of the world, yet are willing to stand on the sidelines: an impossible requirement.

Now add to this parental tightrope the bogey of adolescence. Inevitably there are problems. Anyone who has a child knows that they cannot please all of the time. Anyone who has had any adult relationship knows that it is impossible to please a partner all of the time. What price an adolescent who is one moment a child and the next an adult? Especially when this oscillation happens twice an hour.

It is essential to remember that adolescent problems are more than skin deep. All too often, the apparent problem is a sign of something deeper. That something deeper centres around self-esteem. Problem children frequently feel insecure and unhappy. Parents can respect a child; or the child can attempt to demand that respect through bad behaviour. They can ensure that the child offers them respect, or they can sit back and be trampled underfoot. The byword just now is respect – mutual respect. It won't solve everything, but it will keep some of the problems at bay.

Step-by-step problem solving

If you are in a real *impasse* with your teenager, try solving problems step by step. Some of the steps listed below will seem obvious in isolation, but as part of a strategy, they can have added value.

◆ **Identify and define the problem.** Without blaming, spell out both the surface and the underlying problems. Say what upsets you, what you feel, why you are irritated.

◆ **Brainstorm to find possible solutions.** Express and record all ideas as fast as you each can think of them. Sometimes quite silly ideas make good solutions.

◆ **Evaluate.** Look closely at all the alternatives. Work though all the consequences. What would happen if she had a kettle and tea and coffee in her room? Would a personal stereo be the solution to the noise problem?

◆ **Choose the best solution.** All parties to any conflict need to agree.

◆ **Implement the solution.** What changes does each party need to make. Will they make them? Should the solution be imposed for an experimental period? In some situations, a 'contract' – a memo on a sheet of paper signed by both parties – may eliminate confusion.

◆ **Evaluate again.** Consider the results. Is the situation better or worse? Should a new agreement be made or does it need alteration? Should this solution be scrapped? Why is it not working?

HOW TO FAIL AT PROBLEM SOLVING BEFORE YOU START

✖ *Think or say it is never going to be any different.*

✖ *Think "It's all my fault."*

✖ *Think "It's all her fault."*

✖ *Blame her so that she has to start defending herself.*

✖ *Start by saying "I wish you could..."*

HOW TO WIN AT PROBLEM SOLVING

✔ *Believe that if you change how you interact with your child you can change her behaviour.*

✔ *Consider the limits of your ability to change her. You can support her, but she must learn to make her own decisions.*

✔ *Start by saying "I expect you to..."*

✔ *Make your expectations clear and specific.*

HOW TO GET TO AN *IMPASSE* IN ONE STEP

✖ *"You're all sweetness when you want something."*

✖ *"Where is that jumper you borrowed?"*

✖ *"Get this mess cleared up now."*

✖ *"You'd better call me, or else."*

✖ *"I wish you'd do your homework."*

✖ *"Why can't you get up without me calling you?"*

✖ *"Don't you talk to me like that."*

HOW TO AVOID AN *IMPASSE*

✔ *"I would like to talk to you. Can we set aside some time?"*

✔ *"I expect you to return my sweater by tomorrow. Otherwise I will not lend you my clothing."*

✔ *"I expect this room to be cleared up in the next 15 minutes so that I can prepare dinner."*

✔ *"I'd like you to call me if you are going to be late."*

✔ *"Let me know your plans so I can arrange when we eat…"*

✔ *"I wish you'd go to bed by 11 pm so it would be easier to get up for school."*

✔ *"I don't talk to you like that. And I do not expect you to talk to me like that."*

Teenage problems – a survey

This is not an exhaustive list, but it includes the commonest problems. Each is looked at in terms of the problem-solving principles described above.

We cannot agree about anything

A problem that belongs to both of you. I suggest that you start by attempting a truce that gives you both the right to hold opinions (such as what is great music, what looks good), and requires agreement on lifestyle issues (whether washing up needs to be done once a week or three times a day); and that any agreements on the latter are binding.

Equally, allow her a view on matters that affect the individual (such as what time people get up), but insist on reaching agreement about matters that affect the entire family (such as how long the bathroom is out of action). Say before you begin: "Your thoughts are your domain, and you can think what you like. When it comes to actions that affect other people, changes are requested, and we will discuss them."

Then get down to it. Select one problem, and get out the kitchen timer. Start by taking three minutes to state your case. In this period she may not interrupt. She then has three minutes to state her case. Again, no interruptions are allowed.

Then you each have three uninterrupted minutes in which to respond. During that time you have to propose your own solution.

She is rude to you when she is with her friends

Your problem. Be firm. "I do not like the way you act when you are with your friends. I expect you to be as polite and respectful to me as I am to you. Your friends are banned from the house for three days. If you continue to be rude to me in front of your friends, I will ban them from the house for good." If she continues to be rude, do whatever you said you would do, otherwise you are lost.

Takes all the wet washing from the machine and leaves it in a pile while she washes and dries her jeans

Your problem. "Alice, I understand you needed your jeans washed. However, that is no excuse for leaving the wet washing on the table. In future when you need to use the washing machine I expect you to put any wet washing you find into the dryer, or hang it up."

If it happens again. "Alice, I do not intend to tell you about this again.

383

If I find wet washing on the table again I will throw your dirty laundry into the shed. Irritation and frustration is probably best returned in kind.

If it happens again, carry out your threat.

Never lets you know where she is
A problem for both of you. Divide the problem into her part and your part.

Her part: it is up to her whether or not she tells you what she is doing. Your part: you need to know how to contact her. You need to know whenever she is going to be late.

Solving her part. "Linda, I would be happier if I knew were you were, it is hard sometimes not to worry. I have to keep reminding myself that you are old enough to look after yourself. I understand what you do with your time is your business. I trust you to behave sensibly."

Solving your part. "Linda, can we agree on some ground rules about this? If you are going to be gone for more than a couple of hours I expect you to leave me a contact number, or ring home to say what you are doing. Can we agree that you will let me know if you expect to be more than half an hour late?"

Always stays out later than you allow
A problem for both of you. She wants to be with her friends. She feels you expect her to be in earlier than her friends. You worry when she is late.

Agree that it is her responsibility to ensure she comes home at the time agreed, and always tries to let you know if she is delayed. If she breaks this agreement, she must understand that privileges will be withdrawn.

"Linda, when you are late, we get worried. Being responsible also includes being considerate. I have discussed how late you should stay out with Anna and Sarah's parents and we have agreed that 10.30 is reasonable in the week, and 11.30 at weekends. Obviously there will be some occasions when you may need to be later than this, but on most occasions I expect you to keep to these times. Obviously, you will sometimes be delayed. If possible, you should warn me in advance. If you cannot keep to this agreement, I will have to ground you."

If she still stays out late: ground her. One day for the first time, two days for the second, four for the third and so on.

Wants a part-time job – delivering newspapers
Another problem for both of you. You are nervous about her delivering in the dark, so agree that she can share the work with a friend; or

do it in the summer.

Similarly, if she wants to do a Saturday job, and you don't think she can fit it in with her homework, agree that she can have the job, but if she gets behind with her homework it will have to stop.

Won't do homework

Her problem. Achieving at school is completely bound up in your mind with the child's future. It is hard to let go of this one, but doing so throws the responsibility over to the child, and I think that is where it should rest.

You could: stand over her until she finishes; withhold privileges unless she does her homework every night; bring the household to a halt until she has completed.

Or you could let go of the problem in a way that shows respect, love and trust, and gives her the responsibility.

In doing so, state your feelings: "I am worn out trying to make you do your homework. So from now on I am leaving it up to you. I won't ask, and I won't interfere."

"I know you are capable of doing well academically. I know you are also mature enough and capable enough to make your own decisions. I trust you to do what is best for you."

Address the part of the problem which affects you. "I have explained to the school that I will not sign for homework you have not shown to me."

Not working at school

Her problem. You could nag, plead, get upset; withhold privileges when she gets a poor report; defend her to her teachers, find excuses; blame bad company. Or you could let go of the problem in a way that shows respect, love and trust, and gives her responsibility.

"I am worried you do not work at school. I would like you to be able to get a good job and it worries me that you will not be able to go to college, or have good enough exam grades to choose the career you want."

"I have talked to your teachers. They are frustrated by you, too. But from now on we have agreed that it is up to you to work. They will keep you in detention if you have not completed your work. I won't interfere."

"I know you are capable of doing well academically. I trust you to do what is best for you."

Hold on to your resolve. When faced with making their own decisions, teenagers often try to throw the responsibility back at you.

A bad report

Her problem. You should express sadness at her decision not to work, but don't judge and don't take over the responsibility. "Your report arrived today. I am disappointed to find you have not worked this term. I was hoping you would have started to work harder."

Say what you feel. Acknowledge that you are not in control. "I would like you to do well academically. But I cannot make you study."

Point out the consequences. "At this rate you will not be entered for the top GCSE grades. You may not have the exam grades to get a good job or go to college."

Emphasize that the responsibility is hers. "I cannot make you work. Nor can the school. This is your choice."

Offer, but do not impose, help. "I am willing to help you catch up, but you will have to ask me."

Recognize her feelings. "I understand you feel under pressure, and that you are not very happy at school. I am always willing to discuss problems with you."

Address the part of the problem that affects you. "I want you to know that in future I will only talk to the teachers when you are present."

School phobia and skipping school

Primarily her problem, but she may need help in dealing with it.

There are many reasons why children skip school, ranging from school phobia and victimization to simply opting out. If your teenager is reluctant to go to school, or all too frequently finds an excuse for not going, such as ill-defined pains in the stomach, or headaches, you need to assess the most likely reasons. Obviously, you have to eliminate illness first. Then consider:

Is the child a victim? Talk to the child and the school about the possibility of bullying. Check for obvious signs – taking money into school, or going into school by a round-about route.

The child may be afraid to leave you. This is quite common when there are problems at home. Try to reassure her.

The child may be punishing you. If education is important to you (as it so often is), opting out of school is a very obvious way of protesting against perceived injustice, family trauma, jealousy and general stress and strife.

The child may be very unhappy. Children do not always make an easy transition from a small primary school into a large secondary school, especially if they do not know many other children. Try to help her settle into school by inviting other teenagers at the school to visit, or to go on outings or do activities.

She may prefer to hang around with friends. Once children start opting out of school it can become all too easy to stay out and all too difficult to go back. It takes courage for a child to go back into school after a long absence.

If there is no simple explanation of the child's fear, she may well have a mild school phobia. This is best treated by saying how courageous it is to go to school at all. Praise each small step along the way: getting ready; coping with the journey (you should take her to school yourself); staying at school.

Understand that this is a real fear, however improbable it may seem to you. Teach her how to relax, and show her how to calm herself when afraid. Muscle relaxation is a useful technique, and so is thinking of being on a sunny beach and feeling happy. Since a personal stereo is quite a common accessory for teenagers, you might consider giving her a relaxation tape to listen to on the way to school. Talk to the school about the use of such of personal stereos in school.

If the problem persists, it is one for an educational psychologist.

Never gets up when she is called
Her problem. Buy her an alarm clock. If she isn't up by the time you have to go out, call her once, then leave her. If she is late for school, let it be her responsibility.

Never remembers to organize her books the night before
Stop nagging, and let her take responsibility. She will never remember if she can always rely on you to do it.

You don't like the way she dresses
What she wears is her business. Agree that on some occasions (going out to visit your friends) she should modify his dress so that it is more to your taste, and that she needs to conform with what the school requires. The rest of the time it is up to her.

Won't come on family outings
Trust her to stay at home. Agree, however, that she will treat the house with respect. If there is any damage it should be paid for out of her allowance or Christmas/birthday/holiday money.

Never reads
Her problem. Books on tape might whet her appetite.

Always playing computer games

Her problem. As long as it does not interfere with school work or family meals this is her business. It is usually a passing phase. If it does interfere, address that part of the problem.

"Supper will be ready in 20 minutes. I expect you to stop playing on the computer soon enough to lay the table for supper. If the table is not laid in time, we will eat without you. That is your choice. If you choose to make your own supper I will expect you to clear up the kitchen afterwards."

If she makes her own supper but does not clear up: "I expect the kitchen to be cleared. If it is not I will confiscate the computer for three days."

If a teenager steals

Look at the possible reasons in turn. Is it because she needs money – perhaps because she has less money than her friends; or perhaps to buy drugs? Or maybe she is seeking revenge? An angry or hurting child hits out in ways that hurt and upset. Or seeking attention?

She might be doing it to buy temporary friends; because it is a habit; because it is exciting; because she can see no other way of having her heart's desire. Or she might be doing it to please someone, or to pay off a bully.

◆ **Make your values clear.** At this age there need be no confusion about the moral issues.

◆ **Set an irreproachable example.** Don't ever steal, cheat or accept errors in your favour.

◆ **Make her give it back.**

◆ **Be reasonable about pocket money.** Teenagers need spending money. Look carefully into her money needs.

◆ **Help her.** If she is stealing because her friends steal, talk to their parents.

◆ **Ask for help.** Contact a professional organization before she gets caught by someone less well disposed than you.

Delinquent

You will probably already know if your teenager comes into this category. But many parents worry whether their child is potentially delinquent. It is quite a complicated picture. Plenty of children with a history of hyperactivity, and those with reading and learning problems, become delinquent teenagers. So do aggressive children and those who bullied when younger.

Delinquent teenagers are rarely happy, they are often disliked by classmates and many come from unstable and unhappy backgrounds. Many have parents who seem uninterested and uninvolved in the lives of their children and are harshly punitive, unloving or intolerant. Some of these parents have psychiatric or social problems. However, not all delinquents have such backgrounds. A few are drawn into delinquency by an inability to get on with other children, by weakness, or because delinquency gives them a sense of power.

Sooner or later most delinquents are caught by the police. This may result in an official caution, informal supervision, or prosecution. Occasionally, no action is taken. Of course, delinquent youngsters need firm and confident handling if they are not to reoffend.

Peer pressure

Before complaining too loudly about her being a slave to the fashion dictates of her friends, take a look around your home. Is it typical? Are the meals you cook following the current fads? Few of us are immune to peer pressure or the persuasive powers of the media.

What parents often mean when complaining about the effects of peer pressure on children is that they resent them taking more notice of their friends than of their parents.

◆ **Comment on fashion fads as little as possible.** Green hair and eyebrow studs are usually a passing phase; the less you comment, the quicker the phase will pass.

◆ **Reconsider your belief in peer pressure to do wrong.** It is all too often convenient to believe that your child has been led astray. While some children are easily led, the idea that a strong, secure child can be pressurized into bad behaviour by a friend is a fallacy. Most children do wrong because they choose to act this way. The problem is not that children conform to save face, but that they do things in gangs they would not do by themselves. In this they are no different from adults. Crowds are always dangerous.

The best course is to lobby other parents and agree a common set of rules. Don't let the gang play you off against each other.

Keep it in perspective.

Spending too much time with friends

The first and most obvious answer is to make it your home they use as the base. Accept, too, that spending time with a friends is a welcome sign of growing up. If she needs her friends for company, it does not mean she no longer needs you.

WHAT NOT TO DO ABOUT UNSUITABLE FRIENDS

✖ *Ignore them* – *hope that she will grow out of them. She may, but she may also come to harm.*

✖ *Refuse to meet them. How can you make judgements about people you have never met?*

✖ *Ban them from the house. If they are in your house, at least you know where they are and what they are doing.*

✖ *Run the friends down constantly. This will make your child protective of her new friends.*

Don't like her friends

Your daughter comes home from her new school waxing lyrical about her new best friend. "Invite her around for tea" you say. Perhaps she gives you some warning. Perhaps she simply wheels her in. But her sexually provocative dress, and her heavy make-up makes your heart sink. Is this really the way that your well-brought-up 11-year-old is going?

Answer, no. On the contrary, she is testing your values. Because she is now too old to accept them without question, she needs to form her own view of their worth. This is very different from abandoning your values; it means that she is taking an interest in them.

Remember, too, that attaching herself to an older or more streetwise child makes her seem more grown-up, at least in her eyes. Your shock confirms this.

WHAT TO DO ABOUT BAD FRIENDS

✔ *Get tough. Don't let your liberal attitude stand in the way of your child's safety. If the friendship is dangerous, break it up. On the other hand, if you have no worries about your child's behaviour, you probably do not need to worry about the friendship.*

✔ *Give it time. Wait to see if the phase passes.*

✔ *Warn your child about the danger of being sucked further into trouble. This is a common scenario. If she has gone out drinking with friends in a 'borrowed' car, the next step could well be driving home with a drunk, inexperienced driver at the wheel. Tell her*

✔ *Trust her intuition. Encourage her to get out when she senses things are getting out of hand. Suggest ways of doing this without losing face: 'I've had for the evening – not feeling too good; better go home.'*

✔ *Agree an amnesty code: a word that she can mention down the telephone that means she and her friends are getting into trouble and that she needs help, no questions asked. Assure her that you will respond to the code, without asking questions, as long as she uses it before any real trouble starts.*

Cults

Cults are dangerous because those who mastermind them know how to identify, and prey on, teenagers with low self-esteem. The best protection you can give your child is to ensure that she has high self-esteem; that she is loved. Keep building her up.

It is an obvious and sensible precaution to warn teenagers about friends who invite them to group meetings, especially if they say there will be plenty of interesting people. Explain the dynamics of cults: that they usually have a charismatic leader, who is extremely persuasive and interesting to hear; that they are about exercising power over their members; getting their money; and that although they claim to support their members, those first two aims tends to be the reality.

Tell her not to trust anyone who tries to argue that her family is harming her – despite what she may occasionally feel. How can anyone know about people they have never met? Any stranger who tries to separate a young person from her family and friends must have a sinister motive.

Why do teenagers take risks?

There is a theory that introverted people and extroverted people need different levels of stimulation: that each individual needs to keep brain activity at their own optimal level for performance. Let it drop too low and you are too mellow for action – just as you would be trying to deal with a work crisis in the mid-afternoon lull that follows a fine lunch and a couple of glasses of wine. On the other hand, if you let arousal rise too high, you find yourself panicking, which in turn makes you unable to act – like a rabbit caught in headlights.

Some people, the theory suggests, have a congenitally low level of arousal. They have to 'sail close to the wind' just to keep themselves in functioning mode. These are the extroverts and the risk takers. Others are the opposite, forever needing to calm themselves down. These are the introverts who fade into the background, avoiding too much excitement.

The theory may or may not be true, but it offers one explanation for most people's life patterns. As teenagers, we all behave as if we are more extrovert than we really are. We need loud music, chances, arguments, laughter, and large, gregarious gangs. We get drunk and do not always say "No" to drugs. We dance, we sing, we fall in love, we let hearts break and never do things until the last possible moment. Then, sometime in our mid-20s, we become more introverted – we calm down. We can go to a party and talk rather than dance, our friends do not offer us drugs any more, we prepare for tasks well in advance, make lists and tick things off as we do them. Obviously, there are variations, but this does seem to be the overall pattern.

I think it is easier to deal with teenagers if you keep reminding yourself that they behave as if constantly underaroused. It helps you understand why, when there is nothing going on, they can't be bothered to get up in the morning; and why, once they are up, they blast themselves with constant stimulation as if to keep themselves awake. You, on the other hand, are at the stage of your life when you need to keep your arousal level down. If you can accept this, rather than fight it – just as you had to accept that a baby was a constant tie – then you are some way towards coping with teenagers.

Teenage risk-taking – an honest view

In spite of the intolerable risks they take, the vast majority of teenagers survive. While it is true that teenagers are more likely than the rest of us to have a major accident, acquire a police record, or a drug habit, the odds on your son or daughter reaching 30 without any of these problems are extremely high. For every teenager who dies after taking Ecstasy at a rave, there are literally hundreds of parents winning a major lottery prize. More people are struck by lightning. Although the majority of today's teenagers will probably try at least one illegal drug, the occasion almost always passes without them coming to any harm.

But although in your heart of hearts you expect your children to survive unscathed, the fact that you know they may be doing something silly does not make the waiting easy. When, after two hours' delay, the errant teenager comes smiling through the door, you could hug him – and you could hit him. Like most parents, I have despaired, and considered ringing the hospitals, more times than I care to remember.

Most teenagers – especially boys – do things in gangs. It is not only that chance taking gives young men kudos (although it probably does), simply being in a group makes people feel much safer. Classic psychological studies have shown, for example, that if smoke is pumped into a waiting room via a vent, one person sitting alone will get up and leave immediately. If sitting in a group, that same person will sit and wait for someone else to make the first move.

The environment into which we bring our children often encourages danger. The 'been there, done that' soft drink advertisement and the 'good mates out together' beer advertisements are obvious examples of lifestyle messages which encourage teenagers to take risks because their message is 'Do this and you will be whole, successful, beautiful and admired by your friends.'

From the moment they start to watch TV, children are bombarded with messages about legal drugs. A pill can take away pain, a drink can transport you to a tropical island. If legal drugs have such power, what about the forbidden?

Sex, of course, is central. In reality, you know that sex is usually (but not always) fun and tension-relieving. It is sometimes – but rarely – memorable. When life is good, sex is a necessary part of the background. When life is bad, it can take on a more central, escapist role, like a drug or a stiff drink. It props up a flagging self-esteem.

The sex articles in women's magazines, including those aimed at young teenagers, tend to give a very different message. Here, sex is amazing. Successful people succeed at sex; to be sexy is to be beautiful, admired, desirable. Fail this one, and you fail fundamentally. To disagree with this modern gospel is to be sad, a prude, to live in the Dark Ages.

Yet the majority of women over 30 admit that sex in the teenage years was pretty dull. The earth never moved – it rarely even wobbled. Perhaps we should start telling teenage girls they can indulge boys if they feel like giving them a treat. It would be closer to the mark. Surveys suggest that teenage girls find masturbation more pleasurable and more tension-relieving than intercourse. In girls, the average delay between first inter-course and first orgasm from intercourse is two to four years. For a size-able proportion, it is ten years or more.

It is hard for parents to give a balanced, honest view of the risk their teenagers face when the messages, and the realities, are so different. Only emphasizing the down side, especially exaggerating it, is likely to be neg-ative. For example, implying that all drugs lead to instant addiction, or that many sexual partners will have been in contact with an HIV-posi-tive partner is more likely to lead to the dismissal of sound advice than its acceptance. Teenagers are not fools. They can see that their friends are not addicts and that they are unlikely to know anyone who is HIV-positive. Much better to say that addiction can creep up on one when taking certain drugs, and that although coming into contact with any-one who is HIV-positive is unlikely, the disease is so awful that it is never worth taking the risk.

Then there is the small matter of example. A teenager is, for instance, twice as likely to smoke if both parents smoke. The male Kennedys offer an example of how sexual habits modelled by a father can be passed on to sons.

The risks they take – an instant survey

◆ Mile for mile, young males are involved in more **road accidents** than any other group. In the developed world, 10.3 per cent of males die from accidents, and only 4.4 per cent of females. In the more macho cultures of South America and the Caribbean, the male figure rises to 13.9 per cent. The most dangerous age is 16 to 20.

More than half of the alcohol-related accidents on the roads involve young people up to the age of 24. A substantial proportion of serious accidents involving young drivers occur after the driver has been drinking. A blood alcohol level of 0.15 increases the risk of a car accident by 25 per cent.

Teenagers drink about twice as much as they did 15 years ago. The most alcoholic years are between 16 and 19, and these days both boys and girls drink.

Workers between the ages of 15 and 24 have the highest rate of accidents.

◆ Fewer than 10 per cent of adolescents use any form of contraceptive at **first intercourse.**

◆ **Cigarette smoke** is still the biggest killer drug, although it is unlikely to kill teenagers. Teenagers are more likely to smoke than older people.

◆ **The use of analgesic (painkillers)** is very common in young girls. The risk of damage to the kidneys is high.

◆ **Solvent sniffing** is quite prevalent in 13- and 14-year-olds, particularly those who go out at night, and/or skip school.

◆ **Illegal drug use** is, as everyone knows, a growing problem among teenagers. Marijuana is the most common recreational drug. Reliable figures are hard to get, but it is probably safe to assume that at least one in four teenagers will have tried marijuana by the time they are 17, and about 60 per cent by the time they are 21. Of these, about half become fairly regular, if intermittent, users.

Older teenagers who go to dances and raves are likely to try Ecstasy, also known as E. The use of other drugs, such as cocaine/crack and heroin is less common and obviously more serious.

Illegal drug use is closely tied to social influences. Teenagers try drugs because their friends are trying them. They use them when they get together with those friends. Factors such as social class, peer pressure, low self-esteem, poor family relationships, familial drug or alcohol dependence and stressful life events increase the probability of regular use. The more of these factors are present, the more likely is the move from occasional to regular use of soft drugs, and from regular use of soft drugs to the use of highly addictive drugs – and, eventually, to dependency. The notion that one spiked drink will make someone drug-dependent is a myth.

Drug use: society's attitude

In the Western world there is a very ambivalent attitude to drugs. When people find it difficult to cope with life, they are generally prescribed mood-altering drugs such as sleeping pills, Valium, or Prozac. There are even a few doctors who suggest that most people would cope better with the stresses of modern life and a high-pressure career by having a regular prescription to Prozac.

Many drugs are used for recreational purposes, and we tend to have double standards about these. In the West, three recreational drugs have been legalized, not because they are the safest or least addictive, but because they have been around for a very long time. If we were setting out from scratch, we might still select caffeine as a fairly harmless drug, but we certainly would not choose either alcohol or nicotine as safe recreational drugs.

Alcohol is addictive, causes liver disease if taken to excess, is implicated in violent behaviour, produces serious birth defects when taken in excess by pregnant women, and is known to be involved in a very high percentage of road, household and workplace accidents.

Nicotine is highly addictive, causes circulation problems and, if taken in the form of cigarette smoke, can cause lung cancer. It is harmful to unborn babies. Certain illegal drugs are less harmful and certainly less addictive – which is not to say that they are either harmless or do not produce psychological addiction.

The scale of the problem

Marijuana is California's biggest cash crop. The cocaine industry makes more money than the Ford Motor Company. Controlling the availability of illegal (and legal) drugs is a losing battle. Blocking one drug output simply opens up another. Even if all socially and medically harmful drugs were prohibited, it is unlikely that they would disappear – the profits are simply too great.

The current trend in dealing with drug addiction is to educate adolescents about the problems and dangers that can arise from the use and abuse of drugs, and to combine this with attempts to limit availability. Evidence that either approach succeeds is mixed. The level of addiction has not fallen. In many cases, however, the level of use has fallen. Attempts to control the availability of drugs are largely unsuccessful and availability among the most vulnerable groups remains high.

The problem is that among those groups in which drug availability and use are most common, so are adult drug dependency, unemployment, poverty, social breakdown and feelings of hopelessness. Where hope and self-esteem are low, the temptation for chemical escape is high. If the money from selling drugs brings a lifestyle unobtainable by legal means, the temptation to recruit new drug users and increase income by selling on drugs is obvious.

Once embedded in a drug culture, escape is exceedingly difficult. Coming off drugs does not make a hopeless situation any more hopeful. For almost all heavy drug abusers, unhappiness is so ingrained, life opportunities are so limited, and stress so acute that simplistic prevention programmes are unlikely to have any effect. The outlook once addicted is bleak – but not entirely hopeless.

Can you tell if a youngster is on drugs?

There is no precise set of clues that will enable you to recognize whether your teenager is using drugs. Drugs do not have uniform effects, and the signs of use are not always that different from normal teenage behaviour: abrupt changes in mood or behaviour pattern, secretiveness, and a need for money are the most obvious signs, but many teenagers who show all of these characteristics are not involved in drugs. The following are danger signals – not definite signs:

◆ Be wary if you notice **a change in school attendance,** or a sudden change in schoolwork achievement or motivation.

◆ Take note of **altered sleep patterns,** general lethargy, drowsiness, sleepiness, especially if the change is sudden.

◆ **Poor physical appearance** and an extreme lack of regard for personal hygiene, may indicate drug use, especially if accompanied by sudden highs and lows. Even if such behaviour is not drug-related, it should not be ignored.

◆ **Change of appetite**.

◆ A marked **change in emotional state** with unusual levels of aggression or irritability.

◆ **Withdrawal.** Furtive behaviour; lying; stealing, borrowing money, selling things; unexplained disappearance of money or belongings. Drugs cost money and a serious habit is expensive.

◆ **Loss of interest** in schoolwork, friends or out-of-school activities.

For more specific signs related to particular drugs, see A Parent's Guide to Drugs, pages 398-407.

A parent's guide to drugs

Alcohol

Some drinks – for example alcoholic lemonade – are now specifically produced for youngsters and advertised extensively.

The attractions: An initial high followed by a state of relaxation; decreased anxiety, fear and tension. Because people drink when they are out with friends, an association can be formed between alcohol and having a good time. Alcohol also reduces inhibitions, and, more dangerously, some youngsters take it to increase courage or to escape psychological pain.

Availability: Although shops are not supposed to sell it to teenagers, many do.

Addictive? Yes – for a significant minority of individuals. There is some evidence that there may be a genetic input to addiction. Some races find it difficult to metabolize alcohol and get drunk on quite small amounts. Women can not drink as much as men.

Dangers: This is by far the biggest killer among recreational drugs. It is potentially lethal if taken in large amounts, the danger being that there is little latitude between the dose that makes you to pass out, and the dose that kills. It can cause sickness as well as anaesthesia – a dangerous combination. Choking to death on vomit is not uncommon. Because alcohol affects both attention and judgement, it is frequently implicated in accidents in the workplace, the home and the streets. Nine per cent of all car accidents in the US involve drunken drivers under the age of 20. Also in the US, 40 to 60 per cent of all crashes involving young people happen after drivers have been drinking. As more and more teenagers drive, the figures in other Western countries will probably rise to meet these.

Alcohol depresses the nervous system, but it has a greater influence on unfamiliar tasks than on familiar ones. After drinking, one feels able to drive, and indeed one is often capable; but you are unable to deal with any emergency. It is impossible to calculate how many deaths are caused by alcohol, but it is certain that the figure is higher than for Ecstasy (seven in 1992) or for solvents (about 60 per year).

The plus side: Small amounts of red wine reduce incidence of heart disease.

Has your teenager had a drink? Probably yes. The vast majority of young people have tried alcohol, many before they reach the pre-teen years. Alarmingly high numbers of children are regular drinkers. When asked why they drink, teenagers mention peer pressure, parents' drinking, availability, curiosity and enjoyment.

Recognizing drinkers: Redness of face; smell on breath; bottles or cans in the bedroom.

Discouraging drinking: Set a good example; drink only in moderation. Make sure that youngsters realize the dangers of drinking and driving. Agree upon a code word they can use if they need a lift home with a sober driver. If they ring up to use the word, go and fetch them immediately or order a taxi.

Tobacco

Legal, but relatively expensive. Available not only in cigarettes and cigars but in chewing gum and patches. Campaigns against smoking are working. Young people smoke less than they used to.

The attractions: Nicotine is a stimulant: it wakes you up and helps you to concentrate. Because people smoke while they are out with friends, it is associated with pleasant situations.

Availability: Cigarettes are not supposed to be sold to young people, but small often ignore this.

Addictive? Very. It produces both a physiological and a psychological addiction which can be hard to break.

Dangers: Well known. Cigarette tars and smoke which enter the lungs and throat cause cancer. Chewing gum and patches are safer. Nicotine itself is implicated in heart disease, especially for men.

The plus side: There is some evidence that it protects against Alzheimer's disease.

Has your teenager smoked? In the past, most teenagers would have tried cigarettes. The numbers are decreasing. Girls are more likely to smoke than boys.

Recognizing smokers: Cigarette smoke has a characteristic smell. Smokers carry matches or lighters, and they need money. Even a ten-a-day habit does not come cheap.

Discouraging smoking: Give up yourself. Point out the high level of addiction and the high cost. Advise them strongly not to start. Ban smoking in the house – even by other adults. Smoking in the garden at least keeps the level down.

Cannabis

The leaves and resin from the cannabis plant are readily available. Most teenagers know how to obtain them.

The attractions: Cannabis is the most widely used and probably the most harmless of the illegal drugs. Being 'stoned' makes the user feel peaceful and relaxed and heightens perception. It causes a drop in blood sugar and thus increases hunger. In high doses, it can cause panic attacks and hallucinations. It can also cause vomiting. Because people smoke while they are out with friends and having a good time, it becomes associated with pleasant situations. When people light up, they feel good because this is how they have felt in the past.

Availability: Even if they do not know a dealer, most young people know someone who could obtain some for them.

Addictive? Cannabis is not physiologically addictive. Regular use may produce a psychological addiction. But since it is much more likely to be smoked with other people than alone, psychological addiction is probably rare.

Dangers: Because cannabis is smoked, heavy users probably have a long-term risk of lung and throat cancer. But there is no clear evidence as yet. It affects memory and attention and makes concentration difficult. This can make driving when stoned almost as dangerous as driving when drunk. With excessive and long-term use, memory and concentration may be permanently affected. Some experts think that apathy and ineffectiveness increase with prolonged use; others that ineffective and apathetic people are just more likely to become persistent users. There is no evidence that usage leads to other drugs, although it may bring a teenager into contact with others who use hard drugs. Acute toxic psychosis is very rare but can sometimes occur at high doses.

The plus side: Cannabis can help MS sufferers, and it does not make people aggressive.

Has your teenager had cannabis? Between a quarter and a half of all young people admit to using it at least once. About half this number are regular users.

Recognizing cannabis users: Using words such as dope, marijuana, grass, pot, weed, joints, stoned, or generally sounding like a 1960s hippy. It is usually smoked in a loose cigarette, so drug paraphernalia includes cigarette papers, tins of loose tobacco and bits of card. It comes in two forms: marijuana or 'grass' looks like dried herbs. Hashish comes as a dense, dark block. Hashish is often burned first in a spoon in order to soften it, and you may find this lying about. Because memory is affected, the youngster may forget what he or she is saying. It also causes giggling and an inability to perform simple physical manoeuvres. Hilarity at the top of the stairs and the inability to get down is a likely sign that your teenager is actually stoned. Cannabis has a characteristic smell.

Discouraging cannabis use: Cannabis is illegal. You may not be able to stop your teenager using it occasionally, but this does not mean that you should let them smoke at home. Make sure they understand that driving under the influence of cannabis is as dangerous as driving under the influence of drink. Agree upon a code word they can use if they need a lift home with a safe driver. If they ring up and use the word, go and fetch them immediately, or order a taxi.

Amphetamines

A group of chemical stimulants, either in the form of pills or as powders, these are easily obtained and relatively cheap. Formerly used legally as a diet pill. The powders are snorted, like cocaine. Occasionally injected.

The attractions: Amphetamines keep the user awake and active, speeding up mental and physical processes – hence the name 'speed.' Small doses are sometimes used for swotting or to keep the party going all night. Large doses lead to stereotyped behaviour.

Availability: Quite easy to get hold of, but probably more common in the late teenage years than earlier.

Addictive? Not physiologically, but can be psychologically addictive. After prolonged use, withdrawal is followed by an unpleasant low.

Dangers: Prolonged use can lead to suicidal 'crashes'. Persistent and prolonged use can lead to a psychosis very similar to schizophrenia. Aggression, extreme irritability and violence are common, especially with repeated use. The toxic dose is unpredictable. Overdoses may result in cerebral haemorrhage, convulsions, coma and death.

Recognizing users: They talk non-stop, move about continuously and generally look 'speeded' up. They may grind their teeth, lick their lips repeatedly and make the same movements over and over again. After use, there is often a reaction: the user feels down, depressed and tired. If the 'high' is prolonged by constant use, the downer or 'crash' can be extreme and depression may follow.

Discouraging amphetamine use: Amphetamines are illegal. Make sure teenagers understand that long-term use may cause mental illness and that driving under the influence is as dangerous as driving under the influence of drink. As with alcohol, agree a code word your teenager can use if she needs a lift home with a safe driver. See page 399.

Solvents

Various volatile substances from glue to oven cleaner are popular with some young teenagers. They are taken either by sniffing directly from the container; or by spraying the substance into a polythene bag and sniffing; or by putting it on a rag which is placed over the mouth and nose. Lighter fuel may be spayed directly into the mouth.

The attractions: this is a group activity among young teenagers. Although glue is the most common substance, other volatile substances such as deodorants, hairspray, dry-cleaning fluids, lighter fuels, paint thinners, petrol and nail varnish remover are also used.

They act rather like alcohol, producing a state of excitement followed by a state of calm.

Availability: There has been some attempt to make glue unavailable to youngsters, but many shops will supply it to youngsters. Most sniffers seem to move on to drink or other drugs as soon as they can afford them.

Addictive? No.

Dangers: Suffocation caused by putting a polythene bag over the head in order to intensify the vapour cloud. Spraying substances into the mouth is also dangerous. Large doses can make youngsters confused and uncoordinated, dizzy with blurred vision and slurred speech. Vomiting and coughing is common. Long-term use of petrol and lighter fuel can cause brain and liver damage. In the UK, there are about 60 deaths per year, mostly boys. Death is caused by suffocation, heart failure, or choking on vomit

Recognizing users: Rashes and boils around the mouth, red eyes, red rings around the nose are tell-tale signs, as is the characteristic smell of solvent on clothes.

Cocaine and crack

Available as powders or crystals; relatively expensive. Cocaine is a white powder, snorted up the nose. It may also be heated in aluminium foil and inhaled ('chasing the dragon'). Crack is a crystal which is smoked or burned.

The attractions: A stimulant with effects similar to amphetamine. It is expensive because the effects only last about 20 minutes so repeated snorts are necessary.

Availability: Relatively hard to find, and expensive. Tends to be used by older teenagers who can afford it.

Addictive? Cocaine can produce psychological addiction and dependence. Freebase cocaine, that is, cocaine separated from its salt by the addition of washing soda, is known as crack and is highly addictive.

Dangers: Often adulterated. If you are lucky, with talcum powder.

If unlucky, who knows what it contains? Large doses produce convulsions, insomnia and tactile hallucinations. It also produces aggression, hostility and paranoia.

Recognizing cocaine users: The paraphernalia needed to take the drug includes small mirrors and razor blades for 'cutting' – shaping up a thin line of powder that can be easily snorted; tubes or spoons for snorting. Users rarely eat. They need to snort about every 20 minutes to keep up the effects.

Barbiturates and sedatives

Legal use: as sleeping pills. Usually taken as tablets, but sometimes injected.

The attractions: Can be used in a cycle to create ups and downs: amphetamines (see pages 401–402) give the high, barbiturates bring the user down. Like alcohol, barbiturates provide an initial period of well-being, typically of feeling calm, then a period of lassitude. Quaaludes, chemical name methaqualone, are a non-barbiturate sedative producing a compelling high with a sense of losing one's physical and mental self. It also has a reputation as an aphrodisiac. Other sedatives are popular with some groups. Local youth workers usually know what is available.

Availability: Neither drug is used very frequently by teenagers in the UK.

Addictive? Barbiturates are addictive. Withdrawal symptoms can be worse than with heroin. Quaaludes are also ultimately addictive. They can cause serious withdrawal complications.

Dangers: About 3,000 accidents or intentional deaths occur each year in the USA from barbiturates. Barbiturates produce intellectual impairment and neglect, slurred speech and defective judgement. Quaaludes produce paraesthesia of the arms, fingers, lips and tongue. A sense of invulnerability produced by the drugs may cause accidents. Tolerance develops, and brings the dose needed for a high close to that which kills. Overdose leads to heart failure, convulsions and death.

Recognizing barbiturate users: Sleepiness and extremes of mood are typical signs.

Designer drugs

Ecstasy and angel dust. Ecstasy is MDMA or methylenedioxymetham-phetamine. It is typically used to heighten excitement on a night out at the club. Angel dust is PCP or phencyclidine hydrochloride. Ecstasy was used legally to control appetite. Angel dust is an animal tranquillizer.

Ecstasy comes as pills or powders; angel dust as a powder which is snorted.

The attractions: Ecstasy is widely used in clubs and discos and many use it regularly, without harm. Taken by mouth, it makes you feel alert, sociable, and happy. Angel dust produces a pleasant dream-like state.

Availability: Ecstasy is readily available, angel dust less so.

Addictive? Neither is.

Dangers: Ecstasy can cause serious illness and occasionally death. It has effects on the brain, liver and heart and can affect the body's temperature control system, causing dehydration. Because of this, those using Ecstasy should always drink water in moderation: Ecstasy disturbs the fluid and too much water can be lethal. Otherwise, bad reactions are very rare, but totally unpredictable. Some young people have died after taking their first tablet. Others have taken it quite safely on a number of occasions and then had a serious or lethal reaction.

It is possible that frequent use may cause liver damage. In 1992, seven people died after taking Ecstasy.

Angel dust is also very variable in its action. It can produce paranoia and confusion, muscle rigidity and an inability to recognize danger. In high doses it causes coma and death, especially if combined with other drugs. It is more dangerous than Ecstasy.

Has your teenager had Ecstasy? Since Ecstasy is usually only taken at clubs, you will probably be unaware your child is using it.

Heroin and other opiates

Most teenagers know these are dangerous. Unless they are heavily involved in a drug culture, they do not use them.

Heroin is an opiate derived from a natural source, the opium poppy. It comes as a talcum-like powder sold in wraps or bags; it may be white, grey or pink. It can be taken by mouth, smoked, burned, sniffed or injected. Initially, it is usually smoked as most teenagers realize the dangers of injection. It is, of course, illegal.

Synthetic opiates such as morphine are legal, widely available and used as painkillers. Sometimes people get addicted to them accidentally, or even as a result of abuse; heroin remains the 'druggy's' drug.

The attractions: It produces a 'rush' – a brief but intense feeling of euphoria. This is followed by a feeling of calm and peace.

Availability: Freely available: registered addicts can get legal supplies.

Addictive? A powerful physiological and psychological addiction with unpleasant withdrawal symptoms. However, heroin is not as overpoweringly addictive or destructive as was once thought. One dose certainly does not lead to addiction. About a third of regular users manage to give it up, and can use it again without becoming instantly addicted. Some addicts manage to lead a fairly normal life. About 70 per cent of soldiers in Vietnam became regular users and most managed to give it up or live normal lives while still taking it on their return to the USA. Perhaps the most potent dangers arise from the lifestyle of heavy users, and the cost of the drug, which often necessitates prostitution and crime.

Dangers: The mortality rate is 2 to 3 per cent of users per year. Tolerance builds up quickly and a habit can cost a great deal. Often, the only way to pay for the drug is by crime and/or prostitution.

Recognizing users: It easier to recognize someone injecting drugs than someone taking a drug in other ways. But don't let this put you off the scent of a teenager who becomes withdrawn, solitary and completely demotivated. Addiction saps the will to do anything except obtain the next supply.

LSD, mescaline and other hallucinogens

These tend to be used by an older age group – more of a university than a secondary-school drug. None are legal, or have legal use. They are usually taken as tablets.

The attractions: All hallucinogens produce altered states of consciousness – distortions of reality – although enthusiasts tend to say that it is ordinary reality that is distorted and the drug reality is what it's all about.

Hallucinogens vary from the very mild (cannabis and nutmeg) through the moderate (mescaline, magic mushrooms or psilocybin) to the potent (LSD).

Addictive? No.

Dangers: Unpredictable effects: you can have bad as well as good trips (experiences on the drug). Bad trips can produce frightening and long-term psychological states. Experience of a bad trip can reoccur. In unstable individuals, regular use can lead to psychosis. There is also some evidence of possible genetic damage to offspring after prolonged use by would-be parents.

How to recognize hallucinogen users: Very hard to tell unless actually on a trip. Those on a good trip tend to be deeply preoccupied - 'spaced out'; those on a bad trip also spaced out, but frightened, too.

Can you tell when addiction is setting in?

Not all drug problems are concerned with physiological addiction — which means that the *body* (as opposed to the mind) develops a reliance on the drug and reacts adversely, with unpleasant withdrawal symptoms, if it goes without the drug. Alcohol and heroin can produce physiological addiction. So can nicotine. Most people who use heroin and nicotine become physiologically addicted. Some, but by no means all, drinkers do.

Psychological addiction means that you feel you need and want to take the drug regularly. You may feel unhappy and unsettled without it, but there are no withdrawal symptoms. The signs of psychological addiction are:

◆ Taking drink or drugs when alone.

◆ Finding it hard to turn down the offer of a drink or a drug.

◆ Feeling that drink/drug solves problems.

◆ Drinking or getting high before seeing non-using friends.

◆ Needing drugs or drink to sleep.

◆ Needing drugs or drink to feel alive.

◆ Using drugs or drink before going to school, or skipping school to spend time drinking or using drugs.

◆ Using drugs to improve performance. Being concerned when stocks get low.

◆ Needing something to 'get you through the day'.

Why does addiction happen?

Many teenagers try drugs, but very few get hooked. Most of those who progress from soft drugs such as cannabis or cigarettes to hard drugs such as heroin or crack have other problems; and it is the other problems that make them especially vulnerable.

They may be emotionally disturbed and unhappy with their life in general. Sometimes the cause of unhappiness is obvious. Sometimes you cannot put your finger on it. Most addicts have low self-esteem. They feel they are nothing and nobody without the drug. The sad catch is that although drugs may be a response to this problem, they are not a solution. Drug use leads to more problems.

Since heavy drug users tend to congregate together, addicts spend their time in a culture where everyone has serious problems. Even if the child is relatively well adjusted at the beginning, constant mixing with maladjusted peers lowers hope and esteem. Children get sucked into a drug-based culture from which it is hard to break free.

The only way to minimize the risks is to face up to the problem. Accept that your children are going to be offered drugs. You cannot protect them from this, but you can prepare them.

Discuss drugs with them. Be honest. Make sure they understand the difference between hard and soft drugs. Experimenting with cannabis is one thing. Taking an unknown pill or injecting heroin is something quite different.

Do your best to ensure your teenager does not need to use drugs. Help her to sort out problems. Build up her self-esteem. Don't over-react.

Know what is going on around you. Be well informed.

Emphasize that it is safety and risks that concern you. It may be that the 'wrong drugs' are illegal. But while they are illegal they are probably more dangerous: who knows what they are buying when they come from the street rather than over the counter?

Remember, it is hard to maintain the moral high ground with a glass of whisky in your hand.

Particularly discourage them from taking drugs when alone. Whatever the drug, however harmless, its regular, solitary use is the start of the high road to dependency. This applies to drink and cannabis as much as to heroin.

Helping drug users

Finding fault stops them dealing with the problem. Sympathy and understanding get them nowhere. The only way to deal with drug dependency is for the user to set a goal of stopping, to make a decision to stop and get help. Parents cannot dictate to children who have no desire to stop; teenagers don't catch this: they do it to themselves because they want to. Curing a drug habit is as much about curing the causes and replacing the lifestyle as coming off the drugs themselves. Perhaps it is no coincidence that some of the most successful quitters are those who work to help others quit, and thus retain a degree of existence within the drug culture.

No one who does not want to give up drugs can be made to do so.

Supplies are always available. Crime can always provide the money. Most hospitals and clinics have long waiting lists of those wanting help to give up a drug habit; the same is true of residential rehabilitation centres. If you are faced with the problem, here is a checklist for action – it is no more than that:

◆ **Treat heroin injection as an emergency.** Take the teenager to a doctor. A heroin-substitute may be prescribed, and might help.

◆ Try to persuade persistent users to seek **professional help** and **therapy**, both for the drug habit and the underlying problems.

◆ Help the user to **change their lifestyle** in order to remain drug free. The major problem is keeping the user away from drug-using friends.

◆ **Don't despair.** Many go back on to drugs for a while after kicking the habit. With luck, the off periods get longer and the habit can eventually be kicked.

◆ If you can, help them to **find a job,** or to prepare the ground for returning to **school**. This has the double value of keeping them away from the drug lifestyle and giving them something to do.

A very personal footnote

Far too many of these final pages have had to be devoted to a problem that only affects a tiny minority; and, moreover, a problem that only reflects badly on the world that adults have created. Sadly, the drug problem has to be covered in detail if it is to be covered at all.

In order to correct the balance, I feel it would be just to end this book as positively as I know how. And that means relating my personal experience of being the parent of teenagers.

I am currently the mother of two teenage children and I have to say that they are easygoing, law-abiding and perfectly charming. We calm each other down when we panic (which we do); we laugh when one of us is being silly; and we generally support each other. OK: the school complains that my son does not always work hard enough; there is always music playing (not all of it to my taste), the towels are never in the bathroom and the kitchen is invariably a mess.

But there are more than enough compensations. I am no longer frantic when stuck in a traffic jam on the way home from work, and when I get in there is often a cup of coffee waiting. If I am tired, they say "Sit down, Mum," and one of them cooks supper. Best of all, the flat is usually full of young people who tease and laugh. There is a warm, friendly feeling as I come through the door.

Perhaps it easier because I am doing it alone this time. Perhaps because I have already accepted that I am middle-aged. But the most likely reason for it being easier is that these are not my first two teenagers. I have already seen one through and out the far side. That time it was more turbulent.

My eldest son dropped out of school at 14, frequently stayed out all night, never told me where he was, more than once took money from my purse and ran up gigantic phone bills. He made me angry and drove me frantic with worry.

Yet it was never all pain and worry. I watched his social ease, his charm and obvious zest for life with admiration and respect. When looking at the academic performance of this very intelligent child, his teacher reminded me that there is more than one way to succeed. He predicted that my son would land on his feet, and he was right. I suspect that by the time he is 30 he will be earning more than I do. And I can now say with pride that he is charming, competent, hard-working and fun to have around.

The moral

With hindsight, I believe that accepting – and coping successfully with – teenage children is partly about accepting ourselves. The very fact that we have older children means that we are older parents. As these days many of us have our first child in our late 20s, even in our late 30s, acclimatization to grown-up children is likely to coincide with the mid-life crisis.

What can be more conducive to the realization of lost youth than the presence of real youth in the home? What brings home more painfully the realization of youthful plans never achieved, or only half achieved, than watching teenagers planning, or failing to plan, their futures? They say youth is lost on the young, and some days it certainly feels like it.

Whatever age we are when we meet with the realization of life now being half over, it calls for readjustment – just as the transition from being without children to being a parent demanded adjustment.

The adjustments we are forced to make in the first months of a baby's life start a process of personal and family change that lasts all our lives. For most of the years we are actively engaged in child-raising, we are too busy getting on with the business of living to notice that we are also changing alongside our children. It is only when we meet with friends who have no children that we see the gap between our old selves and the way we are now. In the early years of parenthood we may have envied them their freedom. That few of us now envy their childlessness is, surely, a mark of how rich the experience has been.

However hard the years of child-raising and however turbulent the teenage years, few would have chosen a different route. This does not mean that we are ready to start over again. In this, at least, nature helps us to make the inevitable readjustment.

I am sure I speak for the majority in saying that one of the greatest compensations of parenthood is that because of us, and indeed in spite of us, most children grow up to be normal, happy, well-adjusted people. The disasters that we found so easy to foresee very rarely occurred, and those that did were mostly transient problems: mere blips on our good records.

This may sound like complacency, but any parent will know that it is not. In parenthood you can make regular mistakes and still look back on a job well done: a lasting joy.

INDEX